SOLDIERS & GHOSTS

A History of Battle in Classical Antiquity

J . E . L E N D O N

Yale University Press   New Haven and London

Published with assistance from the income of
the Frederick John Kingsbury Memorial Fund
and from the Louis Stern Memorial Fund.

Designed by Sonia Shannon
Set in ITC Galliard and Trajan type by
Duke & Company, Devon, Pennsylvania
Printed in the United States of America by
Vail-Ballou Press, Binghamton, New York

The Library of Congress has
cataloged the hardcover edition as follows:
Lendon, J. E.
Soldiers and ghosts : a history of battle in
classical antiquity / J. E. Lendon.
p.   cm.
Includes bibliographical references and index.
ISBN 0-300-10663-7 (alk. paper)
1. Military history, Ancient. 2. Military art and science —
History. I. Title.
U29.L46 2005
355'.00937 — dc22
2004021273

A catalogue record for this book is available from
the British Library.

The paper in this book meets the guidelines for
permanence and durability of the Committee on
Production Guidelines for Book Longevity of the
Council on Library Resources.

ISBN-13: 978-0-300-11979-4 (pbk. : alk. paper)
ISBN-10: 0-300-11979-8 (pbk. : alk. paper)

10 9 8 7 6 5 4 3 2

For Elizabeth

CONTENTS

MAPS

FIGURES

PROLOGUE

QUANG TRI PROVINCE,
VIETNAM, 1967

L ordy, Lordy, it's July the Fourth. Here we go again. Hot dog. Hot time in the old town tonight. Bet we make big contact. I'm sure we're going to have an exciting day of fireworks."

"Fuck you, Hatfield, we don't need that."

At dawn on the Fourth of July, two battalions of U.S. Marines began to advance cautiously into the elephant grass south of the DMZ. The regulars of the North Vietnamese army were waiting for them. The Vietnamese were dug in, well concealed, and supported by heavy artillery from North Vietnam, only a few miles to the north. And so it was, that as the Americans pushed forward into the rising heat, Marines began to die. First to fall was Lieutenant Anderson of Kilo Company, 3rd Battalion, 9th Marines, shot in the head leading his troops forward as they opened the battle by walking into an ambush. Anderson had never been much for taking cover: "It's okay. God's going to protect me." By 1115, when it pulled back two hundred meters and artillery was called in to sweep the front, Kilo Company had suffered twelve killed and seventeen wounded. They had not seen a single enemy soldier. As Captain Giles prepared to withdraw, a marine lying in front of his hedge, thought to be dead, sat up slowly and lit a cigarette.

"Are you okay?"

"No, sir, I'm just having a cigarette before I die."

"What I want you to do is roll over on your face and crawl back toward us."

I

"No, sir, just leave me alone. Don't come and get me. Leave me alone. I'm dyin', and I just want to have my last cigarette."

After more futile coaxing and agonizing as to whether to send soldiers out to get the Marine—covered by an enemy sniper, he could not be rescued without exposing other Marines to fire—Captain Giles and his men left their wounded comrade to his fate.[1]

Captain Giles's decision to abandon the dying Marine seems peculiar in light of the purpose of Kilo Company's advance. For the objective of the Marine attack was not military in the strictest sense: it was to recover the dead bodies of thirty-one Marines abandoned on the field after an engagement two days before. But in pulling back hastily to allow a bombardment by artillery and airstrikes (during that four-hour interlude some of the bombs fell short, wounding and killing Marines), Kilo Company had abandoned its twelve new KIAs in front of its lines: now its first task was to recover them. In the process, the company took fire, and the company on its flank took casualties: two dead, four wounded.

"We're taking too many casualties. We're going to pull back."

"*Bullshit.* I'm giving you a direct order under combat conditions to continue to move."

Once the fresh corpses had been secured and manhandled back, the Marines withdrew for the night to the line they had held during the American bombardment. During the morning of July 5, six Marines were wounded by enemy mortar fire, and American artillery and airstrikes pounded the area in front of their lines; now the Marines began to creep forward once again, toward the original bodies. But, as so often in Vietnam, this was to be a battle without a climax. The NVA had withdrawn during the night, and the battered bodies of the Marines killed three days earlier were recovered without further incident. They were bagged by Marines wearing gas masks against the stench, piled high on tanks, and dispatched, by stages, upon their dolorous journey back to the United States.[2]

"We don't leave our people," Lieutenant Howell told the *New York Times* about the operation. "I'm sure they'd do the same thing for me." Insistence on the recovery of their dead has long been part of the code of the U.S. Marines, and this creed has spread through the American armed forces to become a characteristic feature of the American way of war. It is not unusual for the recovery of dead bodies to generate more dead bodies, as it did in Quang Tri Province. Enemies quickly learn that Americans return for their dead: as the Combat After Action Report on this battle observed, "NVA forces seem to be fully aware of the Marine tradition to remove all wounded and dead from the battle field. Evacuation efforts were covered by enemy artillery, mortar, and small arms-fire." This predictability gives the enemy the initiative: baiting ambushes with the corpses of American soldiers or booby-trapping them was perfectly usual in Vietnam and has remained so in subsequent American campaigns, in Somalia, in Afghanistan, and in Iraq.[3]

Soldiers explain the imperiling of live soldiers to bring in the bodies of their dead comrades as fundamental to morale and unit cohesion: it is the pledge of the group to the individual, which allows the group to demand in return that the individual risk his life. This is ample justification, but the practice nevertheless depends upon a particular set of beliefs about the sanctity of the human body (even if the spirit has fled) and of the soil of the United States. "We needed to find this man," said a Marine about the body of an admired sergeant later in the Quang Tri battle. "We needed to make sure that this man came out unmutilated. That's what the enemy did with our Marines, they mutilated them. The most important thing was to find this great Marine and bring him home to the U.S.A." The bodies had to be recovered, even if — given the American reliance on artillery, bombs, and napalm to clear the ground before the infantry advanced — the process of recovering them frequently mangled them far more than the most fiendish enemy could.[4]

American concern for the prompt recovery of soldiers' dead bodies is hardly unique, but it places Americans in the company of peoples with whom they might be surprised to be classed: the Homeric and Classical Greeks, for example (the Romans were far less concerned about recovering their dead), and the warlike tribesmen of highland Papua New Guinea.[5] These are peoples who fight wars in ways we call ritualized, meaning they allow their beliefs to dictate a mode of fighting less ruthlessly efficient than we could devise for them. There are other ways, too, in which beliefs draw modern armies away from purely efficient methods of killing: the reluctance, since World War I, of many armies to employ poison gas and the practice of preserving the lives of prisoners. Such restraints are powerfully reinforced by the scorpion sting of the Golden Rule: soldiers do not want to be gassed themselves, and they want their own surrenders accepted. But such restraints are grounded also in shared belief: the belief that war has rules, however fragile, and that there are appropriate ways of killing and methods of killing too horrible to be used. Where such beliefs are not shared, as in the Pacific theater in World War II, for example, fighting achieves a singular brutality. Nevertheless, from the perspective of several thousand years in the future, an observer might conclude that our contemporary methods of fighting are scarcely less ritualized than those of Greeks and tribesmen of New Guinea. However primitive or sleekly modern the machinery of war, the idiosyncratic beliefs of the men of every time and place play their role in how war is fought.[6]

INTRODUCTION

MILITARY CHANGE IN
CLASSICAL ANTIQUITY

The shrine began as a bubbling hot spring in a peat bog, draining down a gully to the river Avon, and sacred to the Celtic goddess Sulis. When the Romans ruled Britain a great temple was built there, and Sulis, in the comfortable ancient way, was identified with Minerva, the Roman Athena. But amidst the pompous Roman building, the old spring remained the ear of the goddess, and folk threw their coins in for luck and wrote their curses upon sheets of lead and cast them into the water: "I curse him who has stolen my hooded cloak . . . let the goddess Sulis inflict death upon Maximus and allow him neither sleep nor children now or in the future, until he has returned my hooded cloak!" And when their prayers were answered, the votaries of Sulis threw offerings into the spring, a cup or a comb or an earring or a ring or a breast modeled in ivory, to thank the goddess for a divine cure. One day, it seems, a jeweler came into the shrine and cast a whole bag of handsome seal-stones into the spring. Had he been set upon by thieves? And had he vowed his stock of goods to the goddess if she delivered him? And one day a soldier came, and he too cast into the spring a precious votive, a washer from an army catapult, slightly more than three inches across.[1]

Of all the military machines the Romans used on land, catapults were perhaps the most sophisticated. They worked by torsion — by the force produced by the release of twisted cords woven of sinew or hair. The cords had to be kept loose when the catapult was not actually in use, and

5

Bronze catapult washer from the Sacred
Spring at Bath (Institute of Archaeology,
University of Oxford. Photo: B. Wilkins).

the tensioning and untensioning of the cords was the vital function of the washers. The Greeks had reduced the building of catapults to an exact science. The size of the projectile to be thrown defined the diameter of the skein of twisted cords (which was also the diameter of the interior of the washer, through which the cords passed). Every measurement of the catapult was in proportion to that module. With their table of proportions in hand, military artificers could produce a range of catapults, from those lithe and light enough to be carried by one man to gigantic engines casting a stone of two hundred and fifty pounds. The catapult for which the washer dedicated to Sulis Minerva was made was small: the kind of weapon the ancients called a hand ballista (*manuballista* in Latin, *cheiroballistra* in Greek), operated by one or two men.[2]

It is with catapults and the technical treatises describing them that we seem to get closest in antiquity to a modern conception of military technology. But then the catapult washer dedicated to Sulis draws us up short: there is something profoundly alien about this soldier's relationship to technology. However expert an artilleryman he may have been, he remained a Roman and regarded technology through Roman eyes. Weapons were often dedicated as offerings to the gods. Why not, then, a catapult washer?

Unexpected too in his attitude toward catapults is Frontinus, an experienced Roman general and the author of a military treatise in the first century AD. "I leave aside siege works and engines," he wrote, "human invention having been exhausted in this realm long ago: I see no basis for further improvement." And Frontinus was right. In all their centuries and in all their wars, the Romans made only the slightest advances on Greek catapult technology, just as they made only slight advances on Greek naval technology and upon the technology of fighting battles in the open field.[3]

In the twentieth century, warfare changes so quickly that a soldier taken prisoner in 1942 could not recognize the uniforms and equipment of his rescuer in 1945: "I said, 'Hey, who in the hell are you?' The guy had the funniest uniform on, with a funny-looking cap, and he was carrying something that looked like a grease gun, like he was going to grease up a car. He said, 'We're Yanks. Get your ass out the main gate.' This guy is trying to save my life, and I'm sitting there carrying on an argument with him. I said, 'No Yank ever wore a uniform like that.' He said, 'The hell we don't!'"[4]

In classical antiquity, by contrast, technological progress was very slow, and progress in military technology little faster. A soldier who went to sleep in his war gear in the fifth century BC would have been able to fight at no disadvantage in that equipment if he awoke in the fourth century AD, eight hundred years later. Imagine, by contrast, how confused — and soon how dead — a knight of AD 1200 would be if he blundered into a contemporary battle.

There were some slight technological advances in ancient land warfare: the Greeks invented a shield with a double grip, which moved the weight of the implement from the hand to the shoulder (see figures, pp. 54, 64); the Macedonians invented a long pike, the *sarissa*, which gave Macedonian spearmen a longer reach (see figures, pp. 122–23); the Romans invented a heavy, powerful, short-range javelin, the *pilum*. Each of these innovations was used successfully for centuries, but none was so emphatic an improvement that all nations were obliged to adopt it or fight at a severe disadvantage, the situation created in modernity by the firearm and then again by the machine gun.[5]

World-changing improvements were rare and were imported from beyond the Greco-Roman world. In very early times the riding horse and its tack were introduced, freeing Greek warriors from their rattling chariots. Around 300 BC chain mail was invented, perhaps by the Celts, was widely adopted, and was never out of use after. There were less fundamental imports too: from the Celts also, the Romans seem to have borrowed their legionary helmet and the four-horned saddle that made using weapons from horseback without falling off easier in a world without stirrups. From the East came the powerful wood-and-bone composite bow of the steppe nomads.[6]

Some inventions, moreover, were used for a limited time and then mysteriously abandoned: the formidable Roman banded legionary plate armor, for example — known to us as the *lorica segmentata* — appears around the turn of the millennium, is seen on Trajan's Column (see figure, pp. 244–45), and then vanishes in the mid–third century AD. Other inventions went in and out of use, such as bolt-throwing artillery on the battlefield, first seen in the late fourth century BC, not much used in the Roman

Republic but widely attested in the Roman empire. Imports too had the same inconsistent history: Hellenistic armies unleashed elephants on their foes, and so did the Romans for a period in the Republic, but then they abandoned them. The man-and-horse armor of the heavy cavalry cataphract, borrowed from the East by the Hellenistic Seleucid army, was revived by the Romans in the second century AD and was in slowly expanding Roman use thereafter.[7]

Other inventions still, like the sling-dart, seem to have had only a single outing. Sometimes the reason for an innovation's short life is reported: once upon a time a king clad his soldiers in spikes and set them to fight against elephants, but the elephants trampled them all the same. Finally, some proposed inventions were never tried at all, or so one hopes: the chariot that mechanically lashed forward the horses that drew it, the giant squirt-gun that shot poison into the noses of enemy mounts, or the wolf vertebrae cast in front of enemy cavalry that tripped up the horses by their well-known magical vigor.[8]

All in all, there was far less technological change in the eight hundred years from 500 BC to AD 400 than in the forty years from 1910 to 1950; far less technological advance in any ancient century than in one year of either of the World Wars. But if the tools — feet and horses, spears, swords, shields — did not change much, the ways of using them did, if slowly. Horsemen wielding long spears earned a place for themselves beside the javelin-armed. The Greeks learned to fight in a bristling block, with shields and spears: the phalanx. The short-speared Greek phalanx yielded to the longer-speared Macedonian, the Macedonian phalanx to the javelin-and-sword Roman legion. But it is unnerving to find the Romans of the fourth century AD reverting to a spear-and-shield-wall style of infantry fighting that recalls that of the Greek fifth century BC. In technology, then, little change and even less patent progress. In method, more change, but not the kind of unequivocal progress that made older methods unequivocally obsolete.

Nevertheless, ancient people were perfectly capable of thinking of military progress much as we do, with new, better military methods replacing obsolete old ones. Writes the late Roman military author Vegetius (c. AD 400), "On cavalry [the old books] provide many precepts. But since this branch of the service has moved forward in its drill, the nature of its arms, and the quality of its horses, I think that there is nothing to be gathered from books, since current ideas are adequate."[9] The Greeks and Romans understood that some armaments and methods of fighting had an advantage over others and that some might be better suited than others to given circumstances. They understood also that new methods might be adopted (temporarily or permanently) in response to particular threats and that new and better methods of fighting could be copied from foreign peoples: indeed, observers thought this copying a particularly Roman trait, attributing Roman shields and javelins to the Samnites, the Roman short sword to the Spaniards, and Roman cavalry equipment to the Greeks.[10]

More broadly, the ancients understood technological progress: "For it is a rule that, just as in crafts, the new always prevails." They understood that such progress was driven by individual invention, a principle the Greeks hallowed in their myths through such figures as Prometheus and Daedalus, and in myth they applied this theory of progress-by-invention to warfare: "Proteus and Arcisius invented shields when they fought against each other, or perhaps it was Chalcus son of Athamas. Medias the Messenian invented the breastplate, and the Spartans invented the helmet, sword, and spear."[11] Such improvement by invention, they believed, continued in their own day too. So an ancient historian might stop to praise an early fourth-century BC Greek military innovator by the name of Iphicrates: "He is said to have been a man of extraordinary acuity at generalship and to have been by nature fruitful of useful invention. As a result, having had long experience of military affairs in the Persians' War [in Egypt, in the 370s BC], he invented many things useful in war, and was especially ambitious in the realm of armaments. . . . Practical use confirmed the initial impression and from the success of the experiment won great fame for the inventive genius of the general. . . . He also expounded many other improvements to warfare: it would be a great deal of work to write about them." The reformer is described as introducing new equipment, perhaps on the basis of his overseas experience, equipment found to be superior to the old when tested in practice. An ancient author could describe even an entire military technology, catapults, as evolving by human ingenuity responding to successive needs and overcoming successive difficulties.[12]

Given so much ancient encouragement, it is hardly surprising that modern students quietly assume that familiar and contemporary mechanisms of change are adequate to explain transformations in the style of ancient land warfare. Therefore new methods of fighting, whether invented or imported or adapted in the face of new threats, prove more efficient than old methods; then newer, better methods still come along to supersede them. The tale of Greek phalanx, Macedonian phalanx, and Roman legion becomes parallel to the tale of knight conquered by pike, pike conquered by musket, musket by rifle, and rifle by machine gun.

Innovation, borrowing, and adaptation to new dangers certainly played their role in changing military methods in classical antiquity. The question is how large that role was, and what other forces may have been at work. Diodorus, the very same author who describes the genius of Iphicrates, soon turns to a more important fourth-century BC military innovator, King Philip II of Macedon, inventor of the formidable *sarissa*-armed Macedonian phalanx. Philip got the idea, the author says, from Homer, by looking back over his shoulder into epic. And much later, Vegetius, who thought the late Romans had nothing to learn about cavalry from the past, did not think the same about infantry: indeed his *Epitome on Military Affairs* is for the most part a program of reform for contemporary infantry that proceeds by resurrecting the practices of the Roman infantry of old. And Vegetius is not unusual, for most technical military writing that survives from antiquity looks not into the future or even at contemporary methods, but into the past, whether the author collects historical stratagems for the use of contemporary generals, bases a general treatise on the art of generalship on centuries-old examples, describes Macedonian phalanx drill to a Roman imperial audience, or reproduces the plans of catapult designers of old.[13]

Innovating by attempting to recreate what has gone before — going forward by looking backward — is, in fact, entirely characteristic of ancient habits of mind. For the Greeks and the Romans revered the past to a degree that seems unfathomable today. Greek tragedy and vase painting overwhelmingly depict not contemporary events but the age of heroes: writers of tragedy chose settings from the past to treat even contemporary themes, to provide a frame in which to puzzle over current problems of politics and ethics. Much later, in the second century AD, the Greeks based their highest cultural form on reproducing the diction and vocabulary of Athenian rhetoricians of the fourth century BC. At Rome a young man could be imagined to rise in the Senate and propose an idea that he said he had inherited from his great-grandfather. The Romans never knew a progressive notion: their political programs were all conservative — keep things as they are — or reactionary — a return to an imagined past, like the agenda of Tiberius Gracchus. In short, "we face the future resolutely, and the past is behind us. It is noticeable that most modern travelers prefer to sit in a railway carriage facing the engine, to see where they are going; the ancients sat with their backs to the engine, looking at the landscape they had passed through."[14] In modern times the past is usually considered a brake to military change; the cavalryman's attachment to his horse, for example, impeding the development of the tank and its efficient use. Yet in a world in which technological progress was slow (and ancient habits of mind helped to keep it slow) and the progressive thinking that accompanies rapid change was far weaker than in the modern world, a vision of the past could be a powerful engine for change. As we shall see, inherited ethics could encourage soldiers to fight in ways loyal to those ethics and discourage methods that conflicted with them. An admired tradition could inspire military thinkers to imitate it in its details and to advance real contemporary military science by solving the problems presented by trying to imitate an ill-understood or largely imaginary past. Reverence for the past could ease the acceptance of changes or imports that were, or could be presented as, returns to the past, or the past could compel ingenious compromises with imported methods. The past could channel innovation in the face of military crises, offering practical solutions to stark problems. And finally, blind adulation for the past could encourage unwise reversion to the military methods of the past, with somber consequences.[15]

In any society, a great many factors cause, hold back, or influence the change of military methods over time. Advance in any given technology may depend upon a host of other technologies, all of which have histories of their own. Economics too plays a powerful role: a society can have only the army it can afford. In Greece and Rome the poverty of the age meant that cheap infantry always outnumbered expensive cavalry and that cavalry was only fleetingly a decisive arm in ancient warfare.

So too institutions are important: the ability of governments to gather private wealth for military expenditure varies drastically. The ancient Spartans, who used no coinage at all, had to change their ways if they were going to hire mercenaries or rowers, who expected to be paid in good silver. So too politics: the Greeks anticipated the American Founders' suspicion of standing armies, and so the development of military training was hindered. So too social structures: a proud aristocracy and the citizens of a democratic city-state fought their wars differently. And legal structures: the absence of patent protection in classical antiquity encouraged inventors to hide, rather than broadcast, their discoveries. And communications: where communications were poor, innovations were slow to pass from place to place. Many of these considerations appear in the pages that follow. But the overall interpretation of change proposed here proceeds from a conviction that warfare, although it has a melody of its own, is a part of the wider symphony of the society of the combatants, and that among the many themes of that symphony, the one to listen to most closely in understanding military change is the relationship of the Greeks and Romans to their past.

THE GREEKS

They built long citadels, the eldest of the Greeks, and they built them low and strong, not thrusting into the sky but clinging to the rocks, with walls of great stones piled up and cisterns dug deep. In time of peace they laid up chariots in their magazines, their wheels detached, and in time of war rode them forth by their hundreds. They wrought their swords of bronze, these men we call the Myceneans, and they knew the spear and the shield and the bow: all the important tools of ancient combat except the riding horse. Their walls and their weapons and the records of their arsenals reveal a warlike folk, and their relics show that they conquered the Aegean islands and Crete, home to the mellowed-wine civilization we call Minoan. But how the Myceneans wielded their weapons, how they arrayed themselves to fight, and the history of their battles, what we wrest from the earth cannot reveal.

Iron weapons and the riding horse came into Greece in the centuries-long winter after the Mycenean citadels were thrown down in fire. A few weapons survive, and crude pictures on pots of warriors with spears, swords, shields, and bows, but again, how the weapons were used in

Greece and the Aegean

battle cannot be known, or even if the struggles of those hard days should be dignified with the word *battle*. After 750 BC the familiar tools of Greek infantry fighting begin to appear: the round two-handled shield, the all-enclosing Corinthian helmet, and the metal leg protectors known as greaves (see figure, p. 54). When, long after in the fifth century BC, this gear is described in use, it is borne by spear-wielding warriors, the so-called men-at-arms or hoplites, tightly packed together in a block, the phalanx. But this method of fighting evolved in a period from which

written reports of fighting remain desperately scanty. There is rumor of
a major war in Greece around 700 BC, the Lelantine war between the
cities of Chalcis and Eretria on Euboea, which may have been resumed
a number of times in the following century. But there is little to be known
of it except a perhaps legendary treaty banning missiles and an obscurely
related scrap of poetry:

> Not many will be the bows drawn back, nor many
> > slings, when Ares brings the toil of war together
> on the plain, but the work will be of swords, much-sighing,
> > for that is the fighting of which they are masters,
> the spear-famed lords of Euboea.[1]

Brave minds try to pierce the gloom by studying Homer's *Iliad,* the supreme enigma of early Greek history. It tells the story of a Mycenean war
around 1200 BC, the attack on Troy, a city on the west coast of Asia Minor.
But the poem grew up by accretion over the centuries and may not have
reached its final form until around 700 BC (some would say later). The
Iliad may combine material from more than five hundred years and so
presents the historian with one of the slipperiest documents in the Western
tradition. To mine out of the *Iliad* a convincing account of how men of
any specific historical period fought is impossible: here the *Iliad* is important rather for how later men interpreted it.

By the sixth century BC a picture of Greek city-states and their ways
and wars begins to coalesce: the Spartans, austere, brave, and cruel, with
their toiling helots; the men of proud Argos, votaries of Hera and Sparta's
old rivals; the Athenians, who claimed to have slithered up, snake-legged,
from the ground when the world was young; and their neighbors to the
north in Thebes, sprung from dragon's teeth. There are clearer glimpses
now, but still only glimpses, of the wars they fought against each other
and of some details of their battles. But it is with the two Greek wars
against Persian invasions in 490 and 480–479 BC, recorded by Herodotus
(c. 484–420s BC) in his *Histories,* that Greece enters what might strictly
be called its historical period. We see the Persians land at Marathon, and
the phalanx of the Athenians drive them back into the waves. We see the
vast army that Xerxes, Great King of Persia, sent ten years later to avenge

the slaughter on that bloody beach; we see the desperate stand of the long-tressed Spartans at Thermopylae, and the Greeks' victory in the sea battle of Salamis, the ship-wracking triumph foreseen by the oracle: "And with oars will the women of Colias strand do their roasting." In the next year we see the final Greek victory on land at Plataea.

After the defeat of the Persians, a fifty years' shadow covers the military narrative until the detailed account of Herodotus's great successor Thucydides (c. 460–400 BC) begins in 435. Where Thucydides leaves off in 411, the younger Xenophon (c. 428–354) takes up and carries the story down to 362. Thucydides tells of most of the twenty-seven-year-long Peloponnesian War (432–404) between Athens and Sparta, with its great land battles of Delium in 424 and Mantinea in 418, the triumph of light infantry over hoplites at Sphacteria in 425, and the Athenian disaster by land and sea at Syracuse (415–413). When Xenophon takes up the story it is mostly an affair of sea battles, of Arginusae in 406 and the final Spartan victory at Aegospotami in 405. He goes on to describe with a soldier's eye the frequent wars and many battles of the period of Sparta's ascendancy in Greece and in Asia Minor, the generalship of Sparta's greatest marshal, Agesilaus (c. 445–359), the destruction of Spartan power by Thebes at Leuctra in 371, and (bitterly, for the Spartans had been good to him) the short supremacy of Thebes thereafter. Best of all, Xenophon marched with and immortalized the Ten Thousand, the army of Greek mercenaries that marched deep into the Persian empire in 401, then fought its way free to the Black Sea. The changes in Greek fighting that occur in the seventy-year period of warfare Thucydides and Xenophon describe are not revolutions but subtle shifts of emphasis: more and better use of light troops; a shift from the bow to the javelin; better use of cavalry and in greater numbers. But the heavily-armed hoplite remained king of the pride, even if the lesser lions were growing truculent and agile.[2]

When Xenophon flung down his pen in frustration after the Second Battle of Mantinea in 362 — the battle that was supposed to decide everything but decided nothing — another epoch of dimmer light descends, a period that saw the growing power of Macedonia and the depredations of its one-eyed King Philip upon Greece. Nearly lost in the murk are far greater changes than in the times of Thucydides and Xenophon: the new longer-speared Macedonian phalanx and Macedonia's effective shock cavalry. But if the coming of the new Macedonian army is hard to see, its use is not. For the lights come up again, with a glare, upon Philip's refulgent son Alexander (356–323), who led his father's army conquering into the East: upon his victory over the Great King's satraps at Granicus River in western Asia Minor in 334, the triumph over King Darius himself at Issus in 333, the siege and capture of the island-city of Tyre and the conquest of Egypt in 332, and his final defeat of Darius at Gaugamela near the Tigris in 331. Then Alexander's fate took him east into Persia, into Afghanistan, and finally to victory over the Indian king Porus at the Hydaspes River in 326. Both Philip's defeat of the Greeks at Chaeronea in 338 and Alexander's successes in the East show that the Macedonian army was better than the Greek armies that had gone before.

With the death of Alexander the narrative continues for a time. So the great wars of Alexander's generals over their dead king's empire and important battles like Paraetacene in 317 and Gabiene in 316 are well reported. But the record develops large holes after 302, and the battle of Ipsus in 301, the climactic battle of this period, falls into one of them. Thereafter, the evidence casts more shadow than light. After the conquests of Alexander, changes in Greek ways of fighting involved for the most part the integration of the conquered into the Macedonian system: their weapons, their tactics, their sons. But to win their battles, generals after Alexander relied most upon what they had inherited from the conqueror.

I

FIGHTING IN THE *ILIAD*

THE NURSERY OF GHOSTS

I t should have been a moment of high heroism in the *Iliad,* but the gods had a different plan. The wrath of Achilles had set Zeus against the Achaeans, and so the Trojans had driven them back to their ships. As the ships began to burn, Achilles' warmhearted companion Patroclus borrowed the great hero's armor and led Achilles' retainers, the Myrmidons, to drive the Trojans back. Having killed Sarpedon, a great Trojan hero, and turned the Trojans to flight, Patroclus harried them back to the walls of Troy, heedless of his promise to Achilles that he would save the ships but do no more. Thrice the god Apollo, who loved the Trojans, had to knock Patroclus back from the wall of the city. Goaded by the god, Hector, supreme hero of the Trojans, rode out upon his chariot to challenge Patroclus. But Patroclus killed Hector's charioteer and raged through the battle, cutting down thrice nine men of the Trojans. It was then that Apollo struck Patroclus on the back with the weight of his divine hand and splintered his shield and knocked his armor off, stunning him. As Patroclus stood defenseless, Euphorbos speared him in the back with a javelin and fled away. Finally Hector drove his great spear into his belly.

"I with my spear am preeminent among the war-loving Trojans!" crows the victorious Hector over the dying Patroclus. But the gods turn heroism to farce as Patroclus disputes this claim from his bloody span of earth, pointing out rather calmly that destiny and Apollo were chiefly responsible for his defeat, then Euphorbos, and vaunting Hector only third.

He then prophesies that Hector will be slain by Achilles, as indeed soon comes to pass. Only then does his great soul go down to the house of death.[1]

It is not only the dying Patroclus who questions Hector's heroism in the killing. The thrower of the javelin, Euphorbos, a minor hero, has the impertinence to claim Patroclus's armor, thereby insisting he was the chief killer:

> Since before me no one of the Trojans, or renowned
>   companions,
> struck Patroclus down with the spear in the strong encounter.
> Accordingly, let me win this great glory among the Trojans.

But Euphorbos cannot press his title because he is cut down by the Achaean hero Menelaus. And so Hector gets the armor. But the *Iliad* cannot resist a last jab at Hector, when the god Zeus describes the Trojan's taking of the armor as unseemly.[2]

In the wrangle that breaks out here — this argument among men about responsibility for a killing, an argument that even draws in a god — there stands revealed a disagreement in the world of the *Iliad* about what constitutes heroic behavior. Whose deed is higher, that of Euphorbos, the wounder, or that of Hector, the killer? That there should be such a conflict is hardly surprising. Real societies hardly agree on what deeds are admired and to what degree. And the society of the *Iliad* is not a real society, but a fictional, composite one, an epic never-never land that draws elements from the era of the Mycenean kingdoms when the poem is set (c. 1200 BC), through the long Greek Dark Ages, down to the archaic period, when the poem reached its final form. And the *Iliad* was not the work of a single poet laboring at a desk: before it was finally written down it accumulated like coral over centuries through the recitations of generations of bards: so one speaks of the poem rather than of the poet. It is probably impossible to offer a fully satisfactory reconstruction of the real-world fighting that lies behind the poem. Instead the *Iliad,* and its contradictions, must be examined for other, no less compelling reasons: because of the relationship of later Greek warriors to epic fighting and the long-lasting Greek values that epic enshrined. The *Iliad* is the baseline for understanding the military ethos of the Greeks and important for understanding the military methods of historical Greeks.

We mold an *Iliad* in our own image, a tragic poem of character and humanity. We are fascinated by the intrigues of the all-too-human gods. We remember the dispute of Agamemnon and Achilles, the prickliness of Achilles and his proud refusal to fight. We love the compassionate Patroclus, who goes out to stem the disaster that Achilles' pride has caused. We thrill to Achilles' furious return to the fighting and mourn the inexorable doom of Hector, the family man. Finally, our hearts move with Hector's father, Priam, as he begs for the return of the body of his son.

But our *Iliad*, our *Iliad* of human feeling, occupies surprisingly little of the poem: open the work at random and chances are you will come upon the fighting of heroes. To our sensibility fighting is supposed to move along the plot. But the fighting in the *Iliad* goes on for books and books and is totally out proportion, it seems to us, to its significance to the narrative. Evidently the description of the fighting has a purpose of its own, quite apart from the plot. And even the most casual reader of the *Iliad* notices that many of the episodes of fighting are very similar, and the more perceptive reader notices that the fighting is described according to patterns and rules: it is those rules that make most of the combats much the same. Powerful invisible forces shape the descriptions of combat in the *Iliad,* and identifying those forces is the key to understanding not only the killing of Patroclus, but also why the *Iliad* describes fighting the way it does and the legacy of the *Iliad* to Greek military history.

It happens again and again: a major hero encounters a minor hero of the enemy. The minor hero is introduced, and then the minor hero is slain, often with a gory anatomical description of the killing:

> There Telamonian Ajax struck down the son of Anthemion,
> Simoeisios in his stripling's beauty, whom once his mother
> descending from Ida bore beside the banks of Simoeis
> when she had followed her father and mother to tend the
>   sheepflocks.
> Therefore they called him Simoeisios; but he could not
> render again the care of his dear parents; he was shortlived,

beaten down beneath the spear of high-hearted Ajax,
who struck him as he first came forward beside the nipple
of the right breast, and the bronze spearhead drove clean
    through the shoulder.[3]

The encounter between two warriors can be much elaborated. Upon meeting, opposing warriors may exchange threats — "here you will meet your doom!" — defiances — "bragging ox!" — and boastful genealogies. The introduction of the victim and his death are often adorned with epic similes, sometimes heartbreakingly beautiful:

He dropped then to the ground in the dust, like some black
    poplar,
which in the land low-lying about a great marsh grows
smooth trimmed yet with branches growing at the uttermost
    tree top.[4]

The victor may strip the armor of the vanquished and vaunt over his victim: "Carrion-eating birds will drag at you, beating their wings hard about you!" In two cases combats are fought under conditions agreed upon in advance — formal duels, one of which ends in a draw and an exchange of gifts. The most important fights, like the culminating combat between Achilles and Hector, are drawn out to great length with circumstantial details and remarks back and forth, multiple similes, and divine intervention.[5] Yet the one-on-one fighting can also be stripped of all adornment and reduced to a mere list of the slain:

Who was it you slaughtered first, who was the last one,
Patroclus, as the gods called you to your death? Adrestos
first, and after him Autonoös and Echeklos,
Perimos, son of Megas, and Epistor, and Melanippos,
and after these Elasos, and Moulios, and Pylartes.[6]

The pattern of combat as a one-on-one affair is very strong. Even when two warriors gang up to face a single enemy the fight tends to be described as two separate and sequential encounters between individuals.[7]

The heroic one-on-one fighting described in the *Iliad* is, as has long been understood, closely linked to the heroic motives the poem attributes to the fighters. Homeric heroes compete with each other and are conceived as being ranked one against another in a competitive series, each yearning "always to be the best and preeminent above others." At the bottom of the ranking stands the lame, hideous, and craven Thersites, "there is no worse man of those who came . . . beneath Ilion," at the top a man like Achilles, "the best of the Achaeans." Nearly every activity in the *Iliad* can be imagined to be a competition. Soon after the poem's opening the audience meets the seer Kalchas, "by far the best of the bird interpreters." But by far the most important arena for competition is the individual heroic fighting itself. It is in battle that a hero wins the admiration, the glory—the *kleos*, the *kudos*—that conveys high rank, honor, worth, or worthiness: *timē*. In the epic formula, battle is "where men win glory."[8]

Heroes compete in public performance in war and battle, performance which is constantly evaluated by their peers. A hero's high birth and high deeds in the past create a favorable expectation in the eyes of observers, but the hero must uphold his reputation by the continual display of merit in action. Heroes compete in the display of Homeric virtues, *aretai*, which include strength, skill, physical courage, and fleetness of foot, but also cunning and wisdom and persuasiveness in council. The heroic epithets the poem applies to heroes reflect many of the Homeric excellences:

> . . . the son of Tydeus, the spear-famed, and Odysseus,
> and Ajax the swift-footed, and the brave son of Phyleus.[9]

Some heroes excel more in one excellence than in others, like Achilles in strength and Odysseus in cunning. The major Homeric virtues are displayed in fighting and planning for fighting. As heroes slaughter their foes they demonstrate these qualities before their public, the other heroes on both sides, and so establish their claim to relative rank.[10]

Thus, when the armies meet, the heroes compete to be the first one to kill an enemy. To find enemies to fight, leading heroes run out far in front of the rest of the army; to emerge first and run out farthest are competitive acts in their own right. Competitive too are the remarks, the exchange of threats and insults and boasting, that often precede a one-on-

one fight. A hero might boast of his ability in this competitive realm, for this is a world in which a hero can be "best at abuse." Simple numbers slain, too, prove performance: a numerical score can be compared gloatingly to an opponent's inferior score. This is the purpose of mere lists of names of those killed.[11]

Fighting an enemy warrior tests bravery and strength and skill. Only if a god intervenes do "the weapons of all strike home, no matter who throws them, good man [*agathos*] or bad [*kakos*]." A warrior like Achilles, the best, is one whose "spear wings straight to its mark, nor gives out until it has gone through a man's body." The ubiquitous gory anatomical descriptions of killing that are such fundamental elements of the Homeric battle pattern demonstrate the skill and strength of the victor:

> Idomeneus stabbed Erymas in the mouth with the pitiless
> bronze, so that the brazen spearhead smashed its way clean
>   through
> below the brain in an upward stroke, and the white bones
>   splintered,
> and the teeth were shaken out with the stroke and both eyes
>   filled up
> with blood, and gaping he blew a spray of blood through the
>   nostrils
> and through his mouth, and death in a dark mist closed in
>   about him.[12]

If foes flee they must be pursued, testing fleetness of foot. "Ajax the swift son of Oileus killed the most, since there was none like him in the speed of his feet to go after men who ran." Indeed, an especially swift hero might run through the midst of the battle just to show off his speed — and be killed by Achilles as he passed.[13]

Heroes compete not only in open battle, but ambushes and spying expeditions and attacks by night also test strength, bravery, and fleetness of foot as well as the cunning intelligence of which Odysseus is the avatar. War in the *Iliad* also involves meetings, both mass assemblies and conventicles of leading warriors, which give heroes the opportunity to compete in giving good advice and in persuasiveness in council. Like battle, the assembly "where young men compete with words" is also "where men become preeminent" and "where men win glory [*kudos*]."[14]

Yet if gaining glory and thereby rank is a question of performance, it is surprising to discover that heroes believe they have gained glory when they kill unheroically, as when Hector kills Periphetes where he lies helpless on the ground, having tripped on his shield while running away, or when Deiphobos kills Hypsenor quite by mistake, having cast his spear at Idomeneus. Sometimes the glory of the victor depends not only upon his observed performance, but also on the excellence of the defeated; this is a second, quite separate, mechanism for gaining glory in battle. Killing an important opponent constitutes a *euxos,* a "claim to glory," in proportion to the excellence of the hero killed: "We have won ourselves enormous fame [*kudos*]; we have killed the great Hector whom the Trojans glorified as if he were a god in their city." To know how much glory killing a hero brings, the audience must be introduced to the victim, and that is why the poem so frequently gives details about the families and biographies of minor heroes who appear only to be slain. Before Hector slays the helpless Periphetes the poem says he was

> beloved son of Kopreus, who for the lord Eurystheus
> had gone often with messages to powerful Heracles.
> To him, a meaner father, was born a son who was better
> in all virtues [*aretai*], in the speed of his feet and in battle
> and for intelligence counted among the first in Mycenae.
> Thereby now higher was the glory [*kudos*] he granted to
>   Hector.[15]

The victor may also vaunt with boastful speech over the body, claiming the glory due him in proportion to the rank of his victim. "You shall vaunt over the two sons of Hipassos, for having killed two such men and stripped their armor." These proud speeches can seem odd. Sometimes the victor says little about his own achievement and a great deal about the hero he has just killed:

> "Lie there, Otrynteus's son, most terrifying of all men.
> Here is your death, but your generation was by the lake waters

of Gyge, where is the allotted land of your fathers
by fish-swarming Hyllos and the whirling waters of
   Hermos."[16]

But since the victor's glory depends so largely on the quality of the enemy
he has slain, it makes sense for him to add to the details the narrator has
given about his victim.

The two ways in which heroes in the *Iliad* compete for glory in fighting — the slayer's performance and the slain's value — can produce quite
different estimates of the slayer's glory. This is the conflict that drives the
dispute over the killing of Patroclus, for although Hector strikes the final
blow and can glory in the value of Patroclus (high, given his recent rout
of the Trojans), Hector's actual deed is trifling, delivering the coup de
grace to a hero already stripped of his gear, stunned, and wounded. Indeed, the *Iliad* stops to emphasize the special martial skill of Euphorbos,
who threw the javelin that wounded Patroclus before Hector reached
him:

> He surpassed his generation
> with the spear, in horsemanship, and with his swift feet,
> and indeed he had already brought down twenty men from
>   their horses
> since he had come with his chariot, a man learned in war.[17]

So the point is made that all the heroic excellence involved was that of
Euphorbos, rather than of Hector. It is the yawning gap between the distinction Hector earns for killing so successful a warrior — Patroclus's value
— and the unimpressive way he killed him — his own performance — that
lends the force to Patroclus's dying taunt.

These two potentially contradictory ways of evaluating a heroic killing
also pull the actual behavior of the heroes in contradictory directions,
the valuation of performance lending one-on-one combat in the *Iliad*
the curiously formal, chivalrous quality it sometimes exhibits. In the duel
between Hector and Ajax, the son of Telamon invites Hector to deliver
the first blow, and Hector replies by boasting of his performance in war
and proclaiming his refusal to fight by trickery:

"I know well myself how to fight and kill men in battle;
I know how to turn to the right, how to turn to the left
   the ox-hide
tanned into a shield which is my protection in battle;
I know how to storm my way into the struggle of flying
   horses;
I know how to tread the measures on the grim floor of
   the war god.
Yet great as you are I would not strike you by stealth, watching
for my chance, but openly, so, if perhaps I might hit you."[18]

Yet Hector mentions the temptations of stealth and guile: since Ajax is as great as he is, Hector can gain distinction by killing him even without heroic performance. And since fighting Ajax is so dangerous, the prospect of attacking him stealthily is extremely attractive. The valuation of killing in proportion to the excellence of the victim, regardless of how the killing is done, ensures that heroes are elsewhere delighted to kill by surprise, to slaughter the distracted, the terrified, and the dazed, as Hector does to Patroclus. Sometimes individual Homeric combat resembles a series of formal duels, sometimes a wild mêlée: the *Iliad* is struggling to accommodate two different systems of evaluating human beings by their success in combat. It is not that epic attributes to the warriors a system of values that concords with their way of fighting; rather, they are depicted as fighting in a way that accords with their ethics, the two (potentially conflicting) methods they have of establishing relative rank by fighting. Epic wraps a way of describing fighting around a set of beliefs, a set of beliefs sometimes at odds with itself.

The poetic vision of battle as the struggle of individual hero against hero, although overwhelmingly common, does not go unchallenged in the *Iliad*. Before the first general onslaught in the poem, Agamemnon, high king of the Achaeans, circulates among his army, stirring up the Achaean captains for battle:

There he came upon Nestor, the lucid speaker of Pylos,
setting in order his own companions and urging them to battle,

tall Pelagon with those about him, Alastor and Chromios,
Haimon the powerful, and Bias, shepherd of the people.
First he [Nestor] ranged the mounted men with their horses
    and chariots
and stationed the brave [*esthloi*] and numerous footsoldiers
    behind them
to be the bastion of battle, and drove the cowards [*kakoi*] in
    between
so that a man might be forced to fight even though unwilling.
First he gave orders to the drivers of horses, and warned them
to hold their horses in check and not be fouled in the
    multitude:
"Let no man in the pride of his horsemanship and his
    manhood
dare to fight alone with the Trojans in front of the rest of us,
neither let him give ground, since that way you will be weaker.
When a man from his own car encounters the enemy chariots
let him stab with his spear, since this is the stronger fighting.
So the men before your time sacked tower and city."[19]

Nestor's orders are a severe and explicit rebuke to the way most of the fighting in the *Iliad* is actually conducted. Depictions of heroes charging out before the mass in pride of their manhood to fight their opposite numbers — exactly the behavior Nestor forbids — occupy the great bulk of Homeric battle descriptions. Cowards hang back. Chariots mingle constantly with foot soldiers. Although warriors can throw or thrust spears from their chariots, as Nestor urges, they usually dismount and fight individually on foot, using their chariots for transport to and from the field, as taxis and as ambulances. Fiercely critical of the epic practice of one-on-one fighting, Nestor urges a way of war strikingly different from that which dominates the battle scenes of the *Iliad,* and the poem betrays its uneasy awareness of the contrast by having Nestor describe the tactics he is putting into action as those of a past generation.[20]

The way in which Nestor arrays a mass of men before battle is hardly unique in the *Iliad*. In a passage recalling Nestor's orders, Ajax masses warriors to defend the body of Patroclus, forbidding them to withdraw or to sally forth to fight in front. At Poulydamas's suggestion the mounted Trojans dismount from their chariots before the trench defending the Achaean ships and the Trojans attack in five companies.[21] Achilles organizes the Myrmidons to follow Patroclus likewise in five companies, and they go out to fight in close order:

> And as a man builds solid a wall with stones set close together
> for the rampart of a high house keeping out the force of the
>   winds, so
> close together were the helms and shields massive in the
>   middle.
> For shield leaned upon shield, helmet on helmet, man against
>   man,
> and the horse-hair crests along the horns of the shining
>   helmets
> touched as they bent their heads, so dense were they formed
>   on each other.[22]

But right after describing it, the *Iliad* forgets the wall-like assemblage of the Myrmidons and compares them next to a swarm of wasps. And so too is Nestor's array instantly forgotten. Sometimes the heroes appear as leaders marshaling and commanding soldiers. But most of the time in the *Iliad* the heroes appear as fighters, not as leaders, and the mass of warriors is invisible or maintains a shadowy existence behind the heroes. In the *Iliad*'s formal introduction of the heroes on both sides — the Catalogue of Ships — we learn about the large retinues of followers the Achaean heroes and the Trojan allies brought to Troy. But for the most part the heroes fight each other one-on-one quite oblivious to their mass followings, and most acts of mass arraying have little or no consequence in the subsequent battle. Heroes fighting as individuals and those same heroes' role as leaders of men do not fit together well in the poem. With Nestor's complaint about how the heroes fight, the *Iliad* for a moment seems to stand outside itself and criticize, in Nestor's voice, the way things are done within itself. As with the killing of Patroclus, epic seems to be worrying at itself: Nestor's orders seem to draw attention to the conflict that exists between one-on-one and mass fighting in its narrative.[23]

Yet just as the description of one-on-one fighting in the *Iliad* is governed by the values of the heroes, so is the mass fighting. In the first place, masses of warriors commonly participate in the fighting of individual heroes—serve as stage machinery in competitive heroic fighting—by protecting a hero with their shields so he can ply his bow, by protecting wounded heroes, and by forming a collective obstacle to throw back a major enemy hero, often to bar him from the competitive success of despoiling an enemy he has just killed. A hero can win preeminence in rank by holding his ground alone against an anonymous mass. The breaking of such a mass by an individual is a supreme heroic achievement.[24]

But more useful for understanding Nestor's complaint is the fact that one of the excellences, *aretai,* in which Homeric heroes compete is setting troops in order for battle. "Never on earth before had there been a man born like him for the arrangement in order of horses and shielded fighters," the poem says about Menestheus, leader of the Athenians; "Nestor alone could challenge him." So Nestor turns out to be outstanding in this realm. And it is the poem's desire to show off Nestor's preeminence in this excellence that explains the depiction of him giving orders, criticizing contemporary practices, and expounding unusual tactics. The orders given, the array is instantly forgotten. Nestor has shown his excellence by organizing his troops, and after that the poem turns to displaying the different, usually more directly violent, excellences of other heroes. The same oblivion awaits Achilles' array, but the act of arraying shows that he has "divided well." Longest remembered in the poem is the array of Poulydamas, the Trojan Nestor, repeatedly praised for his wisdom. When Ajax masses the Achaeans to defend the body of Patroclus—"such were the orders of gigantic Ajax"—his array, unusually, has immediate consequences in the battle narrative. The Achaeans drive off the Trojan hero Asteropaios and

>   the ground ran
> with red blood, the dead men dropped one after another
> from the ranks alike of Trojans and their mighty companions
> and Danaans also, since these fought not without
>   bloodletting,
> but far fewer of them went down, since they ever remembered

always to stand massed and beat sudden death from each
    other.

What the Achaeans "ever remembered" were the admirable orders of Ajax:
the narrative bends around to signal the hero's excellence in arraying.[25]

    Epic conceives a hero's assembling of an array as a form of competi-
tion with all other heroes who array troops. At the same time the array
itself can be envisaged as the setting up of a competition between those
who are arrayed. So Nestor advises Agamemnon:

> "Set your men in order by tribes, by brotherhoods,
>   Agamemnon,
> and let each brotherhood go in support of brotherhood, let
>   tribe support tribe.
> If you do it this way, and the Achaeans obey you,
> you will see which of your leaders is bad [*kakos*], and which
>   of your people,
> and which also is brave [*esthlos*], since they will fight by
>   themselves."[26]

Arraying, then, tests both those who do the arraying and those who are
arrayed.

The depiction of battle in the *Iliad* stems ultimately from an epic drive
to represent, in the freedom of an unreal world, the heroes excelling in
the full set of Homeric virtues, some of them physical, some moral, and
some intellectual. The result is a confusion of fighting styles, as the poem
moves quickly from the representation of one kind of excellence to another. Yet in its depiction of the wrangle over Hector's killing of Patroclus and of Nestor's admission that his orders do not reflect the practices
of his generation the poem signals that contradictions exist within the
ideals of one-on-one fighting and between the ideals of one-on-one and
mass fighting, between the consequences in the poem of the various kinds
of Homeric excellences. The poem simply chooses not to emphasize them.

    Yet epic *can* choose to emphasize conflicts in the ethics of the heroes.
Indeed, the whole plot of the *Iliad* develops from a profound conflict

between the implications of Homeric values. As the "best of the Achaeans," Achilles maintains that he should receive the most loot and be subject to no man: any other arrangement dishonors him. Yet although an inferior warrior, Agamemnon has other claims to precedence over Achilles. As Nestor says to Achilles,

> Nor, son of Peleus, think to match your strength with
>   the king, since never equal with the rest is the portion of
>   honor [*timē*]
> of the sceptred king to whom Zeus gives magnificence [*kudos*].
>   Even
> though you are the stronger man, and the mother who bore
>   you was immortal,
> yet is this man greater who is lord over more than you rule.[27]

Which one should go without his slave girl when the daughter of the priest of Apollo must be returned to avert the plague the god has brought upon the army? Agamemnon thinks Achilles, Achilles thinks Agamemnon. Agamemnon has the power to enforce his will, and so the outraged Achilles withdraws from the fighting and has his divine mother bring great Zeus in on the Trojan side. The story of the *Iliad* follows from Achilles' and Agamemnon's pressing of what each considers his legitimate claim. Here the poem chooses to stress a conflict in the ethical system because it is essential to the plot of the poem. But this prominent case emphasizes that it is the privilege of a poem to make that kind of choice. Conflicts in outlook do not need to be pointed up: different outlooks can simply motivate different passages of text.

Such is the case with the heroic valuation of archery. Paris hits Diomedes with an arrow and vaunts over him: "You are hit, and my arrow flew not in vain." Diomedes answers,

> You, archer, foul fighter, lovely in your locks, eyer of young
>   girls.
> If you were to make trial of me in strong combat with weapons
> your bow would do you no good at all, nor your close-
>   showered arrows.

Now you have scratched the flat of my foot, and even boast
   of this.
I care no more than if a witless child or a woman
had struck me; this is the blank weapon of a useless man,
   no fighter.[28]

Diomedes' is not an isolated complaint. Elsewhere "arrow-fighters" is a term of abuse, while "[those] who fight at close quarters" is a praising epithet of peoples, and the fact that an individual fights close up, not with missiles, is grounds for pride.[29]

Yet it never strikes archers in the *Iliad* to be ashamed of their craft, or their friends to be ashamed of archers. Quite the contrary. Aeneas asks Pandarus,

Where now are your bow and your feathered arrows;
where your fame [*kleos*] in which no man here dare contend
   with you
nor can any man in Lycia claim he is better?[30]

Despite the contempt in which using the bow is held by some heroes, it turns out to be a heroic *aretē* just like fighting with a spear. When Teucer, "the best of the Achaeans in archery," shoots down many Trojans, he is said to be bringing glory to his absent father, Telamon, and Agamemnon promises him a gift of honor. Archery is an event at Patroclus's funeral games; extreme accuracy is wondered at; in the *Odyssey* Odysseus slaughters the suitors with his bow, having proved his superiority over them as the only man who could string it; in the *Odyssey* archery is a heroic achievement par excellence. In the *Iliad,* moreover, the heroic quality of archery can be admitted even by those on the side victimized by an arrow in battle. Pandarus breaks the truce surrounding the duel between Paris and Menelaus by shooting Menelaus with an arrow. A healer is sent for to attend Menelaus, "whom someone well skilled in the bow's use shot with an arrow, Trojan or Lycian: glory [*kleos*] to him, but to us a sorrow."[31] The poem needs to present both fighters with bows and fighters with spears and swords in a suitably heroic light, and so the heroic evaluation of archery is never settled. By having Diomedes denounce Paris, the *Iliad* betrays its awareness of the contradiction, but otherwise the epic simply tolerates it.

Another unsettled tension, tolerated with an even greater sense of discomfort, is that which exists between the heroes' estimates of a hero's duty to stand his ground in battle. A host of Trojans approaches the lone Odysseus. He wonders whether he should flee such long odds:

> "Yet still, why does the heart within me debate on these things?
> Since I know that it is the cowards [*kakoi*] who walk out of the
>   fighting,
> but if one is to be preeminent in battle, he must by all means
> stand his ground strongly, whether he be struck or strike
>   down another."[32]

A clear statement, or so it seems: according to their code, major heroes, the preeminent, must hold their position; that is what it means to be preeminent rather than a coward. Elsewhere Diomedes echoes the same sentiment. Yet, in fact, major heroes are constantly shrinking back into the mass behind them or fleeing wholesale along with their followers with no sense that they are acting improperly. Epic does not decide whether running away is unheroic or not. When Hector finally faces Achilles and flees from him in terror, the poem seems to consider it a shameful act of cowardice. But as the chase continues the poem compares it to a footrace for a prize and emphasizes Achilles' inability to catch Hector. Running at the same speed as Achilles, Hector displays the same fleetness of foot, the same excellence as Achilles, whose superhuman speed the poem has repeatedly emphasized. Here an honorable contest of fleetness of foot has quietly displaced the ethic that fleeing is dishonorable. And the ethic itself does not go unchallenged. Agamemnon, at least, actually denies that fleeing is against the heroic code. Odysseus then argues the point with him: once again the poem is aware of, and uncomfortable with, the conflict over the valuation of standing one's ground.[33] There is even an attempt to finesse the contradiction. Nestor, in Diomedes' chariot and hoping to ride it to safety, is appalled to discover that Diomedes intends to stand his ground during the Achaean rout because the younger hero fears being mocked by Hector if he runs away, and says to him:

"If Hector calls you a coward [*kakos*] and a man of no
    strength, then
the Trojans and Dardanians will never believe him,
nor will the wives of the high-hearted Trojan warriors
whose husbands you hurled in the dust in the pride of their
    manhood."[34]

Fleeing, in other words, *is* disgraceful, but the heroic audience (here conceived of as consisting of enemies) will consider the whole of a hero's accomplishment, and Diomedes' good performance will outweigh the bad. Here again epic picks at a conflict of values like an itchy scab, betraying a self-conscious awareness of it but tolerating it, letting contradictory positions each play their part in different passages of the poem. Making room for so much contradiction is the privilege of epic, which portrays an ultimately fantastic world.

THE *ILIAD* AND THE GREEKS

The Homeric poems have been called the Bible of the Greeks, an analogy that has lost much of its force in an agnostic age and that was never quite right in the first place. Scripture is far more imperious than epic. No Greek would imagine a duty to regulate his life exactly by the splenetic remarks of the feuding, fallible, lying gods of the poems. Yet as early as can be traced, Homer was the foundation of Greek education — indeed, epic may have constituted nearly all of Greek intellectual education down into the fifth century BC. Homer was "the teacher of Greece," memorized and recited and in later times read and reread with a concentration that no modern system of education devotes to a single set of texts. In the late fifth century it was the sign of a man of standing to be able to recite the *Iliad* and the *Odyssey* by heart, and that fact is evidence that these two epics had already achieved a canonical position quite separate from and above the rest of the prequel-and-sequel Epic Cycle and the swirling clouds of nonepic Greek myth. And at least by Hellenistic and Roman times (when the papyri of Egypt reveal such things) the *Iliad* had established dominance over the *Odyssey* as a teaching text. In all periods Greek authors quote, echo, and allude to Homer in a manner that assumes a warm familiarity in their readers. Homer gave the authoritative account of Greece's early days: epic was the ancient history of the Greeks.[35]

Yet Homer was more, read not only as a way of teaching reading and writing, as a stylistic model, and as what we call literature, but also as a moral text: "One should arrange one's entire life according to this poet." The ultimate origins of the ferocious competitiveness of the Greeks — in human biology? an inheritance of Indo-European codes of masculinity? — cannot be discovered. But without doubt the cult of Homer perpetuated in Greece the competitive ethics embodied in the poems, while the epics remained fundamental educational texts because the poems reflected those familiar, undying, admired principles: epic and Greek competitive ethics walked like conjoined twins through the centuries. And this congruence of Homeric and later Greek ethics ensured that the heroes were not only old, but also admirable, and so the past of the Greeks was not inert, but to be imitated by the men of the present. The heroes of epic always sat invisible upon the shoulders of the Greeks, whispering their counsel.[36]

Yet at the same time the later Greek relationship with Homer gave them a past that was fundamentally textual, fundamentally fixed. A great confection of fast-changing myth could be whipped up around epic, often involving other adventures of the gods and epic heroes; the text of epic could be argued over (of course), and epic could be interpreted (of course). But at the bottom of the Greek past was a little-changing, hallowed set of words. It is notorious that when the Romans, who lacked their own *Iliad* and *Odyssey,* looked into their distant past, their present often looked back at them — later Romans projected their contemporary political problems into the time of their ancestors, about whom they had little authentic information. But epic made the Greek past irreducibly past, and so rather than envisaging the past as the present, they tended rather to understand the present by means of the past. When a Greek sculptor wished to allude to the great wars between Greeks and Persians, he tended instead to depict the combat between the Greeks and Trojans or between Greeks and Amazons, mythic warrior-women, or the combat between the Greek Lapiths and the bestial Centaurs, themes elaborated from epic. Greek tragedy often treated contemporary themes, but with a tiny number of exceptions the plays themselves were set in the heroic era. The Greek epic past, unlike the distant Roman past, had an independent existence outside the needs of the present, and so always exerted a powerful independent traction on the Greek present.

Epic helped to convey the competitive values of the Greeks (older even than epic) down the years. As such, epic was the underlying melody of Greek civilization, for the most part so deep within the symphony of civilization that the Greeks themselves were unconscious of it. Yet where there were ugly clangs and dissonances in the secret melody, epic being so much more forgiving than reality, real Greeks had to work them out in their lives. And so the story of the evolution of warfare in historical ancient Greece is in part the story of the consequences of these epic contradictions in the real world. On the conscious level, moreover, when a Greek faced a puzzle of ethics or writing or even a practical way of doing something, it was to epic he first applied for a solution: the poets (and "Homer is their leader") "know all the crafts." Epic was the "encyclopedia" of the Greeks, and the ways of epic were the good ways. So Greek civilization, and Greek soldiers, also consciously reached back into epic for inspiration. Part of the military history of the Greeks is no more than a particular instance of this pervasive pattern of epic recollection.[37]

II

THE LAST HOPLITE

THE ORIGINS OF THE PHALANX

Diomedes was lord over Argos, sang the poet, and Menelaus ruled Lacedaemon across the hills. And the two princes went forth to Troy with Agamemnon, high king of Mycenae. But this friendship was not to endure, and Argos and Lacedaemon (we know it as Sparta, from its capital) became rivals for the lordship of Peloponnese and long, intimate enemies. Ever jousting for the heirship of Agamemnon, the two proud cities fought many bitter wars against each other, and they battled especially over Thyrea, a bloodstained scrap of land on the coast where their territories met. In the most famous of these meetings, the Spartans and Argives made a covenant that their strife should be settled by a battle of champions, by the clash of three hundred picked men from each city. The rest of the armies, Spartan and Argive alike, retired into their own countries, that none should be tempted to interfere. The champions fought, but neither side could gain the advantage and drive the other from the field. At fall of night only three men still lived: Alcenor and Chromius of the Argives and the wounded Spartan Othryades, lying unnoticed among the corpses. The Argives ran to report their victory to Argos. But the lone Spartan staggered to his feet and stayed upon the field, despoiling the Argive dead of their armor and carrying it back to the Spartan camp. According to one tradition, Othryades, leaning on a broken spear, erected a trophy from the armor of the slain (such was the Greek custom) and inscribed it with his blood.

A poet imagined the return of the two Argives with their army the next morning:

> These arms new-stripped: who nailed them to this oak?
>> Who inscribed this Dorian shield?
> For this land of Thyrea o'er spills with the blood of comrades
>> and we twain alone are left from the Argives.
> Seek out every fallen corpse! lest one, still left breathing,
>> bedizen Sparta with a bastard glory.
> No, stay! For the victory of the Spartans cries from the
>> shield with the clots of Othryades' blood,
> and nearby gasps he whose agony wrought this.

Dawn and the return of the armies to discover the outcome found Othryades standing quietly in his assigned place in the ranks, his rank-mates stretched corpses on either side, a single live soldier in a battalion of the staring dead.[1]

Of Othryades' fate the legends are various: perhaps he died after inscribing the trophy. Perhaps he committed suicide on the battlefield. The Argives denied he had survived the fighting at all: according to them, Othryades had been killed by an Argive warrior, and they had a statue of his killer to prove it. In Herodotus's version the Argives and Spartans fell to wrangling about who had won: two of ours survived, the Argives claimed; yours fled while our man held the field and plundered the bodies, the Spartans replied. Hot words became blows, and there was a great battle between the armies assembled. The gods vindicated the claims of the lone Spartan: the Lacedaemonians bore away the victory.[2]

The battle of champions at Thyrea is an event nearly as mythical as the Trojan War, but it is a myth that imagines a world of warfare far different from that depicted in the *Iliad*. There are Homeric elements, like the despoiling of the bodies, but with new meanings. Othryades' remaining in possession of the field and his taking of the Argives' armor are not only claims to personal glory, but allow the Spartans to claim a national victory. And most arresting of all is the picture the legend conjures in our mind, the vision of the blood-drenched Spartan, wounded, exhausted by a day of fighting and a night of dragging armor from inert, reeking bodies, wandering in the false dawn and turning over the strewn and piled corpses of his Spartan comrades, searching amidst the slaughter to find and reoccupy his exact place in the bright array that once had been.

Othryades' behavior reflects the ethos of the phalanx, the formation which the Greeks were perfecting in his time (around 550 BC). Heavily armored — necessarily with spear, large round shield, and helmet, ideally also with breastplate and greaves to protect his legs — the man-at-arms, the hoplite, went into battle in a tight-knit block, eight or more ranks deep, with men close on his left and right (see figures). Together the warrior and his comrades constituted the phalanx, or "roller," which crashed face to face into the enemy. The phalanx stands in striking contrast to the fighting depicted in the *Iliad,* for it was an ordered block of men expected to maintain its order, a formation. The Greek technical vocabulary for the stages of a hoplite battle — the *othismos,* or mass push, and the *tropē,* or mass turning to flight — emphasize that in phalanx-fighting men acted as a body, not as individuals or temporary bands. Soldiers in the phalanx fought closely packed together, protecting each others' sides, forming a wall with their shields. Perhaps the hoplites in the rear ranks actually pushed their shields against the backs of those in front of them, attempting to drive the enemy back by sheer muscular pressure. In any event, if a warrior left his place in the ranks, whether to flee or go forward to fight in heroic isolation, he placed his comrades in jeopardy. Only when one side was put to flight and the other pursued did the formations dissolve; only then was actual skill at arms very important.[3]

The choice of three hundred champions to represent each side at Thyrea is merely an extreme case of the oddly formal, even ritual, quality that phalanx fighting could display. A "fair and open" battle, that is, a battle without trickery, was the ideal of hoplite combat. The two hoplite armies might approach each other and camp, perhaps for several days, on a mutually agreeable plain. Rules might be agreed upon, as at Thyrea; the inviolability of heralds and sacred places and seasons like the Olympic truce was respected. Battle often came on by tacit agreement, when one army drew up for combat on a flat place and the other accepted the implicit challenge by drawing up in return. If an army consisted of contingents from allied cities, it would array its phalanx according to precedence

Hoplites in battle, aryballos attributed to the Chigi/Macmillan painter,
c. 650 BC (Berlin inv. 3773; drawing from E. Pfuhl, *Malerei und Zeichnung
der Griechen* vol. 3 [Munich, 1923] fig. 58).

from right to left, although often the extreme left wing was conceived
as second in honor. The onset was preceded by sacrifice. The Spartans,
who took the ritual quality of battle to an extreme, went into battle with
their hair combed, their gear polished and decorated, and their heads
garlanded, as if in procession to a religious festival. The paean to Apollo
was sung, there was a shout to Ares, and with an ululating war cry the
phalanxes crashed together. When one side turned the other to flight,
pursuit was usually limited, and the Spartans made a policy of not pursuing far. The winning side remained in possession of the battlefield until
the losing side sent a herald to ask for the right to recover their dead
under a truce, thereby admitting their defeat. Their suit was almost in-
variably granted, the winning side, garlanded and to the music of pipes,
built a monument of captured armor on the field at the point of the *tropē*
(hence the word *trophy*), and both armies went home. By modern standards we often see less than we expect of planning and strategy as the
armies move toward battle or of ambush and of ambuscade in a mountainous country, and in battle itself we see less than we expect of maneuver and tactics. The whole hoplite method of war seems surreally stylized,
apt for comparison to the flower wars of the Aztecs or to a modern team
sport. And the formality and decorum of the Greek way of war struck
the Greeks themselves. The fifth-century Herodotus makes one of his
Persian characters mock it, in exaggerated terms: "When they declare war
upon each other, they seek out the fairest and flattest patch of ground,
and there they set on and fight; as a result the winners suffer great hurt;
and of the losers there is nothing to say, for they are quite destroyed. . . .
[Instead] each should seek out the place where they'd be most difficult
to subdue, and try their chances there."[4] So it is not just to us that the

Hoplite phalanx, Xanthos, Nereid Monument, c. 400 BC
(BM inv. 868; © Copyright The British Museum).

Classical Greek style of fighting seems strange: the Greeks wondered about it too, wondered why they sacrificed advantage for fairness in war.

Even without descending into the mire of Homer and his mysteries, it is possible to catch glimpses from early poetry and Greek vase painting of the kind of fighting out of which the phalanx emerged. Tyrtaeus is the key here, the Spartan war poet of the late seventh century BC, whose elegies urged men to combat in the manner of his day. The heavy-armed warriors in Tyrtaeus's world had ample room to move around, to lurk in the back of the battle out of the range of missiles or to go to the front to fight with thrusting spear or sword, sometimes coming together in clots with comrades to fight side by side. And mingled with them, hiding behind their heavy-armed comrades, were light-armed warriors casting javelins and stones. Vases reveal hoplites regularly armed with javelins or pairs of spears for throwing and show archers as well in the loose, unformed mob in which fighting was conducted.[5]

Yet by the fifth century at the latest, although the changes cannot be shown to be complete until the Peloponnesian War of 431–404 BC, the temporary clots had become an enduring formation, the hoplites had lost their javelins, and the missile-armed light warriors, where they had not been banished from the battlefield altogether, had been expelled from the phalanx and now fought separately. Traces survive, in Classical Greek institutions, of a day when the richest had fought on horseback. Some cities, like Athens, maintained an aristocratic cavalry in Classical times. But when the levy was called, the highborn cavalrymen usually fought as hoplites, even if they rode luxuriously to the battlefield on their high-stepping horses. Athenians of the highest family, men like Cimon and Alcibiades, fought as hoplites. The Athenian politician Pericles, a great aristocrat indeed, is depicted in sculpture wearing a hoplite helmet (to conceal his oddly shaped head, we are told—but a less meaningful cover would have done that as well). In Sparta the "cavalry" had become an élite corps of three hundred hoplites who fought in the phalanx: they may have been the Spartan champions at Thyrea. Sparta's kings too fought in the phalanx, with Spartan Olympic victors standing in front of them. By the fifth century, when we can see the hoplite phalanx clearly, it incorporated the full range of those prosperous enough to afford hoplite equipment.[6]

Aristotle is at the root of a common understanding of the political significance of the phalanx. In the *Politics* he writes, "The first type of constitution in Greece after the age of the kings was founded upon warriors, originally upon cavalry—for cavalry was strong and predominant in war, because hoplites are useless without formation, and in the old days knowledge about formations and the formations themselves did not exist . . .—but as cities grew and hoplites became stronger, more people began to have a share in government."[7]

With these fatal words Aristotle implicated the phalanx in the march of Greek constitutional history and in the rise of the characteristic Greek political organism, the Greek city-state, the *polis*. Aristotle's formulation long enspelled scholars, and only now are the chains enslaving Greek political evolution to military change being loosened. At the root of any constitutional government, scholars argued, be it oligarchy or later Athenian democracy, a cooperative ethic must lie. And they sought the origin of this cooperative ideal in the phalanx: from the cooperation hoplites display in the line they deduced a cooperative ethos to counter the competitive, willful ethos of Homeric warriors. So from the ethos of the phalanx came the ethos of the rising polis. And the Greek phalanx emerged from the story with something of the character of an Israeli kibbutz.

Hoplites cooperated in fact, and their need to rely on one another in battle was clearly understood. "I will not desert the man beside me wherever I may be stationed," swore young Athenians undergoing military training in the fourth century BC. And in the language of Greek tragedy, *paraspistes,* the soldier who carries his shield beside one in the line, became a general term for a loyal companion. But the ethos that lay underneath this cooperation was only superficially cooperative, for those who fought in the seemingly unheroic phalanx conceived of what they were doing in Homeric terms. War poetry down into the fifth century BC continued to use words and ideas taken from the *Iliad*. The gravestones of those slain in battle praise them in words taken from epic — as the best, as *promachoi,* front-fighters — and if grave reliefs were our only evidence we would never imagine that the Greeks fought massed in the phalanx rather than as heroic individuals. Depictions of the mass combat of the phalanx in art are extremely rare: even figures armed and armored as hoplites are depicted on Greek vases fighting one-on-one as if they were Homeric heroes. And when depicted on pots, as they so often were, actual Homeric heroes, often with identifying labels, fight in hoplite equipment, emphasizing the Homeric quality of hoplite fighting in the eyes of the vase-buying public. In the sixth century BC there was even a revival of forging spearheads out of bronze, as they are described in epic, although the iron that had succeeded bronze before 1000 BC was both lighter and sharper.[8]

Performance in hoplite battle was conceived as a great competition between individuals, just as fighting was in epic. In the early fifth century cities made honor rolls of who was bravest in battle, and in some cases who was second bravest, and who third. This fierce culture of competition finds expression in Herodotus, who is careful to indicate who he thought fought most bravely in battles. "Of the Lacedaemonians and the Thespians," Herodotus reports about Thermopylae, "for all that there were so many brave men among them, he that was said to be the bravest was a Spartiate, Dieneces. . . . after him they say two Lacedaemonian brothers were the bravest, Alpheus and Maron, two sons of Orsiphantus." Later in the century Greek cities formally awarded a prize to the man who was bravest in battle. Alcibiades won the prize after an engagement at Potidaea in 432 BC; it should have gone to Socrates, some thought, but the principle is clear. These prizes are not parallel to modern (or Roman) military decorations because they were not awarded according to an abstract standard of achievement. Instead they were explicitly competitive: you get nothing just for being brave, everything for being judged the most brave. Such competitive triumphs might be recorded on the tombstones of those who won them. The competitive ethos of Homeric warriors was still vividly alive in hoplite generations.[9]

Yet if hoplites thought of combat as a competition — indeed in terms actually taken from epic — how did they come to fight crushed in the phalanx? The cramped phalanx is not, on the face of it, a method of fighting congenial to front-fighting Homeric heroes, yet even the best men of Classical Greece, the men who considered themselves the heirs to those ideals, some of whom claimed to be descendants of those very heroes, fought in the phalanx. The answer begins with the need to reconcile the immemorial competitiveness of the Greeks, so powerful a force in epic, to the practicalities of fighting in the real world.

Imagine that real men with the competitive ethos of heroes in the *Iliad* were to fight a battle in the way that battle is depicted in the *Iliad*. In the real world, the iron law of the epic, that no warrior may ever be shown to kill a warrior of greater excellence, is suspended. Amidst the showers of spears and arrows and stones, amidst the running to and fro and confusion and stabbing by surprise, men of high standing would go down, killed anonymously by stray missiles and the spears of low wretches, trampled by horses, or crushed ingloriously by stray chariots. In the confusion the high deeds of the brave would go unnoticed, along with the cringing of the cowardly. The would-be heroes would emerge from battle with the same demoralizing certainty as survivors of a trench bombardment that this kind of combat was chiefly a matter of luck, not a test of excellence; that the strong and weak, the brave and craven can live or die quite at random; that bravery is not necessarily rewarded with glory or cowardice punished with shame. In the real world, Homeric combat would turn the bright colors of epic to gray and would produce that realm dreadful to Achilles in which

Fate is the same for the man who holds back, the same if he
    fights hard.
We are all held in a single honor, the brave man [*esthlos*] with
    the coward [*kakos*].

Moved into the real world and subject to its chaos, the way fighting is
conducted in the *Iliad* would make a very poor contest indeed.[10]

Another society might have rejected individual competitiveness in
battle as impractical or romantic. The Greeks instead maintained their
competitive ethos by simplifying combat and hedging it around with
rules. We can see most clearly the logic behind the abandonment of the
bow. Later Greeks believed that a rule banning the use of missiles had
been agreed upon between Chalcis and Eretria in the early Lelantine war
(c. 700 BC or after). And Thucydides describes an exchange between a
Spartan prisoner of war and an Athenian ally after the surrender of the
Spartan hoplites at Sphacteria during the Peloponnesian War (425 BC).
The ally jeeringly asked the captive Spartan whether the Spartans who
had died on the island, rather than surrendered, had been *kaloi k'agathoi,*
men of aristocratic excellence. The Spartan retorted that a spindle — so
he sneeringly called an arrow — would be worth a great deal if it could
distinguish *agathoi*. But of course it could not, and so to the Spartan it
was a useless implement for an activity in which the participants imagined
themselves engaged in a contest with friend and foe alike to demonstrate
their excellence. The problem with archery, the Spartan is saying, is that
it ruins the competition in excellence that combat is supposed to be. In
an infinitely distant world, a soldier in the American Civil War, his different sense of fairness offended, cursed a shell that landed near him:
"You d--n s-n of a b---h. You haint got no eyes, & would as soon hit a
ambulance driver as anybody else."[11]

The heroic status of the bow was disputed in the *Iliad*. The historical
Greeks made the firm decision about the bow's suitability for competitive
combat that the logic of epic did not require. In his *Heracles* (c. 417 BC)
Euripides stages a debate about the relative merits of hoplite fighting
and archery. "A bow is no test of a man's courage," says one character,
while fighting in the phalanx is. His interlocutor replies that fighting
with a bow is safer, thereby yielding the point that it is not heroic. The

position of Pandarus, Teucer, and Odysseus, that archery is a heroic *aretē* in its own right, had been abandoned. It is significant that while there is a competition in archery at Patroclus's funeral games in the *Iliad*, archery never became an Olympic event in archaic or Classical Greece. The competitive ideals of actual Greek warriors ultimately exiled the bow from the phalanx to reduce the chance that any hoplite would suffer the fate of Callicrates, the most beautiful of the Greeks, shot down with an arrow before the action was joined at Plataea. "He took his death very ill and said to Arimnestus, a Plataean, that he did not mind dying, since it was for Greece; what he minded is that he had struck no blow and done no deed worthy of himself, for all his longing to do so."[12]

Two centuries elapsed between the first appearance in Greece of elements of the hoplite panoply in the late eighth century BC and the final banishment of missiles from the hoplite phalanx: archers still mingle with hoplites on Athenian vases of the late sixth century, and hoplites are sometimes depicted carrying two spears (for throwing) down to around 480 BC. It was slow, this simplification of combat to reduce the role of accident and to create in the real world a better arena for competition between warriors. Old habits died hard, especially old habits enshrined in the *Iliad*. The poem helped to convey Greek competitiveness down the generations, but it also presented models of heroic fighting for the direct imitation of posterity, models whose power is emphasized by generations of Greeks borrowing Homer's words to describe their fighting. The *Iliad* hallowed a mixed mode of fighting—hallowed spear throwing and sometimes archery. The centuries it took the Classical Greek phalanx to mature reflect the duration of the battle between competitive ethics adapted to reality, which tended to simplify combat, and tradition sanctified by Homer, which tended to preserve a diversity of styles of fighting.[13]

Long before Greek competitive ethics drove missiles from the phalanx, those ethics had promoted a single, particular martial competition. While the literary logic of epic could accommodate any number of heroic excellences, and heroic rivalry in them, reality was not so forgiving: in reality such various competitions could not coexist happily on one field of battle. Polydoros, Priam's youngest son, whom Priam would not allow to fight, ran through the battle in the *Iliad* to show off his superb speed of foot. Achilles threw a spear at him as he ran by and killed him. Achilles' desire to compete ruined Polydoros's: the logic of the real world has briefly invaded the poem. Outside the world of epic, failure to rank excellences and resolve the contradictions that simultaneous competition in them caused was as untenable as running all the events at the Olympic games simultaneously in the same stadium, with the charioteers crashing into the all-in wrestlers. In the real world, if battle was to be a competition, it worked best for all the competitors to be competing in the same event.[14]

The Spartan poet Tyrtaeus makes a careful list of Homeric excellences and decides that courage is the chief of them:

> I would not say anything of a man nor take account of him
> for any speed of his feet or wrestling skill he might have
> not if he had the size of a Cyclops and strength to go with it,
> not if he could outrun Boreas, the North Wind of Thrace
> not if he were more handsome and gracefully formed than
>   Tithonos
> or if he had more riches than Midas had, or Kinyras too,
> not if he were more of a king than Tantalid Pelops,
> or had the power of speech and persuasion Adrastus had,
> not if he had every source of distinction except furious
>   courage [alkē]
> . . . .
> *This* is *aretē*, the best possession that man can have,
> the noblest thing that a young man can endeavor to win.[15]

Tyrtaeus's choice reflects a broad consensus, a feeling shared by many Greek warriors. In hoplite generations a soldier's bravery in battle long continued to be valued above other forms of performance and envisioned as the highest human achievement. An Athenian epitaph reads,

> Under this monument lies Aeschylus the Athenian
> Euphorion's son, who died in the wheatlands of Gela.
>   The grove
> of Marathon, with its glories, can speak of his valor [alkē]
>   in battle.
> The long-haired Persian remembers and can speak of it too.

This is the epitaph of Aeschylus the tragedian: even a man of such eminence in another realm — and in two sea battles — wanted to be remembered chiefly for his bravery when fighting as a hoplite at the battle of Marathon. In Classical Greek *aretē* is casually used to mean courage alone, and the rich Homeric status terms *agathos* and *kakos* need mean no more than brave and cowardly, respectively.[16]

Just as the *Iliad* had failed to rank excellences, so it had failed to decide on which behavior really was courageous. In the *Iliad* bravery is manifested mostly in aggressive performance, but holding one's ground is praised as well: "If one is to be preeminent in battle, he must by all means stand his ground strongly." Sometimes the poem treated holding one's ground, what might be called passive courage, as being demanded by the heroic code, sometimes not. Historical Greece decided firmly that it was part of the code; to Tyrtaeus and his contemporary Callinus there is no question that running is disgraceful. Indeed, when defining perfect *aretē*, Tyrtaeus depicts the warrior as a man who

> plants himself firmly and holds his place among the fore-
> > most warriors unceasingly, disgraceful flight completely
> > forgotten,
> and has schooled his heart and soul to endure.
> . . . .
> This is a man excellent (*agathos*) in war.

There are references to attacking in Tyrtaeus — "Let him go close and thrust with his big spear or sword hand to hand, and kill the foeman" — but much more emphasis is placed on holding one's position:

> Let each man plant himself firmly, rooted to the ground with
> > both feet,
> bite his lip with his teeth, and hold.[17]

In the fifth century BC Euripides still identified the test of courage as "standing fast staring at the rushing line of spears, and holding one's place in the ranks." In the fourth, Plato echoes this definition of courage. What is courage, *andreia*? asks Socrates. And his interlocutor answers,

"Whoever is willing to fight the enemy staying in his rank and does not flee, he, certainly, is courageous."

The greatest monument to the courage of holding one's place is the legend of Othryades at Thyrea. To be the sole survivor of the three hundred Spartans cast his bravery into doubt. The way he chose to reemphasize that bravery was to take up his post again in the line to indicate symbolically that he had never left it, that he had not survived by running away. To find and reassume his position in the line was the greatest claim to courage that Othryades could make alive. Only death could prove his fearlessness beyond doubt: going home alive would always leave a suspicion, and so, according to Herodotus, Othryades killed himself upon the field, staking the greatest claim to courage of all.[18]

Othryades' behavior reveals that the courage of holding one's position was no less competitive than the courage of an Achilles running out to seek foes to slaughter. The passive courage, the *aretē,* of Tyrtaeus's warrior is the supreme competitive virtue when placed in contrast to other competitive virtues, such as fleetness of foot, beauty, and persuasive speaking. In the fifth century passive courage was still competitive and was the basis upon which Herodotus describes the prizes for valor being handed out after Plataea. Herodotus, had he the choice, would have given the Spartan prize to Aristodemus, a Spartan who had disgraced himself at Thermopylae and who committed heroic suicide in the fighting at Plataea. But the Spartans gave the prize to one Poseidonius instead, on the grounds that Aristodemus "had plainly wanted to die to escape the disgrace under which he labored, and did great deeds raving and having left the formation." Aristodemus was deprived of the reward for having failed in the hoplites' competition in passive courage. His attempt to win glory according to the Homeric code as a heroic individual impressed Herodotus, but not his countrymen. Sophanes, first among the Athenians that day, was not about to make the same mistake. According to legend he came to battle with an anchor attached to his breastplate. The anchor had little to do with the Persians: it was to emphasize to his fellow Athenians his superiority in passive courage: even if he wanted, he could not leave his position in the ranks, however hard the enemy might press him.[19]

But why choose this particular excellence? The bravery of holding one's position was arguably a venerable Homeric excellence, but to emphasize that excellence to the exclusion of aggressive bravery was a radical shift from epic precedent. Alluding to the way Homer reports combat, Euripides has a character complain, "One thing I will not ask or I'd be laughed at: whom each of these men stood facing in the battle and by what foeman he was wounded. Such a recital wastes the time of both hearer and speaker: can a man stand in battle as the spears fly thick and fast before his eyes and tell us clearly who was brave? I could not ask for such a report nor believe anyone who ventured to give it. When a man stands face to face with the enemy, he is barely able to see what he needs to see."[20] Here Euripides offers a stark practical challenge to the mechanics of Homeric heroic battle. In practice it was impossible to tell who kills whom, so heroic accomplishment could not be judged; or to see who is conducting himself well, so heroic performance could not be judged either. In the absence of the omniscient Homeric narrator, competitive combat as described in Homer simply does not work. If battle is in fact to be a contest between individuals in the real world, it must be possible to tell the winners from the losers.

In the phalanx, the Greeks thought, it was possible. When each man took his place in the grid of the formation, it was possible even in the grind of battle for those beside him to see whether he still occupied it. Before the clash of phalanxes, it was possible to mark the cowards, who dropped out of the line; the Spartans put down as cowards those who failed to keep time to the pipes that were played as the Spartan army advanced. When the phalanxes came into contact it was possible to identify those who fled before the battle was decided; who, knocked down in the fight, rose to fight again; and who was first to die — glorious because it indicated that he had not given ground. When a rout began it was possible to discern who had first turned around to flee, who had fled before one did one's self, and who had hung on longest. After a battle it was possible to identify men who had heroically held their place and died in it or a group that had kept its formation and fought its way free.[21]

After the battle, failure in the contest — cowardly flight — often left humiliating evidence since it usually involved casting away the heavy hoplite shield, an act that became the archetype of cowardice: so the famous instruction of the Spartan mother to her warrior son, to return "with your shield or on it." It is not an accident that in Athenian law cowardice in battle was construed in terms of the obvious acts of leaving one's place and casting away one's shield; an Athenian politician might achieve an invidious fame in comedy as "Cleonymus the shield-thrower." Lesser failures of courage, like trembling (*tremblers* was the Spartan term for cowards), jostling, teeth-chattering, and fouling one's self, might also be detected. The all-encompassing Corinthian helmet, which we associate so closely with the early hoplite, was no doubt valued for the excellent protection it gave (see figure). But not a few hoplites may have valued it also for the way it concealed the expressive face, and so concealed the terror of the wearer — so vivid on the face in Homer, where "the skin of a coward changes color one way and another" — from his competitors in courage. The convenient Greek military jargon of the *tropē*, the turning to flight, suggesting as it does the simultaneous bolt of an entire army, must not be allowed to conceal the fact that the hoplites thought phalanx fighting allowed them to form an excellent estimate of each other's passive courage.[22]

Thucydides has a Spartan general, Brasidas, describe the irregular fighting of the Illyrian barbarians, in which each soldier, like a Homeric hero, decided by his own lights whether to advance or retreat: "Maintaining no formation they are unashamed to leave their post when pressed; flight and advance carry the same reputation for excellence; their bravery is subject to no test. The way they fight — everyone his own master — furnishes each with a good excuse to save himself." A properly competitive way of fighting, then, must furnish none with a pretext to escape the implications of his behavior and so confuse the competition, and must test the competitive excellence of the warrior as directly as possible. To Brasidas, the phalanx, to which he is comparing the barbarians' method of fighting, serves both these purposes. Fighting in the phalanx, unlike fighting in the *Iliad* or among Brasidas's barbarians, allows no excuses for retiring from the fight. Passive courage, moreover, constitutes an excellent subject of competition. Competition in an aggressive martial skill, say ability with the spear, is subject to luck: a critic of spear fighting in tragedy says, "The hoplite is a slave to his arms; if he breaks his spear he cannot ward off death from himself since that is his only defense." Yet it is not in spear fighting in which the hoplite competes but holding his place in the line, and the courage of holding one's place is perhaps the

Hoplite in fighting posture, bronze figurine, Corinth,
c. 500 BC (Antikensammlung, Staatliche Museen zu Berlin.
Photo: Foto Marburg/Art Resource, NY).

form of martial behavior whose success in the real world is most in the hands of the warrior and subject to the least external influence. As such it is the uniquely suitable subject of real-world competition in martial excellence. Whether the courageous warrior lives or dies in his place is, of course, in the hands of fortune, but a warrior can triumph in the courage of holding his place or be shamed for failing in it regardless of whether he lives or dies, a theme upon which Tyrtaeus dwells: whether his wounds are in the front or back will tell the tale. Demosthenes echoes the theme: "When a battle takes place out of necessity one side is beaten, and the other victorious. But I would not hesitate to say that . . . those on either side who die in their place in the formation are victors both alike, and do not partake of defeat." And after their disaster at Lechaeum in 390 BC, where many hoplites had fallen and more had fled, the Spartans showed the power of this code: "There was great mourning in the Spartan army, except among those whose sons and fathers and brothers had died in their place. For they went around like famous victors in games, glorying in the disaster that had befallen them."[23]

The courage of holding one's position should be viewed as parallel to the dignified bravery of the nineteenth-century duelist: the proximity of death is the crucible in which bravery is tested, but who lives or dies is conceived as being quite irrelevant to the outcome of that test. Contemporary accounts of duels dwell minutely on the demeanor of the duelists since demeanor and the moral qualities revealed by demeanor are the subject of the test: marksmanship is the means of the test, not what is being tested. In the day of the musket, immobility under fire also became a competitive military excellence. Of the multitude of possible warlike competitions, competition in self-mastery is the best because it is subject to the fewest vagaries of all.

In the process of simplifying Greek fighting to make it a better competition, all ways of fighting other than the hoplite's were edged out altogether or besmirched. Arrows and stones and javelins became the shameful toys of barbarians and hirelings. Horsemanship had appealing legendary and aristocratic associations; Homeric heroes thought it heroic to fight from chariots; and in Classical times to serve on horseback was delightfully socially exclusive because only the rich could afford to keep horses. But such was the power of the hoplite definition of courage in southern Greece that to volunteer for the cavalry smacked of cowardice. In the *Laches* Socrates' interlocutor gives a hoplite definition of bravery — holding one's position — and then is baffled by Socrates' insistence that he offer a definition that included cavalry as well. When the Spartans found they needed to reestablish a mounted cavalry, only the weakest and those "least avid for honor" would volunteer to fight in a fashion that the ideals of hoplite competition defined as unheroic. The story is told of a lame Spartan who once asked his king for a horse to ride to war. "War needs those who stand their ground, not those who run away!" was the king's answer.[24]

Yet a sign of the power of Homer over the Greeks was the tendency of some Homeric martial competitions which found no place in the phalanx to establish themselves outside warfare. Speed of foot was a particularly prominent Homeric *aretē* because of its association with Achilles. With the emphasis on brave hoplite immobility, the hoplite had little opportunity to demonstrate it in an honorable context, for the halting run into battle was hardly a race, and running in flight was a disgrace. The result was an athletic event, the *hoplitodromos,* the race in hoplite panoply, which was established as an Olympic contest in 520 BC and was widespread in other Greek games. Emphasis on hoplite immobility also reduced the importance of skill with shield and spear, important in Homer. But the need felt to compete in the *aretai* of skill at arms was to a degree filled by antic dances in arms, especially the pyrrhic dance; this dance was competitive and sometimes even an event in games, was conducted in hoplite armor, and, judging by depictions on pots, seems to have involved a wider set of motions than contemporary hoplite combat. The chariot and its associated skills similarly had fallen out of use in Greek warfare. But Athens and Boeotia held competitions of the *apobates,* the dismounter, in which men in hoplite equipment leapt on and off fast-moving chariots being driven by teammates. In their games and dances Greek warriors created warfare as it should have been, a more fully Homeric warfare, as if the shift to the phalanx had never been necessary.[25]

Part of the puzzle of Othryades is solved. The ethos which makes the Spartan a hero arises from the need to make the Greek creed of martial competition work in the real world, to make choices about the value of different military behavior which epic did not need to make. This begins to suggest why Greek aristocrats, men who saw themselves as the heirs of the competitive heroes in the *Iliad,* could endure, could glory to fight in the phalanx. This begins to suggest how the phalanx as a method of fighting could evolve from the mixed fighting that preceded it.

Yet competition between individuals cannot fully explain the strange lumbering dance of the phalanx. For the phalanx is hardly a perfect competition: fortune is not entirely expelled. In the press of bodies many soldiers will have had no choice whether to stand or flee; neither will seeing who stood or fled have been without its problems. At the same time, not all competed under equal conditions: even if the terror of battle affected all, the depth of the phalanx tested the courage of those facing the enemy directly at the front of the formation more than those at the back: a brave soldier might boast that he contrived to be posted to the front. If the Greeks had wanted a more perfect competition between individuals, they could have surrounded one-on-one fighting with rules and taboos and become a nation of duelists, going down the road upon which feudal Europe and old Japan would travel a good distance. There was even epic precedent, not only in the single combats between Paris and Menelaus and Hector and Ajax, with rules set in advance, but in the contest for prizes in armed combat between Ajax and Diomedes which was part of the funeral games of Patroclus. There is a scattering of single combats in Archaic and Classical Greek times (and Alexander and his imitators revived the practice), but only enough to emphasize that dueling was the road not taken. The phalanx needs more explaining; and so does the conduct of Othryades. Why did Othryades' remaining on the field allow his countrymen to claim, and the gods to vindicate, a national victory? The great war of the Greeks against the Persians offers answers to these questions, answers which can be found by understanding the curious behavior of two Spartan warriors, King Leonidas, who fell with three hundred of his countrymen at Thermopylae, and Amompharetus, who disobeyed his superior officer at the battle of Plataea—and was rewarded for it.[26]

III

TWO STUBBORN SPARTANS

IN THE PERSIAN WAR

CITY AND DISCIPLINE IN THE PHALANX

T hey bore shields stretched with the skins of cranes, when they marched against Greece, and they wore horses' foreheads as helmets, with the manes streaming down the back and the ears thrust up in front. They marched with the Indians, with their garments of cotton and bows of reed, but even with the Indians they made but a tiny part of the host that Xerxes, the Great King of Persia, had summoned forth from the recesses of his empire. For there were Persians with golden pomegranates on their spear-butts and Medes and Assyrians with helms of twisted bronze and Bactrians and Scythians and Parthians and Caspians, and Ethiopians in the skins of leopards and of lions: and the Ethiopians bore spears tipped with gazelles' horns, and before they fought they painted their bodies half red and half white. And there were Arabians and Libyans with javelins burned hard at the point and Phrygians and Lydians and Mysians and Thracians with caps of fox skin. And to vie with the horse heads there were proud tiaras and humble snoods and helmets of leather and of wood and of bronze, with the brazen ears and horns of oxen wrought upon them.[1]

Twenty years before, the Greeks ruled by the Great King had rebelled — the Greeks of Ionia, in Asia Minor, now the west coast of Turkey. And some among the mainland Greeks had helped the doomed rebellion, and in the forefront of these, the Athenians. To punish them a Persian force had been sent by sea against Athens, but the hoplites of the Athenians

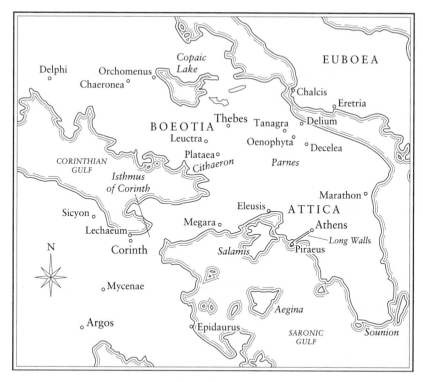

Central Greece

had destroyed it at Marathon in 490 BC. Now Xerxes came to avenge the old insult and the new and to bring all of Greece under his sway. And so the Greeks saw and wondered at the costumes of Asia and of Africa.

With a great army and a great fleet the King descended into Greece. On two bridges made from ships he crossed the Hellespont in 480 BC. Through Thrace he marched, into Macedonia, from Macedonia into Thessaly. In Greek legend, which expanded the King's army to impossible size, cities were beggared by feeding the host, and whole rivers ran dry when it drank.[2]

The Greeks had long warning of the coming of the King, and those in the south agreed, most of them, to set aside their quarrels and combat the common danger. The Spartans would command by land and sea. Athens, although it was to provide the largest number of ships, patriotically yielded its hoped-for leadership of the combined fleet. The proud Argives refused to yield command to the Spartans and so held themselves out of the war, sulking like Achilles in a war long ago. The Greek confederation had attempted to block the passage of the King from Macedonia into Thessaly, but the force they sent there was either daunted by the size of the Persian army or discovered there were too many ways into Thessaly to garrison. They sailed away south, and the Thessalians surrendered to the King.[3]

If Thessaly lay too open to Macedonia in the north, Boeotia, the next broad plain to the south, did not: an army marching down through Greece must pass the narrows of Thermopylae. And the sea thereabouts mirrors the land: the eastward coast of the isle of Euboea is rocky and harborless and stormy, and so sailors yearn to pass through the narrow sheltered strait on the western side. Both at Thermopylae and in the strait, a smaller number could stand against a larger on equal terms. And so there it was the Greeks decided to make their stand. Their strategy was good: lacking adequate anchorage, the Persian fleet suffered terribly in tempests as it tried to force the strait or turn the Greek flank by sailing down the formidable eastern coast of Euboea.[4]

Yet the army that the Greeks sent to Thermopylae was far smaller than it might have been. Those whose lands lay near the pass, the Phocians and Locrians, were there in strength. But the Spartans were celebrating their festival of the Carneia, and so sent their king, Leonidas, with only three hundred Spartan citizens. The rest of Greece was celebrating the solemn Olympic festival, and so the remainder of Peloponnese sent only twenty-eight hundred men. The Greeks were abiding by the easy conventions of hoplite warfare, which forbade fighting during the Olympic truce and usually honored even the local festivals of contending cities. But these rules were meaningless to the Persians. They prepared to attack the narrows at Thermopylae, as Leonidas vetoed a proposal to withdraw and sent desperate appeals for more soldiers.[5]

And so the Persians moved against the Greeks, and the Greeks, fighting city by city in relays, for two days threw them back. And then a Greek traitor revealed to the King a path by which a force could be led around behind the Greek position at Thermopylae. The Greeks knew the path: the Phocians were defending it. But the Persians took them by surprise and drove them off the track. Now word was brought to the Greeks that there were Persians behind as well as in front, and quarreling broke out: all the Greeks except the Spartans and a few others either decamped or were sent away by Leonidas. But the Spartans remained because, in the words of Herodotus, Leonidas "considered it unseemly to leave the post which they had come to defend."[6]

The word Herodotus uses for post, *taxis* (which is related to the English word *tactics*), more narrowly means a position in the hoplite line. Herodotus images an exiled Spartan explaining the Spartan code to Xerxes: "Law is their despot, and they fear it much more than your men fear you. . . . and their law always commands the same thing: that they must never flee from battle in the face of numbers of men, but remaining in their *taxis* they must win or be destroyed."[7] Leonidas decided to stay at Thermopylae, then, in accord with the hoplite definition of courage. But in doing so Leonidas (or Herodotus or his informant) has made a rather unexpected intellectual leap. For leaving their position was disgraceful only if the hoplite definition of courage applied not just to individuals, but to an entire city contingent. The next year, another Spartan commander would appeal to the same code but scale it up even further: he would similarly refuse to retreat, to lead his unit from its *taxis,* "being unwilling to bring shame upon Sparta." The whole city is disgraced if its troops retreat: the hoplite definition of courage applied to all of Sparta. Likewise, in Athenian tragedy, at the climax of an (imagined) hoplite battle, the cry went up, "Keep disgrace from our city!"[8]

THE CITY AS HOPLITE

When the Greeks came to reassemble their world after the shattering of the storied kingdoms of the Mycenean age, they did so in small, independent communities, often centered upon a hill on which the folk could take refuge in time of danger. From the eighth century BC on it is possible to trace the characteristic political community of the Greeks, this *polis,* or city-state, with its territory, its body of male citizens (who often imagined they descended from a common ancestor), its common cults, and its sense of differentness from the next *polis,* which might stand only a few hours' walk away. City-states varied drastically in size and political organization. In most the citizens worked the land; but some *poleis,* like Sparta, were situated atop a class of toiling serfs, the helots. What defined the *polis* most was the citizens' sense of belonging to it and the citizens' fierce, rivalrous pride in the polis to which they belonged.

And so, after a pygmy victory over a rival, tiny Aegium applied to the oracle of Delphi to know who were the best of the Greeks:

> The best of all land has Pelasgian Argos,
> The best horses the Thessalians, the best women the
> Lacedamonians
> Those who drink the water of fair Arethusa are better men,
> but still better than they those who live between Tiryns
> and Arcadia rich in flocks:
> the Argives in their armor of linen, the goads of war.
> But you, men of Aegium, you are neither third nor fourth
> nor twelfth: you are not on the list.

This habit of ranking cities reflects the Greek conception of the *polis* as a mythic collective person whose conduct was ruled by Greek competitive ethics.[9]

The *polis* had a character, like a man: it could be reliable or unreliable, honest or corrupt, just or unjust; it could practice *hybris,* aggressive insolence, or *sophrosyne,* self-control. "In peace and prosperous circumstances both *poleis* and individuals have better ethics," wrote Thucydides. The city could feel emotions like anger and fear and longing. But the *polis* was like a certain kind of man: the personified city was a gigantic Greek aristocrat, proud of its lineage — its founding by gods or heroes or as a colony of an old, distinguished city; loyal to kindred cities who shared the same descent; apt to form aristocratic relationships of formal friendship, or *philia,* and Homeric guest-friendship, *xenia;* eager for glory and anxious to wreak vengeance upon cities that insulted it. The distinctly aristocratic mark of the city's collective identity may well reflect the origin of the Greek *polis* as a collectivity of aristocrats — certainly even democratic Athens continued to imagine itself in the aggregate as an aristocrat — but the darkness of the period when the *polis* was coming into being confounds inquiry. And in historical times, in Athens at least, the sense of belonging and collective pride had extended far beyond the aristocracy.[10]

The quirks of the city and its folk were on display in the way the city fought. The Spartans particularly prided themselves on, and were admired by other Greeks for, their quality of *sophrosyne*. They displayed this in their daily life with their famous terse, Laconic style of speech and in battle in the way they advanced to combat. The phalanxes of other states often broke into a shambling run before contact, overwhelmed by the excitement of danger, so ruining the dressing of their ranks. The Spartans, by contrast, advanced to the tune of pipe players, a practice intended "to remove anger from the warriors," and proceeded at a walk, "without a gap in their lines, and with no confusion in their spirits, calmly and cheerfully," without "excessive fear or passion." It makes sense in this context that when Greeks abandoned the all-concealing Corinthian helmet in the fifth century, it was the Spartans who adopted the most revealing helmet of all, the conical *pilos* (see figure). In the competition of self-control, the *pilos* announced, the Spartans had nothing to hide, no fear or passion in their faces. And, naturally, stung by the challenge, many hoplites all over Greece adopted the *pilos* as well.[11]

This tendency to equate citizenry, city, and army and to regard them all in human terms, and so potentially subject to the same rules and emotions, explains the decision of Leonidas to hold his place at Thermopylae and explains why the hoplite definition of courage applied to Spartans as a whole as well as to Spartans as individuals. But it also completes the explanation of why Greek warriors, so competitive as individuals, fought together in the phalanx. The phalanx evolved not only to allow satisfactory competition between individuals; it evolved also to constitute a symmetrical contest between the contending cities. For in the phalanx, cities competed in the same qualities that individual hoplites did. The hoplite battle simultaneously tested the passive courage of soldier *and* city. The criterion of victory in a hoplite battle was holding the battlefield at the end: the victor was the side that did not give way, just as the hero was the hoplite who held his place in the line, his *taxis*. The trophy—literally, the "turning point"—was placed by the victors at the point where the losers turned to flight, at the place where the civic courage of one state in holding its position overcame the other. The fact that hoplites fought crushed together, hardly ideal for competition between individuals, arose from the

Tegean hoplite in *pilos* helmet,
late fifth century BC (*Bulletin de
Correspondence Hellénique* 4 [1880]).

need for the experience of the macrocosm, the personified city, to be parallel to the experience of the microcosm, the individual hoplite. Like the
hoplite, the state had to enjoy as pure as possible a competition in passive
courage, with clear winners and losers and no excuses for failure. So, by
convention, the losing city publicly admitted its defeat by applying to
the victor for the right to recover the bodies. And in a battle in which
the hoplites of different states fought on the same side, formal recognition
(parallel to the prizes given to individuals) could be given by the massed
army to the most excellent city contingents. The phalanx should not be

viewed as the submersion of the individual in the mass but as creating in mass combat a simulacrum of individual combat.[12]

The phalanx represents the victory of heroic competitiveness over Iliadic methods: but the phalanx makes sense only when it is understood that not only men, but cities conceived as men, were competing. Fighting in the phalanx was hardly a perfect form of individual competition or of competition between states. But it was the best way the Greeks could discover to have man and city compete at the same time in the same way in a form of fighting that worked as a competition in the real world for both. The Greeks' loyalty to their cities — and the way they conceived of their cities — is the final element of the competitive culture that produced the Greek phalanx.

The role of the city may also explain why the evolution of the phalanx culminated when it did, in the early fifth century, when the evidence of vase painting suggests that archers no longer fought alongside hoplites and hoplites no longer carried throwing spears. The mature phalanx is marked by its intolerance of any feature which breaks the exact symmetry of the experience of city and hoplite, of the collective and the individual. And a parallel evolution is observable in the Greek city of the early to mid–fifth century in the realm of grave markers: a reduction of variety in funeral forms, a smoothing out of individual eccentricity, a blending of individuals into a larger whole. Regarding this phenomenon in class terms, an archeologist might present it as an egalitarian triumph of the middle: but it really represents the tendency at this time of the individual, low or high, to affiliate himself more closely with the *polis,* with his fellow citizens. It is the warming of this feeling of membership, this strengthening of identification, that drives the perfection of the symmetry between hoplite and phalanx. Interestingly, the variety of grave monuments, at least at Athens, exploded again in the 420s BC, just when significant challenges to hoplite supremacy by other varieties of soldiers began to appear.[13]

THE *ILIAD* AT THERMOPYLAE

With Leonidas's decision to hold, all that remained was for the Spartans at Thermopylae to die. The surviving Greeks advanced out into the open from the strong place they had been defending. The terrified troops of the great king, fond Greek legend had it, were driven forth to the fray with lashes. Soon the spears of the Greeks were broken, and they were fighting with their swords. Spartan calm was traded for a reckless killing frenzy. King Leonidas fell, and a struggle developed over his body: four times the Persians were driven back, and the body was recovered. But now the Persians from the path were seen, and the Spartans and their Thespian allies withdrew to a hillock in the narrows, and there they defended themselves with their blades, with their hands, and at the last with their teeth, until they were finally overwhelmed. The epitaph over the Spartans read,

> Stranger! Go tell the Spartans
> That we lie here obedient to their orders.

The irony of Thermopylae is that, although the Spartans went to their deaths according to the hoplite code, they did not in their last hours fight entirely as hoplites, bravely holding their ground. Herodotus describes the battle in Iliadic terms, fought with heroic warrior fury: there was hoplite *othismos,* the pushing of shields, but in the context of a fight over a hero's body, "until the Greeks in their valor dragged the body out, and four times turned the enemy to flight." How did he know, given the slaughter? But whether it happened thus or is just a story, it emphasizes that the Greeks did not see any sharp distinction between heroic and hoplite fighting. In their tragedies the Athenians depicted the battles of heroes as hoplite battles with hoplite terminology; on their pots the Greeks depicted the Homeric heroes armed as hoplites; in the *apobates,* a contest which simulated Homeric warfare, athletes jumped on and off moving chariots in hoplite equipment. A triumph of hoplite over heroic thinking? Quite the opposite, in fact: the Greeks of the fifth century simply saw no decisive difference between their fighting and epic fighting. For the *Iliad,* of course, provided plenty of epic precedent for massing of men, especially in arraying scenes:

> For shield leaned upon shield, helmet on helmet, man against
>   man,

and the horse-hair crests along the horns of the shining
  helmets
touched as they bent their heads, so dense were they formed
  on each other.

And these descriptions of masses in the *Iliad* offered down the years a
perennial model for how the phalanx should look and served always to
hide from Greek hoplites — for the most part — that their phalanx style
of fighting was in fact very different from the fighting of the heroes in
Homer. The *Iliad* always stood ready to provide admirable, heroic models:
but it had so many to choose from. Hoplites chose the scenes of mass arraying and combat and so claimed a powerful epic legitimacy for their
way of fighting.[14]

AMOMPHARETUS AT PLATAEA

With the Greeks at Thermopylae killed or fled, Xerxes could march south
and capture the harbors of the Greek fleet defending the narrows of
Euboea: although they fought the Persians to a standstill in two naval
battles off Artemisium, the Greek ships were obliged to withdraw to the
south. Now the Greeks outside the Peloponnese gave the King earth and
water in token of their surrender or fled before his coming: but the Athenians made the courageous decision to evacuate Attica and carry on the
war from their fleet, sending their goods and families over to the close-
by islands of Salamis and Aegina and into the Peloponnese. The Peloponnesians set to fortifying the narrows of the Isthmus of Corinth, and
the Greek fleet made its base on Salamis, somewhat in front of the isthmus but offering a narrow place for defense between the island and the
Attic mainland.[15]

   The Greeks were divided in their counsels, and it took all the guile
of the Athenian commander, Themistocles, to ensure that the climactic
sea battle of the war would indeed take place off Salamis. When the Persians attacked, from dread or strategy the Greeks backed water, drawing
their more numerous enemies into the narrows, where they fell foul of
one another. Now, setting on, the Greeks turned the King's leading ships
to flight, and they spread confusion in the ranks of galleys behind. Soon

the King's great fleet was fleeing south for their harbor in Attica, with the Greeks picking off the hindmost:

> Turned over
> were the hulls of ships, and the sea could not be seen,
> full up with wrecks and the slaughter of men.
> The strands and shoals were filled with the dead,
> and in confusion of flight rowed every ship —
> so many as were of the barbarian host.
> Like tunas, or some net of fish
> with fragments of oars and pieces of wrecks
> they struck, they smote them. Wailing
> and shrieking held the open sea
> until the eye of black night silenced it.[16]

After Salamis the King's fleet was no longer a match for the Greek, and the King's nerve was shattered: with his army he began the long march back from Attica to his own realm, and the remnants of the fleet were sent to protect the bridges of boats over the Hellespont for his coming. The Athenians brought their children and their chattels back to Attica and gloomily surveyed the ruins of their triumphant city.

Yet the prayers of the Greeks for delivery from the Persians were not soon answered. In Thessaly the King split his army, leaving much of its strength with his marshal Mardonius, and continued his march for home. And Mardonius spent that winter of 480/79 BC in Thessaly, intending to complete the conquest of Greece in the next year. The Greeks planned to meet Mardonius in Boeotia: they felt confident enough now to face the reduced Persian army in the open field. But once again the conventions of Greek warfare ruined their plans: the Spartans had another festival to celebrate, the Hyacinthia, and so in the new year Mardonius marched unopposed into Attica, and the Athenians had once again to flee their land in their ships. Only the Athenians' threat that they would make a separate peace with the Persians jolted the Spartans into action. Mardonius decided to meet the combined army of the Greeks in Boeotia, which was more suitable for his cavalry than Attica. He walled a camp in the territory of the small Boeotian town of Plataea and there awaited the coming of the Greeks.[17]

The Greeks assembled in the foothills of Cithaeron, the massif that severs Boeotia from Attica, in myth the haunt of Dionysus and witness to his revels. Mardonius sent forth his cavalry to harass them, to bait them down into the plain. The Athenians told the story that they shot down with an arrow the horse of the Persian cavalry commander, Masistius, and stabbed him in the eye on the ground. A great fight developed over the body, which the Athenians recovered. In its finery it was paraded around the Greek army in a cart, and all wondered at the size and beauty of Masistius. This is another very Homeric scene, like the terrible climax at Thermopylae, and (whatever the value of the story) like Thermopylae a reminder that the Greeks thought they were still fighting like the heroes of old.[18]

Now had come the time to array the Greek army for battle. As *hegemon,* leader of the league army and first in prestige, the Spartans allotted themselves the honorable right wing. It was honorable because it was dangerous, the hoplite shield being held in the left hand, leaving the right flank of the body uncovered: hoplite armies tended to edge to the right as they advanced, as the rightmost soldiers strove to outflank the enemy line to protect themselves, and the rest of the soldiers were drawn right after them, not wanting to lose the protection of the shield of the comrade to their right. Second in honor was the extreme left wing, and the Athenians and Tegeans fell to disputing about who should hold it. Their claims to precedence went back to the days of the heroes, to the hoary legends of the coming of the sons of Heracles to Peloponnese and the Seven Against Thebes, to the war against the Amazons, and to the war against Troy. And, the Athenians added by the way, they had vanquished the Persians alone at Marathon. Again, the seamless quality of the Greeks' understanding of their military history is apparent: men who were brave of old may have become cowards or cowards of old become heroes, the Athenians admit, but even when arraying a hoplite line, they saw no revolutionary change in military method that made claiming heirship to the heroes of old absurd.[19]

The Spartans awarded the extreme left to the Athenians, and the position immediately to the Spartans' own left, third in honor, to the Tegeans. Then came the Corinthians and the Arcadians and the men of Sicyon and others and others still, and finally the Plataeans, upon whose fields the battle was to be fought, nestled up against the Athenians, their longtime allies. Herodotus numbered the Greek army at 38,700 hoplites. And Mardonius arrayed his host opposite to them, with the Persians opposite the Spartans, the other nations of the host in the center, and the King's Greek thralls, the Boeotians and Thessalians and the rest, opposite the Athenians and the Greek left.[20]

Yet the arraying came to naught, for once again hoplite convention intervened. The Greek sacrifices boded well—but only if the Greeks stood upon defense. Mardonius too was employing a Greek seer, and he reported the same omens: Mardonius too was forbidden to advance. So, with the stream of the Asopus between them, the armies sat facing each other for ten days, the Greeks harassed by the Persian cavalry; and on the eighth day Mardonius sent the Persian horse into the pass over Cithaeron that the Greeks were using for reinforcements and supplies, and the Persian horse did great destruction. But finally, as his supplies ran low, Mardonius had done with Greek divining and appointed the eleventh day to begin his attack. On that day the King's cavalry was sent forth to disrupt the Greek lines, and they rode back and forth and shot arrows and threw javelins at the Greeks, and the cavalry choked up the Gargaphian spring, from which the Greek army was drawing its water: cavalry and arrows kept the Greeks from the Asopus.[21]

The army of the Greeks was in agony, disordered by Persian horse, their only source of water fouled, their food exhausted, and their supply route over Cithaeron embattled. The generals of the Greek contingents met in conclave and decided to withdraw by night to a better protected spot near the town of Plataea, to an island formed by a split in the river Oeroe. There would be water aplenty there and protection from the Persian horse; once the rest of the army was safe in that strong place a contingent could be sent to escort in the bearers of food.[22]

The Greek army never made it to the island in the Oeroe. Come nightfall and the withdrawal of the King's cavalry, the allied contingents departed, but toward the town of Plataea, not the agreed mustering point. Pausanias, regent of the Spartans and supreme commander of the Greeks, ordered the Spartans to follow. But a Spartan officer, Amompharetus, Herodotus tells us, refused to shift, saying he would not flee from the Persians. He insisted that the Spartans should not abandon their *taxis:* he swore he would not "bring shame upon Sparta." Through the fleeing night Pausanias and Amompharetus contended; an Athenian messenger sent to find out the reason for the delay witnessed the wrathful Amompharetus cast a great stone to the ground: with this pebble, said he, he cast his vote not to flee from the strangers.[23]

Dawn found Amompharetus unmoved and brought with it the fear of swarms of Persian horse, now likely to catch the Spartans on the march. Pausanias decided to abandon Amompharetus and his contingent — or at least terrify them into motion by casting them away on a Persian sea. He led away the rest of the Spartan army and its Tegean allies, stopping a mile and a half along the route so as to be able to return and protect Amompharetus and his troops if his subordinate did not yield. Thinking himself deserted, Amompharetus at last decided to follow. He caught up with the Lacedaemonians near the shrine of Eleusinian Demeter; at the same time the Persian cavalry found them. And so it was that at the shrine of Demeter the battle of Plataea was joined, and for the decisive hours the Persians strove against the Spartans and Tegeans alone.[24]

Thinking the Greek army was in flight, Mardonius led his Persian infantry over the Asopus and came upon the Greeks at the shrine. The Spartans and Tegeans formed their phalanx, and the Persians pelted them with missiles, striking down many. But once again the Spartan sacrifices forbade attack, and so the Greeks held their posts. Finally the sacrifices turned favorable — Pausanias had appealed to Hera, whose temple he could see at Plataea in the distance — and the tormented Tegeans leapt forward into a charge. The Persians had erected a fence of their shields to shoot from, but the Greeks bore it over and fought hand-to-hand with the Persians, who cast away their bows. When the spears of the Spartans were broken, they pushed the Persians back with their broad shields, in the way of hoplites. Alone or in small clutches Persians essayed to break the Spartan line, but in vain. At the battle's heart Mardonius fought upon a white horse with the pick of his army around him, but he was cut down, and the Persians turned to flight.[25]

The Persians fled to their stockaded camp, but the elated Greeks broke in and caught many within the walls unable to escape and made a terrible slaughter. Such of the King's army as survived made its hard way back into the realm of the King. And so it was that the long-haired Mede was driven from Greece.[26]

The Spartans buried their dead at Plataea in three tombs. Into one of them was placed the body of Amompharetus, who had fallen in the fighting. When the Spartans decided who should be honored for being bravest in the battle, they chose three men of those who had died: Poseidonius was bravest of all, they decided, preferring his claim to that of Aristodemus, who had left his rank and charged out to be killed. Then came Philocyon. And the third was Amompharetus. The Spartan choice fits together well with their passing over Aristodemus: in both cases holding one's position was understood to be the supreme good. But by so choosing the Spartans decided to overlook the disobedience of Amompharetus to the supreme commander, Pausanias, who had described his subordinate as raving and lunatic during their struggle, to overlook Amompharetus's endangering his unit of the Spartan army, and to overlook his endangering of the whole Spartan army, the whole army of the Greek League, and the whole cause of Greek freedom. And the Spartans were hardly indifferent to their officers' scorning to obey commands: on another occasion Spartan officers who disobeyed orders were cashiered and sent into exile; disobedient Spartan officers might even be sentenced to death.[27]

Such tolerance of so blatant an act of insubordination would be surprising in any army, but particularly so in the Spartan army. For the Spartans were notoriously the most obedient of the Greeks, their army a byword for exact submission and stringent discipline. Their treatment of Amompharetus as a hero reveals that the Spartans, and the Greeks in general, understood the obedience owed by a soldier to his commander very strangely.[28]

DISCIPLINE IN THE PHALANX

Before the naval battle of Salamis, the Greek confederates were arguing about what to do. They had just heard of the fall of the Acropolis at Athens. Should the Greek fleet hold its position on the island of Salamis, near Athens, or withdraw to the Peloponnese? The decision was made to withdraw to the Isthmus of Corinth, but the Athenian commander, Themistocles, prevailed upon the admiral, a Spartan and in command of the whole, to summon the representatives of the cities again and reopen the debate. When they were assembled, Themistocles seized the floor and argued at length and with passion that at Salamis they must remain. But a Corinthian interrupted the torrent of words: "In the games, Themistocles, those who start too soon are thrashed." "But those who wait too long are not crowned victors," replied the quick-witted Athenian, and his speech rolled on.

The Corinthian's metaphor is an odd one. To describe harsh punishment for bad behavior the Corinthian reaches into the realm of Greek athletic competition. But there was another realm, and one closer to hand, into which he did *not* reach: that of military discipline. "Those who disobey orders are thrashed," the Corinthian did not say. To the Greek mind it was on the sports field, not in the military camp, that discipline reigned.[29]

This accords with what is known about Greek military discipline from other sources. The writings of the fourth-century Greek military expert Xenophon offer special insight into the subject, which he often discusses, and, given his close relations with Sparta, he is helpful too on how Spartan conceptions differed from those of the rest of the Greeks. Xenophon had good reason to be interested in discipline: when he was a young man, he was placed on trial for trying to enforce it upon troops under his command.

Xenophon had accompanied the Ten Thousand, the Greek mercenary hoplites who had marched deep into Asia in the employ of a Persian prince, Cyrus, to expel his brother from the throne of the Great King (401 BC). In battle near Babylon, Cyrus was killed, leaving the Ten Thousand to shift for themselves in a hostile land, fifteen hundred miles from Sardis, the city in western Asia Minor from which they had set out. The Persians enticed the commander of the Greeks, the harsh Spartan Clearchus, into their hands and slew him along with many other Greek officers. The Greeks, as much a *polis* on the move as an army, elected new leaders, including Xenophon, from whom we have the story. They fought their way through the mountains to the Black Sea. But their troubles were not over: there was rioting in the market of Cerasus. Malefactors among the mercenaries had to be punished; the army had to be ritually purified.[30]

In the context of cleansing the army of misdeeds it was decided to invite anyone who had complaints against the generals to lay charges before a court of officers. Three of the generals were fined. Then a number of mercenaries brought charges against Xenophon for beating them. Xenophon records (no doubt with fond recall) his clever cross-examination of one — a muleteer whom he had struck when he had discovered him trying to unburden his mule of a frostbitten comrade by burying him alive — and his speech of defense: some he beat when they left their positions to plunder, others to get them back on their feet when they had fallen along the route in exhaustion and would otherwise have been killed by the pursuing enemies. He beat them, he says, as a teacher or parent beats a child: for their own good.[31]

Xenophon makes repeated appeals to the horizontal bonds between the mercenaries — their duty to care for each other, their duty to share booty equitably. But wholly lacking is any appeal to Xenophon's right to be obeyed as a general or — the army having many qualities in common with a city on the move — as a civil official. The argument we would expect to undergird Xenophon's defense, that he gave an order as a superior officer and, when disobeyed, enforced that order with his fists, is completely absent. The *eutaxia,* or discipline, which Xenophon is upholding is construed nearly in its Greek root meaning of "holding one's place in the formation well." It is a duty owed to comrades, not to officers; indiscipline is an offense toward equals, not superiors: "If everyone had done this, we all would have perished."

The Greek officer was a terribly lonely figure. "Almost their whole army is made up of leaders over leaders," wonders Thucydides of the Spartans, and Xenophon admiringly confirms that there were five levels of officer between the king and the common Spartan soldier. They are struck by this fact — indeed they mention it at all — because it was so unusual. In the Athenian army only two levels of lofty officers, the taxiarch (tribal regiment commander) and *lochagos* (unit commander), stood between the commanding general and the hoplite: no lieutenants, no sergeants, no corporals. In Xenophon's Ten Thousand the regular officers were generals and *lochagoi,* who received extra pay, and other officers (some on the Spartan model) seem only to have been appointed ad hoc when needed. Soon after he was elected general to replace the generals the Persians had slain by treachery, Xenophon extracted a vote from the Ten Thousand that the soldiers would help their officers punish disobedient comrades: an indication that the officers had no regular assistance and that the soldiers did not consider supporting the officers' authority a normal part of their duty.[32]

Xenophon's lack of a claim to be obeyed as a commander was not a phenomenon limited to the odd marching democracy of the Ten Thousand. In other works, and in terms implying the same lack, Xenophon returns again and again to the problem of how to get soldiers to obey. A commander of the fourth-century Athenian cavalry, he says, must earnestly assure the troopers that their obedience is advantageous to themselves. He must cultivate the troopers' goodwill by kindness. Most of all, the commander must be superior to his men in every warlike skill. This argument appears again in Xenophon's didactic *Cyropaedia:* obedience can be extorted by rewarding the obedient and punishing the disobedient, but willing obedience will be granted only to the leader the soldier recognizes as his superior in military excellence. This is, in essence, Achilles' argument in the *Iliad:* all privileges, including that of being obeyed, come only in proportion to excellence. The counterargument of Agamemnon (or any modern officer), that obedience is owed to office regardless of the man who holds it, does not seem to have been decisive in Xenophon's military culture. Young Athenians undergoing their military training swore to obey the officials of the democracy. But the sharp opposition Xenophon draws between obedience for practical motives, that is, honor, reward, safety, to avoid punishment, and because of the personal excellence of the commander leaves precious little room for any third element, for obeying the office rather than its holder. An Achillean understanding of military authority sharply limited the authority that later Greek commanders could exert over their troops.[33]

With his close ties to Sparta, Xenophon was familiar with the ethic of obedience that operated there. "In other cities," he writes, "the more powerful men do not even wish to appear to respect the magistrates, thinking that to do so is slavish. Yet at Sparta the leading citizens show elaborate respect to the magistrates, and glory in being humble, and running rather than walking in answer to a call." The Spartans made a contest of obedience to authority. There lies the bite of the famous epitaph over the Spartan dead at Thermopylae: the Spartan fallen wanted the Spartans to know that "we lie here obedient to their orders" because the dead had triumphed over their live countrymen in the competition of obedience. "The man whom you choose I will obey as well as I can," grinds out a Spartan exile, the grim Clearchus, organizer of the Ten Thousand, trying to resign his command, "in order that you may see that I know how to *be* commanded better than any man alive." At Sparta obedience was a contest in excellence: it was this competitiveness that made the Spartans the most obedient of the Greeks.[34]

With the Spartan example before them, the other Greeks reflected ruefully on their inferiority in military obedience. To emulate the enviable obedience of the Spartans, Xenophon thinks, they need to emulate Spartan competition. In his *Cyropaedia* Xenophon recommends competitions for all ranks and for all units in military accomplishments, competitions which emphasize obedience. In another work Xenophon reveals that the commander who can inspire competition in his troops can get them to obey even if he is not supreme in each and every martial accomplishment. But these hopeful programs for gaining obedience by inspiring competition serve mostly to emphasize the contrast between Spartan attitudes toward obedience and those of the other Greeks, a contrast that their differing attitudes toward physical punishment confirms.[35]

In Sparta the ethos of competitive obedience lent legitimacy to a harsh regime of corporal discipline. Elsewhere in Greece, where this ideal was lacking, the legitimacy of command, and so the legitimacy of physical punishment, was far weaker: among other Greeks, as Xenophon found out by the shores of the Black Sea, using one's fists or stick to enforce one's commands seemed more like actionable assault. To Greeks other than Spartans, as Xenophon said, exact obedience seemed like the behavior of slaves, and beating treatment appropriate to slaves: the free citizen's sense of aggressive individual autonomy constituted an obstacle to a strong ethical claim that leaders should be obeyed and that they had the right to enforce obedience with force. Where Spartan commanders commanded non-Spartan troops, for example, Pausanias, the victor of Plataea, and Clearchus, first commander of the Ten Thousand, their freedom with their sticks made them very unpopular. For Xenophon to strike soldiers was to behave like a Spartan officer. But Xenophon was not a Spartan, and neither were the men he beat: as his speech of defense reveals, his command lacked the legitimacy that the Spartan system uniquely conveyed. That is why he was compelled to defend himself in such strange terms.[36]

Understanding Xenophon's plight makes it possible to understand Spartan tolerance of the disobedience of Amompharetus. The Spartans were the most obedient of the Greeks, but obedience, although part of the Spartan code (the *kala,* "the noble way") was a competitive excellence that jostled with other competitive excellences, over which it had no necessary precedence. A story was told of a Spartan warrior about to slay his foe in battle who halted his blow when the recall sounded, letting him escape, "for it is more excellent to obey the commander than to kill the enemy." Victory in the competition in obedience ranked higher than that in killing, but both fell along the same continuum of excellence. In the eyes of other Greeks, not leaving one's place in the line seems to have been the supreme commandment of the Spartan code. The Spartans were prepared to disregard Amompharetus's disobedience because they understood he was doing a duty that ranked higher.[37]

Even in Sparta the duty of military obedience was not unchallenged. Elsewhere in southern Greece it was far weaker. And whatever a commander's right to be obeyed, in Athens at least his willingness to compel obedience was limited by prudence: Xenophon's experience of being brought to trial for misconduct as a general was the continual nightmare of the democracy's generals. To the Greek soldier, his commander was far more equal to him than he is to the modern soldier. And this equality might have curious results when Greek soldiers and their generals disagreed on how a battle was to be fought.[38]

IV

THE GUILE OF DELIUM

GENERALS AND TACTICS
IN THE PHALANX

The flight of the Persians left two Greek states great in power and in pride: on the one side Sparta, leader of the Greeks in the war, with her indomitable hoplite army; on the other Athens, with her glittering wealth and great fleet. In the years after Plataea, Athens carried the war against Persia into the east and made the Greek cities of the Aegean her allies and then her subjects. Usually feuding and sometimes fighting, Athens and Sparta fell finally into a fatal contest, the twenty-seven-year Peloponnesian War (431–404 BC), recorded by the historian Thucydides.

In the first year of the war the Spartans assembled their allies and invaded Attica, the territory of Athens. They expected the Athenians would fight to defend their crops. But the city of Athens was strongly walled, and long walls connected Athens to her seaport a few miles away, into which the tribute of empire and the grain of the Black Sea were borne in rich abundance. Pericles, the great Athenian statesman, prevailed upon his countrymen to remain within their walls. This he did with difficulty: as individuals, the Athenians felt keenly the financial loss of the ravaging of their fields, and as a city they felt as keenly the shame of refusing such a challenge to a hoplite contest.

If the Athenians would not come out to fight, the Spartans could do them no fatal harm. The Athenians, similarly, could raid Peloponnese from their ships but inflict nothing upon Sparta or her allies that would compel them to peace. Thus the war went on and on. The actions of the

first year, Peloponnesian invasion of Attica and Athenian raiding of Peloponnese, were often repeated in following years, but as often proved futile. The war became a thing of cruel accidents and fleeting chances. The
Athenians, cooped up within their walls, were struck by a plague in 430
and 429. Mytilene, a city of Lesbos and part of Athens's empire, rebelled
in 428, but the deliberate Spartans moved too slowly to help. Plataea,
Athens's small ally in Boeotia, hallowed as the site of victory over the
Persians, was besieged in 429 and taken by the Spartans in 427; the Athenians could not rescue it without meeting the Peloponnesians in the field.
In 425, the Athenians isolated a force of Spartan hoplites on an island off
Peloponnese, Sphacteria. With a force of light infantry they took them
prisoner (this was the occasion for the bitter Spartan remark on the arrow).
The Athenians threatened to execute the prisoners if the Spartans invaded Attica again; and the Spartans did not, thus freeing the Attic
countryside from Peloponnesian ravage. Athenian spirits soared, and the
Athenians looked ahead to victory: but their hopes were thwarted by an
enemy expedition to Thrace, led by the Spartan Brasidas. Athenian subject
towns in the region defected to him, and he captured the great Athenian
stronghold of Amphipolis in 424. When the Athenians found they could
not recover Amphipolis with the spear, they and the Spartans made peace
in 421—a very temporary peace, as it turned out—in order that the prisoners and Amphipolis be returned. And so ended the first period, the first
ten-year fever, of the Peloponnesian War.

During the period of Athenian optimism after the capture of the
Spartan hoplites on Sphacteria, the Athenians laid a plan to seize and fortify the sanctuary of Apollo at Delium, which lay in Boeotia, enemy territory dominated by Thebes, which was allied to the Spartans. At the same
moment, by plot with Athens, Boeotian democrats were to rise in several
Boeotian cities: Delium was to be a base for a pro-Athenian revolution
against the ancestral oligarchies of the Boeotian plain.[1]

The Athenian general Hippocrates, who had been intriguing with the
Boeotian democrats, led the expedition, which included a mass levy of
mostly unarmed Athenians and resident foreigners to help with the construction of the fort. The army departed in autumn, after the usual campaigning season. But the democratic revolution in Boeotia was stillborn,
and the Athenians faced the unimpaired power of the Boeotians alone.

Speed and surprise got the Athenians safely to Delium. They fortified the temple and drank from the waters of the sacred spring, both acts of atrocious sacrilege, and on the fifth day after entering Boeotia turned for home. Those Athenians without hoplite equipment who had been brought along for the construction hastened back to Athens. The hoplites camped for the night at a distance from Delium to wait for Hippocrates, who was putting finishing touches to the fortifications. And so it was that the next day the Boeotian army caught up with the Athenian hoplite force just on the Athenian border.[2]

The Boeotian commander, Pagondas, drew up his army behind a hill. On the wings he posted his thousand cavalry and his light troops, ten thousand strong. The center was held by seven thousand Boeotian hoplites, drawn up in a conventional phalanx, except that the Thebans themselves — the contingent from the most powerful city in Boeotia, in the place of honor on the right of the hoplite line — drew up their part of the phalanx twenty-five deep. It was perhaps to hide this unusual deployment, unprecedented in previous Greek practice as far as we know, that Pagondas drew up his army in concealment. The Athenians drew up their hoplite line eight deep, with most of their cavalry on the wings. The Athenian army included no regular force of light troops, and the levy of mostly unarmed who had come along for the building had departed. Three hundred Athenian cavalry were left in the fort at Delium with instructions to fall upon the Boeotians during the battle.[3]

After brief harangues from their respective generals (that of Hippocrates was cut short by the Boeotian advance), the armies came together, the Boeotians striding down the hill, singing the paean, the Athenians breaking into a run. The flanks could not engage because watercourses kept them apart. But the hoplite forces fought in earnest in the center, with pushing of shields. The Athenian right had the best of it against the Boeotian left: when those around them fled, the contingent of the brave Thespians was surrounded and cut to pieces. As the Athenian line lapped around the Thespians and met behind them, Athenian slew Athenian in the confusion: "When a man stands face to face with the enemy, he is barely able to see what he needs to see," as Euripides said, perhaps alluding to this very battle.[4]

On the other flank, the fortunes of war were reversed. The deep Theban phalanx on the Boeotian right slowly pushed back the Athenians opposed to them. Seeing that his left was falling back, Pagondas sent a contingent of his horse previously kept from the struggle by the streams around the hill to set upon the victorious Athenian right by surprise. The advancing Athenians, thinking another army had come against them, fell into a panic, which infected the Athenians on the other flank who were being driven back. The Thebans broke the Athenian line, and the Athenians were put to flight.[5]

The Boeotians pursued ruthlessly with their cavalry and slaughtered the fleeing Athenians: only the coming of night (the battle had been fought in the afternoon) saved the mass of the fugitives. One tiny fragment of the shattered army gathered around the philosopher Socrates, who led them to safety, his calm demeanor amidst the cataclysm discouraging their pursuers. The Boeotians set up a trophy on the battlefield, and the Athenians sent a herald to ask for the right to recover their dead. The Boeotians refused: the Athenians must first evacuate the temple at Delium. There was an inconclusive quarrel about whose acts were more displeasing to custom and the gods, the Athenians' for fortifying a temple and using a holy spring as a military watering hole or the Boeotians' for refusing to return the dead under truce. Seventeen days later the Boeotians recaptured Delium with a primitive flamethrower. Then the Boeotians allowed the Athenians to take up their thousand hoplite dead, including their general Hippocrates. The Boeotians had lost somewhat fewer than five hundred men.[6]

There is much unexpected in the battle of Delium, if the conventions of hoplite battle define the boundaries of expectation. The battle occurred after the normal campaigning season. The sanctity of a sacred place and the custom of returning the dead were held in scorn. Pursuit was extended and bloody. Pagondas arrayed his Theban phalanx twenty-five deep and may even have deployed behind a hill to conceal his scheme. Cavalry played a decisive role, and evidently Pagondas expected his light troops to be important as well. The battle of Delium was hardly a solemn ritual of rule-bound hoplite competition. It stands in stark contrast to the conventional, formal ethos of hoplite fighting.

The usual explanation for this fact is to posit a period of decorous hoplite warfare and then suggest that its conventions broke down, perhaps with the coming of the Peloponnesian War. So the outbreak of that war becomes the watershed between strange, archaic, artificial, limited war and real, familiar, gloves-off war, between the ritualized primitive and the efficient modern. But military trickery goes back before the Persian Wars, far into the period of posited formal and rule-bound hoplite combat. In the 490s BC, we are told, the Argives were afraid of being defeated by a trick of the Spartans, with whom they were again at war. To guard against this they ordained that their army should copy every act of the Spartans and use the Spartan heralds' cries as their own commands. When Cleomenes, king of Sparta, came to know of this, he instructed his soldiers to arm and attack when the signal for a meal was given: so the Spartans caught the Argives unawares and drove their army into a sacred grove. First, Cleomenes lured out Argives to their deaths from the precinct by the ruse of having a herald announce that ransom had been paid for them and they were free to go. After fifty had been killed, the Argives caught on and would no longer emerge. So Cleomenes had the temple and its sacred grove burned. Legend has it that no fewer than six thousand Argives were slain in this war, a war in which the Spartans—in some ways the most rigorous adherents to hoplite convention—displayed contempt for convention and the rights of a sacred place and in which we are told that the Argives expected exactly some such deviltry from them. And well they might. For the Spartans had a proud tradition of just such behavior, going back to their legendary King Soüs. He seized a tract of Arcadia and was besieged by the Arcadians in a waterless place. When his force was tortured by thirst, the king agreed he would surrender the conquered territory if he and all his force should drink from a spring: his men drank, but the king did not, and under the terms of the agreement the Spartans kept the land. Herodotus records that at Thermopylae the Spartans did great destruction by pretending to flee and then turning on their pursuers. A later author believed that King Leonidas had ordered the Spartans to make a night attack on Xerxes' camp. If either of these tales is true, they fall into this proud Spartan tradition of trickery. Thucydides has Pericles allude to the Spartan custom of military guile (431/30 BC). Typically Spartan was the saying of the Spartan admiral Lysander, that where the skin of the lion does not reach it has to be patched with the skin of the fox. And it seems there was nothing exceptional about Spartan behavior, because it is easy to build up a dossier of military tricks practiced by a variety of Greek states before the outbreak of the Peloponnesian War.[7]

It is tempting, then, to dismiss the formality of hoplite warfare as a mirage, as a nostalgic fantasy of later Greeks. But the curious way the Greeks fought was pointed to by Herodotus, a contemporary. And the real situation is far more interesting. For most of the evidence for the formality of hoplite battle comes not from the period before the Peloponnesian War, but from late fifth- and early fourth-century battles — Mantinea, Nemea River, Coronea, Leuctra, and Second Mantinea — which also have many unconventional elements. No battle of hoplite against hoplite of which a detailed description survives was fought in a strictly ritualized fashion, but every hoplite battle of which a detailed description survives also betrays some ritual elements. Even at Delium, that carnival of misrule in which every other custom was mocked, the Thebans occupied the place of honor on the right of the hoplite line, and the Boeotians set up their trophy. Tactical generalship — that of a Pagondas or of his Theban successor, the great Epaminondas, victor at Leuctra in 371 BC — was not always answered by tactical generalship on the opposing side. Indeed many of the successes of tactical generalship, like Pagondas's at Delium, depended on taking advantage of the enemy's loyalty to hoplite convention. In reality Greek hoplite warfare existed in perennial tension between battle conducted according to understood rules and the crafty subversion of those rules. Cunning tactics were already in use at Marathon in 490, the very first battle in which Greek hoplites can clearly be seen fighting. Yet in 420, deep into the Peloponnesian War, the Argives and Spartans could agree in principle to a replay of the battle of champions for Thyrea, with rules fixed in advance. The real mystery is how such a mixed picture could arise and persist over time, how the rules could continue to be applied despite the fact that they were frequently broken and despite the advantages that breaking them frequently yielded. When rules are broken, fewer follow them thereafter, and finally none. But in Greece breaking the rules and following the rules coexisted for generations.[8]

Too much had been abandoned as mixed combat was eroded into the phalanx to produce better competition in the real world. The Homeric *aretai* with no place in the phalanx found their champions, of whom Herodotus was one. The Spartans denied the prize for valor at Plataea to Aristodemus because he had left his rank to fight in frenzy, but Herodotus judged him the bravest. The historian was in sympathy with an older, broader, more Homeric conception of bravery. The Athenian Sophanes, who proved his passive courage by bringing an anchor to Plataea, had a few years before triumphed in an arranged single combat in a war against Aegina. This tradition of one-on-one dueling between champions survived in Classical Greece (even if rare) and constituted a challenge to the hoplite compromise, another way of reconciling Greek competitiveness with martial reality.[9]

Yet it was the commanders of hoplite armies who posed a significant challenge to hoplite ideals. "We did not run second to Epaminondas," boasts a memorial to three other Theban generals celebrating the Theban victory over the Spartans at Leuctra in 371 BC. Generals—notice the athletic metaphor—were as competitive among themselves as hoplites. Commanders—Spartan kings and, judging by their frequent deaths in battle, the leaders in other states too—usually fought in the phalanx, participating in hoplite competition: as in the case of Amompharetus an officer might even win the prize for bravery. But generals, like hoplites, conceived of what they were doing in Homeric terms, and the *Iliad* suggested to Classical Greek generals a quite separate set of competitions. To celebrate his recapture of the fort of Eion from the Persians, the Athenian general Cimon erected a monument reading,

> Once from this city Menestheus marched out with the sons
>   of Atreus
>   to the hallowed plain of Troy.
> Of the well-armored Greeks—Homer quoth—
>   he came as the best arrayer of battle.
> So it is meet that the Athenians be called
>   the arrayers of war and manhood.[10]

It is in terms of the Homeric competitive *aretē* of arraying troops, as exemplified by the Athenian Homeric hero Menestheus—outstanding in it—that the Athenian general conceives his accomplishment and that of his colleagues. This reach into the epic past is not surprising, for in Classical Athens Homer was considered a practical guide to generalship, especially to the arraying of troops. In discussions of war, as in so many Greek contexts, the *Iliad* seems to have come up continuously as a model or a tool for thinking. So profound was epic's military authority that a professional singer of Homer, a rhapsode, could claim that his knowledge of epic qualified him to be a general. There was also self-conscious Homeric revival in warfare: a later author mentions that at Delium the Thebans had a unit of three hundred picked hoplites they called the "charioteers and chariot-riders," alluding to the pairing of warrior and driver in chariots as they are described in the *Iliad*.[11]

The tradition enshrined in epic specified for leaders competitions in arraying soldiers (as in the Eion poem). It specified for leaders competition in persuasiveness in council and in giving wise advice: "He was glorious in council: he had the greatest reputation for speaking and advising," says Xenophon about the Syracusan general Hermocrates, in words redolent of epic. It specified for leaders competition in *metis,* the cunning intelligence: "In stratagems you already out-shoot Nicias!" says one character in Aristophanes to another. Thucydides has the Spartan general Brasidas say, "The most successful soldier will always be the man who most happily detects a blunder . . . and who, carefully consulting his own means, makes his attack not so much by open and regular approaches, as by seizing the opportunity of the moment; and these stratagems, which do the greatest service to our friends by most deceiving our enemies, have the most brilliant name in war." So Thucydides places the use of stratagems firmly within the competitive ethos of Greek warfare: the user of stratagems earns a brilliant name by his cunning just as the hoplite does by his courage. In the fourth century the Athenians agreed. They erected a statue of their general Chabrias with his shield leaning against his knees, which alluded to his famous stratagem of ordering his men to lean their shields against their knees in a posture of insouciance. Thinking something must be up, the Spartans did not attack. Celebrating this trick on the statue reveals the fully heroic status of such trickery.[12]

The Spartans agreed that trickery was heroic as well. After the defeat of Xerxes the Spartans gave a prize for wisdom and cleverness to Themistocles, chief intellectual architect of the Greek victory, certifying his triumph in this contest. It was the Spartan custom, moreover, to sacrifice a bull to Ares if a victory was gained by stratagem, a rooster if by pitched battle. This, we are told, was to encourage crafty strategy. Spartan kings, who commanded the army, performed the public sacrifices and received, honorifically, choice portions of sacrificial beasts — and a cow had rather more choice portions than a chicken. Plato associates Spartan institutions, expertise in the "contests of war," and the honoring of military trickery. So cunning was the Spartan king Agesilaus while campaigning in Asia that, as Xenophon reported admiringly, "he showed Tissaphernes," his Persian opponent, "to be a child in deceit." The cultivation of a Homeric competition in cunning explains the old and long-lasting Spartan tradition of trickery in war. In the case of the Spartan general Dercylidas, the Homeric connection was explicit: he boasted the nickname Sisyphus, in Homer "the most tricky of men."[13]

Yet the defensiveness conveyed by Thucydides when he has Brasidas make an overt claim for the heroic quality of stratagem reveals that the historian has entered a realm of hot debate; the same defensiveness can be detected in Xenophon when he urges stratagem upon his reader. Plutarch directs Lysander's tag about the need to patch out the skin of the lion with that of the fox at "those who thought it unworthy of the descendants of Heracles to use trickery in war," and expressions of distaste for military guile are easy to find. During the march of the Ten Thousand, the decision to capture a position by craft rather than by pitched battle, that is, to "steal" it, brings on a jocular exchange: you Spartans are experts at stealing, taught to do it from childhood; no, Xenophon, you Athenians are experts at stealing — public funds at least. The comparison of a military trick to stealing in earnest reveals that the officers of the Ten Thousand thought military trickery had to it something of the moral status of real larceny. Contempt for military trickery is attributed to great marshals like Agesilaus and Alexander the Great. In fact both Agesilaus and Alexander were expert military tricksters — we are not to take the tales about their ideals too seriously — but the placing of such sentiments in such great mouths reveals the continuing power of a body of opinion that discountenanced cleverness in warfare.[14]

Opposition to military trickery was grounded not in some abstract sense of chivalry or fair play, but in the hoplite ideal of competition in passive bravery: competition in guileful generalship was itself in competition with hoplite competition. The Spartan king who won the bull for a bloodless victory by trickery obliterated the competition in bravery between his hoplites. One shift that crafty generalship might recommend was raids on the shore from ships. But this might be objectionable to the hoplite ethos, as Plato reveals by having a character deplore the fact that Athenian naval power compelled Athenian hoplites to act as "marines, instead of steady hoplite foot soldiers, for they are used to jumping ashore frequently and running back fast to their ships, and it does not seem shameful to them not to die bravely standing their ground against the enemy onset, and fair excuses are ready to hand for them when they cast away their arms and flee in what they call 'not shameful flight.' Such phrases are what usually result from using hoplites as marines, and rather than being worth 'a thousand praises' they deserve the opposite. For one should never accustom men to bad habits, especially not the best part of the citizens." Plato could not reconcile raiding to the hoplite ethic; worse, in the eyes of Plato's speaker, raiding habituated hoplites to running away and so sapped their passive bravery, their excellence. Any form of trickery or tactics on the general's part had the potential to ruin the competition of the hoplite in the line or, worse, make a hoplite act shamefully according to his code, and so might be opposed by men with hoplite ideals.[15]

The traces of a long war of ideas between hoplites and their commanders are visible in scraps of the arguments of both sides about wily generalship. Those who advocated generals' ideals insisted upon the practical efficacy of stratagem. This argument was hardly unanswerable: a stratagem gone awry nearly lost the Spartans the battle of Mantinea in 418 BC. But the real vulnerability of this appeal to efficacy in the Greek context was that it revived an Iliadic way of ranking warriors which played little role in hoplite warfare. Epic had evaluated killings both by the performance of the killer and by the value of the defeated: hoplites had made a fetish of performance, while discarding the latter as impractical in the real world. Generalship too was a form of heroic performance — for the general. But this particular defense of generalship attempted to make it more broadly appealing by implying that heroic performance might be sacrificed to results, and glory looked for in those results. As Thucydides had a Spartan king say, "Being aware of how great a city you are marching against, and what a great reputation you will win for your ancestors and yourselves, whatever the outcome, follow wherever you are led, and regard good order and caution as of the utmost importance, and obey your orders quickly." The glory was in defeating so great an enemy, not in how the enemy was defeated: here the soldier's duty is not to fight bravely in the line, but to do as he is told. The same glory is urged which the Homeric hero got by defeating a high-ranking opponent—but in an unheroic way.[16]

In reaction to this, the first counterargument we hear voiced against the appeal to the efficacy of stratagem is that victory by guile is dishonorable. Whatever happy results follow from it, base performance stains. In a mental world dominated by the hoplite ethos this was a powerful objection. Second, it was objected that victory by guile was no victory at all, that, for example, the victory of the Athenian light infantry over the Spartans at Sphacteria "was no victory, but rather a theft of war."[17] This second objection can be expanded by noticing Demosthenes' treatment of the Greek defeat at Chaeronea in 338 BC: "If someone were to ask those in the enemy ranks whether they thought they won by their own courage [*aretē*] or by an unexpected and harsh act of fortune and by the skill and daring of their commander [Philip II], not one of them would be so shameless and bold to claim credit for the result." A victory by the stratagem of a general allowed the defeated to claim that they were not defeated in courage, that they were not defeated according to the hoplite definition of defeat. It allowed the defeated—or Demosthenes, their spokesman— pleas to excuse defeat, exactly those pleas which Thucydides had Brasidas claim phalanx fighting prevented. Victory by stratagem broke the parallelism between the experience of hoplite and city, since an army—so a city —might be defeated without reproach to the courage of its hoplites. This was not a kind of victory that offered the same satisfaction to the victor as victory in a straight-up battle. In a Greek world in which relations between states were conceived in terms of a ranking—a league table in which the relative number of wins and losses in battle played a large part in establishing relative standing—it was a real deficiency if enemies could claim they had been beaten dishonestly.[18]

The odd mix of ritual and trickery that characterizes Classical Greek warfare, the abiding tension between rules and ruthless advantage-taking, is at base the result of an irresolvable conflict between two sets of ideals,

those of the hoplites and those of the generals, the former the child of
Greek competitiveness and closely related to Homer, and the latter taken
directly from Homer. The conflict was perennial because in Greece the
right of the general to command his hoplites against their ideals, that is,
the right of the general's competition to displace or spoil the hoplite's,
was never universally admitted in theory, and his power to enforce his
orders in practice was feeble.

This conflict of ideals could burst into spectacular flame, as at Plataea,
where a Spartan commander attempting a tactical retreat found himself
disobeyed by a subordinate relying upon a very strict construction of
hoplite bravery. More commonly, this conflict can be deduced from its results where the aggressive guile of one general was strikingly not matched
by guile on the other side, and where the general on the other side had
apparently contented himself, willing or perhaps unwilling, to compete
as a hoplite. It is hardly an accident that it was Sparta—where the constitutional position of the king-general was unusually strong, where his soldiers were unusually obedient, his subordinate officers unusually many,
and his authority over the soldiers of other states in coalition armies
unquestioned—that had a particular reputation for guile in battle. It is
not an accident either that other generals famed for stratagem were unusually powerful in their states, men like Epaminondas at Thebes or Pagondas, who could overcome the opposition of all ten other boeotarchs,
representatives of the Boeotian league, to give battle at Delium. It was
a commander lacking such exceptional power, for example, a Pausanias
at Plataea, a mere regent, not a Spartan king, and perhaps still in his twenties, who might meet with furious opposition when he attempted a tactic
(withdrawal to a strong place) offensive to hoplite ideals. Yet this war of
ideals was also a war of many truces, for there were many grounds for
accommodation between generals and hoplites. Generals were drawn
from the ranks of the hoplites, as hoplites they fought; when they ceased
to be generals, it was to the hoplite ranks they returned. Such was the
power of hoplite ideals that many commanders were delighted to compete as hoplites rather than as tacticians, as their frequent deaths in the
line signify. At the same time the tactical general's promise of victory
sparing of blood could hardly fail to be appealing to his hoplites. There
was plenty of grumbling on both sides in the Mantinea campaign when

commanders failed to give battle in circumstances their soldiers thought were tactically advantageous. Nor was fighting at a tactical disadvantage popular among hoplites. Still, there is little indication that this conflict between hoplites and generals shifted much in Classical Greece, that the generals ultimately prevailed over their hoplites, or that the hoplites prevailed over their generals.[19]

In the long war between hoplites and their generals there was little movement of the front over time. Yet the methods by which the Classical Greeks fought did change.

V

THE ARTS OF WAR IN THE EARLY
FOURTH CENTURY BC

PELTASTS, CAVALRY, AND TRAINING

Short and angry was the peace between Athens and Sparta that followed three years after Delium. By 418 BC, Athenian and Spartan soldiers faced each other again at the great battle of Mantinea, which pitted Argos against Sparta in yet another round of their struggle for lordship of the Peloponnese. Thucydides' celebrated description of that combat is the basis of modern understanding of the methods and customs of hoplite fighting. Once again the Spartans prevailed over the Argives. By 415 the Athenians were fighting in Sicily, and by 413 their great expedition there had met with disaster; but even before it did, war with Sparta had broken out again and rolled on for another ten years. Allying themselves with the wealth of Persia, the Spartans could at last carry the war into the Athenian empire in the Aegean. The story of this part of the war is the story of great sea battles, of Cyzicus in 410 and Arginusae in 406, after which the Athenians, over the objections of Socrates, executed their victorious generals for failing to pick up their shipwrecked sailors. In 405, the Spartan admiral Lysander destroyed the Athenian fleet by a ruse at Aegospotami. In the next year a besieged and starving Athens surrendered to the Spartans, and Athens's proud walls to the sea were breached to the festive sounds of pipe playing.[1]

Yet if there was drama and finally decision at sea, when the war resumed there was still frustration on land. It remained out of the question for the Athenians to undertake a war-winning invasion of the Peloponnese;

91

it remained out of the question for the Athenians to fight a hoplite battle in Attica. Rather than invade Attica every year, the Peloponnesians built a fort at Decelea, near the Boeotian border and ravaged the Attic countryside from there. But the fortifications of Athens itself they still dared not assail. Futility so long drawn out was the mother of invention, and the Peloponnesian War saw many experiments in fighting which were harbingers of changes in the following century. In 426 BC, Athenian hoplites were roughly handled by native light infantry in a minor campaign in northwest Greece. Perhaps this suggested to them how light infantry could be used on Sphacteria in the next year, when they captured the force of Spartan hoplites. In 425/24, to counter Athenian raids upon their coasts, the Spartans, their ancient "horsemen" having long fought as hoplites and their archaic archers having long vanished, reestablished a mounted cavalry and a force of archers. The Spartans had trained their hoplites of old, but to the battle of Mantinea the Argives brought a unit of one thousand trained hoplites, the first trained rather than merely "picked" hoplite force known to us who were not Spartans.[2]

In the next century these experiments would amplify into trends. More hoplite training was seen outside Sparta, and finally, in the 330s, the Athenians established compulsory military training for all their young citizen men. By 370 BC a number of Peloponnesian states, in which cavalry had been unusual in the fifth century, had established effective cavalry forces on the model of Athens, Boeotia, and points north, states with old cavalry traditions. At the same time there emerged a sense that an army should consist not essentially of hoplites (with other arms a militarily insignificant afterthought), but of a balance of hoplites, cavalry, and light troops used in close cooperation: so, for example, the charge of the hoplites would turn the enemy light troops to flight, and the cavalry would then ride them down. "The light-armed troops are like the hands, the cavalry is like the feet, the phalanx is like the chest and breastplate, and the general is like the head," the Athenian general Iphicrates is reported to have said. Iphicrates was a famous commander of mercenaries, and in the fourth century many of those who served in all three of these arms were mercenaries, a type of soldier who had been rare, at least in mainland Greece, in the fifth.[3]

The Peloponnesian War was the starting point for many of the military developments of the fourth century BC. But the war does not explain the progress or direction of these developments, or why they were possible in a world dominated by hoplites whose ambitions even generals contradicted at their peril. The river of invention unleashed by the Peloponnesian War was dredged and diked and channeled by the military culture of the Greeks.

Sparta's victory in the Peloponnesian War did not bring peace to Greece. For the next thirty years the Spartans tried to make the Greeks obey them, and for thirty years the cities of Greece formed combinations against Spartan domination. From 395 to 387/86 BC, Thebes, Athens, Corinth, and others fought the Lacedaemonians in the so-called Corinthian war, much of it being fought from rival strongholds in the ravaged territory of Corinth. One of the war's causes was the refusal of the Thebans to allow the Spartan king Agesilaus to sacrifice at Aulis (396 BC) on his way to Asia to fight the Persians. Agamemnon had sacrificed at Aulis on his way to Troy, and Agesilaus wished to sacrifice in the same place. Emblematic of the age was the defeat of a contingent of Spartan hoplites in that war by mercenary light-armed troops near Lechaeum, a port of Corinth's under Spartan control (390 BC).

THE BATTLE OF LECHAEUM AND THE PUZZLE OF PELTASTS

There was war around Corinth, but the god required that the men of Amyclae go home to Lacedaemon for the festival of the Hyacinthia; for it was they who sang the paean to Apollo, and Apollo was not to be denied. With cavalry and six hundred hoplites the Spartan commander escorted them on their way past the enemy city of Corinth. Then, leaving the cavalry with the Amyclaeans, he turned to march back with his hoplites to his base at Lechaeum, scorning the enemy behind the walls. But the Athenians were in Corinth, including their general Iphicrates, commanding a force of mostly javelin-armed mercenary light infantry: peltasts, they were called, from the small, usually crescent-shaped shield, or *pelte,* they carried. Seeing the Spartan hoplites unprotected by cavalry or peltasts of their own, Iphicrates led his men out of the city to do what mischief they could. The peltasts attacked the Spartans with javelins on their right side, unprotected by their shields, and Spartans were wounded. The

Spartan commander ordered the youngest soldiers, the first ten age classes, to run out beyond the phalanx and drive the peltasts off. But at Iphicrates' orders the peltasts fled before them, faster than the heavier-armed Spartans could run, and as the Spartans turned back to the phalanx, scattered from the chase, the peltasts hit more of them with javelins, now outrunning them in the other direction, to hit them again from the right. The Spartan commander then sent the first fifteen age classes out to drive off the peltasts, but the same events played out: seeing them isolated, the peltasts cut down even more of them. By this time the best of the Spartans had been slain, and at last the Spartan cavalry returned to protect the hoplites, but rather than riding down the scattered peltasts, they stayed close to the hoplites, and so were in vain. Under constant attack, taking many losses, becoming fewer as their foes became more, and more timid as their foes became bolder, the Spartans made their way to a small hill near the sea: their allies coasted along from Lechaeum in boats and waited to pick them up. And now the Athenian hoplites from Corinth were seen approaching, and still the Spartans could not avenge themselves upon the peltasts who tormented them, and finally the iron nerve of the Spartans broke, and the storied phalanx of the Lacedaemonians collapsed: some fled to the boats, and a few made it to Lechaeum with the horsemen.

Some two hundred and fifty Spartans were killed in the running battles and the flight. Mourning consumed the Spartan army, except those whose sons, brothers, or fathers had died in their places. "Like glorious victors in a contest they went around exulting," because of the victory of their relatives in the great hoplite contest of the bravery of holding their place, the supreme contest in Sparta. Lechaeum shows the continuing strength of the ethic of hoplite warfare in the early fourth century—but also the grim results that ethic could have when enemies did not abide by it. For the Athenians did not offer a standing hoplite battle but held their hoplites back and instead sent light infantry against the Spartans and harried them to their doom.[4]

The battle of Lechaeum was a famous success for peltasts. But why did the Athenians have a force of mercenary peltasts at all? For Athens had traditionally relied on archers where light troops were needed. An Athenian archer had brought down the horse of the Persian commander Masistius before Plataea. At the opening of the Peloponnesian War Athens

Thracian peltast with javelin and *pelte*, Attic Cup, late sixth century BC
(ARV² 48.159; Antikenmuseum der Universität Leipzig.
Photo: Karin Kranich).

had a force of no fewer than sixteen hundred bowmen (many for use
with the fleet), and in that war units of archers accompanied Athenian
hoplites on campaign.[5]

Peltasts had been known in Greece — and depicted on vases — for a
century before the Peloponnesian War, but they were not, apparently,
much employed by the Athenians. It was during that war the Athenians
began to employ in large numbers peltasts from Thrace, where this style
of fighting was native, and from Greek islands near Thrace. At the start
this may have been fortuitous in that Thracian peltasts may simply have
been easily available when light troops were needed. But soon Greeks

who lived far from Thrace began to fight — and train intensely, under Iphicrates — as peltasts. And this trend toward using peltasts was not confined to Athens: in fourth-century Greece, the peltast established himself as the dominant species of light infantryman, displacing (but never completely) not only archers, but also slingers, who had been common in the fifth century. Both bows and slings had a far longer range than javelins, and they could be very effective. When facing non-Greek opponents armed with bows and slings, the Greeks' neglect of these longer-range missile weapons proved dangerous. To take full advantage of the superiority of bows and slings perhaps required greater training than throwing javelins, but this had not posed a problem to the Athenians before the Peloponnesian War. Even if wielded by the poorly trained, bows and slings still had a great advantage over javelins in the number of missiles a user could carry.[6]

Peltasts were not uniformly armed: in addition to the *pelte* most carried javelins, but some carried thrusting spears (see figures, pp. 95, 97), and peltasts also threw stones. Thracian peltasts rushed out to attack and then pulled back into clumps for mutual protection. Whether by accident or long survival, the peltast way of fighting — of running and throwing or stabbing, of individual attack and protective defensive massing — was very similar to most of the fighting depicted in the *Iliad*, indeed far more similar to most of the fighting in the *Iliad* than the massed array of the phalanx, which had only a few passages to justify it. The Thracians even threw their *pelte* shields over their backs for protection when they ran away, like Ajax in the *Iliad*, and performed a dance in which one dancer mimed killing another with his sword and then stripped the body, a very Homeric vision. Peltasts, like generals, had epic legitimacy ready to hand. The use of slings, by contrast, had only the slightest epic precedent, and archery's heroic status was disputed in the *Iliad*. Once the exigencies of the Peloponnesian War brought large numbers of peltasts into Greece and introduced large numbers of Greeks to this way of fighting, peltast fighting fit far more comfortably into Greek military culture than slings or archery.[7]

The peculiarly Homeric quality of the peltast may also make sense of a very murky story told about Iphicrates, that in the 370s he altered the equipment of the peltasts, giving them round shields, longer spears,

Thracian peltast with thrusting spear and *pelte,* skyphos
(*Annual of the British School at Athens* 14 [1907–8] pl. 14).

and longer swords. No doubt he had practical reasons, but the *Iliad* was
ready to hand as inspiration. "Round" (expressed in various ways) is the
most frequent epithet of shields in the *Iliad,* while the *pelte* inherited from
the Thracians was scalloped or crescent-shaped. Longer swords brought
peltast equipment more in line with Iliadic description, in which long
swords were very often used to gory effect; but in recent times the Greeks
had carried a very short sword or dagger. Longer thrusting spears gave
the peltasts a longer reach. But such spears also accorded with the spears
described in the *Iliad,* so frequently "long" or "far-shadowing."[8]

Their epic legitimacy may also begin to explain the advance of the
peltast at the expense of the proud hoplite, an advance archers and slingers had been unable to achieve. Even in the prosaic sentences of Xenophon the disaster at Lechaeum takes on a heroic quality. Again and again
the Spartans pursue swiftly, as swiftly as they can, but again and again the
peltasts, "the swiftest," outpace the hoplites and run back faster than the
foe and kill them with skillful casts from the side. The pursuit is especially
tense because young Spartan hoplites sometimes could catch fleeing peltasts: they had done so earlier in the war and killed some. When Xenophon
notes that "the best" of the Spartans were killed in these chases he is
hardly striking a consciously epic note, but he is swept up by the epic

quality of the scene, for the peltasts are victorious because of their supreme fleetness of foot and their skill at arms. Half-unknowing, Xenophon is unveiling the heroic code of the peltast: the peltast took up those epic competitions, in running and in spear-throwing, which the hoplite had let fall to the ground.[9]

JASON OF PHERAE AND THE PUZZLE OF CAVALRY DRILL

If southern Greece was the realm of the hoplite, northern Greece was the realm of the horse. Central Greek states like Athens and the Boeotian cities that had hoplite forces and hoplite outlooks nevertheless also had ancestral cavalries, which they had wielded at Delium. But north of Boeotia lay the broad plain of Thessaly, famed for its cavalry, where leaping off horses to wrestle bulls was the national sport and where haughty barons in wide-brimmed sun-hats raced their horses over serf-tilled fields. Thessaly was horse-breeding country, like its northern neighbor and ancestral enemy, Macedon, also ruled by an equestrian aristocracy. Thessaly's defense lay in the hands of its cavalry; its nobility rode with their retainers to battle.

When the horsemen of southern Greece went to war, they arrayed themselves for battle in a square or a wide, shallow rectangle. The Scythians and Thracians used a wedge, or triangle, which Philip II of Macedon adopted from them. The wedge is better than the square, the ancient tacticians say, because it offers a point for penetrating enemy formations and gathers the leaders in a group at the front. It is easier to turn than a square because all follow the commander at the apex, "like a flight of cranes." But the supremely skillful horsemen of Thessaly disposed themselves in a rhombus, shaped like the diamond in a deck of cards. It was one Jason the Thessalian who invented the formation, the tacticians say, and this must be the formidable Jason of Pherae, the grim strongman who briefly raised Thessaly to power in Greece until his murder in 370 BC.

The rhombus offered the advantages of the wedge—the spear-wielding Thessalians could make good use of the penetrating point—and added security in flank and rear, with leaders posted at all four corners. And the tactical authors speak admiringly of its maneuverability, its ability to wheel quickly in any direction: to turn left or right or backward the wedge had to be led around in an arc, a slow procedure that required much room.

But with leaders at all four points the rhombus could turn left or right or backward simply by having each trooper in the formation turn his horse in place, the old left, right, or rear point becoming the new front of the formation.[10]

Yet the most wonderful quality of the Thessalian formation was its ability to change shape. For the rhombus was really four different formations in one. It could be packed as tightly as possible to deliver a charge with spears, each horse with another in front and on both sides. Or it could spread out back and front, while drawing in left and right, to pass through narrow places and fit in the gaps between units of friend and foe. Or, to protect a longer section of the line, it could elongate left and right, while drawing in its front and back (see figures). Finally, to move quickly across the ground, a looser order could be adopted, with more space between the horsemen. So elegantly simple was the array that it is likely the Thessalians could change its shape on the fly. The rhombus was supremely maneuverable on the field of battle, a flash of drilled riders moving with the sparkle of a school of fish.[11]

But such virtuosity came at the cost of sweat. "It is necessary to try out each of the formations often in daily exercises," advises a tactical writer. Riding in formation is far harder than marching: horses do not always do as they are told — the brutes are savage by nature, a tactical author complains — and the tacticians knew full well the chaos that resulted if horses got too close together and began to panic and kick. An exemplary member of the fourth-century Athenian cavalry, which essayed nothing as sophisticated as the rhombus, could be imagined practicing the riding needed in simple cavalry maneuvers nearly every day. One of the reasons the southern Greeks preferred to send their cavalry to battle in square formations was that they were easy to form and easy to preserve once formed, each rider having both the visual cues of comrades beside him and a comrade in front to follow: not so in the rhombus, where the rider might have to keep station with rank-mates beside him only, or file-mates front and back, or those in a diagonal relationship to him, and where he might have to shift from one to another, all the while controlling his warhorse without the benefit of stirrups. Yet by the second century BC the Thessalians had taken formation riding to such a pinnacle of excellence (although they had seemingly abandoned the rhombus by then) that

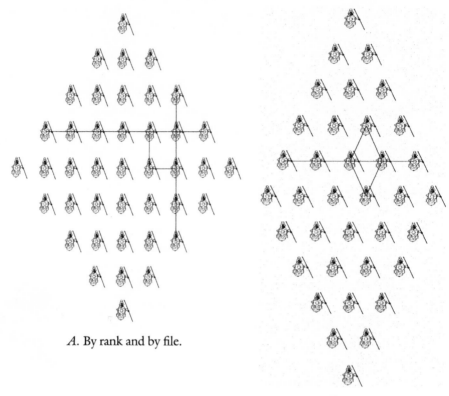

A. By rank and by file.

B. By rank but not by file.

Thessalian cavalry formations (SeungJung Kim)

Polybius could describe them as irresistible when arrayed in their squadrons but quite useless when trying to fight one on one.[12]

The horsemen of Thessaly, then, were not only practiced in riding (like all equestrian aristocracies), but they must have come together from their towns and estates to practice riding in the rhombus. Unlike the phalanx of amateur hoplites, the rhombus required exacting drill, and Jason of Pherae was a famously stringent trainer, of his mercenaries at least. Yet in Athens at any rate it was very hard to get the cavalry to train. Horsemen were the richest citizens and were so grand and independent-minded that Xenophon assumes the cavalry commander will have only the slightest authority over them. To get the troopers of the Athenian cavalry to drill required not commanding but cajoling: exercise in horsemanship is

C. By file but not by rank.

D. Neither by rank nor by file.

fun, the commander should say—riding is like flying! But despite the pleading only unusually influential Athenian cavalry commanders could prevail upon the cavalry to practice new and flashy parade maneuvers.[13]

Many of Jason's horsemen were mercenaries, but the core of his cavalry was necessarily the truculent baronage of Thessaly, "not tractable, but arrogant and full of strife," as an orator calls them, far harder to handle even than the Athenian wealthy. Horsemanship was ancestral to them, but so too was indiscipline. To other Greeks the wealth, feasting, and drunkenness of the Thessalian nobility were proverbial. They behaved more like the willful heroes of the *Iliad* than the circumspect citizens of the Classical Greek city-state. Customs that recalled Homer, in fact, survived in Thessaly: the avenger of a murder pulled the murderer around the victim's tomb behind his horse, just as Achilles had pulled Hector in the *Iliad*. However grinding a despot Jason may have been, it is nearly as difficult to imagine the Thessalian nobility drilling in formation as it is Achilles, the particular hero of the Thessalians and a native son. And Jason's cavalry is a microcosm of a wider puzzle: in a Greece where hoplite training was rare, how was cavalry training, which involved a far richer class of men even less inclined to take orders, ever possible? But Athens had public cavalry training before it had public hoplite training, and no doubt other Greek states with cavalry forces did as well.[14]

By the fourth century Athens had a great public spectacle, the *Anthippasia*, or "riding against," which pitted the ten tribal contingents of cavalry against one another in a contest of riding in exact formation. Performed at the festivals of the Greater Panathenaea and the Olympieia, it involved two teams of five tribal units riding through one another. A fourth-century relief celebrating a tribe victorious in the event represents the contest: the four horses that survive are in identical postures, perhaps suggesting the precision of their drill (see figure). And it may be that a party of the riders on the sculpted frieze of the Athenian Parthenon represents this contest in the mid–fifth century, an idea supported by their artful and meticulous overlapping. Advising the commander of the fourth-century Athenian cavalry, whose weak authority he takes for granted, on how to get the Athenian cavalry to practice drills of this type, Xenophon places his greatest confidence in competition: "If you offer prizes to the tribal units in all the feats the cavalry are expected to practice in festivals, this

Marble relief commemorating a victory of the tribe Leontis
in the *Anthippasia,* Athens, c. 400 BC (Agora Museum I 7167;
American School of Classical Studies at Athens: Agora Excavations).

would appeal greatly, I think, to the spirit of rivalry in every Athenian."
Indeed, Xenophon urges the hiring of foreign mercenary cavalry chiefly
to inspire a sense of rivalry in the Athenian cavalry. Even when two cavalrymen went out to train alone, he says, they should make a competition of it: one rider should chase the other and try to hit him with blunt
javelins or his spear.[15]

Elsewhere in Greece as well, cavalry drill might be made attractive
by making a game of it. On the eve of a great campaign on the west coast
of Asia Minor, the Spartan king Agesilaus in 395 BC gave prizes to the
Greek cavalry unit that displayed the best horsemanship. And while cavalry
drill in Greece hardly depended entirely upon a series of formal contests,
the existence of such contests reveals that participation in such drill was
in Greece conceived as competitive. The Greek culture of competition

extended even to exact drill, to our minds the definition of a cooperative, rather than a competitive, activity. This accounts for the orderly rhombus formed of disorderly Thessalians: the rambunctious nobility of Thessaly reconciled themselves to the practice required to fight in the rhombus by conceiving that drill as a contest in horsemanship, a quality in which they particularly prided themselves. The pride and independence of the Thessalian nobility did not work against their riding in exact formation but were rather its basis.

The next century offers a parallel, in Philopoemen's training of the horsemen of the Achaean League. This was a cavalry idle and undisciplined; "the commanders overlooked these vices because the cavalrymen were the most influential men among the Achaeans, and rewards and punishments depended chiefly upon them." These are exactly the problems earlier Greek cavalry presented. Philopoemen went the round of the cities of the league, and "whipped up the competitive ambition of each of the young men individually, punishing those in need of coercion, and employed exercises and processions and competitions against each other, in places where many would watch them, and in a short time imbued them all with amazing strength and zeal and — this is of the chiefest importance in tactics — made them nimble and swift in wheeling and deploying by squadrons, and wheeling and turning by a single trooper, making the dexterity of the whole mass in its evolutions to be like that of a single body moved by a voluntary impulse." By making drill into a competition in front of an audience, Philopoemen appealed to the powerful competitive spirit of the Greek aristocracy.[16]

When they drilled, Greek cavalrymen competed in horsemanship. When one praised the Thessalian riders for their performance in battle, one praised not only their bravery but also their maneuvering of their squadrons; one praised them for their bravery and their skill, for their bravery and their horsemanship. The excellence of horsemen had two different aspects. The horsemanship of which they were proud was a venerable Homeric *aretē*, and it never seems to have worried the Classical Greeks that they rode their horses, while the Homeric heroes drove chariots behind theirs.[17]

Competing in a skill thus allied the cavalryman with the peltast against the hoplite and his conception of excellence. When Agesilaus held the games in which he gave prizes for horsemanship, he also gave prizes to light infantrymen and archers for their skill but rewarded hoplites for their physical fitness: there was no exacting art to being a hoplite. Competing in a skill made the light infantryman vulnerable to hoplite sneering: "The skill [*techne*] I practice is no working-class one," an archer can be imagined growling, defensively. *Techne* could be a fighting word, implying the lowly craft of a manual laborer. But the peltast's or cavalryman's conception of martial competition was different from the hoplite's (and far closer to the *Iliad*): rather than trying to reduce all competitions to a single common one, as the hoplites did, each type of soldier competed against his fellows in his particular excellence. A Greek sea battle was expected to work in much the same way: "On either side the rowers showed great zeal at bringing up their vessels when ordered, and the helmsmen great skill in maneuvering, and great rivalry with one another, and once the ships were alongside each other, the marines on board did their best not to let the service on deck be out-done by the others; in short, every man strove to prove himself the best in his particular department."[18] Each man competed in his particular department against those in the same department (on either side of the battle), and department competed against department. The competition in some departments of nautical endeavor, moreover, was in quick obedience to orders. And so it was on land for peltasts as well, and likely for drilled cavalry too. A late author reveals that during the Corinthian war "no soldiers in Greece were ever better trained or more attentive to the orders of their leader" than those of Iphicrates, "and he inculcated in them the habit, that, when the general gave the signal for battle, they would array themselves, without the intervention of the general, such that each seemed like he had been arrayed by the most skillful possible general." The generals' competition in arraying was mirrored in the peltasts' competition in exact drill and obedience to command.[19]

Greek armies of the first half of the fourth century BC consisted of two opposed interests, the hoplites and the rest. All claimed Homeric legitimacy for the way they fought, but their different ideals set them in conflict. The hoplite stood at the end of a long historical process of simplification that had tended to make combat a more adequate competition between men and cities. Generals, peltasts, and cavalry represented a fundamentalist reaction: they rejected hoplite simplification and looked directly to Homer for justification of their methods and competitions. Leaders and non-hoplites were natural allies. Commanders' competition in tactics and trick-ery encouraged the use of a broader range of arms (as Iphicrates implied, with his body metaphor for the army), and if leaders competed in array-ing, nonhoplites competed in being arrayed and doing as they were told with dispatch. But the hoplite outlook conflicted with both, by denying the heroic status of nonhoplite fighting and resenting the world of strata-gems, tactics, and nonhoplite troops, which undermined the perfection of its competition.[20]

The reason cavalry had not been prominent in the fifth century BC is that those at the top of society — for only they could afford horses — preferred to fight as hoplites in the phalanx. But the advance of cavalry in the fourth century means that some part of the aristocracy had changed their minds. Hoplite ideals too were changing, weakening.

THE BATTLE OF LEUCTRA:
SPARTA, HOPLITE TRAINING, AND MERCENARIES

The power of Lacedaemon was shattered by Thebes upon the field of Leuctra. Although an ally of Sparta during the long Peloponnesian War, Thebes had become the lodestar of resistance when victorious Sparta be-came an angry tyrant in her turn. When an exhausted Athens made peace with Sparta in 371 BC, the Spartans moved in this moment of tranquillity to bring the isolated Thebans to heel. Although the desperate Thebans struck a treaty with Jason of Pherae, now at his brief climacteric in the north, when it came to combat in Boeotia, they faced the Spartans with only the other Boeotian cities at their side, and some of them wavering. But the Theban commander was Epaminondas, a crafty general in the tradition of Pagondas, the victor at Delium. He got a slim majority of his fellow boeotarchs to endorse battle, however outnumbered the Boeo-tians might be, and (the story is) worked on the spirits of the Boeotian army: victory was certain, an oracle was produced to say, if the battle was fought near the memorial to virgins who had killed themselves in shame after being violated by Lacedaemonians. The temples at Thebes had opened their doors by themselves, it was reported to the army, and the arms of Heracles, whom the Thebans claimed as native, had vanished from his shrine—so the Thebans' heroic countryman had marched forth with the army to war.[21]

Cleombrotus, king of the Spartans, drew up his phalanx with the Spartans in the place of honor on the right, twelve deep. Sparta's allies formed the left. There were also mercenaries in Spartan pay present at the battle and allied peltasts. For reasons unclear the Spartans posted their cavalry in front of their phalanx. The Lacedaemonian cavalry was poor because good Spartan warriors still insisted on serving as hoplites and was unpracticed because those Spartans who served on horseback applied to the richer Lacedaemonians who actually kept the horses for their mounts at the very last minute. The Thebans, by contrast, had an old cavalry tradition, and their excellent horse, much exercised in recent wars, quickly routed the Spartan cavalry and drove them back into the phalanx, confusing its order.[22]

Epaminondas grasped the chance and led his Theban hoplites on, perhaps catching the Spartans with a change of their formation half completed and so in further confusion. He had learned from Pagondas and arrayed his Theban phalanx deep—fifty deep, even deeper than Pagondas's twenty-five. But this deep phalanx he had disposed on the left of the line, not in the position of honor on the right but directly opposite the Spartans themselves. "Crushing the head of the serpent," the Theban was said to have called his plan, and Epaminondas may also have told his right wing, which was manned by Thebes' Boeotian allies, some of them unreliable, to hang back so that the battle would be decided on the left. None of these tactics, individually, was new by 371 BC. But in combination they brought a singular concentration of force upon the king and hoplites of Lacedaemon.[23]

A drastic struggle unfolded as the phalanxes strove against each other. Cleombrotus, fighting in the phalanx as Spartan kings did, was struck down and was carried dying out of the battle. Xenophon insists this meant that the Spartans had the best of it, at first. Other leading Spartans were soon killed fighting as well. "Grant me one step, and we will have the victory!" shouted Epaminondas (the story is), and the Thebans pushed the Spartans back one fateful step—and then the leaderless Spartans were in flight and their allies with them. Of the seven hundred full Spartan citizens at the battle, four hundred died. The thought of admitting defeat by sending a herald to ask for the bodies, in accord with hoplite ritual, appalled the Spartans, who had known so few defeats. It was urged that the army should be arrayed again and the bodies regained by fighting. But the allies had no heart for another battle, and the herald was sent, and the Thebans built their trophy and gave back the bodies under a truce. Word of the disaster came to Sparta on the last day of the Laconian festival of the Gymnopaidea, when the Spartans wore wreaths of palm in honor of those who died in wars over Thyrea, long ago. The festival was not suffered to end early, and the next day the stark emotions of hoplite Sparta were seen once again: "The relatives of the killed bustled about in the open with bright and shining faces, but of those whose relatives were reported alive, few were seen, and they went about sad and lowly."[24]

"Pushed by the mob" is Xenophon's clipped and dismissive diagnosis of the Spartan defeat at Leuctra: the Theban mass did the deed. But he does not mention that at the front of that Theban mob stood the Theban Sacred Band, an élite unit of three hundred, kept in continual military training at the expense of the city. Later authors say that they struck the Spartan line first and that it was their fighting that overcame the Spartans.[25]

The Sacred Band represents a wider tendency toward hoplite training. In the fifth century only the Spartans had regularly trained their whole hoplite force. Such training meant that (in the fourth century), "the Lacedaemonians conduct with the utmost ease [drill motions] that instructors in tactics regard as very difficult." In other cities a program of general training might be undertaken in an emergency, as when the Syracusans found themselves unequal to the invading Athenians in 415/14 BC, or a rare élite unit might receive training at public expense: the Argives had such a unit, one thousand strong, at Mantinea in 418. The bloody coup of this Thousand at Argos after Mantinea (bloodily reversed eight months later) must have made many Greeks wonder about the wisdom of keeping a standing force in continual training, likely composed of young men of oligarchical sympathies. But nevertheless the fourth century saw the gradual spread of trained élite units, including the Sacred Band. Such change was slow because training was opposed, and not only on political grounds: Thucydides has Pericles jeer at Spartan training and insist that the Athenians, who took none, were just as brave. In Plato's *Laches* a serious argument could be made that training in the technique of hoplite fighting was worthless. That training was irrelevant to military success was not a position Xenophon shared, but in his generation he had to argue for the importance of training in his polemical *Cyropaedia* because in his day the value of training could not be taken for granted. But by the 330s Xenophon's position had triumphed. The Athenians had established a compulsory program of public military training for all their eighteen- to twenty-year-old citizens, the *ephebeia* (perhaps adapting it from a less rigorous or comprehensive institution that had existed before). The first year the ephebes spent in the gymnasium being instructed systematically in hoplite fighting, the javelin, the bow, and operating the catapult. Upon completing their training the ephebes displayed their drill in the theater and received a hoplite shield and spear from the city. A second year was spent patrolling the countryside and manning the border forts. Having been presented with hoplite equipment, ephebes could have fought as hoplites: that they nevertheless were to be trained in light-infantry skills illustrates the rise of those skills in prestige. That they were also *trained* to fight as hoplites suggests that the old definition of hoplite excellence as the natural bravery of the élite — and so untrainable — had been greatly alloyed.[26]

A peculiar quality of the Theban Sacred Band helps to explain this wider move toward training: the corps of three hundred was made up, we are told, of one hundred and fifty pairs of male lovers. Among the reported advantages of this arrangement was that of exaggerating competition between the warriors: lovers competed with each other and dreaded to be shamed in the presence of those they loved. Once again the competitive ethos of the hoplite emerges. But using such relationships between men as a font of military excellence is a transparent borrowing from Sparta, where such relationships were institutionalized, played a large role in the training of boys, and were thought to contribute to bravery in combat. At Sparta lover and beloved stood beside each other in the hoplite line: before battle the Spartans sacrificed to Eros, to love.[27]

The idea for the trained Sacred Band, then, came from Sparta. "You'd think everybody else mere improvisers in soldiering, and the Lacedaemonians the only artisans [*technitai*] of war," said Xenophon. Not only were the Spartans the most practiced in war, he is saying, but they seemed to him to envisage war as a *techne,* a learnable craft. Elsewhere in Greece there had always been some who conceived of hoplite fighting as a teachable skill, rather than as a pure expression of courage. In the last generation of the fifth century, although the Athenian state provided no public training, expert tutors, *hoplomachoi,* could be hired to teach rich young men hoplite techniques. Such professional instruction seems at first to have been jarringly newfangled, judging by early references to it. But it gained acceptance over time: Plato is probably reflecting fourth-century reality when he refers to competitions in hoplite fighting, one on one or two on two or up to ten on a side—competitions with rules and presided over by *hoplomachoi*. The appeal of this training at Athens is probably also to be attributed to the example of Sparta, the spell her lifestyle cast on the aristocrats of other cities, and the evident success of her training as proven by Sparta's victory in the Peloponnesian War and her subsequent decades of military dominance over Greece. In Athens the legacy of Spartan success was experts in hoplite technique available for hire; in Thebes, it was the trained Sacred Band of three hundred lovers.[28]

At the same time as Spartan-style training in the technique of hoplite fighting was spreading through the aristocracy of Greece, the Spartan example made clear the potential of training poor men in mass as hoplites. For during the Peloponnesian War, the Spartans had used thousands of their own serfs, their helots, as hoplites. Their need was great: the Spartan population of citizen warriors was dwindling. But the decision is astonishing, nevertheless, standing as it does athwart the whole Greek conception of slavery and martial excellence: how could one send the basest of men to fight? Those by definition wholly lacking in the *aretē* that made a hoplite hold his place in the line? But Spartans could conceive of it because they were open to the possibility, radical in the fifth century, that physical courage itself was a consequence of training, rather than inborn. "Man differs little from man by nature, but he is best who trains in the hardest school," Thucydides has a Spartan king say. It is probably from the Spartans that intellectuals of the fifth and fourth centuries got the idea that courage was a function of experience or a mixture of training and inborn quality, an idea elaborated in philosophy into the doctrine that courage was a function of knowledge. And if it was accepted that bravery could be acquired, either by training or experience, then it was possible to imagine employing helot soldiers and hiring mercenaries.

Indeed, if both technique and courage could be acquired, then experienced mercenaries, whose technique was admirable, could be better soldiers than citizens, a view that had advocates in the fourth century and in the Hellenistic period. Given their views, it is hardly surprising that the Spartans made the largest use of mercenaries on land during the Peloponnesian War and that the Spartans were the first mainland Greek state to hire a large force of mercenary hoplites — the remnants of the Ten Thousand — upon their return from Asia. The Spartans had mercenaries at Leuctra as well. Supply of mercenaries was never a problem in Greece, as political turmoil and rocky soil ensured that there were always men eager to sell their swords. Greek mercenaries had long campaigned in the East and in Sicily. For their widespread use in Greece all that was needed was a willingness to hire them and a system of gathering and holding money to pay for them. The Peloponnesian War, so much of which involved ships and paying crews of rowers, presented the same problem, and made the Spartans at least develop the necessary infrastructure. And the Spartan example and Spartan success gave the rest of the mainland Greeks the necessary willingness.[29]

Where did the Spartans get the idea of mass hoplite training and the notion that courage could be taught? They hardly thought of hoplite fighting as a low craft, like making shoes: Spartan citizens were forbidden to work with their hands and were famous for their contempt of those who did. Facing complaints about the small number of Spartan soldiers on a confederate expedition, the Spartan king Agesilaus is said to have set aside the soldiers of the allies craft by craft — potters, smiths, carpenters, builders — leaving only the Spartans, the only pure soldiers who practiced no base handicraft. And they were extremely suspicious of martial activities they did feel smacked of handicraft: so Spartan contempt for the "spindle" of the arrow at Sphacteria, and their reluctance to serve as cavalry. It was, of course, out of the question for Spartan citizens to fight as light infantry.[30]

Yet one thing that set the Spartans apart from the other Greeks was their belief that many noble excellences could be taught, and their public care to see to it that they were. At seven a Spartan boy was taken from his mother and raised in barracks, beneath the eyes of older boys. Boys were whipped to inculcate respect (*aidos*) and obedience; they went ill-clad to make them tough; and they were starved to make them resistant to hunger. They were schooled to silence and taught to look at the ground while walking to train them in the supreme Greek civic virtue of self-control (*sophrosyne*). The cruel Spartan regimen was believed to make Spartans brave. In short, as a frantic Athenian admirer of Sparta put it, "more men are excellent [*agathos,* the Homeric term] from practice than from nature."[31]

The particular learned *aretē* that may be involved in Spartan training in military drill and skill-at-arms was *metis,* cunning intelligence. Greeks widely esteemed this Homeric virtue and honored its exemplars, like the wily Themistocles. But at Sparta this admiration was extreme and institu-tionalized. Only at Sparta were steps taken, in the system of public edu-cation, to teach *metis.* One of the reasons Spartan boys were starved was so they would be compelled to steal, and if they were caught, they were beaten, to compel them to steal better. Young men lurked through the countryside, as part of the Spartan *krypteia,* the "time in hiding," to catch the helots plotting. Young husbands had to sneak out to visit their wives. Yet *metis* was not only the cunning of the thief and the warrior, but also, in Homer particularly, the skill of the tool-user, the secret technique of the heroic artisan, the hidden craft within craft. To the Spartans hoplite training was not a low *techne,* but rather training in the secret craft of warriorhood. And as a secret craft Spartan training had to be kept from others, which is one of the reasons foreigners were not allowed into Sparta, and why the Spartans had an old rule which they attributed to their lawgiver Lycurgus that they were not to campaign too frequently against a single enemy, lest their enemy learn how to fight as well as they did.[32]

Spartan training in bravery, hoplite drill, and hoplite skill-at-arms was merely a subset of Spartan education of boys and young men, the old system of public upbringing (at whose origins we cannot guess) that notoriously set the Spartans apart from the rest of the Greeks. But being wrapped up tightly within that system, Spartan military training was not easy to imitate. Other states lacked the financial infrastructure needed to support training—the Spartans, of course, had the helots—but, more important, despite their admiration for the Spartan system, the rest of Greece was never prepared to take up Spartan ways wholesale. For Spar-tan military training to spread, a few strands only of the strange Spartan cosmos had to be teased out and made comprehensible in the rest of

Greece, the Greece without the Spartan system of education, and the beliefs that went along with it.

In the wake of the Spartan victory in the Peloponnesian War, and in a world with many admirers and imitators of Sparta, hoplite training began to spread; the Spartan example justified the widespread employment of mercenaries, and the financial arrangements necessary for both were perfected where they had previously been lacking. But in the rest of Greece hoplite drill, skill-at-arms, and, over time, even bravery were understood in terms that made sense there, as *technai*. When Xenophon, an outsider, looked at Spartan war making, it was *techne*, craft, that he saw and admired. And it was as a craft that hoplite training spread through Greece.

To many hoplites fighting as a craft was unobjectionable: *techne*, as Hesiod reminded the Greeks, was just as competitive as *aretē* and potentially as gratifying to Greek competitive ethics, which is why competitions in martial *technai* were possible. Many hoplites, as Agesilaus had revealed, practiced handicrafts in their daily lives. To mercenaries such a definition was welcome, for the craft of fighting, learned especially by long practice, was what they had to sell. And at the same time a distinction had arisen, perhaps prompted by this very question of military training, between noble, that is, military and intellectual, and degrading, banausic *technai*. So when in the late fifth century the science of generalship began to be systematized and taught, and when in the fourth century guidebooks came to be written and the stratagems of admired generals collected and written down, these developments, despite their Homeric antecedents, were quite casually gathered up as the *techne* of generalship, with no sense of contempt.[33]

But some of the wealthiest Greeks felt that *techne* stained the phalanx: and those Greeks forsook the phalanx for the cavalry. Thus the change in the culture of the fourth-century rich, to make cavalry a possibility where it had not existed before. With its taint of low *techne*, the coming of training was damaging to hoplite pride and precedence, which is why hoplite training was so long resisted. An endpoint for this development was the Athenian *ephebeia* of the 330s, in which the ephebes were trained to fight interchangeably in hoplite equipment, with the bow, with the javelin, and with the catapult. At last the predominance of the hoplite was gone, his fighting conceived as a craft like any other. The remaking of the fourth-century Greek army as a cooperative of trained hoplites, peltasts, and cavalry, many of them mercenaries and all obedient to a general, required not only the assertion of the Homeric legitimacy of peltasts and the reassertion of the Homeric legitimacy of cavalry, but also cracks in the supreme legitimacy that hoplites had long asserted for their particular way of war.

The Spartan legacy of hoplite fighting as a skill, at least in part — and of courage, at least in part, as a consequence of training — had the potential to reconcile the hoplite and his nonhoplite rivals. But this reconciliation was long in coming. For generations the rival visions of hoplite, general, and nonhoplite fought for place; for generations Greek warfare played out this uneasy coexistence. Perhaps the competing Greek outlooks would eventually have achieved harmony on their own. But the reconciliation implied by the Athenian *ephebeia* was not the product of internal evolution, but of an exterior shock. The mature system of Athenian mass military training was a consequence of the defeat of the Greeks by Philip II of Macedon at the battle of Chaeronea in 338 BC, where the Theban Sacred Band died to a man defending Greek freedom. And Philip's formidable new Macedonian military system becomes clearly visible in accounts of his son Alexander's campaign into the East to conquer the known world.

VI

ALEXANDER THE GREAT

AT THE BATTLE OF ISSUS

HOMER AND MACEDONIAN WARFARE

On the European side of the Hellespont arose a great barrow, shaded by a stand of elms. The trees that rooted there grew up just high enough to catch a glimpse of Troy across the water — before dying away in sympathy, it was said, with the hero buried beneath the mound. For this was the tomb of Protesilaus, by far the first of the Achaeans to leap down into the surf upon the Trojan foreshore, and the first to go down in death, when a Trojan man slew him. And at this tomb Alexander, the young king of Macedon, sacrificed before crossing over the Hellespont in order that his own landing in Asia might prove happier than that of his distant predecessor.[1]

An advanced force had secured the landings, and a fleet of warships and cargo vessels carried Alexander's army the few miles to the eastern shore. They were ferried over at Sestos, where once Xerxes and his innumerable host had crossed the other way, dry-shod, on bridges of boats. But Alexander and his companions crossed over farther south, to Troy, to the harbor where according to legend the Achaeans had made landfall. And like Protesilaus, Alexander leapt first from his ship, men said, in full armor.[2]

At Troy the king sacrificed to Trojan Athena. In her temple he dedicated his armor to the goddess and took down in exchange a panoply of arms said to date back to the Trojan War. Then he sacrificed to Priam, patriarch of the Trojans, to soothe his vengeful ghost: Alexander's mother

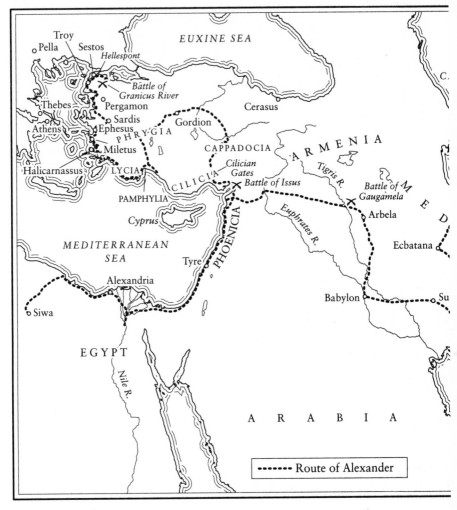

Campaign of Alexander the Great (334–323 BC)

claimed descent from Neoptolemus, the son of Achilles, and at the sack of Troy, Neoptolemus had slaughtered Priam at the altar of Zeus. Alexander also made offerings at the tombs of the Achaean heroes, Achilles and Ajax and the rest. The king was said to have crowned the tomb of Achilles with garlands, his best friend, Hephaestion, crowning that of Achilles' best friend and retainer, Patroclus. And it was reported that Alexander and his friends ran a race in honor of Achilles before the hero's tomb.[3]

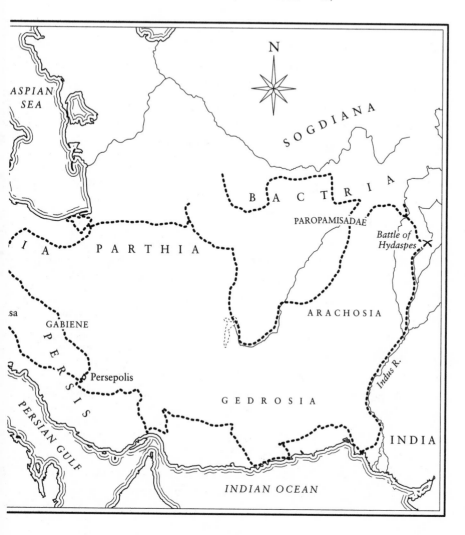

The heroes of epic were always present to the Greeks as companions in the mind and models of conduct, but the Greek love of Homer seems to have been unusually passionate in the royal Macedonian house of Philip — and strongest of all in Philip's son. Alexander's tutor found favor at court by calling his young charge Achilles; his friend Hephaestion, Patroclus; King Philip, Peleus, who was Achilles' own father; and himself, Phoenix, the tutor of Achilles. When Hephaestion died on campaign far in the East, Alexander mourned him there as Achilles had Patroclus, cutting off his hair over the body. According to rumor he offered the shade of Hephaestion the bitter sacrifice of human flesh, as Achilles had done for his friend. There was even a bloody legend that Alexander had dragged an enemy leader behind his chariot around the walls of a city, as Achilles had the dead Hector. As these stories show, the ever-growing jungle of Alexander's myth found rich soil in the association with Achilles, for everybody knew the historical truth: Alexander felt he "had a rivalry for honor [with Achilles] from the time of his youth." This was not merely an eccentricity without consequence: Macedon's relationship with Homer, in all its ramifications, made Alexander's army the most fearsome the Greeks had known.[4]

That the West was on the march to avenge Xerxes' invasion of Greece a century and a half before was not a secret to the lordly satraps who in 334 BC ruled western Asia Minor in the name of Xerxes' successor, Darius III, Great King of Persia. Memnon, a Greek mercenary captain in Persian service, advised the satraps to retreat before Alexander and destroy the forage, so that Alexander would be driven out of Asia without a fight. But the satrap whose territory would have been ravaged pitied his subjects, and the Persians decided to make their stand behind the shallow Granicus River.[5]

Accounts of the battle on the Granicus, the first of the four great battles Alexander fought in Asia, are muddy. But Alexander's role in its terrible climax shines through the murk. Alexander led his Macedonian cavalry through the riverbed and directly at the position of the satraps and Persian grandees on the other side. When the two lines struck, Alexander broke his lance in the fighting. He cried to a groom for another, but the groom's own lance was broken, and he was defending himself bravely with the broken stump. "Ask somebody else!" he shouted. When another of his retinue finally surrendered his lance to the king, Alexander spied Mithridates, a son-in-law of Darius the Great King, advancing. Riding out from his guard, the Macedonian drove his lance straight through the Persian's face, flinging him to the ground. Now Rhoesaces, brother of the satrap of Lydia, struck Alexander on the head with a sword. The blow wrecked the king's helmet, yet the helmet saved the king. Clearing Mithridates' gore off his lance, Alexander took Rhoesaces in the chest, piercing his cuirass, and hurling him to the ground as well. From the mêlée behind the king, the satrap Spithridates swung back to deliver a great blow to avenge his fallen brother, but Alexander's companion Clitus was there first with his own sword and clove off at the shoulder the arm upraised to fell the king. It was from this point in the fighting—this cascade of arterial blood—that panic began to spread among the Persians, until it carried them fleeing from the field.[6]

An ancient author attributes the victory at Granicus to Alexander's hand-to-hand fighting. But even in antiquity voices were raised against the risk to which the king exposed himself. He had been strongly advised, tradition holds, against trying to force the crossing of the river at all. Granicus River was not a victory of tactics, then, but of sheer pluck: that of the king, who risked his glittering hopes in the grind of the fight, and that of his cavalry troopers who forced their way up the riverbank, cut their way into the Persian spears, and turned the Persians to flight.[7]

What was on Alexander's mind as he charged the Persian commanders may be guessed from the fact that he fought the battle arrayed in the ancient armor he had taken from the temple of Athena at Troy. Wearing a heroic panoply, Alexander fought in rivalry with his ancestor Achilles, seeking out the heroes of the enemy to slay in single combat, as Achilles had once cut down Hector, son of Priam, the bulwark of the Trojans. In the battle, Alexander took two blows to the breastplate, one on the helmet, and three upon the shield, a testimony to his Iliadic heroism. In later battles he did not wear this battered gear but nevertheless had it carried before him as a reminder.[8]

Alexander's defeat of the satraps left Darius's possessions in Asia Minor without an army to protect them. Through the summer and fall of 334 BC the Macedonians marched south down the western coast, setting free of their Persian garrisons the Greek cities of Ionia—grave Ephesus, proud Miletus, Magnesia on the Meander—so fulfilling an immemorial yearning of the Greeks. Then, after taking Miletus, Alexander disbanded most of his fleet. This was not a sign of discouragement, but a signal that his ambitions were not limited to liberating the Greeks of Asia Minor. He meant to march upcountry, deep into Darius's realm, where his fleet could no longer follow him.[9]

Memnon, the Greek mercenary captain who had so wisely advised the Persians before Granicus, had gathered the remnants of the Persian army of the western satrapies behind the walls of Halicarnassus, at the point where the Ionian shore, having run south with many harbors from the Hellespont, turns east and becomes unwelcoming to mariners. There Alexander brought up engines against the walls, and the defenders sallied bravely forth to burn the machines. A full and bloody siege was necessary to drive Memnon out.

On a quiet day between assaults two of Alexander's infantrymen sought excitement in wine, which led to boasting and, in turn, to rivalry in courage. Alone they armed themselves, alone they quit the camp, alone they charged the city's walls, to settle who was braver. Seeing their approach, the defenders sent forth a party to assail them. But the Macedonians killed all those who came close and pelted the timid who hung back. And so for a time these soliders fought their two-man war beneath the walls, defying their foes' attacks and missiles, until their comrades came up from behind, more enemies emerged from the city, and a full fight broke out, with the defenders finally forced back behind the gates. Alexander's infantry left no diaries, but this outburst of rivalry reveals the competitive quality of their fighting prowess.[10]

Once Halicarnassus was taken, Alexander marched east through Lycia and Pamphylia and then struck northeast into the interior of Asia Minor. In the summer of 333 he marched south again toward the coast and by speed and terror seized the formidable Cilician gates, the sheer pass through the Taurus mountains, which could be defended by a mere handful against an army advancing from central Asia Minor into the East. Defense against Alexander after Granicus had been sporadic—here a town held or a tower, there a levy of brave locals offering futile battle. Darius first depended for the protection of his realm on the indefatigable Memnon, whom he sent into the Aegean with a great fleet. The obedience of mainland Greece to Alexander was unwilling, imposed by Philip's defeat of the Greeks at Chaeronea in 338 BC, and confirmed by Alexander with minatory slaughter. Darius hoped to drive Alexander back into the West by raising Greece in revolt. This plan might have succeeded, for the Persians quickly captured islands and cities in the Aegean, but Memnon, upon whom the strategy depended, fell ill and died, and the King finally recalled most of his mercenaries into the East. Darius was assembling a host to meet Alexander in Cilicia. Finally the King himself would fight for his kingdom.

Alexander marched east and south, following the curve of the Mediterranean down into the Levant. Darius slipped in behind him and camped upon the Macedonian communications. The Persians butchered the sick and wounded whom Alexander had left in the town of Issus. The next day Darius moved out and took up a position along the Pinarus river. Hastening back to meet him, Alexander was forced to rest his troops in the high passes. Now he had to defeat Darius, or his army would starve. In acute anxiety Alexander sacrificed to useful gods by night: to Poseidon, since the morrow's battle would be fought upon the seashore; to Nereus, the Sea's Ancient; and to his daughters the Nereids, and especially Thetis, the sea-nymph who had lain with Peleus and so had become the mother of Achilles.[11]

The next day Alexander descended into the plain, and the long, snake-like marching order of the Macedonian phalanx wheeled into its line of battle, the royal foot guard in the place of honor on the right, then the élite battalion of Shield Bearers, hypaspists, then the other battalions of Macedonian phalanx: the battalion of Coenus, then that of Perdiccas, then Meleager, then Ptolemaeus, so soon to die, then Amyntas; finally, on the left, the battalion of Craterus. Arraying the phalanx first in the narrows of the valley, Alexander formed it thirty-two men deep. As he advanced into the broad, Alexander unfolded the phalanx left and right, making it wider and shallower, first sixteen men deep and then eight.[12]

The phalanx which here so deftly doubled and redoubled its frontage as it advanced was not the traditional formation of the Greeks, but the improved Macedonian phalanx Alexander had inherited from his father, Philip, its creator. The Macedonian pike, or *sarissa,* was much longer than the Greek spear and was wielded with two hands. The first few ranks of the Macedonian phalanx were slightly offset so that the points of four or five spears extended in front of the first rank, a militant porcupine (see figures). With this new phalanx Philip had defeated the venerable phalanx of the Greeks at Chaeronea and become master of Greece. And so well drilled was the phalanx by the time Alexander inherited it that simply by putting it through its paces of raising pikes, lowering them to the charge, swinging them right, then left, he could drive Balkan foes fleeing in terror.

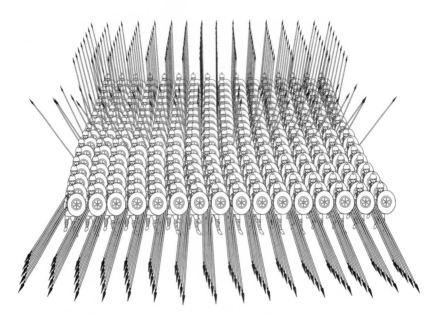

Macedonian phalanx, reconstruction (SeungJung Kim after S. Anglim et al., *Fighting Techniques of the Ancient World* [Amber Books, London, 2002] p. 21).

Prior to these improvements, the Greek phalanx had changed very little for more than a century. It was a style of fighting deeply rooted in the warrior code of prosperous and powerful Greeks. So perhaps it was only natural that change, when it came, should occur in a northern land lacking a strong and conservative hoplite tradition, a rough land where cavalry was king, a land like Macedonia.[13]

Accident had also given Philip a sense of the possibilities offered by inventive military thinking. As a teenager, the Macedonian prince had been held as a hostage in the Thebes of Epaminondas, that Thebes whose training and tactics had destroyed the power of Sparta. He lived in the house of the Theban general Pammenes, who had a formidable reputation for military cunning. In Thebes, it was said, Philip learned many lessons.[14]

But the direct inspiration for Philip's new phalanx, later Greeks maintained, was Homer, probably the very passage which the Greeks had recited for centuries and applied to their own phalanxes:

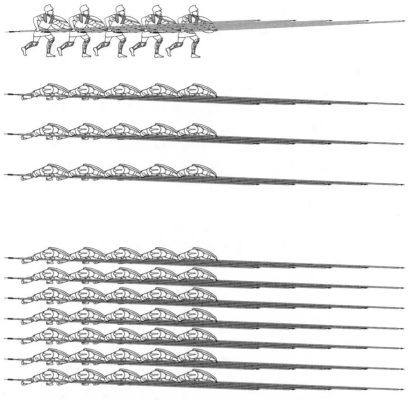

Macedonian phalanx, reconstruction, detail of files
(SeungJung Kim after P. Connolly).

Locking spear by spear, shield against shield at the base,
    so buckler
leaned on buckler, helmet on helmet, man against man,
and the horse-hair crests along the horns of their shining
    helmets
touched as they bent their heads, so dense were they formed
    on each other.[15]

Philip's phalanx was an attempt to recreate this description more accurately than the Greeks had: with its offset ranks, Philip's phalanx was

more tightly packed than the Greek. When Philip's phalanx assumed its closest formation, the *synaspismos,* or locking of shields, men stood mere inches apart, far closer to spear locking spear, helmet leaning on helmet, and man upon man.[16]

One detail of equipment, moreover, may confirm Philip's Homeric inspiration. The length of the Macedonian *sarissa* required that it be wielded with both hands, leaving no hand free for the large round shield the Greeks had carried in their phalanx. The shield of the Macedonian phalangite may therefore have been attached to his body with a strap around the neck and shoulder: he marched with it on his back and pulled it around front for combat. Classical Greeks, in contrast, used shields with handgrips only. Like the phalanx that used it, this Macedonian strap may have been borrowed from the *Iliad,* for that is how shields were carried in epic:

> Ajax and Teucer aimed at him together, and Teucer
> hit him with an arrow in the shining belt that encircled his
>   chest to hold the man-covering shield.[17]

Any Greek soldier recalled Homer when he thought about fighting: Homer was the mirror into which Greek warriors looked to see themselves. And it was perfectly natural that Philip, who chuckled at being called Peleus by his son's tutor, whose family claimed to be descended from Heracles, and whose host at Thebes was famous for comparing the élite Theban Sacred Band to Homer's heroes, should take the kernel of his new phalanx from Homer.[18]

When there was finally space on the field of Issus, Alexander ordered the cavalry up to the flanks of the phalanx, the Macedonian Companion Cavalry under his own command and the crack Thessalians on the right, the lesser allied cavalry on the left under his marshal Parmenio. With the arraying of the Companions next to the phalanx, the ethnically Macedonian center of Alexander's line was complete. In each of his four great battles in Asia, Alexander drew up his Macedonians in a similar fashion, the Macedonian Companion Cavalry led by Alexander himself arrayed on the right of the phalanx. Where fuller details survive, the similarity between deployments stands out even more starkly. At the battle of

Gaugamela two years later, Alexander disposed the battalions of the phalanx in exactly the same order from right to left as he had at Issus. When units did not fight in their normal position in the line, the fact was remarked upon by the tradition. But the array was not wholly unchanging, and the way the dispositions shifted in the course of the Asian campaign hints at the logic of the system.[19]

Always to the right of the other battalions of the phalanx stood the Shield Bearers, an infantry *corps d'élite* chosen from all of Macedonia on the basis of their strength and size. To the left of the Shield Bearers came the six (later perhaps seven) battalions of the Macedonian phalanx of the line, the *pezhetairoi,* or Foot Companions, each recruited from a different area of Macedonia. The Foot Companions fought in the same relative order at Issus and Gaugamela, first the battalion of Coenus on the right beside the Shield Bearers, then that of Perdiccas, all the way over to that of Craterus. But earlier, at Granicus River, the positions of the first two units had been reversed: Perdiccas had held the right, followed by Coenus. Between the dates of Granicus and Issus, moreover, when Coenus replaced Perdiccas on the right of the Foot Companions, Coenus's battalion also earned a new title, becoming the *asthetairoi,* which may mean the "best companions." In time this honor was granted to other battalions of the Foot Companions as well. The order of the battalions of the Foot Companions in the line, then, reflected their fighting quality and might be adjusted on the basis of their performance. A penal unit of discontented Macedonians that Alexander formed was called the *atakton,* the "out-of-the-line" unit, their punishment being to be taken out of their place in the Macedonian array and so to lose the status that place implied. The tradition is that, inflamed by the insult, they fought with exceptional bravery.[20]

Performance was not the only criterion for the position of units in the Macedonian line. To the right of the élite Shield Bearers, on the extreme right of all the infantry, marched the infantry *agema,* the royal guard, a small formation recruited not from the commons of Macedonia, like the rest of the infantry, but from the nobility. Their social standing earned them the position of honor among the infantry. This suggests why the Companion Cavalry, also recruited from the highborn, lined up to the right of the infantry. The king, finally, the very top of society, occupied the extreme right even of the cavalry, surrounded by his royal Horse Guard, the cavalry *agema*. The Macedonian battle order thus had much in common with the processions of a medieval town, which carefully replicated the social order in their progress around the streets. But within each social division the order of the Macedonian deployment could be varied to reward those who had done well and to punish those who had done badly. If the evidence to judge survived, we might discover that the relative order in the line of the seven territorially based squadrons of Companion Cavalry, an order of which we catch only a single glimpse, was regulated in the same way as the order of the battalions of the phalanx. For there does seem to have been some system of ranking among the cavalry: by 328 BC the old cavalry squadrons had been reorganized into hipparchies, "horse commands," or cavalry brigades, and it was meaningful to speak of "the most distinguished hipparchy."[21]

Alexander did not use his Macedonian array exactly as he had inherited it from his father. At Philip's great victory at Chaeronea the cavalry seems to have charged from the left, not the right, and Philip may himself have preferred to command the phalanx, rather than the cavalry. Neither, so far as can be told, did Alexander borrow his array from the practice of any single Greek city. For the Spartans lined up for battle in an order that varied according to the direction from which the enemy came, the Athenians seem to have lined up their tribal units by the number assigned to each of the ten tribes, and the Thebans, after gaining their great victory at Leuctra by weighting the left end of their line, continued to favor the left.[22]

The Macedonian array, on the other hand, recalled the arrays formed when different Greek cities went to war as allies, contending fiercely with each other over their relative place in the line, because each place conveyed a corresponding rank of honor. This was the system that produced such wrangling between the Athenians and Tegeans before the battle of Plataea. What Alexander seems to have done is adapt this rivalrous procedure to the single national contingent of the Macedonians. And this array must have evolved over time in Alexander's own hands, for it cannot be detected in his early battles in the Balkans.[23]

What was in Alexander's mind when he settled upon this arrangement? As befitted a king who yearned to rival "the best of the Achaeans," Philip's son had a predilection for explicit rankings of human excellence and an old-fashioned, Homeric conception of excellence that combined social status and performance — or in which high social status implied excellent performance. So on one occasion on his march Alexander "gave presents, honoring each in accord with his standing or his bravery if he had been remarkable amidst dangers," and granted gold crowns to a series of men: "Peucestas was first, for having shielded him [with the shield taken from Troy, in a nasty piece of fighting among the Mallians] and then Leonnatus, also for having shielded him, and for the risks he had run in India and his victory in Ora. . . . Next he crowned Nearchus for his coasting voyage from India by the great sea . . . and next Onesicritus, the steersman of the royal ship, and also Hephaestion and the other bodyguards."[24] Not only were the heroes rewarded, but their merits were examined and weighed, and the brave were placed in rank order. This tendency to rank could extend to Alexander's appointment of officers. Deep in Asia, Alexander established a new tier of officers for the phalanx:

> He appointed judges, and proposed a . . . prize for military courage: those judged the bravest were each given command of one thousand men, and called chiliarchs [commanders of a thousand]. . . . A great crowd of soldiers gathered to participate in this excellent contest, both as witnesses to the deeds of each candidate, and to offer their opinion about the judges: they could not fail to know whether the office was given justly or unjustly. First of all the prize for bravery was given to old Atarrhias, who especially fired up the younger soldiers to action when they were giving up the battle near Halicarnassus; next came Antigenes; Philotas Augaeus got third place, Amyntas fourth, Antigonus came after these and after him Lyncestian Amyntas; Theodotus the seventh place, and Hellanicus got the last place.[25]

It was not enough merely to choose new officers on the basis of bravery, but they must be placed in order from first to eighth. The Greeks had long given prizes for excelling in battle but usually only first prize, and they never seem to have ranked prizes deeper than third. Homer, on the other hand, had Achilles give prizes for first through fifth place to charioteers at the funeral games of Patroclus. And if it was no part of Homer's poetic art to rank warriors other than best, second, and worst, it remained for Alexander, so keen an enthusiast for Homer, to bring out the more un-poetic implications of the Homeric system and apply them to his army.[26]

Such spectacles of ranking had a practical purpose, of course, inas-much as they served to inspire emulation in those not included in the roll of honor as well as rivalry among the favored. All of this was part of Alexander's ceaseless effort to reinforce the spirit of competition in his army. The king offered prizes for unusual feats of bravery, he watched for the brave deeds of his men in battle, and after victory he visited the wounded to hear them recount their exploits.[27] He publicly recited the brave deeds of his officers and men and honored and rewarded those who had acted courageously, whether living or dead. To the first twenty-five cavalrymen who fell forcing their way up the bank at Granicus River, for instance, Alexander paid the extravagant honor of commissioning bronze statues of them by Lysippus, his favorite sculptor, for "he was keen to put his soldiers in heart to face the dangers of battle with honors."[28]

All Greeks were competitive, but rivalry among the Macedonians had a rawer edge. In Alexander's camp, a disagreement over wine might be settled the next morning by a formal duel with weapons before a great audience of rapt soldiers. In old Macedonia a man who had not yet killed an enemy in battle was obliged to wear a horse halter on his person as a sign of his humiliation. A man who had not killed a boar in hunting might not recline at dinner, and the brute had to be killed bravely, with a spear, not tangled up in a net. Hunting was fiercely competitive in the Greek tradition, and Alexander and his companions in Asia were addicted to it, hunting not only noble beasts but birds and foxes and weasels too, any forlorn creature that offered a chance of sport. There were ball games as well and drinking competitions. Moreover, Alexander's campaign was repeatedly interrupted for formal athletic games—we hear of ten such events. Greek athletes and performers might be imported to star, but Alexander's army supplied most of the competitors. Marching along with his army, Alexander himself practiced archery and trained himself in leap-ing off and on a moving chariot, that appropriately bronze-age revival Greek sport.[29]

As the story of the two drunken heroes who attacked Halicarnassus shows, the lower ranks of Alexander's army competed not only in sports but in bravery. Even the camp followers fought mock battles between gangs, setting a humble "Alexander" and "Darius" over themselves as leaders. Alexander was delighted when he was told of this and had the two leaders fight a duel before the watching army. Discussions of relative excellence of the type which gave rise to the attack at Halicarnassus seem to have been a preoccupation of the Macedonian camp: a similar wrangle over whether the deeds of Alexander or his father, Philip, were greater resulted in Alexander's drunken murder of his comrade Clitus, the very friend who had saved his life at the Granicus. The willful barons who kept their rude state in the glens and gorges of highland Macedonia had never learned the gentler ways of the Greek city. Their ways were the old ways, more nearly the ways of epic. Alexander was a master at exploiting the coarse, hand-on-sword competitiveness of his Macedonians, as his father had been before him: when Philip had wished to train his truculent and ungovernable countrymen, he had done so by making their drills into competitions, a practice Alexander inherited.[30]

Alexander's array of his Macedonians was a motivational tool, a technique to make the Macedonians fight at their best. The array expressed the relative quality of Alexander's Macedonian units, and so set the units and their soldiers in competition with each other to prove themselves worthy of their place (or worthy of a higher place), for their competition was exacerbated by the possibility of the promotion or demotion of units within social categories. No ancient author reveals where Alexander got the idea for this arrangement, but it is not far to seek in the mind of a man who called the *Iliad* his "commissary of military excellence" and who slept with it under his pillow—superfluously because he had it all memorized; who, having captured Darius's most priceless casket and wondering what contents could be worthy of such a receptacle, placed his copy of the *Iliad* within; who quoted the *Iliad* when he was wounded and was reported to have chosen the site of Egyptian Alexandria on the basis of a passage in the *Odyssey*. Alexander's interest in Homer extended to fine details, and he even became involved in issues of textual editing. He may have noticed and imitated not only what was present in Homer, but also what was absent. Perhaps he noticed that the Greeks' sacrifice immediately before battle could not be paralleled in epic, and so eliminated it in his own army. Perhaps he noticed as well that the younger heroes in the *Iliad* are not described as having beards (whatever the reality in Dark Age or Archaic Greece) and so ordered his soldiers to shave, as he did himself, in striking contrast to the bristly Macedonians of his hirsute father's generation.[31]

The Macedonian array was a gigantic Homeric ranking system. In principle, every soldier was placed in rank order relative to every other, from the haughty Ajax in the royal Horse Guard on the extreme right to the Thersites, "the worst man who came beneath Ilion," in the humble foot battalion of Craterus, forever at the left of the line. In Homer, standing implied performance and performance standing — the best men were also highborn and rich — and Alexander's array combined performance and social status in the same way, a way no doubt perfectly natural to the old-fashioned, aristocratically minded Macedonians.[32]

It may be that just as Philip had elaborated the Macedonian phalanx from one suggestion of Nestor's, so Alexander had found inspiration for the Macedonian array in another of Nestor's ideas, also much loved by Greeks who thought of warfare:

> "Set your men in order by tribes, by brotherhoods,
>   Agamemnon,
> and let each brotherhood go in support of brotherhood,
>   let tribe support tribe.
> If you do it this way, and the Achaeans obey you,
> you will see which of your leaders is bad [*kakos*], and who
>   of your people,
> and which also is brave [*esthlos*], since they will fight by
>   themselves."

Dividing up his line of battle by contingents would allow Agamemnon to distinguish his good troops from his bad. And it was a short jump from learning who was good and bad to making all better by setting the contingents to compete against one another, a jump made even shorter by the fact that of the five contingents in which Poulydamas formed the Trojans to attack the walls of the Achaean camp, the first was singled out as containing the best men:

They who went with Hector and Poulydamas the blameless,
  these were the most numerous, and best [*aristoi*], and beyond
    others furious
  to smash the wall and fight their way among the hollow ships.[33]

Alexander's ranked array, separating out the best of the Macedonians, was available to him from the *Iliad*.

At Issus, as Alexander's army slowly approached the Pinarus River and the Persian force beyond it — with many halts to dress the ranks of the phalanx, so easily disordered by marching over landscape in line of battle — Alexander adjusted his dispositions in light of what he could see of the Great King's. Darius had concentrated his cavalry on his right, opposite the Macedonian left. Alexander sent the excellent Thessalian cavalry from his own right to reinforce Parmenio on the left, passing them behind the phalanx to conceal the transfer. The heights behind the Macedonian right were held by the Persians. Alexander posted a mixed force behind the right wing to deal with them, extending from the rest of his army at an angle "so that the right of his line was deployed separated into two wings," into a fork, in other words. This flank guard promptly ejected the Persians from the nearer heights and, having posted a few horsemen to keep the Persians from coming back, were soon available to extend the main line to the right. The Persians overlapped the Macedonian army in that direction, and Alexander feared being outflanked. To the further right wing, he added Greek hoplites from the reserve phalanx behind the Macedonian phalanx, bolstering them with archers and light infantry and two squadrons of the Companion Cavalry.[34]

When Alexander wanted, as he did here at Issus, he could be a subtle tactician. But even so he preferred to maneuver the forces of his Greek and barbarian allies and perhaps some Macedonian light troops which had no normal position in the line rather than the central array of his Macedonian phalanx and Companion Cavalry. The importance of keeping the Macedonians in their ranked array created a tension between Alexander the tactician and Alexander the motivator: his decision to send two squadrons of the Companion Cavalry far to the right at Issus suggests how serious he felt the danger there was.[35]

Now, as the Macedonian army approached the Persians, Alexander reverted from tactician to inspirational leader, riding up and down the front, calling upon his men to be brave. He not only appealed by name to his marshals with all their distinctions, but singled out too the commanders of each battalion of the phalanx and each squadron of the cavalry and even individual mercenaries, if they were outstanding in rank or bravery. Thus he whipped up the spirit of rivalry between men and, through their commanders, each unit of the Macedonian array. The soldiers roared back: No delay! They wanted to attack. The trumpets sounded the charge, and the horns and the battle cries of both hosts echoed and reechoed from the surrounding mountains.[36]

As the Macedonians drew within range of the Persians behind the river, Persian arrows began to fall among them. Then, on the right of the Macedonian array, at the head of his Horse Guard, Alexander himself began the onset, rushing forward into the riverbed to terrify the Persians and to allow the Persian archers no time to shoot. The Persians fell back in front of the Macedonian cavalry. On the other wing of the battle, the Thessalian horse defended themselves grimly against superior numbers of Persian cavalry, who had crossed the river to attack them. The Macedonian phalanx in the center advanced into the riverbed of the Pinarus and upon emerging found itself face to face with a phalanx of Greek mercenary hoplites, the infantry in which Darius, wisely, placed the most confidence. There was no love lost between Greeks and Macedonians. The Greeks could imagine this battle as a second Chaeronea, and Greece as free if they could destroy Alexander and his army. The riverbanks disrupted the Macedonian formation, and the mercenaries exploited the holes, pushing the Macedonians back into the river.[37]

The phalanx could make no progress. Men began to die, and the commander of a battalion, Ptolemaeus, fell fighting bravely, along with one hundred and twenty other officers. But although the fight was unequal, the phalanx did not flee. They were aware of the success of Alexander and the cavalry and yearned "not to be left behind by the success of Alexander, already apparent, and that the reputation of the phalanx — much cried up before as unconquerable — not be obliterated." So Alexander's ranked array revealed its value: the rivalry between the Macedonian phalanx and the cavalry, with its more honorable position in the line of battle, was fierce. When Alexander was wounded, both phalanx and cavalry demanded the honor of carrying his litter, and Alexander had to settle the potentially explosive contention by having them take turns. In the fighting right after Alexander's death ten years after Issus, the mutual detestation of horse and foot led them to support different marshals.[38]

Competitive pride made the phalanx hold its place, even as its formation came apart and its leaders fell. Now Alexander and his cavalry, having driven off the Persians in front of them, turned left and took the Greek hoplites in the flank and rear. Suddenly it was the Greeks who were in confusion: they turned to flee, and the Macedonian phalanx scrambled up the bank in pursuit. Finally the cavalry on the Persian right, who had distinguished themselves against the Thessalians, realized that all was lost, and they too fled the field, only to be cut down in flight by their vengeful foes.[39]

"It fell out just as Alexander had conjectured," wrote Arrian about Alexander's decisive charge across the river at Issus, for he had expected the Persians would flee where he attacked. To the historian, the charge of the Companion Cavalry was a brilliant instance of cerebral generalship, an example of the same tactical finesse Alexander had displayed when re-ordering his flanks as he approached the river. But how cerebral was Alexander's plan? For Alexander led his cavalry in a charge from the right in all his four great battles in Asia. And his motive, as his conduct at Granicus River reveals, was not narrowly tactical. There he had sought out combat with the enemy leaders arrayed in equipment he believed had been worn by a hero at Troy. At Gaugamela, Alexander's final victory over the Great King, Alexander led the Companion Cavalry directly at Darius in search of single combat. Darius turned and fled. And so the tradition about Issus, that there too Alexander had charged straight at Darius trying to engage him in single combat, is likely to be true.[40]

A terrible struggle developed around Darius's chariot (such is the story). Darius's brother and other noble Persians fought to protect the King, and the Macedonians fought to break through; bodies piled up like the pieces of a collapsed building, for "in their rivalry to reach the Great King, the Macedonians were heedless of their lives." Alexander was wounded in the thigh, by Darius himself in one version, but then the wounded horses of the Great King's chariot panicked, and Darius lost

Battle between Alexander and Darius, usually identified as Issus,
mosaic after a painting, Pompeii

(Inv. 10020 Museo Archeologico Nazionale, Naples.
Photo: Erich Lessing/Art Resource, NY).

his nerve and fled. His flight from Alexander's onrush is immortalized in the famous Alexander Mosaic from Pompeii (see figure).[41]

The commanders of Greek armies had often fought in person in battle but usually as part of the phalanx. Eager to show their bravery and inspire their troops but not to kill any specific enemy, they contented themselves with hoplite courage and Homeric generalship. Alexander's desire to fight enemy leaders in single combat, by contrast, is a reversion to a Homeric strain long nearly hidden in Greek warfare: the desire to be judged not only by performance but also by the achievement of defeating high-ranking enemies, the Homeric principle that required the poem to provide so many details about warriors before or after they were slain, so that their value could be judged. Legends about Alexander fall easily into this epic mode, depicting Darius as a worthy foe, "the fairest and largest of men." A parallel story was told of the young Alexander: would he enter the Olympic games as a runner? Of course he would, he replied, if his competitors were kings.[42]

The Homeric standard of excellence that later Greek civilization had chosen to emphasize was not enough for Alexander. He sought to combine it with the other Homeric standard as well, by defeating worthy opponents with his own hand. No doubt he hoped too that if he could kill or drive off the enemy leader, the enemy army would flee. But there is a significance in Alexander's habitual charges from the right deeper than his rivalry with the shade of Achilles and deeper than any strictly tactical reason one might assign to it. For Alexander was a relentless seeker after danger in battle, even when his opponents were not satraps or kings. Plutarch puts into Alexander's mouth a list of all his reported wounds: "First, among the Illyrians my head was wounded by a stone and my neck by a cudgel. Then at Granicus my head was cut open by an enemy's dagger, at Issus my thigh was pierced by the sword. Next, at Gaza my ankle was wounded by an arrow, my shoulder was dislocated, and I whirled heavily round and round. Then at Macaranda the bone of my leg was split open by an arrow. . . . Among the Aspasians my shoulder was wounded by an arrow, and among the Gandridae my leg. Among the Mallians the shaft of an arrow sank deep into my breast and buried its steel; and I was struck in the neck by a cudgel."[43] Alexander's officers and friends did not behave much differently. They left the safety of their formations to fight in person like their king, seeking out single combat with enemy leaders and, judging by the high casualties among them — including the slaughter of the officers of the phalanx at Issus — behaved extremely aggressively in battle. Evidently, a personal rivalry with Achilles was not necessary to make a Macedonian officer bold.[44]

As in Greek armies, formal discipline was loose in the army of Alexander. But Macedonians were "wont of old to consider the mightiest in arms the most kingly." Macedonian leaders had to fight with their own hands because that is how they commanded the obedience of their soldiers. We have seen this same idea in Xenophon, who believed that the surest way to get soldiers to obey was to be better than they in martial accomplishments. This is perhaps the oldest type of legitimate authority the Greeks knew, going back to Homer:

> Indeed, these are no ignoble men who are lords of Lycia,
> these kings of ours, who feed upon the fat sheep appointed
> and drink the exquisite sweet wine, since indeed there is
>   strength
> of valor in them, since they fight in the forefront of the
>   Lycians.[45]

It was this authority of the heroic warrior that Achilles defended against Agamemnon's claim to a primitive divine right. Likewise it was by his fighting in person, by leading the charge that opened the battle, that Alexander, heir to a weak monarchy but also to an army that preserved Homeric ideals, earned the right to be obeyed by his army, earned the right to lead them beyond the ends of the earth.[46]

At the same time Alexander's personal participation was the keystone of the ranked array of the Macedonian army. Alexander rode with his guard at the extreme right of the long line. The array of the army from worst to best implied that he was the single best of the Macedonians. And as a device to inspire competition, the array would be ridiculous unless he vindicated that expectation in battle. If he himself led and fought, his soldiers, like the phalanx at Issus, would fight better in rivalry with him. And fight he did, with great success, loudly praising his own feats to his army afterward. For Alexander had no Homer to sing his deeds, as he was said to have complained, so he served as his own Homer. Not only Alexander's rivalry with Achilles, but the way authority was earned in Macedon, and the very logic of his Macedonian array, required that Alexander fight like Achilles.[47]

The army of Alexander the Great was the most successful army the Greek world ever knew. Its soldiers were brave because their parents raised them brave, because out-of-the-way Macedon had preserved the warrior values of an older Greece — the Greece that Thucydides remembered with a shudder — when men still wore swords. Macedon was a society of noble companions and riotous banqueting, a society of untamed emotion, of boasting, of drunken murder, a society that recalled that of epic. Philip and Alexander harnessed this traditional ethos by bringing the world of Homer back to life and so turned the ramshackle levy of old Macedonia into an army of world conquest.[48]

After the victory at Issus, the army of Alexander marched south, capturing Tyre by siege and seizing Egypt. Then it marched up the Levant again and turned east into the heart of the Persian empire. Darius gathered a great polyglot army from many lands to face Alexander in a final decisive struggle. But when they met upon the fatal field of Gaugamela in 331 BC, Alexander charged from the right directly at Darius's position: the Great King fled and his army fled after him. Darius was soon murdered. Now Alexander was lord of the Persian empire, and he marched east, ever east, setting his realm in order and placing garrisons. For the broad demesnes of the Persians were not the limit of Alexander's ambition. Out of Persia he marched into what is now Afghanistan, out of Afghanistan into India. There he won the last of his great battles, against the Indian king Porus and his host of elephants, at the river Hydaspes (326 BC). He wanted to march on into India, but his soldiers refused. After more than eleven thousand dusty miles — half the orb of the earth, if their king had led them straight — they longed for the friendly hearths of Macedonia. Furious, Alexander was nonetheless compelled to turn back. Of Alexander's plans, had they not been thwarted, his historian despairs to guess, "but they were neither small nor trivial: and he would not have stopped quietly however great his conquests, but even if he had added Europe to his conquest of Asia, and added the Isles of Britain to Europe, he would have striven for the unknown in regions beyond the beyond, and failing anyone else, he would have done it in rivalry with himself."[49] After a long march back from India, Alexander died at Babylon of a fever. Asked to whom he left his empire, he replied, "To the strongest." He was thirty-two years old.[50]

VII

HELLENISTIC WARFARE (323–31 BC)

COMPETITION, COMBAT, AND

INNOVATION

The death of Alexander in 323 BC left his gigantic conquests without a steersman, but with plenty of his hard-eyed friends eager to try their hands at the helm. Alexander's body was hardly cold when the fighting began. For twenty years Alexander's generals and governors fought over his sprawling empire. After the battle of Ipsus in 301 BC, three major successor states emerged, ferocious Macedonia, rich Egypt of the Ptolemies, and the vast Seleucid realm based upon Antioch, slowly shedding its eastern extents as if afflicted by political leprosy. These kingdoms fought each other. They fought internal wars of succession. They fought rebellions of the Greeks and natives they held in thrall. They fought the lesser powers who struggled to exist in the spaces between them. They fought invaders from outside their world. And finally they fought, and finally they were conquered by, the Romans, who brought their world to an end.

If Classical Greek history is a still life that can be taken in with a sharp glance, and the campaigns of Alexander are an old-fashioned history painting that kindly guides the viewer's eye, the Hellenistic era, the history of Greece and the Greek East after Alexander, is a titanic, smudgy, abstract canvas. The eye wanders and rebounds and hunts in vain for comfort and rest. Best to understand this brushwork by looking at one tiny corner.

THE GAMES OF SAMOS

A finger traces the familiar words on the second-century BC stone from the Aegean isle of Samos: the footrace. Demetrius son of Democrates won that. The double-distance footrace. In that, Aretus son of Minnion was the victor. But soon the finger runs into trouble and crooks in puzzlement and has resort to the Greek lexicon. *Euexia,* a male beauty contest: Oh, those naughty Greeks! Apollonius son of Posidippus won it, lucky boy. *Eutaxia.* Discipline? Kallidromus son of Exacestes. *Philoponia.* Love of effort? No one seems to know what that is. But Exacestes' other son, Sopater, won it. What a tediously admirable family Exacestes must have had. *Lithobolos.* Stone throwing. But how? with the hand? the sling? perhaps a stone-throwing engine? Anyway, Mentor son of Zoilus won that. The catapult, Asteriscus son of Asteriscus; the javelin, Asclepiades son of Democrates; the bow, the same. Fighting in hoplite gear, Sostratus son of Sostratus. *Thureomachia?* Fighting with a door? Ah, fighting with a long shield that someone once thought looked rather like a door. In that, Apollas son of Apollonius was triumphant.[1]

The Greeks loved their games and often inscribed lists of victors upon stone: it is no surprise that a set of monthly local games on Samos should leave a set of victor lists. But many of the events are surprising. To the sports one expects to see at Greek games — running, boxing, wrestling, the *pancration* (all-in wrestling) — a set of competitions in military skills has been added. And this development is not confined to Samos, although the Samian games are an especially striking instance. With the spread of public training for young citizens, ephebes, through the Greek world in the Hellenistic period came special games (often with a military flavor, as at Samos) for ephebes, and for those about to be ephebes, and former ephebes; military events became more common at nonephebic games as well.[2]

The number of martial skills thought worth teaching had increased since the Athenian *ephebeia* of the 330s BC, but just as then, even the sons of the wealthy were to learn not only hoplite fighting but also how to use light-infantry weapons. In a set of regulations for a gymnasium in second-century BC Macedonia, slaves, freedmen, their sons, and tradesmen were banned. No riffraff need apply! Only the quality were allowed. But the presiding official was to ensure that the ephebes practiced daily with the javelin and the bow. The social differentiation of types of infantry fighting, so evident in Classical Greece, seems to have vanished. In the Samian games, too, fighting in hoplite equipment had no precedence over fighting with other weapons. It was a technical skill, learned by painstaking practice, in Athens as in other cities, under the instruction of an expert instructor provided by the city. Over time Greek hoplites had come to share the outlook of nonhoplites and prided themselves on their skill and obedience, competing in the precision of their drill like the men of Philopoemen's phalanx in the late third century BC, whom "he drilled, and they obeyed his commands for drill evolutions zealously and in a spirit of ambitious competition." They constituted a force that could "perform, as it was used to, its tactical movements quickly and vigorously."[3]

Thus the prize at Samos, as in other Hellenistic cities, for *eutaxia* (narrowly, "drill," broadly, "discipline"). Now all young warriors, hoplite or not, were expected to compete in following orders. As in Classical Greek armies, the formal discipline of Hellenistic armies was loose: a Greek observer like Polybius was awed and astonished by the severity of Roman discipline. Hellenistic soldiers, at least those of broadly Greek background, were expected to fight and obey not because they were compelled to do so, but because of their culture. And it was this competitive culture the games of Samos were designed at once to inculcate, exploit, and test, encouraging not only skill at arms, but discipline, too, and zeal. The Hellenistic army was an army of professions, an army in which the fighting quality of troops of many types was a function both of their competition in skill at arms and of the competition of all soldiers in precision of drill and obedience to command.[4]

Such a finale could perhaps have been predicted from the advance of all forms of military training during the fourth century BC and from the growing importance of mercenaries, light infantry, and cavalry. But the example of Philip of Macedon was no doubt decisive. It was Philip, who took the tough peasants of his realm and made them hoplites by training them in his new phalanx, who took the logic of training to its end by decreeing it for his whole Macedonian army, and who defeated the Greeks at Chaeronea in 338 BC with a trained phalanx of some twenty thousand men, much the largest trained army ever seen in Greece. Philip's example spawned systematic training at Athens and after that throughout the Greek world.[5]

The games of Samos, then, stood at the end of one road in Greek warfare, that of regarding warfare as a set of teachable skills, *technai*, and competition in those skills. But they stood at the end of another as well, for the games of Samos were yet another solution to the problem of how to organize competition for soldiers in the world outside epic, the problem Greeks had been wrestling with since the birth of the phalanx.

THE BATTLES OF PARAETACENE AND GABIENE (317–316 BC)

Of the characters struggling over Alexander's leavings, the two most appealing were Antigonus the One-Eyed, Alexander's satrap of Phrygia in central Asia Minor, and Alexander's secretary, Eumenes. The pair were old, dear friends, but an odd couple. Antigonus was a Macedonian's Macedonian, big, fat, tough, ribald, and with a great booming laugh. But someone had once presumed upon his good humor to call him Cyclops behind his back, and that someone was no more. Eumenes was a rare Greek who had won Alexander's confidence, and late in Alexander's campaigns had held military commands. But he was small and boyish, quiet, elegant, and intellectual, a master of artifices and inventions. Despite their friendship, the lottery of successor politics made them rivals for control of Asia, and on one occasion, when Eumenes' fortunes were low, Antigonus had him trapped in an inaccessible castle (320–319 BC). The fat Macedonian proposed a meeting, and the slender Greek agreed but cautiously required hostages to guarantee his safety when he emerged from the walls. When he did come out, he was warmly greeted by Antigonus, but so many soldiers rushed up to catch a glimpse of him that Antigonus feared for his old friend. He shouted at the men to go away, then tried to drive them off by throwing stones, and finally threw his arms around Eumenes to protect him.[6]

Two years later the friends met in battle deep in Asia at an unknown site in the province of Paraetacene, in what is now Iran. The armies camped close together, but a deep riverbed separated them. Supplies were short on both sides. Antigonus sent messengers to tamper with the loyalty of Eumenes' army. They failed. Then deserters came from Antigonus's side with the intelligence that he was going to march his army away by night into the unplundered province of Gabiene. The cunning Eumenes sent pretended deserters the other way: Eumenes would attack his camp during the night, they lied to Antigonus, to confine him to his camp so that Eumenes could reach Gabiene first. Sending his baggage on ahead, Eumenes had a lead of two watches before Antigonus smoked the ruse and set out in pursuit. Leaving his infantry to make their slow way, Antigonus led on his cavalry. In the dawn Eumenes saw the horsemen on a ridge behind him and, thinking that all Antigonus's army was there, ordered his forces into line of battle and so wasted his lead. "In this way," wrote the historian, "the leaders of both armies each out-generalled the other, as if in a preliminary contest of intellect."[7]

Now it was time to array the armies for battle. This was a complex operation, given the large number of units — differently equipped and from different parts of Alexander's empire — that often made up Hellenistic armies like those of Eumenes and Antigonus. Eumenes' left wing rested upon the high ground and was held by the hundred-and-fifty-man cavalry guard (*agema*) of Eudamus, one of Eumenes' marshals, with two small squadrons of lancers posted in front of it. Then came several units of Asian cavalry from Mesopotamia, Paropamisidae, and Arachosia in far Afghanistan (and if we do not recognize some of these place-names, neither did the Greeks) and then a unit of Thracian cavalry. In front of this flank Eumenes placed forty-five elephants at an angle, with archers and slingers between them. A phalanx of more than six thousand mercenaries was the furthest left unit of the center, then a phalanx armed in the Macedonian manner but drawn from many Asian nations, then the vaunted Silver Shields, veterans of Alexander's campaigns, and then the phalanx of Shield Bearers, who formed the right of the infantry. Forty elephants were lined up in front of these phalanx units, again with light troops between them. The right wing was cavalry, first a unit of Iranians, then Companion Cavalry, then the Horse Guard of Peucestes and Antigenes, and finally Eumenes with his own Horse Guard. Posted in front of them and echoing the left flank were two small cavalry units formed of Eumenes' pages. Behind the Horse Guard, close to Eumenes in case he should need them, was a picked cavalry reserve. Some distance away,

not forming part of the line, was a small cavalry flank guard. Forty elephants, no doubt interspersed again with light infantry, stood in front
of this wing.[8]

The similarity of this array to that of Alexander is obvious: Shield-
Bearers still stand on the right of the phalanx, Companion Cavalry is set
to the right of the infantry, and the Horse Guard forms their right wing.
Eumenes was still drawing strength from Alexander's ranked array. And
so too was Antigonus. Of his phalanx, ethnic Macedonians held the right.
On the right wing, Companion Cavalry were rightmost, except for Antigonus's own Horse Guard. But there were unfamiliar elements too, in both
arrays: not only elephants from India, but elephants and light troops forming a whole first line in Eumenes' army and covering the center and right
of Antigonus's host. There were not only the javelin- and lance-armed
cavalry of the Greek tradition, but horse archers as well and the cavalry
of Media and Parthia with their practiced technique of false flights and
Tarentine mercenary light cavalry, who had a special fighting technique
(presumably invented at Tarentum, in the south of Italy) which is obscure
to us but may have involved dismounting to throw javelins. Each warlord
might have his own Horse Guard, a cavalry *agema*. There were three in
Eumenes' army, all in positions of honor: that of Eudamus anchoring
the left, that of Eumenes himself anchoring the right, and that of Peucestes and Antigenes just to the left of him. Mercenaries and Asian units
were intermixed in both armies with Macedonian-style units (whatever
the actual ethnic origins of those who made them up). Antigonus, who
had made his dispositions after careful study of Eumenes' from the higher
ground, thrust forward his powerful right wing but ordered his left to
hang back, posting there light cavalry and mounted archers who were
supposed to thwart the charge of Eumenes' right by harassment and
wheeling maneuvers. While ultimately based on Alexander's, the arrays
of Eumenes and Antigonus were carefully adapted by active minds. Having
proved equal in stratagems before the battle and having failed to get an
advantage one over another in that arena, the two generals "used different arrays, vying with each other in this skill as well."[9]

Just as in Classical Greece, the idea that generals competed with each
other was a Hellenistic commonplace. Generalship was an art, a *techne*,
and a competitive one. Hellenistic generals conceived of themselves in a

rank order of excellence and debated who of them was the best. The competition of opposing commanders was conceived as being a dynamic potentially independent from the simple desire to win their country's battles: "Many men were killed on both sides, such was the extremity of the ambitious rivalry of the generals."[10]

The historian's commentary on the behavior of Eumenes and Antigonus at Paraetacene reflects the division of Hellenistic generals' competition into two main departments, the same ones as in Classical Greece. "Tactics is the highest *techne* of war," and tactics was the deployment, formation, and movement of troops on the field. Second was stratagem, or trickery: "In war, less is achieved openly and with force than with guile." Commanders sought to "outgeneral" each other with stratagems. A competition between enemy generals in stratagems might be compared to that between ambitious and rivalrous boxers. It was quite possible for a commander to be good at stratagem and bad at tactics.[11]

The crafts both of tactics and of stratagem could be learned from tactical manuals and collections of stratagems, which had by now become common. So an author will mention in passing the use of "stratagems from history." The general's craft was learned by such reading, by apprenticeship to other generals, or by experience in command. The knowledgeable Polybius had the greatest confidence in experience — generals could be practiced "athletes" of war. But service as a common soldier was not enough, for the art was a cerebral one, like playing checkers.[12]

The Homeric roots of this Hellenistic science, betrayed by the departments into which it was divided, were self-consciously asserted by contemporaries. A tactical manual might trace the art of tactics right back to Homer, to the inevitable Menestheus — "never on earth before had there been a man born like him for the arrangement in order of horses and shielded fighters" — and in Hellenistic times written collections of Homeric tactics were compiled. Hellenistic stratagem too was considered the legacy of Homeric cunning. A manual might open with a series of citations from Homer on the value of the art. Polybius urges the expert in stratagem to be knowledgeable about geometry and astronomy. For hadn't Odysseus, that "best of commanders," observed the stars? Polybius, an experienced soldier and himself the author of a manual on tactics, sprinkles his military narrative with citations from Homer. The power of Homer was not limited to thinking about warfare in this era. Hellenistic times saw not only a rash of intellectual interest in Homer, but royal and popular interest as well in the form of royal benefactions to Troy, the revival and creation of cults to Homeric heroes, and the erection of buildings that looked like Bronze Age edifices.[13]

The Achaean marshal Philopoemen was an exemplary Hellenistic commander: a lover of Homer, a reader of histories of Alexander, his copy of Evangelos's *Tactics* ever at his side, wandering over the land and discussing with his friends how he would form a phalanx to get it up slope or down defile. When his services were not wanted by his native Achaean League, he took employment as a mercenary captain on Crete to keep up his dexterity as a commander and to hone his skills in the cunning ambushes and ambuscades for which Cretan warfare was famous. Because of the weakening of the old hoplite ideals, the general's arts were not opposed by his troops, and indeed, soldiers might demand generals thought especially crafty, like Eumenes. During the Lamian War (323–322 BC) the soldiers of Phocion wearied the Athenian commander with their advice on artful generalship. "How many generals I see, and how few soldiers!" he complained. A general who showed aptitude at tactical commands might be cheered by his troops.[14]

At Paraetacene, the cunning plan of Antigonus to win with his right wing while craftily holding his left back was thwarted by Pithon, his own commander on the left, who advanced aggressively with his light cavalry upon the line of elephants in front of him, wheeled around the wing, and took Eumenes' elephants in the flank, keeping out of harm's way while wounding them with arrows. To drive the horsemen away, Eumenes needed light cavalry of his own to pursue them, and this he summoned from his own left wing. Attaching them and the light infantry to the lance-armed cavalry around him, he led the cavalry charge against Pithon's light cavalry, with his elephants lumbering behind. Antigonus's left flank, which he wisely had hoped would not engage seriously at all, was routed and pursued to the hills.[15]

In leading his cavalry in a charge from the right, Eumenes was acting in the high tradition of Alexander, who had led the charge similarly and sought out combat with his own hands. Hellenistic commanders sought to excel at skill at arms and personal bravery as well as in command, and kings and commanders took training in arms and, like Eumenes, fought in person in battle. Indeed, in an earlier battle Eumenes had fought an enemy commander one-on-one (always Alexander's ambition). When Eumenes and the hated Neoptolemus recognized each other, "there arose a great display of rivalry for honor as the leaders charged at each other." They fought with swords and then grappled hand to hand, falling from their horses. Eumenes was up first and stabbed Neoptolemus in the back of the knee: he could not stand but fought on from his knees, wounding Eumenes in the arm and thighs. Finally Eumenes caught him in the throat and killed him.[16]

Duels between commanders were not uncommon on the Hellenistic battlefield. A Hellenistic commander yearned both for victory by intellect and to do great deeds with his own hands, to be "most capable in fighting and in generalling." When men ranked the commanders of their time they thought in terms of personal prowess as well as intellectual quality: cleverness and courage are the qualities that describe a good commander. This yearning to compete both as commander and fighter at the same time presented severe practical difficulties. Polybius complained of commanders who put themselves in danger and thus placed the entire enterprise at risk. Yet he could not conceal his admiration for commanders who did so. How could a general keep his mind on the overall progress of the battle while fighting with his own hands? It was noted of Pyrrhus that he managed this difficult balance: "Placing his hands and body in the fight and stoutly repelling those who attacked him, he did not become confused in his thinking nor lose his reason, but steered the battle as if he were looking on from a distance, rushing here and there and bringing succor to those who seemed overpowered."[17]

These two contradictory roles that Hellenistic commanders felt obliged to play were consequent in the first place on their emulation of Alexander (and so a Homeric reconstruction at second hand). But commanders also conceived of their deeds in directly Homeric terms. Pyrrhus, the greatest Hellenistic hand-to-hand fighting commander, boasted,

> These shields, Pyrrhus the Molossian as a gift to Itonian
> Athena

hung here, taken from the brave Gauls
after he had vanquished the army of Antigonus: and no
  wonder!
The sons of Aeacus are warriors still, as they were
  of old.

"Of old" meant the days of Achilles, from whom Pyrrhus claimed descent.
The name Pyrrhus was another name of Neoptolemus, son of Achilles,
the killer of Priam, and Pyrrhus depicted Achilles on his coins. The victor
in a commanders' single combat might personally strip his enemy of his
armor. Commanders in Homer both planned and fought: the easy logic
of epic allowed them to. And the strength of the Homeric model compelled commanders thereafter similarly to attempt both at once, however
difficult it was to reconcile them in reality. The contradictory culture of
Hellenistic command is a singularly powerful illustration of the continuing
sway of Homer, supercharged by the example of Alexander, over Greek
warriors.[18]

Now at Paraetacene the infantry phalanxes had come to grips and fought
for a considerable period, until at last the phalanx of Eumenes got the
better of that of Antigonus. Decisive were the Silver Shields, Alexander's
veterans: "Because of the mass of battles they had fought, they were outstanding in bravery and skill at arms." Such an analysis is very much characteristic of its epoch, following naturally from the growing Greek conviction that skill at arms was important, even in the phalanx, and that it
could be taught and learned. Slingers from the Balaeric islands, for example, "contribute greatly to victory in battle, because they have applied
themselves continuously to practicing with the sling from childhood."
And so Hellenistic officers trained their troops not only in drill but in
the use of their weapons. As in the fourth century BC, superior technical
skill was especially associated with mercenaries. In the exactly arrayed
phalanx, technical skill was a matter of keeping and changing formation
and following orders precisely. As a later author wrote of the phalanx of
Alexander, "Intent upon the order of their commander, they have learned
to follow the standards and keep their ranks. What is ordered, all obey.
To stand fast, to surround, to make a flank march, to change formation:

the soldiers are as skillful as their commanders."[19] Attributing the courage of the Silver Shields to their experience follows in the wake of the opinion of advanced thinkers of the fifth and fourth centuries that courage was also, at least in part, a function of training or experience, that courage also was part of the "craft" of war. In general, then, training made one's own units better than enemy units, and training made armies win battles. Experience made soldiers "athletes" of war and formidable.[20]

The phalanx of Antigonus was in flight, and his advisors, thinking the battle lost, told him he should retire to the high ground to rally his defeated army. But Antigonus saw that the advance of Eumenes' center had opened up a gap between the phalanx and the cavalry on Eumenes' left, commanded by Eudamas. So Antigonus led his powerful cavalry right wing through the gap and into Eudamas's flank. Eudamas's force was soon put to flight, and when he heard the news, Eumenes had the recall sounded on his trumpets, breaking off the pursuit of the rest of Antigonus's army. With the pressure removed, Antigonus then managed to rally the rest of his army on the high ground. As dusk fell the armies faced each other again, as they had in the morning, and slowly came into battle order, "so great a spirit of rivalry filled not only the generals, but also the mass of the contestants."[21]

As here, Hellenistic battles are sometimes described as involving the competition of soldiers, but this is nowhere near as common as envisaging battle as a competition of generals. And for good reason: amidst the chaos of a Hellenistic battle, with so many types of soldiers fighting in so many ways, who could tell who was the best? Who was the bravest or the most skillful? how, as Euripides had once asked, could anybody see? Hellenistic battle had finally obliterated the hard-won clarity of competition in the classical phalanx. When competitions between man and man, unit and unit, and types of armament on the same side are described in accounts of Hellenistic battles, they usually occur under the eyes of a commander, who serves as a judge of excellence. This betrays that the Hellenistic battlefield was a poor arena for competition between soldiers, despite their competitive outlook, and at the same time hints at why it had become so: the commander had risen to a more lofty plane, and the commander's conception of battle had finally prevailed over that of his soldiers. The varied troop types of the Hellenistic army represented the final victory of the commander's competition in arraying over his soldiers' need to have a battle that allowed them to exercise their individual competitiveness. Such was the legacy of Philip and Alexander, such the consequence of armies made up of subjects and mercenaries, rather than of citizens.[22]

Hellenistic martial games followed, in part, from the degradation of competition between soldiers on the field of battle. In time of old, when Greek battle had evolved in such a way that valued martial competitions were excluded, competitive Greek soldiers had simply moved their competition outside battle. Thus, in an earlier day, the *hoplitodromos*, the run in hoplite panoply, the competitive pyrrhic dance, and the competition of the *apobates*, who leapt on and off chariots, the sport Alexander practiced on long marches in Asia. And the same happened in the Hellenistic era, when there arose athletic competitions in every possible martial skill, minutely subdivided. So Hellenistic soldiers did not need to compete in skill on the field of battle because they already knew who was best: their training was competitive. Unlike hoplites, who went into battle to find out who was bravest, Hellenistic soldiers went into battle already knowing who among them was most skillful, which unit's drill was most exact, and which unit hopped to obey commands fastest. Hellenistic soldiers were no less competitive than Greek soldiers in any generation, but their competitions were conducted for the most part away from the field of battle on the drill field. One competition, of course, could never be shifted from battle, for the bright pavilions of a contest in courage could be erected only in the valley of the shadow of death. But even for hoplites, that contest, once at the center of their world, was now only one contest among several. And even courage could be understood to be, at least in part, a consequence of experience and training.[23]

It took until midnight to get the armies of Eumenes and Antigonus back into line of battle and then to advance until they were some four hundred feet apart and ready to renew the fighting. The night was clear, the moon was full, and the sound of the enemy's gear made them sound even closer than they were. But human weakness finally cried a halt. The troops were exhausted and had not eaten since the morning. In the end, they would not fight and moved away to camp. Thirty-seven hundred infantry and fifty-four horsemen of Antigonus's army had been killed, while Eumenes had lost five hundred and forty footmen and only a handful of horse. By the numbers this was a lopsided victory for Eumenes. But not in the eyes of Greeks, for whom victory was still defined according to hoplite rules. Eumenes yearned to camp around the dead bodies, to stake his claim to victory in the ancestral Greek way, but his troops refused and insisted on camping with the baggage train. The more authoritative Antigonus did compel his forces to camp near the bodies, and so, by the odd, old rules of Greek warfare, he was the victor because Eumenes had to send a herald to ask for the return of the corpses. This suit Antigonus granted, after a wily delay to allow him to bury his own, more numerous, dead and so conceal his losses from Eumenes.[24]

The armies of Eumenes and Antigonus now went into winter quarters, but the winter was spent by both generals practicing tricks and counter-tricks upon each other. Antigonus plotted to fall upon Eumenes while his troops were still scattered in their winter camps. Advertising that he was marching away toward Armenia, in December Antigonus instead forced a march through the desert (the shortest route) directly at Eumenes, carrying his water and supplies with him. His soldiers complained audibly of the hardship. "You'll be sorry if you don't stand farther off when you curse me!" Antigonus shouted merrily from his tent. But the cold forced his soldiers to disobey Antigonus's order against fires, the fires were seen, and his advance was reported to Eumenes. How to slow down Antigonus's army until Eumenes' forces could gather? With a few men Eumenes set up a large camp and lit the fires of a great host. Antigonus feared to face what he thought was Eumenes' whole army right after his grueling desert march and turned off his route to refresh his army by plunder. Thus Eumenes "out-generalled" Antigonus and gained the days he needed to assemble his scattered units.[25]

And so Antigonus and Eumenes met again in battle, in Gabiene, and fought to another bloody draw in the winter dust of the salt plain, Eumenes' phalanx and Antigonus's cavalry each prevailing, and Eumenes trying to reach Antigonus to fight him hand to hand in the confusion. But taking advantage of the blinding dust, Antigonus sent cavalry unseen and captured the baggage and so the families of Eumenes' Macedonians. To get their families back after the battle, the Silver Shields seized their own general Eumenes and handed him over to Antigonus. And so the crafty Macedonian mastered Eumenes "of many wiles," the successor who had failed in the end wholly to master the balancing act of Greek generalship, to be a tactician and a fighter at the same time. At Gabiene, Eumenes had wanted too much to win glory by his right arm and too little with his mind. Seeing Antigonus with his cavalry on the right, in Alexander's fashion, Eumenes set himself with his cavalry on the left, directly opposite Antigonus, breaking with Alexander and with the tactics that had worked well against Antigonus at Paraetacene. He wanted to charge directly at Antigonus, wanted to kill Antigonus hand to hand as he had Neoptolemus in an earlier battle. But as Eumenes played Alexander, Antigonus, sober amidst dangers and with less to prove than a former secretary, calmly won the war with the gambit of sending horsemen to seize the precious baggage train.[26]

The big Macedonian agonized about what to do with his slender captive, so brilliantly talented, so useful, yet so dangerous. His son Demetrius, a great captain in the next generation, which would know him as Demetrius the Besieger, pleaded for Eumenes' life. But Antigonus's Macedonian officers, who had suffered so much at Eumenes' hands, wanted the Greek dead, and Antigonus finally ordered him executed. As a token of their old friendship Antigonus allowed him proper funeral, and his ashes were delivered to his family in an urn of silver. The tarnished Silver Shields, the graying traitors who had betrayed their general, received no reward from Antigonus. He burned their commander alive and sent them out to Arachosia, to Afghanistan, that "none of them might ever return home to Macedonia, or gaze again upon the Hellenic Sea."[27]

MILITARY INNOVATION IN THE HELLENISTIC ERA

A consequence of the Hellenistic conception of warfare as a congeries of competitions in technical skills is that change in military technique was comparatively rapid in the Hellenistic centuries. The old hoplite definition of courage and the vision of ritualized battle it created had held back change, much as the anchor the Athenian Sophanes brought to the battle of Plataea had prevented him from leaving his position. The most powerful citizens identified themselves as hoplites, and the hoplite definition of courage was fundamental to their self-perception. Hoplites resisted change. But as the training of Athenian ephebes and the games of Samos show, in later times one martial craft came to be considered much the same as another. It had been remarkable, a sign of the extremity of the situation, when prosperous Athenians had consented to row in the fleet at Arginusae, an act unthinkable except when the very survival of the state was at stake. But the soldiers in the phalanx of Philip V of Macedon took cheerfully to rowing in his galleys and even to lowly construction work.[28]

The competition of generals in tactics and stratagems encouraged experimentation in the arming and training of their armies. So, as seen at Paraetacene, the tactics of the cavalry of Tarentum in the south of Italy could be taught to others, and Tarentine cavalry could appear all over the Hellenistic world. *Thureomachia*, fighting with a large shield (one of the competitions at Samos), came to battle in the person of *thureophoroi*, large-shield-bearing soldiers. These shields and the method of fighting with them appear to have been borrowed from the Gauls. One could hire Cretan mercenaries, or train non-Cretans to fight in the Cretan style, as "neo-Cretans." Ptolemy IV (221–205 BC) trained Egyptians to fight in the Macedonian phalanx and used them to win a great victory over the Seleucids at Raphia in 217 BC. Over time the ethnic names of units became less and less meaningful, now referring to styles of fighting, whosoever might be doing it. Ptolemy IV's generals could take a large, diversely armed force of mercenaries, divide them by age and nationality, and re-train them, "paying no attention to how they were armed before."[29]

Predictably, the hoplites of old Greece changed slowly. But in the mid–third century BC, Boeotia took up the Macedonian phalanx, and later in the century so did Sparta, and then the Achaean League. It was more than a hundred years since Philip had invented the Macedonian phalanx, but finally the old hoplite code had passed away. Outside Greece itself, change was easier. Hannibal, a commander in the Hellenistic tradition, could have his soldiers cast away their arms in Italy and fight instead with Roman equipment. It has been argued that in the 160s BC the infantry of the Seleucid Empire and Ptolemaic Egypt were reorganized on the Roman model, and that by the time the Romans swept the world of Hellenistic armies, they were for the most part fighting with Roman arms and in the Roman fashion. The Hellenistic culture of war was so friendly to new methods that in the end it could adopt another culture's methods wholesale and cheerfully watch its own methods pass into extinction.[30]

THE GREEKS

CONCLUSION

Try a thought experiment. Suppose a modern, familiar dynamic of technological progress in which better methods are invented or imported and drive out the old, and then are replaced in turn by still better, had applied to ancient Greek warfare. What would Greek military history have been like if the Greeks had climbed a set of well-defined steps to ever more efficient ways of killing?

In such a world the classical phalanx, the close-knit, exclusively spear-armed phalanx of Thucydides and Xenophon, might have been expected to prevail soon after the appearance of hoplite equipment before 700 BC. But in reality the final expulsion of missile-armed soldiers and their associated confusion from the phalanx appears to have taken more than two centuries and was not complete until after 500 BC. In such a world generals might have been expected to establish their unquestioned authority over their soldiers early, but they did not do so in fact until the generation of Philip and Alexander. Similarly the "combined arms" tactics of phalanx, light troops, and cavalry, operating in separate units but cooperating, would not have taken until the fourth century to prevail. Light troops and cavalry depended on technology older than the phalanx, and so their efficient use together with the phalanx would have been coeval with the coming of the phalanx. If the training of the Spartans can be regarded as a military technology, it would have been widely copied, and early: it would not have taken until the last decades of the fourth century BC for military training to become general in Greece. And when the phalanx of Philip showed itself to be decisively superior to the phalanx of the Greeks, all the Greeks would have adopted it immediately, not piecemeal and inconsistently as they did in the next century and a half.

A simple conception of the march of technology is a very poor explanation for Greek military developments. Only in Hellenistic times (and then only enabled by the particular culture of the era) does one get the sense of Greeks experimenting freely with different modes of fighting to find the best. In earlier epochs change and continuity in military technology and method had different causes.

In actual Greek history the story of military change was more complicated and more interesting. In real Greek history poverty stifled innovation, and primitive communications discouraged imports. In real Greek history institutions, or the lack of them, politics, and social pressures sometimes promoted, sometimes prevented, and always affected innovation. In real Greek history the shock of events encouraged changes, and the vagaries of human genius had a great impact. Finally, in real Greek history, Greek culture, and especially the legacy of the Greek past, had a pervasive influence on the way the Greeks fought and how their methods of fighting changed over time.

The first powerful cultural force was primordial Greek competitiveness. Watch a troop of urchins playing, and the direction of competition's historical force is quickly seen: rivalry generates rules and rivalry simplifies play, so that winners and losers can be identified. Strife, the poet sang, was the mother of Oath. This particular power of human rivalry, operating in the Greek case between both men and cities, was responsible for the slow evolution of the like-armed hoplite phalanx out of the confused and mixed fighting that came before. And competition was also responsible for Greek military discipline, at least at Sparta, and for Greek drill as well, since the most reliable way of getting Greek soldiers to do anything disagreeable was to make a competition of it. It was their competitiveness and their kings' ability to exploit that competitiveness that made the Macedonians invincible.[1]

Mixed and mingled with competitiveness was reverence for epic. Epic was a vital conveyor of Greek competitive ethics down the generations, but such was the cultural authority of Homer that epic also offered models to be directly imitated. Thus the long evolution of the phalanx. If fighting in a mass could claim epic legitimacy, so could the old ways of fighting that the mature phalanx displaced, and thus they were a very long time departing. Thus too the competing ideals of the general, who looked back directly to the Homeric competitions in guile and in arraying troops. And thus the competing ideals of the peltast, whose way of fighting was so much like that of the heroes in Homer, and of the cavalryman, who could look back to the heroic virtue of horsemanship. In the case of the peltast Homer helped to naturalize an imported way of fighting and helped it edge out methods with an inferior epic pedigree. Subtly, epic may have turned the minds of Greek warriors away from certain possible ways of fighting. But so varied was the fighting in Homer — and so many possible ways of fighting did the poem seem to endorse — that Homer could not provide a compelling mechanism for choosing between later men's different reconstructions of epic. That was the role of events: the Peloponnesian War, the victory of Philip II over the Greeks at Chaeronea in 338 BC, and Alexander's conquest of the East.

With Philip and Alexander came another set of Homeric reconstructions, the Macedonian phalanx and the Macedonian array. What followed after them was the Hellenistic army of professions, with its many specialized troops, carefully disposed to best advantage on the battlefield by competitive commanders. The conflict between hoplites and commanders and between hoplites and other kinds of troops was finally over, but at the cost of making battle so imperfect a competition for soldiers that they moved such of their competitions as they could outside battle, into training and games. The insistence of Alexander on fulfilling both sides of the Homeric vision of leadership, commanding and fighting in person, enforced that vision too upon Hellenistic commanders. Hellenistic warfare is the result of an accumulation of attempts, some recent, some long forgotten, to preserve or return to Homer.

Epic provided Greek soldiers with both inspiration and legitimacy for the ways they fought, and from so tremendous a distance it is hard for us to tell inspiration and subsequent justification apart. No direct communication by ouija board reveals the Homeric inspiration of Philip II's phalanx: later Greek authors attributed that inspiration to him. Was he really so inspired? or did Philip present an idea from elsewhere in Iliadic terms? or was it merely the later authors who made the connection? But the habit of looking to epic for sanction reemphasizes the power of epic over the Greek mind. A folk who so relentlessly turned to the *Iliad* for justification are exactly the folk who will have turned to it also for inspiration. In no individual case can Homeric inspiration conclusively be proved, but the wider pattern is beyond doubt.

In as grim a business as war the force of cultural influence is limited at every turn by harsh reality. Wars must be won, or at least survived, or culture may become extinct. Few soldiers, however brave, yearn to die or are happy to fight in a fashion they think places them at a disadvantage relative to their enemies. Yet few Greeks would have seen a distinction between re-creating Homeric warfare and fighting in the most effective way possible, however they may have defined effectiveness. The fighting in Homer was the fighting of the heroes and was therefore not only the most prestigious way of fighting, but also the most effective. Philip II created a new phalanx that was both Homeric and better. And the excellence of the Macedonian phalanx convinced Greek observers, like the expert Polybius, that it was indeed Homeric.[2]

But if Homeric fighting was conceived of as the most effective, why was the re-creation not more thoroughgoing? Why, for example, did the Classical Greeks not fight from chariots? Greeks did use chariots, of course, in some places, as in Cyrene on the coast of North Africa, for example. Chariots were revived in some Hellenistic armies, and they are mentioned in the tradition of Hellenistic tactical writings, if briefly, with allusion to their Homeric and Persian use. Xenophon, too, may be advocating their use by Greeks when he discusses them at length in the *Cyropaedia*. But the tactical author Asclepiodotus dismisses chariots (along with elephants) as "not naturally suited for fighting," and this seems to have been the general opinion of the mainland Greeks as well. Perceived practicality triumphed. Greek competitiveness and the Homeric model channeled Greek thinking but did not prescribe it. Much of Greek military method and change had nothing to do with Homer, however many Iliadic passages might be adduced to endorse them. And the Homeric model might be criticized or improved upon, as when the Theban general Pammenes, alluding to the homoerotic bonds that held together the Theban Sacred Band, joked that Nestor "was no tactician when he ordered the

Greeks to dispose themselves in units by brotherhoods and tribes, 'and let each brotherhood go in support of brotherhood, let tribe support tribe,' because he ought instead to have stationed lover by beloved."[3]

The way epic could shape Greek thinking about warfare is perhaps best grasped on the largest scale by comparison of the practices of the Greek battlefield with Greek siege and naval warfare. Greek siegecraft constitutes a particular puzzle. The art of attacking walled cities was well developed in the Near East. The Assyrians knew rams and ladders and siege towers and ramps and tunnels. The Persians inherited this knowledge from the Assyrians, as the excavations of tunnels and a siege ramp at Paphos reveal. The Greeks had continual contact with the Persians, both in peace and in war. Yet the technologies of eastern siegecraft do not appear in mainland Greece until the mid–fourth century, trickling over from Sicily, where Dionysius of Syracuse had begun to use them around the beginning of the century. He probably learned them from the Carthaginians, who, being settlers from Phoenicia, had presumably brought them from the East. It can hardly have been from lack of need or wholly from poverty that the Greeks were so backward in siegecraft. For years during the Peloponnesian War, the Peloponnesians glared angrily up at the walls of Athens and for years the Athenians glanced scornfully down, both thinking the walls of Athens impregnable. The Persians, Sparta's allies in the later years of the war and paymasters of the Peloponnesian fleet, knew better. But somehow the information was never transmitted to the Spartans.[4]

Why were the Greeks so blind for so long to what was going on elsewhere in their world? The question about siegecraft may only be part of a larger one, and that one perhaps insoluble. The Greeks for generations failed to adopt many useful things they saw on their travels to the East, the arch, for example, and the barrel vault. But if Greek blindness in siegecraft is not just part of a wider blindness, it may be possible to posit a reason for it. The Greek epics described the progress and results of a siege at which machinery was wholly absent. Could it be that the power of the Homeric model channeled the Greeks away from thinking in terms of mechanical attacks on walls? What *was* well developed among the Greeks, by contrast, was thinking about taking besieged cities by trickery. The surviving fourth-century treatise of Aeneas Tacticus is nearly fixated upon forestalling betrayal and acts of guile. Could the development of this facet of siegecraft, and only this facet, be a consequence of the fact that Troy was taken by trickery?[5]

Contrast the Greeks at sea. At the first sea battle of which a detailed description survives, the battle of Artemisium in 480 BC, the Greeks formed their triremes into a defensive circle. Although Greek sea fighting had its ritual aspects — trophies were set up on convenient shores — it was more consistently tactical than land fighting, from an early date a matter of clever deployment, fast maneuvers, and trickery. Indeed, it has been proposed that tactical fighting on land grows from the example of tactical fighting on the sea. One suspects that the ruthlessly tactical quality of sea fighting was a by-product of the social makeup of Greek fleets, which consisted of rich trireme commanders who viewed their duties in Homeric terms of guile and arraying, few hoplites, and poor oarsmen without the clout to impose an alternative vision of combat even if they had one. When fleets did ship a significant number of hoplites — what Thucydides calls "the old, unskillful method" — the triremes closed and the hoplites fought a hoplite battle on their decks. If numerous enough, hoplites could impose their model of fighting even at sea, despite its impracticality. But the contrast between the aggressively tactical quality of sea fighting, the puzzling, mixed, semitactical, semiritual quality of land fighting, and the long primitiveness of siege warfare may again have its roots in Homer. For if the Iliadic model discouraged siege techniques not in Homer and channeled techniques of land warfare along Homeric lines, the model left sea fighting wholly free and ingenuity unconstrained: there are no sea battles in epic.[6]

Cultural vector, cultural model, cultural constraint, and cultural justification: the Homeric epics were all these to the later Greeks. And the power of epic is nowhere more evident than in its sway over warfare, the most serious and practical of human arts. It hardly surprises if a painter paints a scene from epic or a sculptor carves one. But a soldier acting out epic in his own person: that vision enlightens and amazes.

THE ROMANS

A grimy village huddled against the river Tiber, young Rome gazed out with fierce love and hate at similar villages near and far, villages that spoke the same tongue and shared familiar rites: the Latins. Across the Tiber the proud, alien Etruscans held their sway and collected their Greek vases; upriver, in the Apennine hills, lurked tribes of brooding strangers. The Latins rustled and raided ceaselessly among themselves, their combats more like murderous feuds than the wars of nations. In early days the Etruscans pushed over the river, perhaps ruling Rome itself for a time, and in latter days the Latins pushed over the river in their turn. Sometimes the hillmen coveted the rich plain of Latium or the fat beasts that grazed there to repletion and descended to take them. Rome was born fighting.

In this early warfare Rome had only a very slight advantage over her neighbors. By 509 BC, when, by tradition, Rome expelled the kings who had ruled her since her founding, Rome was much the largest state in Latium, with slightly more than three hundred square miles of territory. But to achieve that predominance had taken, if we accept the traditional date for her founding, two hundred and fifty years. Although Rome had

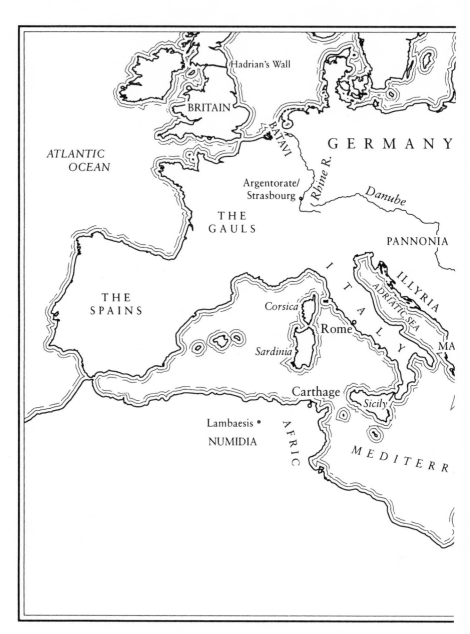

The Roman World

N

DACIA

BLACK SEA

CASPIAN SEA

THRACE
Adrianople
CEDONIA

ASIA

CAPPADOCIA

COMMAGENE

Antioch

SYRIA

Cyprus

Crete

ARMENIA

Amida

Tigris R.

KINGDOM
OF
PARTHIA/
PERSIA

Ctesiphon

Euphrates R.

ANEAN SEA

Jerusalem JUDAEA

Alexandria

EGYPT

Nile R.

RED
SEA

managed to survive the vortex of old Latium (many of the Latin towns succumbed), she had managed to add only slightly more than one square mile to her territory for every year of her existence. In the decades after 507 BC, Rome continued, still slowly, to expand her power and her land. There were setbacks, such as Rome's sack by marauding Gauls in 390 BC, but also wars with enemies further afield, like the Samnites, the stern and numerous hill people down the Apennine chain. Decisive local superiority came only with Rome's final victory over her Latin neighbors in 338 BC; now she had a territory of more than two thousand square miles and a population of warriors equal to that of any power in Italy.

After the Latin War, Rome's rate of expansion exploded. The Samnites and Etruscans were crushed, the Gauls driven back into the north and marked down for the slow attrition of yearly campaigns. The Romans could not easily defeat King Pyrrhus of Epirus, a Hellenistic warlord in the tradition of Alexander, summoned as a savior by men of the south of Italy. But the Romans could die at his hands with terrible conviction. Fighting the Romans, it seemed, was like fighting the mythical hydra: there were always more heads to cut off. In the end Pyrrhus departed in despair of overcoming a folk so profligate of their lives, and the Greeks he abandoned soon learned to obey their relentless northern neighbors.[1]

Next the Romans fought Carthage, an old colony of Phoenicia that was reaching greedily for more of Sicily from the craggy shore of Africa. The First Punic War was fought mostly on Sicily and the sea from 264 to 241 BC, the Second in Italy, Spain, and Africa from 218 to 201. To defeat the lords of the western sea was a long fight and a cruel one. Carthage made war much as Pyrrhus had, in the Greek way. Inferior in the art of war, the Romans resisted Carthage, as they had Pyrrhus, by replacing fallen fathers with their willing sons. Eventually, the Romans found in Scipio Africanus a general who could defeat the guileful Carthaginian marshal Hannibal. But before Hannibal was called home to defend Carthage, Roman stubbornness had made him a military gypsy, wandering the south of Italy with a tired and tatterdemalion army. With Hannibal's final defeat, for the defeat at Zama in 202 BC was the defeat of Carthage, the western shores of the Mediterranean were Rome's, although it took the Romans centuries of slaughter to subdue the interior of Spain.

Now the Romans turned their eyes upon the East. The legacy of Alexander, the Greek powers of the Hellenistic world, fell one after another to Roman arms: first, the phalanx of brave Macedon was defeated at Cynoscephalae in 197 BC; next, at Magnesia (190 BC), was King Antiochus, heir to Seleucus, who kept his state at Antioch in Syria. A resurgent Macedon was defeated at Pydna in 168 BC. It was Hellenistic Egypt's Macedonian pharaohs who took the longest to succumb, not because they were strongest, but because they were weakest and knew to obey and because the Romans were occupied elsewhere. Finally, the Romans looked north into the mists of Europe. In seven bloody years Julius Caesar conquered Gaul to the Rhine. Although brave Vercingetorix, the best hope of the fractious Gauls, threw Caesar back at Gergovia, Caesar later captured him at Alesia in 52 BC. Caesar's victories in Gaul were followed soon after by victories in civil war against his rival Pompey the Great. But Caesar had barely defeated Pompey and his followers when his murder in 44 BC set off another round of civil wars, wars in which his grand-nephew and adopted son Octavian (Rome's first emperor, under the name Augustus) was the eventual victor. Augustus extended Roman sway in the Balkans to the Danube.

The Romans had already sparred with their next ring of enemies, the Germans beyond the Rhine and the Parthians across the Syrian desert, when change in aims and zeal came over them. A realm ruled by a single man, an emperor, was less aggressive than a republic in which the competition among general-politicians had fed, vampirelike, upon the blood of defeated enemies. After Augustus, emperors feared victorious generals, and generals feared to be victorious. A great defeat could threaten the regime. In AD 9, Varus's three Roman legions were ambushed and destroyed beyond the Rhine — the site has been identified from the scatter of coins and equipment discarded by fleeing men, the heartrending remains of disaster — and Augustus immediately posted guards against a rising in Rome. And in the prosperity of conquest, a martial folk was becoming more civilian. Roman manhood no longer demanded killing, and there was less drive for conquest from above and from below. Rome still took great meals — Britain (after AD 43), Dacia (after AD 101) — but they were fewer and separated by longer postprandial naps. Natural dividers — the Rhine, the Danube, and the eastern desert — became de facto borders. From time to time the Roman armies crashed over them to conquer, plunder, and punish, but the Roman army now defended more than it attacked. From time to time there were also civil wars and revolts within the borders, revolts the Roman army put down with exemplary brutality, as it did the Jewish uprising (AD 66–70), so vividly narrated by the historian Josephus.

In no generation was Rome's military superiority absolute; there were always reverses, even disasters. Before 338 BC the balance had been slightly in Rome's favor and after that date more heavily so. But at some point during the later Roman empire the balance began to swing again, away from Rome. At first the swing was only temporary. The third century AD saw terrible civil wars, barbarian sack, and twenty-five emperors, all between AD 235 and 284, but the borders were finally restored and held again for another century. Yet by the end of the fourth century AD the advantage had shifted decisively to the enemies of Rome. An invasion of Persia in AD 363 ended in defeat, and after the fatal battle of Adrianople (AD 378) Rome could no longer protect her long borders in the West. Barbarians crossed frontiers and were not cast out again. Finally, the empire in the West was divided among petty barbarian kings. Trees took root in the fields; men gaped at the ruins; and sheep nibbled grass in the forum.

The relative military superiority of Rome in its first four hundred years was so slight and Rome's expansion so slow that their causes might well elude historians with a perfect set of records. But reports of those early days are meager and little to be trusted. The rapidity of Roman expansion after 338 BC, by contrast, cries out for an explanation. In this period the Romans were militarily superior to all the enemies they faced, western and eastern, Greek, Carthaginian, and barbarian, who fought in a wide variety of styles. The Romans won neither all their battles (and they probably lost even more than the patriotic sources reveal) nor quite all their wars, but they defeated most of their enemies in the end and nearly always won the last battle. A large population combined with the simple unwillingness of the Romans to surrender or withdraw is much of the reason. Rarely would they come to terms, even after suffering disasters by land and sea. But Roman stubbornness alone would not have conquered the Mediterranean world if the Romans had not been able, decade after decade with rare exceptions, to win more battles than they lost. If they had not won, the Romans, however stubborn, however numerous, would eventually have run out of Romans.

The Romans' military superiority continued into the centuries of the empire. If Rome no longer expanded so greatly, it was for reasons of politics or outlook or geography, not because of the inability of the army to win most of its battles. The capacity of Rome to defend her long borders for centuries was almost as strong a proof of her military superiority as her centuries of rapid expansion. But the reasons for Rome's edge over her opponents must be reexamined. The armies of Republic and empire were very different, the former a citizenry in arms, the latter a paid force of long-service professionals, many of them barbarian mercenaries. An explanation for the superiority of the army of the Republic may not necessarily apply to the empire. And an understanding of the Roman imperial army must incorporate an explanation of its decline.

Why did the Romans, for so many centuries, enjoy a military advantage over their enemies? how did this superiority come to exist? how was it preserved as the Roman army evolved and Rome's enemies changed? why did it pass away? A general explanation (or perhaps several of them) seems to be required. Fortune plays its role in history, and the Romans won battles by luck, but it was not given to the Romans more than to any other people to have the coin turn up heads century after century. Genius too played its role. Sometimes the Romans were led by geniuses, like Scipio Africanus, but more times not, and their empire expanded or held regardless. Theirs, also, was not an adventitious superiority over a single, sad, unlucky folk. They began by fighting the Latins, men like themselves in arms and manners. As their power grew, their enemies grew more exotic: the somber, drilled pikemen of the Greek East, the hooting blue-painted savages of Britain in their woods and their war wagons, the quicksilver horse archers of Parthia. All of these they defeated — or at least held at bay.

Roman discipline. This has been the explanation for Roman success at least since Machiavelli's *Arte della Guerra* (1521). For its discipline, modern soldiers emulate the army of the Romans; for its discipline, scholars praise it; for its discipline, the public admires it. Iron discipline is basic to the odd popular appeal of the Roman army. A perfectly disciplined, machinelike Roman army long ago became an intellectual navigational marker for those who think about armies, a beacon that all other armies approach far or near. Its traditional role as a tool for evaluating other armies places the discipline of the Romans beyond analysis: Roman discipline is useful, so it must be true. But where did Roman discipline come from? and how did the Romans come to have the most of this essential quality? and why, if discipline is the key to Roman success, was discipline allowed to decay? To be grasped and evaluated, Roman discipline must be seen not as a platonic ideal, shorn of its Roman identity, but instead placed in the wider realms of the Roman army and the Roman mind.

Stress on Roman discipline has a good ancient pedigree. Polybius, the major source for the army of the mid-Republic, praises Roman military punishments. He is particularly impressed by the good attitude inculcated by decimation, the execution of every tenth soldier after a unit had broken in battle, and the execution of negligent sentries. Josephus and Vegetius, under the empire and late empire, respectively, praise the early imperial army's discipline and especially its training. But few have stopped to ask how the perspective of these observers affects their conclusions: Polybius, an officer of the Achaean League, whose army was badly trained and intermittently cowardly and whose officers had only a very limited disciplinary authority; Josephus, a leader of the Jewish levies hastily raised to resist the Romans, a militia whose insubordination, indiscipline, and infighting appalled him; and Vegetius, a would-be military reformer and starry-eyed lover of things past.[2] Polybius, in fact, did not think Roman discipline the key to Roman success, although it was praiseworthy: he thought the soldiers of Macedon more orderly and obedient than the Romans. The Romans defeated the Macedonians, he says, not because of their discipline, but because of the superiority of their formation. And a close look at the record of the Roman army, a litany of mutinies, rebellions, and individual and mass disobedience, can easily raise doubts as to whether the army of the Romans was, by the standards of modern armies, very well disciplined at all.[3]

Now, after centuries, the consensus about Roman discipline is beginning to crack. The peculiar historical origins of the sixteenth-century emphasis on Roman discipline are coming to be understood. The truculence and disobedience of early modern armies, their legacy from the Middle Ages, disposed early modern students of ancient fighting especially to admire the training and discipline of ancient armies. And now other factors contributing to Roman success are being advanced. The psychological analysis of warfare, for example, has directed the attention of professional soldiers to investigate cohesion as a key to military success. Cohesion is the strength of horizontal bonds of affinity between soldiers. Soldiers fight well not because they are compelled from above but because they do not want to let down their comrades. Armies, in this school of thought, are evaluated by their ability to create and preserve those bonds; to portray the Roman army as a singularly tight-knit community is to explain its success. And so the role of military discipline as a fully adequate explanation of that success is called into question.

Those who admire the cohesion of the Roman army, just like those who continue to admire Roman discipline, have part of the answer. Yet cohesion, like discipline, is not an unchanging biological absolute, the same in all societies, but rather is grounded in a society's unique habits of sociability, its ways of forming links between men, in its culture. Both discipline and cohesion assume their proper role in Roman military success when they are understood in the context of a fundamental Roman cultural drive: competition in aggressive bravery arising from a heroic tradition of single combat. For as with the Greeks, the Roman past, real or imagined, combined with the admiration of later men for that past, is a powerful tool for explaining how the Romans fought and how the way the Romans fought changed over time.

VIII

EARLY ROMAN WARFARE

SINGLE COMBAT AND THE LEGION OF MANIPLES

VALERIUS THE RAVEN, 349 BC

The Romans told a curious story about how Marcus Valerius Corvus, "the Raven," got his nickname. A vast host of Gauls was camped in the Pomptine country to the south of Rome. The Gauls, Rome's most feared enemies, had sacked the city forty years earlier, vagrant armies of Gauls wandering over Italy brought frequent panics, and Gallic attacks had brought Rome's neighbors to the north, the haughty and refined Etruscans, to the verge of destruction. The Roman army marched against the Gauls, but the Roman war leaders, the consuls, were alarmed by the number and strength of the ancestral foe. In the Roman army there was a young officer, a military tribune, Marcus Valerius by name. According to the oldest surviving written account, in wonderful creaky archaic Latin,

> The chief of the Gauls, gigantic and tall in size, his weapons agleam with gold, coming on in great steps and shaking his spear in his hand, advanced glaring around with contempt and arrogance and scorning everything, and commanded anyone from the whole Roman army who dared to fight him, to come forth and fall to. The others were torn between fear and shame, but Valerius the tribune—having first asked the consuls for permission to fight the Gaul, so vainly vaunting—set forth bravely but quietly against him. They come together! They stop! They are fighting!

When, Lo! a divine power intervenes. Suddenly a raven — none had seen it — flies in and perches on the helmet of the tribune, and from there begins to assail the face and eyes of his adversary. It leapt at him, distracted him, mangled his hand with its claws, and blocked his view with its wings. When it had savaged him enough, it flew back to the helmet of the tribune. And so it was that the tribune, with both armies watching, relying on his own courage [*virtus*] and protected by the help of the bird, defeated and slew this most ferocious enemy leader, and for this reason took his nickname. This happened four hundred and five years after the founding of Rome.

A later version of the story adds that after this victory the Romans, elated by the triumph of their champion, swept the dejected Gauls from the field.[1]

In the next year the twenty-three-year-old Valerius Corvus was elected consul for the first time. That was the year of Philip of Macedon's sack of Olynthus (348 BC), the year when many Greeks first felt the cold wind blowing out of the north. By the time Valerius Corvus held his sixth and last consulship, forty-nine years later in 299, Philip had conquered Greece and been murdered, Philip's son Alexander had conquered the East and died at Babylon, and Alexander's generals had been fighting over their marshal's empire for more than twenty years.

In Italy as well, Marcus Valerius Corvus's career spanned momentous years: terrible wars with the Latins, the Samnites, the Etruscans, and the Gauls that laid the foundation for Rome's dominance over the peninsula. But whereas the history of Greece and the East in this era is spotlit, the age of Corvus in Italy is murky. Reliable accounts of Roman affairs begin with Rome's wars against Carthage, more than thirty years after Valerius's last consulship. For the nearly five centuries of Roman history before that, Roman writings, all from centuries later, preserve a rich mixture of truth and fable, with myth predominating in earlier times. The story of Valerius and the raven is a typical relic of those dim days, a legend passed down from the dreamtime.

The story of Valerius and the raven is not, alas, one we should believe. Not only is it implausible on its face, but it has all the traces of a tale invented to explain a puzzling fact. Later Romans knew that an early worthy of their nation bore the nickname "the Raven" and guessed at how it had come about; and so over time there evolved the tale of the raven assisting Valerius in battle. The story tells us nothing directly about events in the past. Its historical significance lies in the frame, a heroic duel, later Romans imposed upon it to explain the name Corvus. A boundless realm of guesses was open to the Roman storytellers who wondered about the nickname Corvus. Perhaps Corvus sported a raven sculpted on his helmet. Perhaps he had a long nose, or talked too much: the origin of most Roman nicknames lies in cruel mockery. Or perhaps, since the Romans examined the flight of birds, including ravens, as indications of the will of the gods, they might have deduced the appearance of an auspicious raven at a crucial moment in Valerius's career. The historian Livy seems to be edging in that direction in his account. But they chose instead to tell a story about a single combat between Marcus Valerius and a Gaul.[2]

For the Roman storyteller the choice was natural because this was a kind of tale he had told many times before. In the stories Romans told about their past, accounts of challenges and resulting duels are common. Perhaps the most famous is that of Titus Manlius Torquatus, a decade or so before the exploit of Corvus. Then also a gigantic Gaul — "naked, except for his shield, two swords, his torque [metal collar] and arm-rings" — had challenged the Romans to send forth a champion to face him. "No one dared because of his size and savage appearance. Then the Gaul began to laugh at them and stick out his tongue." Offended at the insult to his country, the young Titus Manlius answered the challenge, and when the Gaul came on singing, the Roman rammed the barbarian's shield with his own, driving him back and throwing him off balance, eventually getting under his guard and stabbing him in the chest and then the shoulder with his sword. "When he had overthrown him, he cut off his head, dragged off his torque, and put it, bloody as it was, around his own neck. For this act he and his posterity bore the nickname 'Torquatus,'" the Torqued One. The story of Corvus echoes that of Torquatus at many points — and may be no more than a shadow of this more famous tale.[3]

Later Romans believed that this practice of one-on-one dueling on the battlefield was sanctified by immemorial tradition. Romulus, they believed, the very founder of Rome, had been the first to dedicate to

Jupiter the *spolia opima,* the "noble spoils," a special honor for a Roman commander who had killed the opposing commander with his own hand. And the Romans told a story about olden times when they were ruled by kings, a story about a duel between two sets of triplets, the brothers Horatii and Curatii. Two of the Roman brothers were cut down, the tale went, but all three of their opponents were wounded, and the surviving Roman brother fled. This was a ruse to spread out his attackers, and the Roman killed them one by one as they pursued him. And so the town of Alba, whose sovereignty was the stake for which the champions fought, was made part of Rome. When Romans imagined the fighting of their distant ancestors, they imagined it had allowed for and demanded formal combats that arose from challenges. Later Romans, in short, imagined a heroic culture not too far distant from the military culture depicted in the *Iliad* but even more ceremonious and ritualized.[4]

In projecting heroic dueling back into their very earliest days, later Romans were doing nothing more than projecting back in time the military ethos by which they actually lived in the late third century BC. From the well-attested age of the Second Punic War come credible reports of single combats and of heroes who fought in many of them, including the Roman marshals Marcellus and Marcus Servilius, consul in 202 BC, who had killed twenty-three men in various duels. He had despoiled every one of those he slew of his armor, Livy has him boast. Like Homeric heroes, Romans of the Republic claimed the armor of their victims. The Romans hung such armor on their houses as "witnesses to their bravery." Under the Roman law such spoils could not be removed even if the house were sold, and in an emergency, when the Roman Senate needed to be replenished after a slaughter, those who displayed such spoils on their houses might be enrolled in that august body. There was a special term, *spolia provocatoria,* for spoils taken after a single combat that issued from a formal challenge. Polybius, our best witness to the way Romans fought in the Republic, described the seeking out of single combat as especially characteristic of the Roman way of war. He was looking into the past, but he was also describing his own generation in the second century BC, when Romans, Polybius's own protector Scipio Aemilianus among them, still regularly sought out single combat. Excelling in single combat might launch a young Roman aristocrat upon a meteoric political career.[5]

Seeking out single combat was hardly confined to the Romans: it was part of the Celtic warrior tradition as well and the Greek, revived by Alexander and part of his legacy. Perhaps the most eager Greek emulator of Alexander in this regard was King Pyrrhus of Epirus. But when he found himself fighting the Romans and their allies in Italy (281–272 BC), although he fought in battle with his own hands, he proved less eager for single combat than the natives. After an Italian cavalry captain who charged him was killed, Pyrrhus nervously gave his own conspicuous equipment, no doubt including his famous helmet with its enormous crest and goat horns, to a friend, who was attacked and killed in turn. Greece offers no tales of multiple duelists to approach the Romans, nor the sense that single combat was a common rite of passage for young men of the ruling class. Seeking out single combat was a more prominent characteristic of Roman military culture than of the Classical or Hellenistic Greeks.[6]

The force driving the quest for single combat was the yearning to demonstrate the human quality that Romans of the middle Republic most admired, *virtus,* or martial courage. As a wife sings in Plautus,

> I want my man to be cried as a victor in war: that's enough
>   for me.
> *Virtus* is the greatest prize,
> *virtus* comes before everything, that's for sure:
> liberty, safety, life, property and parents, homeland and
>   children it guards and keeps safe.
> *Virtus* has everything in it: who has *virtus* has everything
>   good.[7]

Compared to the display of *virtus,* "everything else is subordinate, and hides in dark night." *Virtus* was the root value of the Romans of the middle Republic — Romans wore iron rings to symbolize it — and like the martial excellence of the Greeks, *virtus* was par excellence a competitive quality:

> I'm the one, I do declare; it is just that I should enjoy them:
> my kinsman's arms should be adjudged to me,
> either because I am kin or a rival in *virtus.*[8]

It was the fiery ambition of Romans, especially young Roman aristocrats, to excel those around them in *virtus* that led them to seek out single combat. In the historian Livy's version of the Corvus story Valerius accepts the challenge out of a sense of rivalry with the older duelist hero Manlius Torquatus.[9]

There is a detail in the account of Valerius and the raven that the modern eye can easily pass over, but that no Roman would ever miss. Before Valerius went forth to fight the Gaul, the young hero scrupulously asked the permission of the consuls. To a Roman this detail resonates terribly with the stark story — Romans set it in the same generation as Corvus's fight — of a young man who fought in single combat against the orders of his commander. This was the son of the very Titus Manlius Torquatus who had claimed the Gaul's torque in the earlier duel. As Livy tells the tale, the son proudly presented his father the consul with the spoils of an enemy warrior he had slain, "in order that all report that I am sprung from your blood." But the consuls had forbidden the seeking of single combat: this was the Latin War, fought against an enemy alike in language and equipment, and the consuls feared the resulting possibilities for error. "You have destroyed military *disciplina,* by which up to now the Roman state has stood firm," replied his implacable father, "and you yourself, I think, if there is truly any of my blood in you, will not refuse to restore by your punishment the military *disciplina* which has collapsed on account of your crime. Go, lictor, bind him to the stake!" And so Manlius Torquatus ordered the torture and execution of his own son before his own eyes, not for cowardice, but for misplaced courage.[10]

The old stories of the Romans, then, are not just a Roman rumination on their aggressive, competitive military ethos, but also a way of worrying at the tension between that ethos and another fundamental Roman military value, *disciplina.* "Discipline," the flat English translation, fails to convey the full force of this Roman concept. For *disciplina* was not primarily a system of imposed or felt rules to make an unwarlike people place themselves in danger, to do something unnatural to them. In the old stories the Romans used to think about *disciplina,* tales like that of the son of Manlius Torquatus, it is conceived primarily as a brake to overly aggressive behavior. The tradition as it came down to the first century BC could be summed up thus: "In war, fighting against the enemy without orders, or retiring too slowly when recalled from the fight, was more often punished than fleeing the standards or abandoning one's position when pressed." Roman *disciplina* was understood to be more a curb than a spur, and it formed an opposed pair with Roman *virtus*.[11]

Details of early Roman legends are a dangerous sand upon which to build an enduring historical castle. But conceived as the dreams of men who, early and later, passed them down, elaborated them, and often invented them they reveal the concerns of those who dreamt them. The story of Corvus and related tales suggest a military culture at war with itself. The Romans had two contradictory sets of imperatives, both the heroic ethos of the single combatant and the stern code of *disciplina*. This latter did not just coexist with the ethos of single combat but was exactly set against it. The discovery of such a contradiction makes one wonder as to its origins and practical results. For that, it is necessary to pass from the realm of legend to the way the Romans arrayed themselves for battle.

THE LEGION OF MANIPLES, THIRD AND SECOND CENTURIES BC

The first detailed description of the way the Romans fought their battles comes from the mid–second century BC, when the Greek historian Polybius described the Roman army of his day. We call this array the manipular legion, the legion — literally, "levy" — made up of maniples or "handfuls" of Roman warriors. It was while fighting in the manipular legion that the Romans went from being a minor power in Italy to being the masters of the Mediterranean basin; it was while fighting in the manipular legion that the tricks of Carthage were confounded and the phalanx of Macedon overthrown.

In Polybius's day the manipular legion consisted of forty-two hundred men deployed into four echelons (see figure). At the front were twelve hundred *velites*, "fast men," armed very similarly to Greek peltasts with a small shield, javelins, a sword, and a helmet. Behind them stood the line of the *hastati*, the "spearmen," also twelve hundred strong, organized into ten maniples of one hundred and twenty men each. They were armed with a large oval shield, the *scutum*, helmet, greaves, breastplate, sword, and two *pila*, heavy throwing javelins. Behind them came twelve hundred

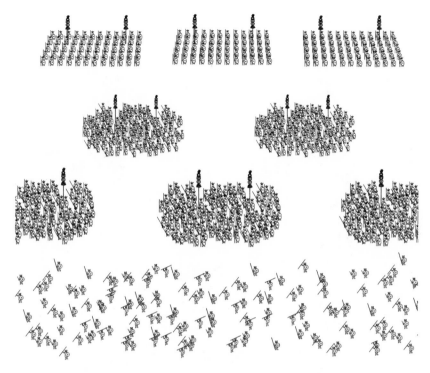

The manipular legion. *Velites* (front), maniples of *hastati* followed by maniples of *principes* (middle), and maniples of *triarii* (rear) (SeungJung Kim).

principes, "first men," armed like the *hastati*, also in ten maniples. Behind them in turn came six hundred *triarii*, "third men," in ten half-strength maniples of sixty men each. They were armed like the *hastati* and the *principes*, except that they carried a longer thrusting spear, the *hasta*, rather than the *pilum* (see figure).[12]

The *velites* seem to have fought individually as an irregular swarm, without officers or standards of their own, although they might be dispatched en masse or in groups on special missions, often with the cavalry. They also might be set to throw javelins in volleys to disrupt and discourage the enemy, like light-armed skirmishers in a Hellenistic army, although unlike Greek skirmishers they were eager to fight hand to hand as well. The maniples of the *hastati*, *principes*, and *triarii* were cohesive bodies of men, but the *hastati* and *principes* at least fought as individuals, maneuvering with sword and shield against the foe. Before it came to sword point,

Soldiers of the manipular legion: *hastatus* or *princeps* (left), *triarius* (center), and *veles* (right) (SeungJung Kim after R. Hook).

at least some of the *hastati* and *principes* threw their javelins, but the throwing of javelins seems to have continued all through a Roman infantry fight.[13]

The maniples of *hastati, principes,* and *triarii* appear to have formed on the battlefield with gaps between them, the maniple of the echelon behind covering the gap between the maniples of the echelon before. Groups of maniples were thus disposed like the spots on the five of a die. The *velites* withdrew into the gaps between the maniples behind them, ebbing when they were pressed, then flowing forward. The engagements of the *velites* could be long. After this opening act, when the *velites* had withdrawn for good, the *hastati* engaged the enemy. Livy describes a procedure by which the *hastati*, when pressed, fell back between the maniples of the *principes*. Similarly, the combined *principes* and *hastati* could fall back between the maniples of the *triarii,* who then "close the lanes, as it were," and so compressed, the legion fell upon the enemy one last time. When the *triarii* finally came into action the Roman legion could aptly be described as a phalanx.[14]

The brevity of the surviving descriptions of the manipular legion presents notorious and ultimately insurmountable obstacles to understanding exactly how the legion operated in action. Did the *hastati* fight with maniple-sized holes between their maniples? If so, soldiers in each maniple presented their "open," shieldless side to the enemy, which later Roman soldiers were alarmed to do. If not, how did the maniples expand to occupy the whole frontage and then shrink again to withdraw into the gaps between the maniples of the *principes?* How did the combined *hastati* and *principes* fall back on the *triarii* without collision, without a "passage of lines," the infiltration of a formed group of men through another formed group, a notoriously difficult evolution to perform without confusion? Were these maneuvers undertaken by the two centuries, each of sixty men in the *principes* and *hastati* and of thirty in the *triarii,* of which a maniple was made up, but of which Polybius seems only dimly aware? Some of these problems might be solved if the physical shape and size of a maniple deployed on the field were known. But we also do not know how much space a Roman soldier normally occupied in the maniple or the shape of a maniple in action or even whether it was a drilled, rectangular formation or a shapeless mob gathered around a standard or standards. Men have been puzzling over these questions since commanders yearned to re-create Roman formations with musket and pike. Controversy over some of these conundrums was old by Shakespeare's day.[15]

Yet the manipular legion presents more interesting and deeper puzzles, puzzles from which these intractable mechanical questions are a distraction. What *is* the manipular legion? That is, to what conceptual category does it belong? Is the manipular legion tactical doctrine, a set of self-conscious standing operating procedures arrived at on the basis of experience and intellection? Or did the Romans fight in this way for other reasons? Why was it adopted? Why, in a world where even keeping a reserve, a second line, was hardly usual, did the Romans fight in so deep an array, depriving themselves of the services of so many of their soldiers and making their army vulnerable to being outflanked? Why, in a world where everybody else seems to have understood the first rule of command in war — Keep It Simple — did the Romans fight in so complicated an array, an array with so many moving parts, and so requiring hazardous evolutions in the face of the enemy? Why did they fight in an array premised on successive, calm withdrawals under enemy pressure? This was "a motion peculiar to Roman fighting," as Polybius described it, and peculiar for good reasons. For such withdrawals might encourage the enemy and discourage those withdrawing, a phenomenon warned against in a Greek tactical handbook. In ancient battles any movement backward was apt to become a rout, and the fleeing soldiers were apt to infect those behind them with their fear. The fundamental issue, in short, is not the details of how the manipular legion worked, but what the manipular legion was and why the Romans employed it upon the battlefield in the first place.[16]

The Romans believed their predilection for single combat went back to their earliest days. But the first reliable indications have the Romans fighting in the phalanx. A set of early Roman census classes survives, which is likely to bear a relationship to historical reality. The men of the first class, that is, those with the most property, were armored with helmet, greaves, breastplate, and a round shield, the *clipeus*. They were armed with a spear, the *hasta,* and a sword. They were clearly hoplites. Tradition associates this census with King Servius Tullius (trad. 578–535 BC). By that time hoplite equipment was present in Italy not only in the Greek settlements to the south, but to the north of Rome, in Etruria. Indeed, an ancient tradition (much later and not worth a great deal) insists that the Romans learned the phalanx from the Etruscans and learned it so well that they defeated the Etruscans with it. In any event it appears that by the mid–sixth century BC at the latest, the Romans, a folk just beyond the edge of the Greek world, had adopted the contemporary Greek method of fighting in the phalanx. The phalanx they adopted was not the close-arrayed mature fifth- and fourth-century phalanx of Thucydides and Xenophon from which missile-armed troops had been excluded. At this date it was necessarily the looser archaic phalanx of Greek vase painting, in which missile-armed troops still jostled with the hoplites; such weapons are stipulated for the lower census classes in the Servian list.[17]

The manipular legion betrays its origin in the phalanx. The last echelon, the *triarii,* continued to be armed with the hoplite thrusting spear, the *hasta,* even in Polybius's day. A fragment describing Rome's war against Pyrrhus has the *principes,* the next echelon forward, still using a thrusting spear in the 270s. The name of the first formed echelon, *hastati,* may suggest they too were once armed with the hoplite spear. If the formation were compressed all the way back by the enemy—if it had "come to the *triarii*" in the Latin proverb for a critical situation—the legion finally fought like a phalanx in *pyknosis,* in close order. The transformation of the old phalanx into the manipular legion consisted of collapsing the phalanx out front into successively more open order, as though rocks had fallen from a solid cliff face to form a tumbled scree before it.[18]

According to one much later ancient tradition, the Romans abandoned the phalanx for manipular tactics during their war with the Etruscan city of Veii, after 406 BC, when they started paying their army. According to another version, of no more merit, they invented the equipment characteristic of the manipular legion to fight the Gauls, perhaps in 367 BC. A third legend holds they adopted it from the Samnites during their long wars against them in the late fourth or early third century BC. The ancients, in short, did not know. But whenever it happened, modern students agree that "the reason for the new formation was a tactical one." The phalanx, the story goes, proved defective against Roman enemies who fought in open order or on rough terrain, so the Romans invented or borrowed a more spread-out, flexible formation. Thus the manipular legion appears as an intellectual adaption of doctrine to changing military circumstances, although neither ancients nor moderns can agree on what the circumstances were or when they came into play.[19]

More helpful, perhaps, is to reason backward from a day about which there is reliable ancient testimony. Begin by considering the way Polybius describes soldiers being assigned to the legions, a picture he paints at length, perhaps because as a Greek he found Roman methods so odd. Once the military tribunes, the officers, had been elected and assigned to their legions, the thirty-five tribes of Roman citizens were called forward in an order decided by lot. From a tribal contingent groups of four men, chosen as reasonably alike in age and body, came forward one after another for inspection by the tribunes. The tribunes of the first legion chose one man, then the tribunes of the second, then the third; the fourth was left with the last. When the next four men came forward, the second legion got first choice and the first legion was left with the last. And so it went around until the legions had their full complement of men. This guaranteed, as Polybius says, that each legion got men of the same caliber.[20] Yet this system was not only laborious and time-consuming, but also ensured that each soldier would serve among strangers. This method of selection cut across all previous bonds of attachment, splitting fellow tribesmen, fellow villagers, fellow tenants, clients of the same patron, even comrades in arms who had served together in the previous year. Contrast Macaulay's description of the Highland clans forming themselves into regiments for war:

> As the individual Celt was easily turned into a soldier, so a tribe of Celts was easily turned into a battalion of soldiers. All that was necessary was that the military organization should be conformed to the patriarchal organization. The chief must be colonel : his uncle or his brother must be major : the tacksmen, who formed what may be called the peerage of the little community, must be the captains : the company of each captain must consist of those peasants who lived on his land, and whose names, faces, connections, and characters were perfectly known to him. . . . In such a regiment was found from the first moment that exact order and prompt obedience in which the strength of regular armies consists. Every man, from the highest to the lowest, was in his proper place, and knew that place perfectly. It was not necessary to impress by threats or by punishment on the newly enlisted troops the duty of regarding as their head him whom they had regarded as their head ever since they could remember anything. Every private had, from infancy, respected his corporal much and his captain more, and had almost adored his colonel. There was, therefore, no danger of mutiny. There was as little danger of desertion. Indeed, the very feelings which most powerfully impel other soldiers to desert kept the Highlander to his standard. If he left it, whither was he to go? All his kinsmen, all his friends, were arrayed round it.[21]

Modern armies endorse Macaulay's judgment, carefully preserving and encouraging horizontal links between soldiers, for example, by raising regionally based regiments and by keeping units together over time so that bonds of mutual loyalty and affection can grow up. And so did the Greeks, for Classical Greek armies took care to reproduce the micro-communities of their *polis* in the army. An Athenian, for example, could always fight alongside his fellow villagers, his demesmen, because at Athens the tribes, constituted of demes, formed the military units. Nothing prevented the Romans from doing the same, but they did not. All the cohesion born of previous civilian connection and previous military service the Romans cast away in selecting men for legions. This Roman system of selection, which so curiously prefigures the way athletes are drafted onto American professional sports teams and the way children are divided up for schoolyard games, suggests that the Romans of the middle Republic conceived that a soldier's qualities as an individual were far more important to his military potential than his membership in a cohesive preexisting group.[22]

This vision of the Roman soldier fits well with the competitive pursuit of *virtus* which the highborn youths of the Republic, youths like Valerius Corvus, manifested in their quest for single combat. The Roman soldier did not primarily think of himself as part of a team, and he was not treated as such by his officers. Rather, he regarded his comrades as his competitors in aggressive bravery. This was also how a Roman of the first century imagined the early fighting of his countrymen: "Their greatest contest for glory was with each other: each hastened to be the first to strike down a foe, to climb a wall, to be witnessed while doing such a deed." In this army a commander might have to ride up and down in front of an advancing legion beating eager soldiers back into their lines with the shaft of his spear. If this aggressiveness characterized the generations when the manipular legion was evolving (and certainly the Romans thought it did) the manipular legion appears not as a rational adaptation to changing military circumstances, but as the direction in which the competitive ethos of the Roman soldier drove the Roman phalanx.[23]

Whether the Roman phalanx or the Roman culture of single combat was older it is impossible to say. Single combat seems the more primitive, and to make it senior appeals to a modern sense of the natural order of things. Certainly the Roman army of the Republic had its primitive qualities, including the totem beasts that adorned the Roman standards, the wolfskins that some Roman warriors wore upon their heads, and the fact that early Roman cavalrymen went into battle with their torsos bare like Germanic berserkers. To imagine that single combat was a survival from a primeval, tribal past appeals because it offers, as Frazer put it, "the flavour and freshness of the olden time, some breath of the springtime of the world." Yet single combat and its ethic could also have been learned later, especially from the Gauls, whom the Romans began to fight in the early fourth century BC and who are the challengers in the most famous Roman single-combat stories. In that case the stories of Corvus and Torquatus, the stories of Gauls taunting the Romans until young Romans came forth to fight one-on-one can be taken as Roman reflections upon a wider Roman cultural change.[24]

Yet whatever the order of their coming, the phalanx and the ethos of single combat were in conflict. Even the archaic phalanx had no great place for offensive prowess or heroic dueling, for aggressive *virtus* as the Romans understood it. To employ the phalanx in the face of this culture therefore required severity from above and self-discipline below, that is, *disciplina,* set in opposition to the individual ambitions of the warriors. And in fact there is a Roman story set in the mid–fifth century BC, in the age of the Roman phalanx, about another exemplar of *disciplina,* the dictator Postumius Tubertus, who executed his son for advancing beyond the lines without permission. It is from this dimly seen conflict between the phalanx and the culture of single combat that the singular Roman code of *disciplina* may derive and the odd sense, which the Romans worried at in their old stories, that for young men to disobey and fight against orders was justly punishable but at the same time right and natural.[25]

But *disciplina* alone did not settle the conflict. Rather, the manipular legion in particular should be understood as the result of this conflict between methods and ideals playing out over generations of Roman warfare. That is why Roman soldiers were assigned to their echelons in the manipular legion on the basis of age. The *velites,* in the first line, were the youngest soldiers, the *hastati* the next youngest, the *principes* the next, and the oldest the *triarii*. This system of age classes is especially striking because it seems to have been superimposed on an older system based on wealth, traces of which survived in it. The *velites* combined the youngest and the poorest soldiers, the latter those who could not afford the equipment needed to serve in the other echelons as they got older, and soldiers in the *hastati, principes,* and *triarii* belonging to the first Servian class wore a full coat of mail rather than the small metal chest protector that their less affluent comrades wore.[26]

No ancient author gives an explicit rationale for the division into echelons by age. Modern students tend to interpret it as an issue of physical suitability, and they can find parallels from antiquity. But Polybius hints at another justification: the young *velites* often covered their heads with a wolfskin or some other distinguishing mark so that their superiors could identify individuals and see how bravely they were fighting. This detail is to be connected to Polybius's description of the criteria by which Roman decorations were handed out: "To the soldier who has wounded an enemy, a spear is given; to the soldier who has struck down and despoiled an enemy, a cup is given if he is an infantryman, and horse ornaments if a cavalryman. . . . These are not given to a soldier if in the formed array or in the storming of a city he should wound or despoil one of the enemy, but to those who in the skirmishing or in similar circumstances in which there is no need to engage in single combat, have voluntarily and by choice placed themselves in danger."[27] It is not the soldiers of the echelons behind, those who fought in the formed array, but the young *velites* who skirmished individually in the front who were rewarded especially for engaging in single combat, for defeating and stripping their foes in the heroic way. Not all would, of course, for in a swarm there "is no necessity to engage in single combat." There were no officers or centurions among the *velites* to compel them, no standards to urge them: the *velites* fought in a realm of artificial equality and self-motivation. But the lack of compulsion allowed them to make the heroic choice to seek out single combat, decorations lured them, and their headgear allowed them to be recognized when they did so. The manipular legion was arranged so that the *velites* could fight as individual duelists before the pitched battle in accord with the ideals of *virtus*. And when there was no pitched battle, the *velites* might skirmish with enemy light troops between the camps or when sent on independent missions. Periods of skirmishing between fortified camps, combined with foraging and bushwhacking of enemy foragers, could be extended, lasting days, months, and in one case three years. Roman commanders were expected to allow challenges during such standoffs, which accounts for the stress placed in the tradition on the rare occasions when they forbade them.[28]

Decorations were also given to cavalrymen who distinguished themselves in skirmishing. It is cavalrymen who fight many of the reported single combats, often on horseback. Nearly all reported single combatants, whether they fought on foot or horseback, were members of the aristocracy and so cavalrymen. This is natural given the concentration of the sources on the deeds of the grand. But evidently even among the cavalry there was an old prejudice in favor of fighting single combat on foot. For the aristocratic cavalry of the mid-Republic often dismounted to fight on foot, to duel man to man, indeed, might even fight on foot among the *velites,* confirming that even in the eyes of the aristocrats the fighting of the *velites* was marked as special.[29]

A frequent theme in Roman legend is the aggressiveness of young men in war. Heroic duelists like Corvus, Torquatus, and Torquatus's son were usually young. Youth, in the Roman tradition, is *ferox,* ferocious, and embodies *furor,* savage passion. This became a tired literary topos, but there is significance behind it. In a society in which fighting is competitive, young men will in fact be more aggressive in war because of the way the competition is structured. The race for distinction does not begin anew each year: older soldiers carry over the reputation for great deeds performed in years past, and plunder and decorations keep those deeds in the public eye. At Rome age gave a warrior a long head start. Imagine the despairing thoughts of the son of Marcus Servilius, growing up in a house creaking with twenty-three sets of enemy armor. And so the young were more aggressive so as to equal or surpass their elders, each son striving, in the words of the Roman playwright, to be "equal in *virtus* to your father." In the tradition of the son of Manlius Torquatus, sons even strove to duplicate their fathers' deeds. "We were heroes once, and young," sings the chorus of old warriors at Sparta (the principle applies across cultures). The young warriors respond, "So we are now: look, if you would, and see." And then the chorus of boys pipes up: "But we'll be better by far."[30]

The different need for opportunities to gain distinction manifested itself institutionally in the age echelons of the manipular legion. In the old phalanx days the Romans had simply divided the army between young and old, *iuniores* and *seniores,* and left the *seniores* at home to guard the city. In the manipular array the older men, "veterans of known valor," Livy calls them, weighed down with honors and victories already, were posted at the back. Having proved themselves of old, they fought most rarely and in the phalanx, the least heroic mode. As one moved forward in the array, younger soldiers were offered more opportunity to fight because they were closer to the enemy, and their method of fighting became looser and freer — from phalanx to formed array to catch-as-catch-can — and the chance for individual distinction was accordingly greater as the opportunities for individual dueling and despoiling increased. However the maniples of *hastati* and *principes* were formed, there were evidently plenty of opportunities for individual distinction. Livy preserves an old oath that Roman soldiers swore to the other men of their century, that they "would not withdraw from fear or flight or leave the *ordo* except to seize or seek a weapon or smite a foe or save a fellow citizen." However *ordo* is to be translated — rank? formation? company? — evidently the Roman soldier expected to go beyond it to attack the enemy.[31]

What, other than their aching bones and mellowed glory, reconciled the older men to their role in the phalanx at the back? Why did the older men and commanders allow the young men to fight in front? Sons' desire is hardly answer enough in a society which placed such terrible power in the hands of fathers; young soldiers' desire is hardly an answer in an army which placed such cruel power in the hands of commanders. But a fragment of the Twelve Tables, Rome's earliest written law, indicates that a father could wear the crown won by his son for bravery in battle. This accords, of course, with the Roman legal principle that whatever a son under *patria potestas* may gain is his father's property. But the situation would never arise unless the father was thought to participate in the glory of his son. Old men as well as young were eager for young warriors to fight in the heroic style.[32]

The manipular legion was a solution to the problem of how to reconcile a competitive culture of individual dueling with the unaggressive mass fighting of the phalanx. It was the archaic, mixed phalanx that the

Romans learned from their neighbors, one in which missile-armed troops mingled with hoplites. In Greece this evolved under peculiar Greek cultural pressures into the mature phalanx, from which missile-users were excluded, but in Rome the aggressive cult of *virtus* exerted a quite different cultural pressure, not expelling missiles but finally dissolving the phalanx toward the front into the manipular legion. The ideal of *virtus* required the youngest men to sally forth in front of the phalanx, to gratify their yearning for individual distinction. The power of the same ideal compelled their elders to allow them to go, to satisfy what they too considered a legitimate ambition, and to gain glory through them. By this logic the manipular legion was not an abstract tactical system developed by a mythical Roman general staff. It was not a phalanx rationally adapted to rough terrain or to enemies who fought with irregular tactics, although perhaps it proved useful in such cases. The manipular legion was the fruit of compromise resulting from the meeting of an imported method of fighting, the phalanx, with a people whose martial values, whether inherited or new-acquired, made fighting in the phalanx a heroic challenge for them.

The manipular legion was a successful way of fighting. Polybius attributes its advantage over the Macedonian phalanx to its adaptability and its advantages on rough terrain. But Polybius also notes that the manipular array had defeated all Roman enemies in the West as well, few of whom used the phalanx. And the formal advantages of the manipular array to which Polybius points were not as obvious to everybody: most Greeks, in Polybius's telling, still thought the phalanx superior, even after Roman victories. It has been argued that some Macedonian-style eastern armies began to convert to Roman methods of fighting, but not before the 160s BC, a full century after the Greeks became aware of Roman methods through Pyrrhus's fighting the Romans in Italy. Hannibal, in Italy, did change over to Roman equipment, but his example was not soon followed, even though Greeks at least were quite willing to try other nations' methods of fighting in the third and second centuries BC. If the advantages of Roman armament and the manipular array as a formation were as obvious to the rest of the world as they were to Polybius, one might have expected enemies both west and east to adopt them.[33]

That Rome's defeated enemies were slow to borrow Rome's way of fighting argues that the advantages of the manipular system were more subtle than Polybius indicates. The manipular legion was a way of fighting deeply rooted in Roman martial culture, a way of fighting that worked well—for Romans. By allowing Roman soldiers to fight according to the ideals of their society the manipular array encouraged the individual Roman soldier to fight with a feral courage. The true secret of the manipular legion—the true advantage it gave to the Romans—was that it made the soldiers in it braver. Viewed simply as a formation, the manipular array, with its narrow frontage, its multitude of moving parts, its evolutions in the face of the enemy, and its dangerous backing-up-inchworm motion, might have placed the Romans at a disadvantage relative to many of their enemies. But this disadvantage was overcome by the advantage the Romans gained from fighting in a style that brought out the very best in them as warriors.

THE ROMANS AND THEIR PAST

Lacking an *Iliad* and *Odyssey,* the Romans' relationship with their past differed from that of the Greeks. Rather than a set of ancient stories from which they derived ethics and ways of doing things, the Roman past was a set of admired ethics around which they later wove illustrative stories, and a set of ways of doing things to which they were strongly attached. Romans of the Republic were no less past-minded than the Greeks, and in some ways far more, but they tended more toward conservatism, preserving the past, than re-creation of it. So the Romans for centuries began their public auctions with the cry that they were selling the property of Lars Porsena of Clusium, against whom they believed they had fought a war in the late sixth century BC. So Roman officials continued to levy fines in animals centuries after the fines were paid in good silver money. And the Romans could hardly understand some of the prayers they offered to their gods, having preserved their archaic Latin formulae long after linguistic change had made old Latin a foreign language.[34]

Lacking epic, the Romans of the Republic did not contrive ingeniously to re-create epic methods of fighting. But change in Roman military methods was always resisted, and everything possible held on to: that is the story of the coming of the manipular legion, which preserved in it so much of the old phalanx. And that too would be the story of the Roman army for centuries to come. The early Roman phalanx was organized by centuries, each commanded by a centurion. There were also military tribunes, six per legion. And, astonishingly, this venerable command structure was preserved and added to as little as possible for at least five hundred years, even as the tactics of the Romans changed and changed again and even though it bore no relationship to the tactical needs of the evolving legion. The centuries and centurions came to bear the names of their positions in the manipular legion — *hastati, principes,* and *pili* (another term for *triarii*) — and they kept those names into the third century AD even though the maniples to which they alluded had long lost their military function.[35]

Conservatism is not the whole story of the Roman relationship with their past. In time the Romans would develop a past enshrined in texts, the history of their own conquests. And they would borrow Greek history too. Under the empire, history became the epic of the Romans, and like the Greeks before them they began to experiment with ways of bringing that epic back to life. But in the shorter term, under the Republic, Roman conservatism was mighty. The inherited ethics that dominated Roman warfare were the opposed ones of *virtus* and *disciplina*. The Romans struggled to keep both, and those principles struggled against each other down the bloody years. Much of the history of the Roman army of the Republic is the history of that struggle.

IX

THE WRATH OF PYDNA

COMMAND, DISCIPLINE, AND
COURAGE IN THE ROMAN REPUBLIC

T he Romans knew that a war against Macedon would be great and terrible. The consul who led the Roman army over to Greece in 171 BC was authorized to enroll especially large legions and forces of Italian allies, to draft tough veterans and centurions past the legal age limit, and to handpick his officers, the tribunes of the soldiers. So many grizzled senior centurions were called up that there were not posts for all, and some were ordered to serve in lesser capacities. A political furor erupted, with the tribunes of the plebs taking the side of the aggrieved centurions. But eventually the centurions waived their privileges in the interests of the Republic. Such was the magnitude of the war and such the anxiety of the city that an unusual number of Romans of all classes escorted the consul on his way when he set off for the Adriatic.[1]

The war was to be fought against Perseus, the king of Macedonia, and the tough Macedonians arrayed in their formidable phalanx. It was the young king's father, Philip V, who had first set Rome and Macedon into collision of strife. He had grasped a shining opportunity in 215 BC, allying the storied kingdom handed down to him from Philip II and Alexander to Rome's enemy Carthage. These were the darkest days of Rome's Second Punic War (218–201), when Carthage's general Hannibal was rampant in Italy, and the power of Rome seemed shattered at Cannae (216). How prudent, then, how admirable, to join with the new power rising in the West, and what a moment as well to seize Illyria, the coast where northern Greece looks over to Italy, when Rome, its master, could not protect it. But in the resulting and fitful First Macedonian War (215–205), Rome achieved with ships and the blood of Greek allies her limited goal: to keep Philip distracted in Greece while Rome defeated Carthage. But when Carthage surrendered in 201, the Romans called to mind the king who had joined their enemy when Rome was at her nadir. Defeating Philip at Cynoscephalae in 197 in the Second Macedonian War (200–196), the Romans stripped Macedonia of the lordship of southern Greece that Philip II had won more than a century before. Surviving after defeat by Rome required a lowly humility, as Carthage too was to discover, for the Romans were acutely sensitive to signs of a reviving spirit, which they construed as arrogance and aggression. Philip's son Perseus proved insufficiently abject, and the Romans resolved that Macedon must be destroyed.

In addition to the special care they took in levying their own troops for Macedonia, the Romans summoned foreign auxiliaries to the war: savage Ligurians from the north of Italy, Numidian light cavalry and ponderous elephants from North Africa, and archers from Crete. These last were light infantry much sought after by Hellenistic Greek commanders, and the Roman decision to seek out such troops suggests the increasing influence of Greek military ways upon the Romans. While the Romans were making their long preparations, Perseus — ready for war in the winter — was prevented from advancing to seize strong places by the lies of Roman envoys who held out to him false hopes of peace. Returning to Rome, they boasted of their guile to an approving Senate, but found themselves, so the story goes, reproached by the older senators for their "new and too-clever wisdom": "Our ancestors did not wage war by ambush or night battle, nor by pretended flight and surprise return catch the enemy off his guard, so that they could glory in craftiness rather than real *virtus*."[2] Whatever the value of this tale, it does suggest that the Romans saw *virtus* and cunning tactics in battle as in some way opposed to one another, an opposition that must be grasped to understand the way Romans fought wars in the middle Republic. For this opposition made the underlying and contrasting ethics of *virtus* and *disciplina* push very hard against one another and contributed, as we shall see, to the angry and critical quality of Roman military life — and to Roman success in war.

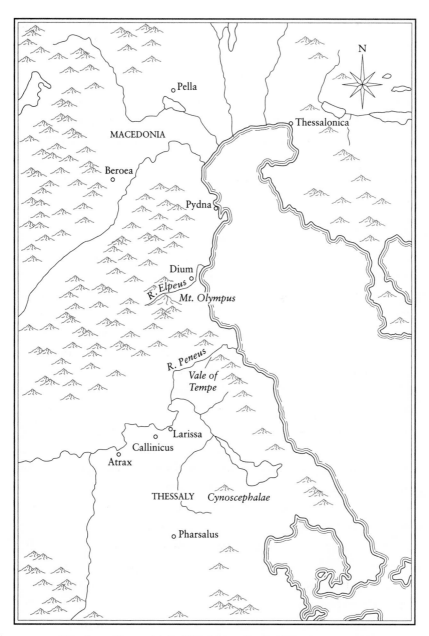

Northern Greece in the Third Macedonian War (171–167 BC)

Perseus descended, plundering, into Thessaly, and the Roman consul rushed to meet him. The king won a cavalry and light-infantry battle at Callinicus but declined to commit his phalanx to seek a decisive victory in the vain hope peace could still be negotiated. The Romans withdrew behind the Peneus river and turned to reaping the grain round about. Perseus followed and harassed them, but after losing a skirmish over forage, he fell back into Macedonia. After an abortive attempt to force the Vale of Tempe, a passage from Thessaly into Macedonia, the Romans went into winter quarters. And so the first year of the Third Macedonian War ended in stalemate.[3]

The Romans were not more fortunate in the second year, 170 BC. The new consul tried twice to break through from Thessaly into Macedonia. The first attempt was defeated, and in the second Perseus offered battle and the Romans withdrew. The Romans consumed much energy this year in investigating accusations against their commanders: a rash attack had been made on a fortified town, leaves had been granted to a large number of soldiers in hopes of winning their political support, and allies in Greece had been plundered. The Cretans were upbraided in the Senate for the fact that more of their soldiers were serving with Perseus than with the Romans. They must have been mystified by the complaint: Cretans served anyone who paid them and often fought on both sides. Although eager to use Greek light troops, the Romans were not yet comfortable with the easy loyalties of Greek mercenaries. Perseus took advantage of the Roman muddle to campaign successfully against the Dardanians, enemies on the opposite border of his embattled kingdom.[4]

In the third year of the war a new consul crossed over to Greece with generous reinforcements for the Roman army. His plan was to strike at once from Thessaly into Macedonia. Perseus occupied all the passes, but the Romans forced their way through. Tidings were brought to Perseus in his bath: he leapt up crying out that he had been defeated without a battle. Panicked, he withdrew the outposts on his borders and ordered the Macedonian royal treasure to be cast into the sea. In the confusion the Romans got as far north as Dium but had to retire south again for want of supplies. The consul's Roman critics were divided on whether cowardice or stupidity had prompted his retreat, for the Romans were not slow to judge their generals. Perseus regained his composure and re-occupied Dium, establishing his line of defense upon the Elpeus river. Divers brought up most of the chagrined king's briny riches. Subsequently the Romans raided the coast of Macedonia by sea and attacked remaining Macedonian garrisons south of the river. They gathered supplies for winter but made no further advance into Macedonia that year.[5]

It fell to Lucius Aemilius Paullus, consul of 168 BC, to bring Perseus finally to a decisive battle. Around sixty years of age, Paullus was a harsh old veteran. As praetor in 191, Paullus had been victorious in Spain. As consul for the first time in 182, he had defeated the Ligurians. When selected for the Macedonian command, Paullus pointedly refused to thank the Roman people for electing him, scorning the immemorial custom of the Romans. He was doing them a favor by undertaking to finish the war against Perseus, he said, rather than receiving a favor from them. Then he warned them brusquely against second-guessing him, gossiping about the war, forming ill-informed opinions, and offering useless advice.[6]

Paullus's curmudgeonly outburst was a reaction not merely to the widespread criticism, mostly justified, of his predecessors in the war against Perseus, but also to the wider Roman habit of testing a commander's performance in war in the fires of Roman public opinion and politics. In 187 BC, L. Furius Purpurio and Paullus himself had opposed the grant of a triumph to C. Manlius for his campaign in Asia Minor, not excluding — if the details of the speech Livy gives them have any basis in reality — criticism of his tactical arrangements. Nine years before Pydna there had been a scandal when a victorious proconsul had returned to Rome and demanded a triumph, but a tribune had threatened to veto the proposal, not because the triumph was undeserved, but because the current consul campaigning in Greece, an old enemy of the proconsul, wanted to speak against it when he returned home. The Romans were a martial people led by a warrior aristocracy: there was no large body of civilians at Rome who conceded that they had no right to an opinion about the making of war. Talk about war, often ignorant talk, given the distances and poor communications, and criticism of commanders were constant, and war and public opinion and politics were inextricably bound up with each other.[7]

Once again the Romans made arrangements appropriate to the gravity of the war. Only experienced men were elected or appointed military tribunes in that year, and Aemilius Paullus was invited to select the best of them for his legions. The legions themselves were reinforced to exceptional strength, and a large draft of men dispatched to Greece. Once again an unusually large crowd of Romans escorted the consul on his way out of Rome.[8]

When he arrived at the Roman camp in Macedonia, Aemilius Paullus discovered that the Roman army was tormented by lack of water. He used his knowledge of geology to dig wells in well-judged places and relieved the crisis. He reconnoitered, and he also made minor changes to Roman military procedure — to the way orders were passed among officers and to the way sentries were posted. But the soldiers complained and offered impractical suggestions. Aemilius was obliged to summon the army and rebuke it, as he had the Roman people before, telling his soldiers to mind their own business — their weapons, their bodies, their rations — and leave the generalling to him. In exchange he would do his duty and, in Livy's words, "provide them with an opportunity for a successful action."[9]

The river Elpeus rises in a gorge of Mount Olympus. Swollen by rain in the winter, its banks were sheer, and its bed in the summer, when it was dry, was wide and deep, a maze of pits and strewn boulders. Perseus had fortified the far bank of the river and placed catapults. Paullus despaired of crossing the river against such obstacles natural and man-made. What was to be done? At the Roman council of war some officers urged a concerted attack on the Macedonians behind the river, while others suggested the Roman fleet be sent ranging up the coast toward Thessalonica to draw the Macedonians off their line. Instead, Paullus merely feinted right, pretending to embark a force to outflank Perseus by sea, and then sent a flanking force far to the left, around Mount Olympus, to get behind the river. To cover this move Paullus had the Roman *velites* skirmish for two days in the wide riverbed against Perseus's light infantry. In the exchanges of missiles the Macedonians had the better of it, not least because they were assisted by missiles cast from the Macedonian fortifications. But when it came to hand-to-hand fighting the Romans proved superior, protected by their larger shields and aided, one suspects, by the Roman *velites*' habit of fighting hand-to-hand, a habit Greek light infantry did not share. On the third day Paullus distracted Perseus by pretending that he was going to make a full-scale attack on the Macedonian lines.[10]

Despite all Paullus's precautions a Cretan in Roman service deserted to Perseus and reported the Roman flank march. The king sent a column of his own to block the Romans, but the Romans overcame it: the Roman commander of the expedition, Scipio Nasica, boasted that he had killed a Thracian mercenary in single combat. His position forced, Perseus retreated upon the Macedonian city of Pydna. Paullus crossed the river and followed, and the king offered him battle in the plain before the city. The Roman army had marched far that day, and it was blazing hot. But the men and the officers wanted to fight, so Paullus had to trick them to prevent a battle against his orders. The consul drew up the legions for battle and rode the lines encouraging the troops just as a Roman general did before giving the signal to engage. As time passed, the sun melted the ardor for fighting out of the Romans, and eventually Paullus was able to give the order to make camp. But the instant it was clear Paullus was not going to fight that day, his officers swarmed in to remonstrate. After three years of frustration he must not let Perseus escape! The consul was unmoved. His withdrawal of his tired army from battle order into camp — from the back, the *triarii*, then the *principes*, then the *hastati*, in case Perseus made a move — was a masterpiece of tactics.[11]

That evening in camp Aemilius Paullus gave permission for the astronomer C. Sulpicius Gallus to deliver a lecture to the soldiers on lunar eclipses: there was to be one that night of June twenty-first, and the Roman leader wished to inoculate his army against interpreting it as a sign of divine wrath. To reassure those unimpressed by science Paullus nevertheless sacrificed opulently to the moon in the wake of the eclipse. The Romans, according to their custom, set up a clangor of bronze and held torches skyward to entice the moon back, and back she came. The Macedonians were unsettled: eclipses forebode the fall of kings.[12]

At dawn the consul sacrificed to secure the blessing of the gods upon the battle. An hour passed, then another, and another: the dead beasts piled higher and higher until finally the twenty-first ox proved propitious, but only, the consul said, if the Roman army stood on defense. Paullus was already much blamed in the talk of the camp for refusing action the day before, and now he seemed to be delaying even more over his sacrifices; then he called a council of war — more delay, some complained — and argued with his officers about yesterday's refusal to fight. And he did not convince them all that he had acted wisely.[13]

ROMAN GENERALS AND SOLDIERS
IN THE SECOND PUNIC WAR

Although Paullus's relations with his soldiers and his officers — their wrangling with him, his tricking them — seem surprising, especially to a modern observer with visions of the iron discipline of the Roman army, they were nothing unusual to the Romans, merely the normal environment in which a Roman commander exercised his command. The criticism of generals that throve at Rome (and against which Paullus railed before his departure) was no less pervasive in the army. And although some of this criticism was rooted in genuine strategic and tactical disagreement, it was rooted primarily in impatience at the slightest apparent lack of aggressiveness on the part of a Roman general: the discontent was not chiefly the result of an alternative strategic vision, but of impatience with any strategic vision at all. When Paullus deviated from the quickest route toward a pitched battle with Perseus there was protest and remonstration, remonstration which is all the more remarkable when one realizes that Paullus fought Perseus at Pydna only twenty-five days after his departure from Italy and only fifteen days after he arrived to take up his command in Macedonia. Paullus had particular reason to be resentful of the Roman culture of impatient aggressiveness, for when Aemilius Paullus had been about twelve, that culture had killed his father.[14]

L. Aemilius Paullus the elder had been one of the consuls elected in the fateful year of Cannae (216 BC). He continually urged caution, deliberation, and precaution against the ambushes of the guileful Hannibal. His colleague in the consulship, Terentius Varro, supported by the soldiers, sought instant battle. When the elder Paullus and Varro came face to face with Hannibal, it was on flat ground that gave the Carthaginians the advantage because of their superiority in cavalry. Better, the elder Paullus urged, to fight on broken ground, where the more numerous Roman infantry would be decisive. But neither Varro nor the soldiers would brook delay. On a day when he had command, Paullus's colleague in the consulship offered Hannibal battle. The result was the greatest catastrophe in the history of Roman arms. Aemilius Paullus's father fell bravely along with tens of thousands of his countrymen.[15]

Livy preserves a tradition that the dying consul had sent to his men-

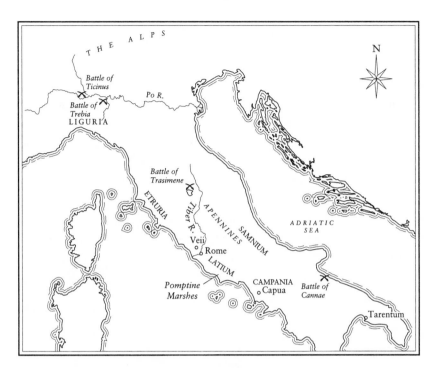

Italy in the Second Punic War (218–201 BC)

tor Fabius Maximus at Rome a message that he had lived to that hour and now died according to his precepts. Fabius was the dictator who had been appointed for six months after the Roman disaster at Lake Trasimene in the previous year. He had seen the aggressive expectations of the Roman army and people and the competitive tenor of Roman command contribute to two great Roman defeats. The lost battle of Trebia was fought in December—and the Romans had to ford a frigid river to get at Hannibal's army—because one of the consuls of 218 BC, Tiberius Longus, wanted to win a victory before he was superseded and before his wounded colleague recovered enough to share his glory. Flaminius, consul of the next year, rushed into Hannibal's ambush at Trasimene for fear of the reproach to which he would be subject in his army and at Rome if he let Hannibal plunder Etruria. Contrary to the expectations of the majority of Romans, Fabius refused to face Hannibal in open battle, preferring to follow him

and wear out his army — so originating "Fabian tactics." But Fabius's logistical strategy was offensive to Roman martial values and so faced a
whirlwind of criticism. He was accused of cowardice. His handpicked
subordinate, the Master of Horse Minucius, joined in the chorus against
him. Master of Horse, tribunes, and centurions all urged battle, and battle
was what the Romans at home wanted too. When Minucius won a skirmish in Fabius's absence (and against his explicit orders), the Romans
raised him to parity in power with Fabius — made him codictator, in a
constitutional innovation. When Fabius returned to the army, he was
able to save Minucius and his army from the consequences of Minucius's
rashness. But when the six-month term of the dictators came to
an end the Senate showed what they thought of Fabius's policy by giving the new consuls clear instructions to seek a battle with Hannibal —
instructions which they followed to Cannae.[16]

Nor did the Romans entirely learn their lesson at Cannae. Subsequent
Roman armies still threw themselves upon Hannibal and kept being defeated. A former centurion, the story is told, applied to the Senate for
five thousand men, was given eight thousand, accumulated as many half-
armed volunteers on his march, and led them to their destruction. Eight
years after Cannae the Senate, by now slowly accepting reality, puzzled
as to where it could find cautious generals. No surprise: a Roman leader
who was unwilling to commit his troops to combat or to continue fighting
in circumstances he thought unequal was disobeyed by soldiers and officers alike. At Herdonea in 212 BC, the praetor Fulvius's soldiers were so
eager for combat that they drew up the line of battle according to their
own lights, despite the pleading of the military tribunes that the line was
too thin. The tribunes proved right, and yet another Roman army was
slaughtered. Here Roman soldiers aggressively asserted their right to
fight as they saw fit, even down to the tactical details. A Greek writer reported of the Gauls that "the whole Gallic race . . . is mad for war and
brave and quick to go to battle; otherwise they are frank and not malicious.
As a result when they are aroused to anger they assemble in crowds for
battle, openly and without planning, so that they are easily handled by
those who want to fight with stratagems." But he might have been describing the Romans in the first years of the Second Punic War: Hannibal
found the aggressive Romans very easy to beat with simple stratagems.[17]

Generalship that tended to delay battle was offensive to the inherited Roman ethic of *virtus,* and its practitioners were suspected of cowardice. To get their way generals had to rely on the old opposing ethic of *disciplina* and the power it gave them. But when generals forced the two hallowed principles against each other, as in the war against Hannibal, *disciplina* was often the loser. The Romans, like the Greeks before them, never made the decision that obedience was the overriding military duty. Their discipline, as Polybius reveals in amazement, was far harsher than that of the Greeks. But *virtus* had legitimacy as well, and legitimacy not inferior in kind.

THE BATTLE OF PYDNA AND THE
ROMAN TRADITION OF COMMAND

We do not know why the battle of Pydna finally began. In one tradition Aemilius Paullus sat in his tent waiting for the sun to decline into the west, so that it would shine in the eyes of the Macedonians. When the time was right he brought on the battle with the ruse of having the Romans pursue a runaway horse toward the Macedonian lines. In another version, Paullus did not wish to fight at all that day because he was waiting for his foragers to return, and the battle began accidentally as the result of a skirmish between drawers of water. But this we know: the Roman army deployed in the conventional manipular formation and fought Perseus's phalanx nose to nose on the plain.[18] And, predictably, the Romans began to lose. When the Romans met the Macedonian phalanx the spears of the Macedonians pushed them steadily back: "At the onset, Aemilius arrived and discovered that the Macedonian units had already planted the tips of their *sarissas* in the shields of the Romans, who could therefore not get forward and reach them with their swords. And when he saw the rest of the Macedonians drawing their shields around front off their shoulders [in preparation for combat], and that the *sarissas* leveled at a single signal were withstanding his shield-armed soldiers, and when he saw the strength of the locked-shield formation and the harshness of the attack, astonishment and terror seized him, because he had never seen a sight more fearful. And later he often used to recall his emotion and what he saw."[19] The Romans were driven to extremities to break the

Macedonian formation and stop the relentless pressure. The commander of a contingent of Rome's Pelignian allies cast his soldiers' standard into the midst of the phalanx, and the Pelignians tried heroically to thrust the Macedonian spears aside — with swords, shields, even their bare hands — to recover it. But to no avail. The Romans were soon in full retreat. Aemilius Paullus rent his garments in despair.[20]

Why Aemilius Paullus was willing to fight a frontal battle with Perseus's phalanx is a mystery. Plutarch attributes to Paullus awareness of the special dangers presented by fighting the Macedonian phalanx: and well might he have been. The Romans had been fighting the Macedonian phalanx for more than a century. Pyrrhus defeated the Romans with it in the early third century, the Carthaginians in Africa in the middle of the century did as well, and Hannibal did the same later. In 197 BC the Romans had won a terrifying victory against Perseus's father at Cynoscephalae, a battle that vividly illustrated the terrible power of the phalanx's charge, even on unsuitable ground. In the year before Cynoscephalae, the Roman siege of Atrax had failed when a Macedonian phalanx drawn up in a breach in the wall had proved quite impervious to Roman attack. Polybius's judgment that "when the phalanx has its characteristic virtue and strength nothing can sustain its frontal attack or withstand the charge" will have been no news to Roman commanders. The phalanx's fatal flaw, Polybius says, is that it requires flat terrain so that it can preserve its close order. Perseus's father's unwise decision to fight on broken ground allowed the Romans to defeat him at Cynoscephalae. But Aemilius Paullus consented to fight the Macedonian phalanx on a plain, ideally suited to it, on ground that Perseus had chosen for exactly that reason.[21]

There was nothing in Aemilius Paullus's record to suggest he was rash or inept: quite the opposite. When campaigning in Spain, he had chosen his battlefields with a careful eye toward advantage. Later he had defeated the Ligurians with a complicated stratagem, issuing forth from a besieged camp from all gates at once to catch the enemy by surprise, here carefully having the *hastati* of one legion lead the charge, there the *principes* of another. After his victory over Perseus men remarked on the careful preparations Paullus made for throwing dinners in Greece, and the Roman general joked that he took as much care over ordering dinners as he did in marshaling a line of battle: a remark that loses its force unless he was thought an especially careful tactician. "A really good general," Paullus was apt to tell his own son, "does not commit to a pitched battle at all, except in cases of the greatest necessity or the greatest advantage." Neither was the case at Pydna.[22]

The outlook, past conduct, and behavior of Aemilius Paullus in the days before Pydna—his feints and ruses on the Elpeus—place him squarely in the Roman tradition of crafty, strategy- and tactics-minded generals, in the tradition of Fabius Maximus and the great Scipio Africanus. Rome was old in the use of tactics: there is no reason to suppose there was ever a generation of Roman fighting without tactics, any more than there was in Greece. Guile in war was as ancient as Roman legend: in the fabled duel of the brothers Horatii, the surviving brother overcame the Curatii by the trick of false flight. At the very first Roman land battle of which there is a reliable, detailed account, Bagradas River in 255 BC in the First Punic War, the Romans are already found varying the standard manipular deployment in the hope of gaining a tactical advantage. By the Second Punic War and the early second century, commanders like Scipio Africanus managed to adapt the many moving parts of the manipular legion to sophisticated tactical battle plans: varying the checkerboard disposition of the maniples, deepening the array, wheeling the array, using the lines of *hastati, principes,* and *triarii* independently, detaching maniples to flank the enemy, deploying a second line of legions as a reserve, and approaching the enemy in a battle-ready marching formation. Other sections too of the Roman army were creatively exploited by tactical Roman commanders. Cavalry made flank attacks, and the *velites* were detached from their legions and used as independent forces of light infantry. Such tactics played a crucial role in defeating Carthage and featured largely in the great victories of Scipio Africanus at Ilipa in Spain in 206 BC and Zama in North Africa in 202. Cato's battle of Emporiae in Spain in 195 may display the most complicated Roman tactics of all in this period.[23]

Although tactics were native at Rome, by the late third and second century BC there is clear evidence of Greek influence on Roman generalship and methods of fighting. Scipio, we are told, was a keen reader of Xenophon's *Cyropaedia,* a work in which the Greek expert offered in Persian guise his proposals for Greek military reform. By Paullus's day Roman cavalry equipment had been reformed on the Greek model. The Romans had also begun actively seeking out specialist Greek troops, like the archers from Crete, rather than merely using them when sent by their allies. Elephants too were part of an integrated Hellenistic army. A force of them had been brought from Africa at the beginning of the war against Perseus, and Aemilius used them at Pydna. Thirty years before, Flamininus had used elephants to fight Philip V at Cynoscephalae. The Romans may have learned more about elephants from fighting Carthaginians than from reading Greek manuals, but this was Greek doctrine at second hand: the army of Carthage was modeled on Greek armies, and Hannibal himself was a Hellenized commander. Now the Romans were using Greek stratagems; now the Romans knew Greek lore like the path around the back of the pass at Thermopylae. Now Romans could be imagined debating questions like, Who is the greatest general of all time? — questions that implied that some of them at least had come to share the Greek conception of generalship as a competition in technical expertise.[24]

Greek influence on Roman command is hardly surprising: it is merely a small instance of the gigantic phenomenon of the Hellenization of the Roman aristocracy in the late third and second centuries BC. This cultural transformation affected nearly every aspect of upper-class Roman existence — from education and language to entertainment, decoration, clothing, and housewares. And many of Rome's tactically minded commanders were leaders of the philhellenic movement, Scipio Africanus (Hannibal's foe) and Aemilius Paullus among them. After his victory over Perseus, the Greek-speaking Paullus took a long tour of famous sites in Greece and offered Greek athletic games. He gave the Macedonian royal library to his sons. When Paullus made his grim way home after being appointed to fight the Macedonian king, he found his small daughter in tears. Her little dog Perseus had died. "Good fortune, my daughter! I accept the omen!" crowed the consul (how his weeping daughter greeted his glee is not recorded). But a dog named for a Greek hero is also a small yapping sign of how pervasive Greek influence on Rome had become. When we see Paullus not only employing military tricks and ruses, but also applying natural science to war — geology to dig wells, astronomy to reassure his men — we can be certain that he was up to date with the most advanced trends in Greek generalship.[25]

Yet cerebral generalship was strongly resisted at Rome. Trickery and tactics, as the old senators had complained when the envoys reported the lies they had told to Perseus, could be viewed as opposed to *virtus*. "Among the Romans, a bit of a trace of the old philosophy of war is left," wrote Polybius of the Romans of Aemilius Paullus's day. "They declare war openly, rarely use ambushes, and fight their battles hand-to-hand at close quarters." Many Romans preferred a battle, as Livy put it, "with standards set against standards, on a clean and open field, where without fear of ambush the affair could be settled by true *virtus*." The general, in this view, was to lead the army directly at the enemy, to allow his soldiers to display their *virtus,* and to display his own. After a loss a Roman general might be prosecuted for personal cowardice, but not for tactical stupidity. Terentius Varro, the aggressive consul who committed the Roman army to the disaster at Cannae, was not punished for his bad planning but thanked when he returned to Rome for "not despairing of the Republic." It was far more important to the Romans that their generals be plucky and adventuresome than that they be skillful strategists and tacticians.[26]

An unusual general like Scipio Africanus could regularly prevail in this conflict over how wars and battles should be fought. His personal heroism at the battle of Ticinus, where he was said to have saved his father's life, and in the wake of Cannae, where he rallied a party of survivors when they threatened to surrender or flee from Italy, gave him at least partial protection against charges of personal cowardice. But even Scipio was severely criticized at Rome for lack of aggression, for moving too slowly, and for spoiling his soldiers. And he was sometimes obliged to trick his troops into obeying him by pretending that his plans were suggested to him by the gods. A less charismatic figure like Fabius Maximus, by contrast, could exert only an intermittent sway over his army in the face of the Romans' aggressive culture, despite the supreme constitutional power the awe-evoking office of dictator supposedly conferred.[27]

Many Roman generals shared the common Roman distaste for strategy and tactics; others were impatient of slow strategy but not of tactics which did not delay the battle: the aggressive Varro deepened the Roman manipular array at Cannae. Still others, politicians in a city where politics and reputation were so wound up with war, will have been unwilling or unable to resist the impatient expectations of their soldiers and officers, whatever their private views: as long as the general and the soldier both followed the banner of *virtus,* the conflict between *virtus* and *disciplina,* for the most part, slept. But to make sophisticated plans — to fight like a Greek — might require that *disciplina* be set against *virtus,* and so produce the baying of angry voters, that sound so dreaded by the politically ambitious. Frequently, therefore, in the Roman army, as Livy had Paullus complain, "the soldiers do the thinking, and the commander is led around by the gossip of the rankers." Roman command gyrated between tactical ingenuity and tactical simplicity.[28]

It is the conflict between the ancestral Roman value of *virtus* — and the impatient aggressiveness which grew from it — and the opposed tradition of cerebral generalship, which *disciplina* made possible, which explains the Romans' facing the Macedonian phalanx head-on upon the plain of Pydna. On the day before the battle, Paullus had had to trick his own soldiers to prevent an engagement: a bald order to go into camp would not, it appears, have been obeyed. And soldiers' entering battle against the orders of a commander was hardly uncommon in the Roman army. On the day of the battle both Paullus's long sacrifices and his council of war were denounced as yet more delay. As long as possible Paullus lingered upon the rough ground: perhaps Perseus would advance and fight where the Romans had an advantage. But finally Paullus's power to restrain his soldiers was at an end, and the Romans fought on ground of Perseus's choosing. Ferociously denounced by both his officers and men, Paullus finally could resist no longer the *virtus* of his army. Before the Macedonians and Romans fought at Pydna the Roman ethics of *virtus* and *disciplina* fought their own battle, and in that battle *virtus* won.[29]

Having finally got the battle they yearned for, the young aristocrats of Paullus's army took to the contest with a will. Having lost his sword in the fighting and so fearing disgrace, the son of Cato the Elder (who was also Aemilius's son-in-law) ran along the ranks summoning his friends to help him recover it. This mob of noble youths attacked on their own the section of the Macedonian phalanx where the sword had been lost, pushed it back, and recovered the lost weapon amidst the carnage; then they attacked the Macedonians again, singing in their triumph.[30]

Despite Roman bravery, ground and equipment favored the Macedonians, and they steadily pushed the Romans back. Finally the Macedonians' very success was their undoing. Their advance met more or less resistance at different points, and so some parts of the phalanx pressed forward and some held back. Their progress also took them onto higher and less regular ground which interrupted the exact dressing of their ranks. Aemilius was able to rally enough troops to attack vulnerable points in the phalanx as it lost its order. Once the flanks of individual members of the phalanx were exposed, they were vulnerable to Roman swords. The elephants in the Roman service helped to disrupt the Macedonian left, and it was there that the rout began. And so, barely, desperately, the Romans began to win the battle. As the phalanx came apart the Roman advantage turned into a slaughter. More than twenty thousand Macedonians were slain and only a handful of Romans. When the next day the Romans crossed over the river Leucus, its waters were still tinged with blood. Some Macedonians fled all the way to the sea and waded in, hoping to surrender to the Roman fleet that was standing by. But the Romans sent boats to kill them in the water. They fled back to land only to be trampled in the shallows by the Roman elephants.[31]

After the battle one of Aemilius Paullus's sons, a teenager, was found missing and searched for; hours later he returned safe with a few comrades, drenched in blood, having slain many when carried away in the killing joy of the pursuit. This young man was Scipio Aemilianus, later the destroyer of Carthage and Numantia, and almost twenty years later a single-combat victor in early middle age. Scipio Nasica's killing of the Thracian, Cato's son and his friends' recovering his sword, and Paullus's son's blood-mad pursuit of the enemy are tokens of how strong the heroic, competitive culture of Roman *virtus* still was among young Roman aristocrats in 168 BC.[32]

King Perseus fled the stricken field. Within two days nearly all of Macedonia surrendered to the Romans, who were to divide it into four feeble republics to ensure it would never make trouble again. Perseus abandoned his kingdom to seek asylum on the sacred isle of Samothrace, his only escort his Cretan mercenaries. Abandoned finally by all, the king surrendered himself to the Romans. Brought before the consul's council, the king was peppered with questions by Paullus, but he stood in silence and wept and then flung himself upon the ground as a suppliant for his life. Paullus lost his Roman temper. Didn't Perseus understand that by cringing in public he was detracting from the reputation of his conqueror? But then he remembered his Greek culture and lectured his young officers in Latin on the mutability of fate, offering Perseus as an object lesson — a very Greek moment, despite the language. Such was the end of the kingdom that had bred Alexander the Great.[33]

Before Paullus could lead his victorious army back to Rome, his soldiers' greed had to be satisfied. The cities of Epirus that had defected to Perseus were granted by the Senate to the army to plunder. But how to sack them without having to besiege each one? One last time Paullus's guile was called upon. He told the men of Epirus that they would have to pay a fine, but in exchange they would have their freedom. Ten men from each city were summoned and told to collect all the gold and silver in each town. Then Roman units were sent out at different times so that they would arrive at cities near and far on the same day. At dawn of the day appointed the Romans received in each town all the treasure that had been collected; then, at the fourth hour, the troops were unleashed to sack. One hundred and fifty thousand were taken as slaves and seventy cities were destroyed. It was a suitably horrible end to a singularly cynical Roman war.[34]

Still, the soldiers were unhappy at the sums they received: the gold of Macedon was headed for the public treasury; they were permitted merely to squeeze the stone of Epirus. And so when an enemy of Paullus, one of his own handpicked military tribunes, tried to defeat the proposal granting Paullus a triumph, the soldiers paid him eager heed. Besides, they had resented the strictness of his discipline; it was time to teach commanders a lesson. In the end Aemilius Paullus got his triumph — the voting was suspended and the great Marcus Servilius, victor in twenty-three single combats, harangued the crowd, and finally the triumph was voted. But it is satisfying that the Pydna campaign should have ended as it was carried on — in angry conflict between the general and his army.[35]

Roman warfare of the mid-Republic was a product of fierce division over how war should be fought. The vision of generalship that Aemilius Paullus embodied, that is, the Hellenistic conception of the general as the master of trickery, tactics, flanking maneuvers, and applied scientific knowledge, was conceived as illegitimate on its face by a large proportion of his army and his officers, at least if it delayed their getting to grips with the enemy. To them the duty of the general was to lead his army straight at the foe and to fight as soon as possible. The willful *virtus* of the soldiers and officers pounded like a siege ram against *disciplina,* the ethic the general relied upon to command the obedience of his soldiers and to put his plans into action. Yet this very conflict underlies the success of the army of the middle Republic, for despite the disasters it sometimes produced, the result of the conflict was a balance between qualities essential to Roman victory: on the one hand, the bravery and aggressiveness of Roman soldiers of all ranks, and on the other the ability of commanders to use that bravery and aggressiveness. The Roman army was disobedient because it was brave: a less brave army might have been more obedient but would have won fewer wars, while an army whose bravery broke entirely through the bonds of *disciplina* would have been uncontrollable and so would have won fewer wars as well. In a world where their enemies often represented extremes — brave but ungovernable Gauls, drilled but sometimes timid Greeks — the secret of Roman superiority was that the Roman army, although often inferior in respects in which their enemies excelled, was adequate in respects in which their enemies were not.

Tactical generalship was old at Rome, and native, but Roman generals' eagerness to maneuver and trick was multiplied by Roman contact with Greek habits of command, just one aspect of the far greater transformation of Roman society that world power and Roman plundering of the world's treasures brought in its train. Greek generalship was new and foreign, but the conflict it exacerbated was old and Roman: the conflict between *virtus* and *disciplina* that the Romans explored in their stories about their early heroic duelists, the conflict that had created the manipular legion.

Roman success in war would eventually destroy the constitutional Republic that created and nourished that success. A state that could manage wars so well could not in the end manage either the wealth and pride of conquest or the discontent and misery. Rule by Senate and people gave way to rule by solitary emperors. What effect did the whirlwind of change that we call the late Republic have on the odd, delicate, fertile balance between discipline and bravery, and between soldier and general, the singular moral alloy that had allowed the Romans to conquer their world?

X

CAESAR'S CENTURIONS AND

THE LEGION OF COHORTS

MILITARY CULTURE AND GREEK

INFLUENCE IN THE LATE REPUBLIC

O ne hundred and ten years and over ninety significant Roman battles separated Aemilius Paullus's departure from Macedonia from Julius Caesar's arrival in Gaul: battles in Spain, Gaul, North Africa, Italy, Greece, and Asia Minor; battles against German marauders, the Cimbri and Teutones; battles against foreign magnates, Jugurtha and King Mithridates of Pontus; battles against impertinent Greeks and Carthaginians — and Greece was made subject, and Carthage destroyed; battles against Roman slaves, brave Spartacus and others; and battles against Rome's own Italian allies, the tragic Social War. And if all that were not enough, this was the era when the Romans learned to fight against each other, and Sulla, Marius, and their followers fought Rome's first civil wars.[1]

This long century saw great changes in the way Romans fought their battles — but not changes that can be inspected as they happened. With the loss of Livy's manuscript after 167 BC the military world goes dim. Wars and battles can be named but not studied in the detail that an account of Roman military evolution demands. The historian Sallust casts one brief ray — on the Jugurthine War of 111–105 BC — but otherwise the lights come up again only with Julius Caesar's account of his campaigns in Gaul, from 58. We can only recollect the army of Aemilius Paullus, then examine the army of Julius Caesar, see what has changed, and venture a guess at the reasons why.

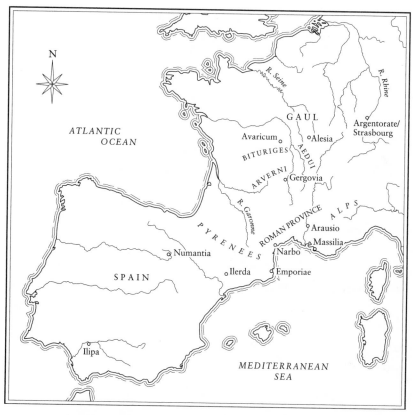

Gaul and Spain in the Time of Julius Caesar (58–45 BC)

THE SLAUGHTER OF CENTURIONS:
JULIUS CAESAR AT GERGOVIA, 52 BC

The nations of the Gauls were nations of warriors, forever fighting against their neighbors or against invaders from afar, forming and breaking leagues, and summoning the Germans from over the Rhine. When Julius Caesar led his army into their realm to defend Rome's allies and punish Rome's enemies, he must have seemed just another player in the ancient bloody confusion of Gallic politics. But as he marched and fought and took surrenders — and punished with terrible Roman cruelty those who, in the old Gallic way, fought against him again — the Gauls came to understand that Caesar intended nothing less than their subjection or their doom. Yet the old hatreds between the Gallic states, their eagerness to enlist Caesar in their feuds, their lack of national feeling, and Caesar's deft diplomacy prevented them from acting in concert against him. Gallic chiefs like Indutiomarus of the Treveri and Ambiorix of the Eburones struggled to assemble confederates. With fast marching, Caesar and his lieutenants thwarted their plans. But in the winter of 53–52 BC, the charismatic Vercingetorix, hero of the Arverni, raised against Rome the Gauls from the Garonne to the Seine.

News of the new war reached Caesar in Italy, and he hastened north. The snow was still heavy on the ground when Caesar rushed to join his legions, which were camped for the winter in Gaul two hundred miles from the border of the Roman province in the south. Taking advantage of the bitterness of the season, Vercingetorix settled upon a logistical strategy and ordered towns and villages near the Romans destroyed to deny them supplies. But the Bituriges, allied to Vercingetorix, refused to abandon Avaricum, their capital. This Caesar besieged, and Vercingetorix moved his army to relieve it. The Gaul disposed his forces upon a hill behind a marsh — impossible to attack without great loss. Even so Caesar's soldiers cried out for the signal to charge, and Caesar refused it because of the ground. Like Aemilius Paullus before Pydna, he was obliged to reason with his soldiers and explain his decision. After a siege of twenty-five days the Romans forced their way into Avaricum and slaughtered its whole population, which Caesar numbers at nearly forty thousand.[2]

Avaricum was in the geographical center of the hostile Gauls. After his victory, Caesar divided his army, sending four legions to put down the tribes to the north and taking the other six south with him to attack Gergovia, capital of the Arverni and the firepit of Gallic resistance to the Romans. When Vercingetorix attempted to block his advance at a river, Caesar concealed two legions at the crossing and then marched the rest of his army along the bank, luring the Gauls away by the venerable Greek stratagem of spreading marching soldiers out to make fewer appear like more.[3]

When Caesar arrived beneath Gergovia he discovered that the town was set upon a height and so despaired of storming it. To blockade the city Caesar would need secure supply lines, but he was camped in the country of the enemy. Vercingetorix had occupied the slope beneath the town and all the hills around with his army. Attacking by night, Caesar seized and fortified a steep rise at the base of the ridge of Gergovia and connected it to his camp by fortifications. Now the Gauls would find it much harder to secure water and forage.[4]

Further plans against Gergovia were thwarted by a diplomatic crisis. The powerful neighboring Gallic state of the Aedui was allied to the Romans: Caesar had just settled a dispute there over who should hold the supreme office. But Vercingetorix had tempted the victorious leader into his fold, and the Aeduan had arranged in turn that the troops the tribe was sending to Caesar should be led by like-minded chiefs. On the march, those officers attempted to bring the force over to Vercingetorix, pretending that Caesar had massacred their countrymen already in his camp. The marching Aedui turned upon the Romans who were traveling with their column. When this defection was reported to Caesar, he set out instantly with four of his six legions, Aeduans in his suite exposed the massacre as an invention, and the defection was reversed. But while the legions were away, Vercingetorix attacked the Roman camp, and because of its size — a camp for six legions defended by two — the Romans had suffered many casualties. Caesar had to march back through the night to relieve his beleaguered forces.[5]

By this time Caesar realized he would have to withdraw from Gergovia. Word of the defection of the Aeduan troops to Vercingetorix had set off an orgy of killing and plundering of Romans in the neighboring Aeduan country: when the Aedui were informed that Caesar had their troops in his power they begged for mercy, but Caesar no longer trusted them. Caesar feared that a wider war was brewing in Gaul. Fearing he would be encircled at Gergovia by a great league of Gallic states, he decided to abandon Gergovia and reunite his divided army.[6]

Yet Caesar was in agony lest word of his retreat — his failure, his flight — be the omen that brought all Gaul to arms against him. Many tribes had already pledged their swords to Vercingetorix, but others plotted and yet others waited. Caesar needed to escape Gergovia but appear not to have been defeated. The Roman therefore planned a limited action to snatch a victory before he led his forces away. The camps of the Gauls extended halfway down the hill from Gergovia to a low stone wall. Caesar knew from deserters that Vercingetorix was worried about a point at the back of the town where access was easy. Caesar encouraged these worries by feinting toward the vulnerable spot, drawing more and more Gauls away from their camps to fortify it. Then he smuggled his soldiers in small groups to the small camp nearer the foot of the slope. Finally he revealed his plans to his officers.[7]

Caesar proposed a limited attack directly up the slope at the Gallic camps, which were nearly denuded of defenders by the frantic work being carried out on the other side of the town. The Romans would take the camps by surprise, plunder them, and retreat before the Gauls could come over the ridge. This was to be a smash-and-grab raid, a cheap victory to cover Caesar's withdrawal from Gergovia. If the Romans lingered, and the Gauls came up, the Romans would be fighting a larger force up-hill, a considerable disadvantage in a world of thrown missiles. Caesar instructed his officers to restrain the troops and make sure they got back in good time.[8]

When the signal was given, the Roman legionaries rushed up the six hundred paces of slope to the low wall, vaulted it, and quickly got possession of the camps: Teutomatus, a Gallic king, was jolted from a daytime slumber and fled half-naked upon a wounded horse. Now Caesar sounded the retreat and stopped the Tenth Legion, with which he had advanced. But the other legions did not hear the trumpet and forged on up the hill toward the walls of the town. The military tribunes and legates — the aristocratic officers — tried to hold them back, as Caesar had ordered, but in vain. Centurions led the unordered assault on the wall of Gergovia. Lucius Fabius, a centurion of the Eighth Legion, was lifted up the wall by three of his legionaries and then pulled them up after him. Marcus Petronius, of the same legion, tried with his men to cut down a gate.[9]

Gergovia was in tumult: most of its defenders had been lured away by Caesar's feint to the other side of the hill. The inhabitants began to flee the town or, from the wall, beg the mercy of the Romans: the people of Gergovia dreaded suffering the fate of the folk of Avaricum. Gallic women cast their treasures from the wall as a plea for mercy: some were let down from the ramparts by hand and surrendered themselves to the Romans. But desperate messages summoned the Gauls from over the hill, and they rushed to Gergovia's defense, arriving beneath the town wall to confront the Romans. The women of Gergovia turned from imploring the Romans for mercy to calling upon their own men to destroy the hated enemy, loosing their hair and holding up their children after their savage custom. A pitched battle — exactly the pitched battle Caesar had schemed to avoid — broke out under the walls. The Romans were tired, the Gauls fresh; the Romans were few, the Gauls many; the Romans were lower, and the Gauls higher on the hill. Now the Aedui, Rome's dubious Gallic allies, appeared to help the Romans on the Roman right (the side their shields did not cover); but in the confusion they were mistaken for foes. Shaken, the Romans began to be pushed down the slope. This left the foolhardy centurions isolated: Lucius Fabius and his men were surrounded, slain, and cast from the wall. Marcus Petronius urged his troops to abandon him, charged the Gauls single-handed, and by his death got his soldiers safe away. The Romans began to cascade down the hill, and extended pursuit was only prevented by the looming presence of the Tenth Legion and some other cohorts which threatened the pursuers from the flank, cohorts Caesar had summoned for the emergency from the Roman camp. At the bottom of the hill the defeated Romans formed again and turned their standards toward the enemy: Vercingetorix led his troops back into the town. Slightly fewer than seven hundred Romans, including forty-six centurions, were lost.[10]

The casualty figures from Gergovia confirm the anecdotes Caesar tells about the aggressive bravery of his centurions at the battle. Nearly one in fifteen who died was a centurion. But only one in eighty of the soldiers of a legion was a centurion. At Gergovia the centurions placed themselves in danger to such a degree that they were nearly five times more likely to die than the rankers they led. And the special bellicosity of Caesar's centurions was hardly limited to Gergovia. In Caesar's victory at Pharsalus (48 BC), two hundred of Caesar's men fell, but around thirty centurions, an even more striking proportion than at Gergovia. At the Sambre (57) when the Nervii were pressing the Twelfth Legion, "all the centurions of the fourth cohort had been killed . . . and of the remaining cohorts almost all the centurions were either wounded or killed."[11]

In addition to the exploits of Lucius Fabius and Marcus Petronius at Gergovia, Caesar tells other tales of the feats of his centurions. At Pharsalus, Crastinus, a former centurion, led a forlorn-hope charge into the Pompeian lines and, fighting heroically, was cut down by a sword-stroke to the face. When a Roman winter camp was besieged by Gauls in the winter of 54 BC, Pullo the centurion challenged his rival in courage: "What are you waiting for, Vorenus? Or what better occasion to prove your *virtus* do you expect? This day will settle our dispute!" And with that he left the rampart and charged the enemy all alone. Stung by fear of what men would think if he refused, his fellow centurion Vorenus followed him out. A Gaul advanced from the pack to fight Pullo in single combat: Pullo struck him down with his javelin, and the protective shields of the Gauls closed over him. Now the Gauls showered Pullo with spears; now one dislodged his scabbard so he could not get at his sword; now the Gauls were surrounding him: but Vorenus came to his rescue and drew the foes away. Vorenus killed a Gaul, but slipped and was surrounded in his turn. And now Pullo rose up to rescue him, and both fought their way unhurt back within the Roman fortifications. "And it was impossible to judge which of them should be considered superior in *virtus*."[12]

Rome had a tradition of brave centurions, extending back centuries: centurions had always been expected to lead from the front and place themselves in danger to steady and inspire their troops. And centurions aggressive to the point of disobedience are attested earlier too. But such reports are not common, and, writing a century before Gergovia, Polybius was struck by — and remarked upon — how phlegmatic the Roman centurions of his day were, writing of the Romans, "They do not want centurions to be bold and danger-loving as much as authoritative and steady and calm in spirit." Yet by Caesar's day, centurions had taken up the role of the young aristocratic heroes of Paullus's, not merely acting bravely to spur their men, but brave out of rivalry in bravery, brave for bravery's sake. By Caesar's day many centurions had crossed the line from those who restrained to those who needed to be restrained, from the exemplars of *disciplina* to the exemplars of *virtus*.[13]

Caesar's aristocratic officers were headed in the opposite direction. As a cunning, tactical, stratagem-minded general, Caesar fought in the tradition of Scipio Africanus and Aemilius Paullus. And Caesar's ad hoc legionary commanders, his legates, and his military tribunes were his assistants in tactical generalship and tried desperately to restrain the aggressiveness of the soldiers and centurions. These were not the tribunes who in time of old sought out single combat, or young men like Cato's son seeking his sword, or Aemilius Paullus's son returning from the pursuit drenched in blood. In the writings of Caesar and his followers, when aristocratic officers — tribunes and their superiors and Caesar himself — display personal bravery, their bravery is usually the calculated courage of a commander, leading and rallying, rather than the heedless bravery of a heroic fighter. Caesar's aristocratic officers had for the most part ceded the old heroic role to the centurions. A quaint exception proves the rule. Before the bloody battle of Munda in Spain (45 BC) a soldier, Antistius Turpio by name, came forth from the Pompeian ranks to challenge a champion on the opposing side to single combat. An aristocratic, equestrian Caesarian met his challenge, and they fought on foot between the lines. But the contemporary author who described this encounter considered it an eccentric throwback, comparing it to the mythic fight of Achilles and Memnon. And the armies contending had long forgotten the tacit protocols that made such artificial encounters possible. The duel seems to have been abandoned — the corrupt text allows no certainty here — when a cavalry skirmish collided with it.[14]

The attitudes of upper-class Romans toward military service had changed. At some time between 102 and 58 BC the Roman cavalry, made up of Roman citizens of the highest census class, was abolished. Now Rome's allies would supply the cavalry. Those aristocrats who still went to war were appointed as military tribunes of the legions or prefects commanding allies, or they served as supernumerary staff officers, *contubernales,* "tentmates" of the commander. In that same period, or perhaps slightly earlier, the requirement that a young Roman serve in ten campaigns before he could run for public office was allowed to lapse. In the course of the first century BC the social standing of young men who became military tribunes or prefects declined — fewer nobles, fewer patricians: more young men of equestrian, rather than senatorial, birth. The higher reaches of the aristocracy increasingly shunned such posts, leaving them to the lower. The late-Republican Roman aristocracy had become increasingly civilian in outlook and ambitions, many preferring advocacy, moneymaking, and leisure to military service. More important for military affairs, however, was the secession from actual fighting with their own hands of the aristocrats who continued to go to war — they no longer served five years as a ranker in the cavalry before election to a military tribunate. By the first century the Roman aristocracy had become an officer class: when at war they did not fight but commanded or assisted as *contubernales* those commanding. Aristocratic officers and followers of the army still felt very much at liberty to debate strategy and tactics with their commanders, as Pompey found out before the battle of Pharsalus when his camp was filled with Roman senators, all complaining and pressing their opinions upon him. But if aristocratic officers differed about tactics (or suspected Pompey's motives or wanted the war to be over before the Tusculan fig season ended), they were not opposed to the idea of tactics or strategy. There are still stories of aristocrats seeking out single combat in the late second and early first centuries BC: the young Marius fought one, and Pompey several. But judging from Caesar's accounts, aristocratic heroism was no very large part of his experience of war. Caesar, indeed, thought many of his aristocratic officers deficient in military qualities: he pointedly notes that the panic that infected his army at the prospect of fighting the Germans began with the tribunes, prefects, and *contubernales* "who had little military experience." It was the shift in aristocratic interest from fighting to commanding that allowed the centurions to invade the old prerogative of their betters and become the models of brave aggression. When the aristocrats abandoned this realm of admired behavior, the centurions, still driven by the traditional values of Roman soldiers, hastened to take possession of it.[15]

The day after his defeat at Gergovia, by his own account, Caesar paraded his troops and reproached them for their temerity and passion: "They had decided for themselves where to go and what to do; they had not stopped when the recall was sounded, nor could they be restrained by the military tribunes and legates. . . . As much as he admired the bravery of men whom no camp fortifications, no height of hill, no city wall could slow, he blamed to the same degree their license and arrogance, that they thought that they knew more about victory and outcome than their commander. He wanted from his soldiers obedience and self-control as much as *virtus* and greatness of spirit."[16] Success in war, Caesar insisted, depended not on *virtus* or *disciplina* alone, but upon maintaining a balance between these two opposing drives. Despite his complaint about his soldiers' insubordination, the terms of Caesar's reproach indicate the tremendous military importance he still attributed to his soldiers' culture of *virtus*. Caesar was horrified by—and at the same time enormously proud of— the behavior of the fallen, foolish, brave centurions Marcus Petronius and Lucius Fabius: what his centurions did at Gergovia was wrong, perhaps, but still admirable. Caesar and the authors who completed the account of his wars tell with delight stories of the bravery of his soldiers, of heroic standard-bearers and the soldier who fought in single combat with an elephant. And a close examination of Caesar's battle descriptions reveals how important he considered the *virtus* of his soldiers as an ingredient of victory, how he tested the *virtus* of his own forces and the enemy, and how he worked to call upon the *virtus* of his troops.[17]

So the old aggressive culture of the Roman army—eager to fight, impatient with tactics—remained strong among the soldiers and centurions of the Roman army of Caesar's day. At Gergovia this culture broke through the restraints of discipline; so too at Thapsus (46 BC) in the Civil Wars, although there the centurions tried to hold back the advancing troops; so too at Forum Gallorum (43 BC). At other times Roman soldiers were held back but were unhappy about it (as they had been for centuries): as at Avaricum they demanded the signal to attack, even at disadvantage, and commanders denied it to them. The desires of his soldiers might still compel a commander to offer battle against his better judgment, and a commander who seemed too timid, when his soldiers wanted to fight, might still be jeered by his own troops, recalling the behavior of Roman soldiers in the Second Punic War. But judging by his remarks to his troops after Gergovia, it is unlikely that Julius Caesar would have preferred to replace his brave, and so sometimes insubordinate, army with a less brave but more obedient one. Caesar puts in words what acts displayed in the days of Aemilius Paullus: the superiority of the Roman army depended on a hard-fought compromise between *virtus* and *disciplina*, competitive bravery and subordination. What had changed was the position of officers and centurions on either side of that compromise, a shift that, as we will see, had important consequences for Roman tactics.[18]

After his setback at Gergovia, Caesar twice offered battle to Vercingetorix in the plain—and twice it was declined, allowing Caesar to claim boasting rights. Then the Romans marched away from Gergovia. Yet Caesar's fear that his failure to win a victory would cause wobbly tribes

to side with Vercingetorix proved only too justified. The treacherous Aedui, among others, now declared for Gallic freedom. Caesar was surrounded by hostile tribes and running out of food. The Roman proconsul extricated himself by forced marches and made rendezvous with
his other four legions. Vercingetorix now threatened the Roman province in the south. Caesar marched south to protect it: Vercingetorix led
his cavalry out to stop him but was defeated. He fled back to Alesia,
where Caesar besieged him, raising a double ring of siege works, both
against the town on its hill and against the vast army of relief which soon
gathered to rescue the Gallic captain. Mighty attempts to relieve Alesia
were beaten away, and finally Vercingetorix and his starving men surrendered themselves to Caesar. The rebellion was over.[19]

THE LEGION OF COHORTS: JULIUS CAESAR AT ILERDA, 49 BC

Three years later, as he gazed up the hill at Ilerda, Julius Caesar might
have been forgiven a pang of cruel recall. He was fighting Romans now,
rather than barbarians, his victorious Gallic campaign having passed almost seamlessly into civil war against Pompey and the Senate. And he
was fighting in Spain rather than Gaul, having driven Pompey out of
Italy and having decided to clear Spain of Pompey's followers before
chasing his rival into Greece. But here too there was a hill. And here too
soldiers of Caesar's who had advanced too eagerly up it were being showered with missiles from higher ground.

It was at Ilerda that Pompey's marshals had gathered their five legions,
and so it was to Ilerda that Caesar came to fight them. The Pompeian
army was camped on a low hill, which was connected by a saddle to the
loftier hill of the town of Ilerda. Marching up, Caesar offered battle on
the flat: Afranius, Pompey's general, accepted the challenge but only to
the extent of drawing up his line in an advantageous position on the hillside beneath his camp. As at Avaricum, Caesar declined to attack with the
ground against him but decided to camp a mere four hundred paces from
the base of the slope. Suspecting the Pompeians would try to hinder the
construction, Caesar kept his army in array and dug a trench to defend his
camp — a trench, rather than the expected rampart, which would be noticed by the enemy. Like Aemilius Paullus, Caesar used craft to fortify his

camp in safety. The next day Caesar continued to surround his camp with trenches, and the Pompeians came down to terrify his troops — but once again would not advance off the hillside. On the third day the rampart was finally erected around Caesar's camp and the baggage brought up.[20]

Caesar had noticed that on the saddle between the Pompeian camp and the town of Ilerda stood a knoll. If he could capture this and hold it, he thought, he could cut his enemies off from the town, their supplies within it, and the bridge over which their supplies were carried. Drawing up three legions near the place, he sent the *antesignani* — those deployed "before the standards," the *hastati* in the time of Aemilius Paullus — of one of the legions to seize the mound. But in vain. The Pompeian camp was closer, and Caesar's intention was quickly suspected. Cohorts on guard at the camp reached the hillock first and threw back Caesar's men, and with the help of reinforcements pursued them back to their legion. But now that legion too began to waver. Not without admiration, Caesar explains that the Pompeian troops, from long service in Spain, had adopted Lusitanian tactics and "charge at the beginning with great force, boldly seize a position, do not care to preserve their formation, and fight spread out and scattered; if pressed they retreat and do not think it disgraceful to abandon their position." Caesar's more conventional legionaries, believing "they should preserve their formation, not abandon their standards, nor, once they had captured a position, leave it without a grave cause," thought they were being outflanked by the light-infantry tactics of the Pompeians and withdrew to a nearby rise.[21]

This retreat threw the rest of Caesar's line into a panic, and he had to lead the Ninth Legion to the rescue. The enemy attack was stopped and thrown back upon the hill of Ilerda, the Pompeians turning to fight again beneath the walls. Now it was that the Ninth Legion advanced too far up the hill against them, and now it was that the ghost of his defeat at Gergovia must have risen to torment Caesar. The rise toward the town was narrow, and there were steeps on either side. In this space only three cohorts could fit, fighting shoulder to shoulder, under a constant hail of missiles. There was no room on the flanks to send up support, no room for cavalry. And it was far from clear how Caesar's men could be extracted, for when they tried to retreat they were punished severely from the higher ground.[22]

Rather than withdraw and risk the rout he had suffered at Gergovia, Caesar decided to fight this unequal battle in place. Fresh cohorts relieved tired cohorts on the slope, and the enemy kept replacing their cohorts as well. And so the battle was extended for five hours. Eventually, their javelins exhausted, Caesar's cohorts drew their swords and charged the Pompeians, driving them away and herding some within the walls of the town. Now, finally, the Caesarians could escape down the slope as the cavalry rode in to cover their retreat. Caesar tactfully fails to give full details of his casualties in this debacle, but in the initial fight for the mound seventy fell and more than six hundred were wounded. Among the killed was a high-ranking centurion of the Fourteenth Legion. The Pompeians lost more than two hundred men and five centurions — centurions dying at twice the rate of the rankers they led.[23]

What distinguishes the battle of Ilerda from Gergovia was Caesar's decision to fight on the slope, a decision made possible by his ability to maintain the battle for five hours by relieving tired cohorts with fresh. This is not something Aemilius Paullus could easily have done and reflects an enigmatic change in the way Romans fought, the shift from maniples to cohorts. The legion of maniples which Paullus had led used a system of line relief whereby the *principes* replaced the *hastati* and the *principes* fell back on the *triarii,* but all the pieces of the manipular legion were not as casually interchangeable as Caesar's cohorts. The manipular legion also required large gaps between the maniples for line relief to work, gaps which the relief of cohorts, as the compressed circumstances at Ilerda reveal, did not need.

Caesar's ability to keep up the fight at Ilerda was a triumph of the way the Romans were fighting by his time, when the significant subunit of the Roman legion had ceased to be the maniple of one hundred and twenty men and had become the cohort of four hundred and eighty. When Caesar looked at a legion he saw not thirty maniples but ten cohorts. When the new legion drew up in three lines — in the *triplex acies,* as was usual — four cohorts held the front, and there seem to have been three cohorts in each of the second and third lines (see figure). The differentiation of equipment between the echelons of the manipular legion had disappeared. The special roles of the *velites* and the *triarii* were gone:

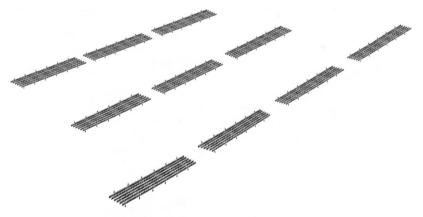

Legion of cohorts arrayed for battle
(SeungJung Kim after P. Smith and M. Swanston).

now all soldiers carried the heavy javelin, sword, and oval shield of the old *hastati* and *principes* (see figure, pp. 226–27). Now all legionaries, unless they had taken up barbarian ways, like the Pompeians at Ilerda, fought as heavy infantry in formation, keeping to their standards and posts. And the age echelons had been swept away as well, unless the *antesignani,* who rushed the knoll at Ilerda, were younger soldiers.[24]

The legion of cohorts, as depicted in Caesar, allowed the commander a great deal of flexibility in arraying his line of battle. The cohorts of the legion could be disposed in a single line, in two lines — which seems to have been common under the empire — or in three lines, the *triplex acies* or "triple battle line" — usual in Caesar. As at Ilerda, rear cohorts could relieve those in front of them one for one by a process we are never privileged to witness. Cohorts could be drafted from the rear lines to form a flank guard, or the cohorts of a legion could be split five and five and set to guard both flanks. The cohorts of the third line of a *triplex acies* formed by several legions could be detached to form their own *triplex acies* on the flank.[25]

But cohorts did not merely articulate the legion: they fought in other combinations as well. At Ilerda, in a place too narrow to fit a legion, three cohorts were sent forward to form their own array. In describing a complicated engagement around the fortifications of Dyrrachium (48 BC), Caesar

Two legionaries (left) and a Roman officer (right, sometimes interpreted as the god Mars). The so-called Altar of Domitius Ahenobarbus, first century BC (Louvre, inv. MA 975; Réunion des Museés Nationaux / Art Resource, NY. Photo: Chuzeville).

thinks as much in terms of multiples of cohorts as in terms of legions: sixty cohorts, twelve, thirty-three. Fighting in the streets of a city was done by cohorts. In a pitched battle, cohorts and groups of cohorts could take on independent functions: they could encircle the enemy, be detached to capture a strategic hill, be sent on a surprise attack, be sent to the support of units in distress. In an emergency cohorts could form a circle, and individual cohorts could make sallies from it. When cavalry attacked, cohorts might charge in sequence to drive them away. If a line was attacked from both sides, alternate cohorts could face in either direction to fight off the enemy. Outside battle, groups of cohorts could be sent on independent strategic expeditions or to forage.[26]

The cohort fought as part of a legion, with other cohorts, and by itself. An army made up of cohorts gave its commander flexibility in planning for battle and options to deal with battle's vicissitudes. The characteristics of a mature way of arraying an army for battle may not have had anything to do with the origins of that array. But it may not be an accident that in the two earliest circumstantial mentions of the cohort — those of Polybius, describing the Second Punic War — it appears as a unit of maneuver. Polybius describes the cohort when he depicts a dramatic flank march at Ilipa and later has four cohorts make a surprise attack which is combined with a cavalry envelopment. At Muthul River in 108 BC Metellus deployed for battle in the old manipular formation. After a great part of the day had passed fighting, his infantry formed into cohorts to attack a hill on which the enemy infantry had taken refuge. In the earliest accounts, then, cohorts seem to be temporary gatherings of maniples for the purpose of maneuver, whether ad hoc or practiced we cannot tell. And Caesar's legion of cohorts is the legitimate heir to these early maneuvering cohorts.[27]

The change to the dominant use of cohorts is nevertheless extremely puzzling. It was slow: it took at least forty years in the second half of the second century BC and probably far longer. Polybius reports cohorts in use in 206 BC, yet it is only with Caesar's campaigns in Gaul beginning in 58 that the cohort clearly has replaced the maniple as the principal subdivision of the legion. The cohort was not the kind of invention that quickly and emphatically replaced what had gone before.

The change is also unexpected: the Romans had come to dominate the Mediterranean world with the manipular legion, perhaps varying it with cohorts for special purposes. Despite a spotted record against the phalanx, the manipular legion had proved itself over generations of victories: it had conquered Carthage in the West and the Greeks in the East; it had campaigned successfully against Spanish tribesmen and Italian Gauls. The maniple, in fact, was finally submerged in the cohort only when the maniple had already nearly conquered the world. If Roman doctrine had developed according to modern notions, the Romans would have kept the victorious manipular legion in the late Republic (just as they might have abandoned it earlier when Pyrrhus and Hannibal defeated them with the Macedonian phalanx). The Romans were a ferociously conservative people: they did not accept change easily. The maniple did not die a natural death: someone had to murder it.[28]

The maniple was finally killed by the same shift in culture that made the tribunes and centurions exchange their roles in battle. Abandoning a successful old system of fighting for one that allowed easier maneuver suggests the decisive influence of a powerful body of men who viewed maneuvering troops as a great part of their role. These were the Roman commanders, their attitude the result of ever more intense Greek influence in the second and first centuries BC. For generation after generation Romans fought and learned from armies practiced in the Greek tradition of command — in the twin arts of tactics and stratagem. By the first century it was unsurprising if a large part of a general's military education came from his reading. Roman officers read Greek military treatises — there was only one notable textbook in Latin, that of Cato the Elder — and it was a matter of boasting if a commander had learned his trade by fighting rather than by reading Greek experts and Roman history. Brutus was copying out Polybius, the Greek historian and tactical writer, on the eve of the battle of Pharsalus. The way Julius Caesar, who seems the most Roman of authors, thinks about battle, that is, about the crash of formations into one another and about morale, was profoundly influenced by Greek models.[29]

Not only was Greek influence stronger by the first century BC, but its audience was wider as well. The Greek example held sway not only over the commanding general, but over all the aristocratic officers of the Roman army. In an older time an Aemilius Paullus or a Fabius Maximus stood nearly alone against the massed opinion of his soldiers and officers, who were nearly unified in their devotion to the old ways of *virtus* and the ways of fighting *virtus* urged. Then the generals' chief allies had been the centurions, the exemplars of the *disciplina* upon whom the general relied to get his way — if he did. In the old days the argument over how to fight battles had been an argument with aristocratic officers on both sides. But now the aristocracy was for the most part arrayed on the side of the general and against the soldiery and centurions. In a deferential and hierarchical society like that of Rome, this communion of the higher-ups had its predictable result, as they were able slowly to transform the legion in accord with their ideals. And so the single combat of the *velites* and the system of manipular age echelons — the hard-won result of the primeval battle of *virtus* with the phalanx — finally yielded to the ambitions of commanders for interchangeable units they could array and maneuver more easily.

Aiding this transition — an enabling factor — was a shift over time in the relative power of aristocratic officers and the soldiers who served under them. To fight in the Roman army of the middle Republic required a property qualification. Originally this qualification will have required ownership of a farm ample enough to support a family, and so excluded landless laborers. This system of property qualification reflected the social reality that soldiers were long expected to provide their own equipment, but also the old Roman sense that military service, offering the opportunity to display *virtus* and collect plunder, was a desirable privilege that should be confined to the more desirable citizens. Yet by the late second or early first century BC — both the stages of reduction and the reasons for them are irremediably confused — the property qualification was gone, and any physically suitable Roman citizen, however humble, could join the legions.[30]

The frightening political consequences of this "proletarianization" of the Roman army — *proletarii* being the Latin term for Rome's poorest citizens — are celebrated. Soldiers with no farms to return to became political dependents upon their generals, who called upon them in the civil wars that broke the Roman Republic. Soldiers turned to generals and demagogues because, being poor and weak, they had nowhere else to turn. And that same weakness fundamentally altered the relations between soldier and commander in the Roman army. From a military standpoint the proletarianization of the Roman army meant it was no longer socially a cross-section of the middling-to-upper ranks of Roman society, as it had been when the destitute were turned away. Now an army of poor men, with its centurions drawn from the same humble background, was led by military tribunes and higher officers drawn from at least the petty aristocracy: an army of the weak led by the sons of the strong. The middling had largely departed to civilian pursuits, undergoing the same cultural transformation as so much of the Roman aristocracy. Thus the soldiers of Caesar's day were in a weaker position to dictate to their commanders than soldiers had been in the days of Scipio Africanus.

As Gergovia, Ilerda, and countless other incidents in the late Republic show, Roman soldiers remained dangerously willful and assertive. When they found champions, like the warlords of the first century BC — Caesar, Pompey, Antony, Octavian — their passions threatened the state and played a large role in the bloody passage from Roman Republic to empire. But on questions of military organization, the warlords stood arm in arm with their officers against the soldiers, and the soldiers of the late Republic were no longer powerful enough to resist them, except by open mutiny. The late Republic saw a slight but significant shift in the old battle between the opposing ideals of *virtus* and *disciplina:* as soldiers became weaker, *disciplina* gained ground.[31]

This was a long struggle, as manifested by the long coexistence of maniple and cohort. The aristocracy never entirely won this struggle. For centuries to come the cohort continued to be viewed as somehow temporary, ad hoc, alien, and unloved. Even under the empire the legionary cohort never developed officers of its own, or a standard of its own. Centuries and centurions continued to be called by their place in the older manipular array. Imperial soldiers expressed their sense of attachment to a group by worshiping its collective divine spirit, its *genius*. But although the *genius* of the venerable century (and the legion, and of groups like standard-bearers and centurions) commanded warm devotion, the *genius* of the legionary cohort was not worshiped.[32]

The coming of the Roman empire brought great administrative changes to the Roman army. It became by rule and regulation what it had been becoming in practice during the long wars of the late Republic, a professional regular army with a long, set term of service, with systematic training and a regular rank structure. In principle, under such conditions one might expect *disciplina* to continue to advance at the expense of *virtus*. To test that theory it is best to leap forward over a century to the Roman siege of Jerusalem.

XI

SCENES FROM THE JEWISH WAR, AD 67–70

FIGHTING, WORKING, AND TRAINING
IN THE ROMAN IMPERIAL ARMY

I n AD 67, Levantine Ptolemais looked seaward to the calm of the
Roman Mediterranean and inland to the storms of a rebel Galilee.
The year before, the province of Judaea had flown to arms against
a monstrous Roman governor. The hapless legate of Syria had
descended with a legion to suppress the revolt but had been driven
back with loss, abandoning his siege engines. Now Nero's new
general, Vespasian, marched south from Antioch with two of the legions
of Syria, and his son Titus marched north to meet him at Ptolemais with
a legion from the garrison of Egypt.[1]

His army united, Vespasian marched inland into Galilee, which was
defended by a scratch force led by the Jewish notable Josephus. After the
Romans captured him, and he began to assist them, the flexible Josephus
was eventually to chronicle the war, first in Aramaic, then in Greek. The
Romans had fought many wars and countless battles since Caesar's day —
had captured Britain, completed the circuit of the Mediterranean, extended their power to the Danube, been thrown back from beyond the
Rhine, and fenced with the kings of proud Parthia in the eastern wastes
— but the *Jewish War* of Josephus is by far the most detailed written description of Roman fighting that survives from the first three centuries
of the Roman empire.

Josephus had striven mightily to organize and drill his Galileans, yet
at the approach of the Romans most of his army deserted and fled to
fortified places. This humiliation is significant because it, as well as the

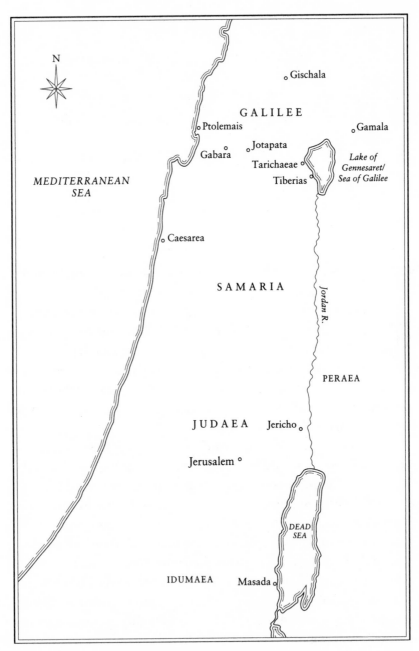

N

GALILEE

Gischala

Ptolemais

Gabara   Jotapata

Taricheae

Tiberias

Gamala

Lake of
Gennesaret/
Sea of Galilee

MEDITERRANEAN
SEA

Caesarea

SAMARIA

Jordan R.

PERAEA

JUDAEA   Jericho

Jerusalem

DEAD
SEA

IDUMAEA   Masada

The Levant in the Jewish War (AD 66–70)

unruliness of the Jews throughout the war and their fierce internal battles, provides the context for Josephus's one-dimensional evaluation of the Roman army. To Josephus — and he has convinced many of his modern readers — the army of the Roman empire excelled because of its relentless, realistic training and the exact obedience to orders that training inculcated: "To the Romans the beginning of war is not their introduction to arms. . . . Instead, as if they had grown with weapons in their hands, they never have an armistice from training, never wait for crises to arrive. Their exercises lack none of the vigor of true war, but each soldier trains every day with his whole heart as if it were war indeed. . . . He would not err who described their exercises as battles without blood, and their battles as bloody exercises."[2] Of this same training the fourth-century Vegetius gives details, looking back longingly to an earlier day: marching in regular step and quick time; marching with kit, with three long route-marches a month; running; jumping; swimming; throwing javelins; endless attacks with mock shield and sword on a wooden post; mass drill in keeping ranks and formation; and finally, mock battles. When it was fine the Romans trained out-of-doors, when foul, under roofs. Even experienced soldiers, Vegetius tells us, were expected to exercise with their arms every day. The reality of such training is confirmed by the excavation of drill grounds and cavalry riding areas, of catapult ranges, by the traces of countless "practice" camps — sometimes many on the same plot of land — that Roman units built on maneuvers, and of elaborate practice siege-works built around pre-Roman hill forts. "I praise [the commander] because he turned your efforts to this exercise, which is similar to a [real] combat," said the emperor Hadrian upon witnessing an exhibition of drill at Lambaesis in North Africa (AD 128).[3]

"The Romans are unbeatably strong," Josephus says, "especially because of their obedience and practice at arms." In the Roman camp "there is nothing that happens without the word of command." In short, "no disorder disperses them from their usual formation, no fear confounds them, no labor exhausts them, and certain victory follows against those unequal in these respects." In fact, disorder, fear, and exhaustion were the Romans' constant companions in the Jewish War, as the detailed narrative of Josephus reveals. Roman training and discipline were certainly admirable in comparison to that of Josephus's countrymen, as he pointedly told them, and especially valuable in a world where many opponents undertook cursory training or none. But training and discipline alone do not account for Roman success, and training and discipline are themselves a puzzle: how did they fit in the wider culture of the Roman imperial army? What was the fate of the balance of *virtus* and *disciplina* in a professional army?[4]

Gabara was the first strong place in Galilee Vespasian captured. All the men were killed and the city burnt and also the villages and country towns round about: the Romans had become no kindlier since Caesar's day. Next the Romans moved south to the well-protected town of Jotapata, as Josephus rushed to oversee its defense. The siege of Jotapata was bitter and lasted forty-seven days. Finally the Roman earthworks were built up to the height of the walls. The Romans rushed the town before dawn, when they hoped the sentries would be drowsing. Vespasian's son Titus and a military tribune were the first on the wall; others followed, and the city was captured before most of the inhabitants were awake. There was a general massacre. The dead were calculated at forty thousand. Josephus was captured.[5]

After a pause to rest his troops, Vespasian turned his attention to eastern Galilee. After some indecision the town of Tiberias surrendered and so preserved itself from destruction. Tarichaeae by the lake of Gennesaret was the center of what resistance remained, and Vespasian moved toward it. A body of Jews attempted to resist the Romans in the field outside the city, and Vespasian sent Titus with cavalry against them. Titus led the charge in person and killed many by his own hand during the pursuit: it may be in this battle that, as Suetonius records, he had a horse killed under him and mounted another in its stead. The survivors fled into the town, and dispute about whether Tarichaeae should surrender soon became an uproar audible even to the Romans outside. Titus, taking advantage of the chaos, led his cavalry into the shallows of the lake and so into the town, it not being walled on the lakeward side. Thus Tarichaeae was captured.[6]

Next came Gamala, on the other side of the lake and beyond. Soon the Roman rams had broken through the walls, and Roman columns were in the city, advancing without orders to the higher reaches of the steep place. But the Jews rallied and threw them back. The town was narrow and sheer: it was hard to retreat except onto the roofs of houses where they were flush with the slope, and these soon collapsed under the weight, killing many Romans in the avalanche. In anxiety at the crisis Vespasian himself had advanced heedlessly within the walls. Suddenly he found himself in the front lines and under attack. He formed those near him into a shield wall and stopped the Jewish onrush and then retired slowly, front to the enemy, until he was outside the city.[7]

There could be no doubt that Vespasian and Titus were father and son: both looked as if a giant had seized them by the ears and stretched their faces broad, leaving deep creases in their brows from the pulling. But father's and son's sense of their roles in battle were far different. Vespasian fought like Caesar, close enough to the front to command and encourage — at Jotapata he had even been hit in the foot with an arrow — but not to fight. Titus, by contrast, fought at the head of his troops and cut down enemies with his own sword. And the contrast was not merely because one was a cautious fifty-eight-year-old supreme commander and the other a carefree twenty-seven-year-old: Titus too had grave responsibilities, as commander of the Fifteenth Legion.[8]

The Roman setback at Gamala, with soldiers out of control and driven down the hill, was very similar to that at Gergovia, and Josephus's account of it is much like Caesar's of his defeat in Gaul: alike even in the tales of courageous individuals Josephus tells, a brave cavalry officer slain, a centurion saved by derring-do; alike even in the speech he gives to Vespasian to correct and reassure his troops afterward, carefully balancing the need for discipline with the need for courage. But if Vespasian gave such an address, his men paid it little heed. Soon after, three soldiers of the Fifteenth Legion crept by night to the base of one of the towers of Gamala and quietly dug out five great stones: they leapt back as the entire tower, and the sentries atop it, crashed to the ground. The Jews were in a panic. No less surprised were the Romans: no plans had been made to exploit the collapse and the chaos, and, remembering their previous failure, the Romans did not try to enter the city for a full day after. So this appears to have been a private enterprise on the part of the three legionaries. When the Romans did enter the city again, they were led by Titus (he had been away during the first attack), who once again cut down those he met. Even women and infants were slaughtered in this sack, in revenge for the earlier defeat: nine thousand were killed or threw themselves from the walls into the ravine that bordered the town. Only two women survived. After the capture of Gischala in the north, which surrendered to Titus after the warriors escaped by a ruse, all of Galilee was in Roman hands.[9]

It was now November and time to send the legions into winter quarters. In the new year the strategy of Vespasian was to put down the revolt outside Jerusalem and drive all the surviving rebels into the seething city. While it was still winter he quickly seized the Jewish towns of the Peraea, to the east, across the river Jordan from Jerusalem. Those downstream learned of his coming when thousands of bodies floated down the river and washed up on the shores of the Dead Sea. In the spring Vespasian struck south into Idumaea, then north into Samaria. By June he had captured Jericho, completing his circuit of ravaging around Jerusalem. Vespasian was told that nothing sank in the nearby Dead Sea: he had prisoners cast in with their hands bound, and lo! they floated. Now all that remained was to march directly to Jerusalem and lay it under siege.[10]

But now fate put a halt to the campaign. Far away in Rome Nero was overthrown and Italy cast into the confusion of the year of the four emperors. In the East, Vespasian waited upon events, and so the summer of AD 68 passed into winter. In June of the next year he moved to reassert his hold on Judaea outside Jerusalem, wasting the countryside and taking some towns he had neglected before. He rode with his cavalry up to the walls of Jerusalem as well and then rode away again. He avoided a major campaign in AD 69 because he had his eye on higher things: on July 1 the carefully instructed garrison of Egypt proclaimed Vespasian emperor, and his own legions and the powerful Syrian army soon followed suit. Away went Vespasian to manage a civil war against his rival emperor Vitellius, and by December Vespasian's lieutenants in Europe had made him master of the Roman world. Rome's new emperor sailed for the capital and left Titus to bring the war against the Jews to an end.[11]

Two years had now been squandered. Titus would delay no longer and ordered his legions, now reinforced to four by another from Syria, to advance on Jerusalem from both east and west. Approaching the city, he rode ahead with six hundred horse to reconnoiter, but, riding too close to the walls, he was cut off by a Jewish sally that broke the head of

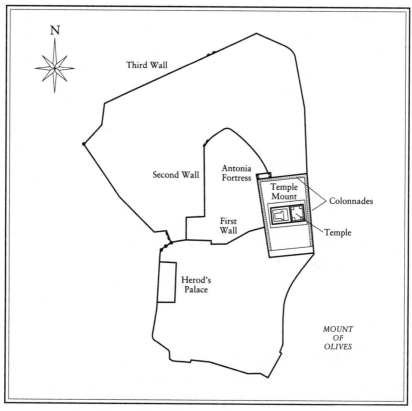

Jerusalem during the Roman Siege (AD 70)

his cavalcade from the body. Titus could not go forward — garden walls and trenches blocked that path. The only way to safety was through the enemy, and through them he led his companions in a breathless, headlong charge, killing those who tried to block his onrush. Although unarmored, for this was no more than a reconnaissance expedition, Titus came through unscathed. Two of his companions were killed.[12]

Now the legions came up, and Titus ordered them to camp around the city: the Tenth — not Caesar's old Tenth, now called X Gemina, but X Fretensis, founded by Octavian — was assigned the Mount of Olives. While the Tenth was fortifying its camp, the enemy unexpectedly struck against it from the city. After a confused struggle the legion was turned to flight but was rallied by Titus, who took the Jews in the flank with his personal guard. Having restored the situation, Titus established a protective line nearer the city and sent the Tenth back to build its camp. But the Jews thought the legionaries were fleeing and attacked again, and the forward Roman line collapsed before them, leaving Titus isolated with his companions on the slope. Now, and not for the last time in this war, Titus's friends and staff begged him to take care: he was the general-in-chief, not a soldier, they said. Everything depended on him, and he should not risk himself. This was the standard advice of Greek tactical writers and the principle to which Julius Caesar had adhered. But Titus was having none of it. He held his position, himself fighting by hand. In their eagerness to chase those in flight the enemy split around his small band like a torrent around a rock, and so Titus and his guard charged them in the flank. Once again the Tenth was in a panic — so much for Josephus's "no disorder disperses them from their usual formation, no fear confounds them" — and it began to flee, but then Titus was noticed in the fight on the slope below, and (Josephus says) pure shame at having abandoned their general rallied the legionaries, and they pushed the Jews back down the slope.[13]

With the legions encamped, the Romans turned to clearing the ground before Jerusalem, shifting their camps closer to the walls and bringing up the baggage. During this work, the defenders worked a ruse upon the besiegers. The Romans knew from defectors that the Jews inside the city were riven by religious and political faction and that some yearned to come to terms with Rome. So when a body of men appeared to have been ejected from the city amidst a shower of stones and appeared to be trying to force their way back in while cowering from the Romans who looked on, and when those who had expelled them shouted, "Peace" and offered to open the gates to the enemy, many Romans were deceived. Titus suspected a trick and ordered no move to be made, but the guards of the Roman works made a rush for the gates without orders. Now those who had pretended to be expelled attacked them in the rear, and now those who had promised to open the gates shot them down with missiles from the ramparts: only slowly and with great loss did the Romans fight their way free. The defenders jeered and capered on the walls.[14]

This was Titus's Gergovia, and the sequel was the same as at Gergovia. Titus fumed and ranted — "among the Romans even victory without orders is a disgrace!" Josephus has him insist — and terrified the disobedient soldiers by threatening the terrible penalty for fighting without orders: death. But then he allowed the pleas of the legions to soften his anger, and no one was punished: like Caesar at Gergovia and like Vespasian at Gamala, Titus contented himself with a lecture. At the climax of the siege he would have reason to rejoice that he did not bloodily stamp out his soldiers' initiative.[15]

Having selected what he hoped was a weak stretch of the fortifications, Titus ordered the erection of three siege ramps. With their throwing engines, towers, rams, and ramps, the Romans were fully up-to-date besiegers, but fully up to date in a technology of siege that had advanced hardly at all since Greeks made a science of it in the Hellenistic period. An engineer employed by Demetrius Poliorcetes at his great siege of Rhodes (305–304 BC) would have been quite at home before Jerusalem with Titus, more than three and a half centuries later.

The Jews attacked the builders with engines, missiles, and sallies, but to no avail, and rams were brought up on the ramps. The defenders charged out against them but were thrown back, Titus leading the relief in person. Again they sallied against the rams, and again Titus led his cavalry in, killing with his own hand. Towers were built to defend the rams: at night one of these, badly constructed, collapsed with an enormous crash. The Romans panicked, thinking the Jews were inside their camps, and confusion reigned until the truth became known. The Greeks had a saying they often applied to the blind and inexplicable panics that afflicted armies: "There are many empty things in war." Despite Josephus's editorializing, the Romans of the empire were no less vulnerable to empty panic than any other ancient army.[16]

With the towers brought up, the Romans swept the walls with missiles, and so the rams could work in safety. When a ram nicknamed Victor made a breach, the Jews abandoned the wall: behind it two more remained. The Romans established a camp inside the wall they had taken, and during their preparations to attack the next wall there was skirmishing in the open between the Romans and the defenders. During a combat at range with javelins, Longinus, a cavalryman, leapt out from the Roman lines and charged the mass of the enemy. He killed one, pulled his spear out, took another in the side, and then made his way safely back to his

comrades. Others subsequently emulated his deed. On one occasion a
Jew challenged any Roman who dared to single combat. Pudens, another
cavalryman, answered the challenge but tripped during the fight, and the
Jewish challenger killed him, only to be shot down in the act of vaunting
over the body by a Roman centurion with a bow. So much for the chivalrous old rules of single combat.[17]

The old competitiveness in bravery of Roman soldiers was still strong in
the army of Titus. But Josephus's account of the Jewish War hints at a
change in the identity of the Roman army's heroes. The type of reckless
bravery once practiced by young Roman aristocrats, the heroism that
Caesar's centurions inherited from them, was in Josephus's account primarily the province of the Roman army's auxiliary soldiers. Pudens was
certainly an auxiliary; Longinus probably. During a Jewish sally an exceptionally strong auxiliary cavalryman reached down from his saddle and
grabbed a fleeing enemy by the ankle and then bore his armored captive
off just as he was to be admired by Titus. Such behavior is part of a wider
trend: the Romans increasingly relied on auxiliaries to do their hand-to-
hand fighting. This trend is most remarkably illustrated on Trajan's Column, that enigmatic monument which depicts in astonishing detail on
a huge spiral relief the Roman conquest of Dacia, in two wars of AD
101–102 and 105–106. So detailed and circumstantial is the sculpted narrative that it is nearly irresistible to suppose that it adapts to pictures a
literary account of the war, perhaps that of Trajan himself.[18]

In the standard type of battle scene on the column, auxiliaries and
bare-chested barbarian allies fight at the front, while at the back legionaries
stand or build or lurk in fortifications cosseting their ballistas. Pointing
up the contrast between the roles of auxiliary and legionary is a scene
high on the column in which auxiliaries attack Dacians on top of a wall,
while a party of legionaries, right beside them, attack the wall itself with
picks; just up the spiral more legionaries cut and stack wood for use in
the siege (see figure, pp. 244–45).[19]

On all of Trajan's Column legionary and nonlegionary infantry (auxiliary infantrymen, conical-helmed eastern archers, bare-chested barbarian allies) play very different roles. Put simply, legionaries parade, march,
and work — and nonlegionaries fight. There are more than fifteen scenes

in which legionaries build fortifications, sometimes with auxiliaries as sentries, or cut wood or clear forests or harvest grain or conduct supply wagons, fatigues that are depicted in seemingly demented detail over yard after yard of stone. But legionaries are depicted as fighting in only four scenes, while nonlegionary infantry fight in fourteen. Moreover, nonlegionary infantry engages in fatigues in only a handful of scenes, and when they do so the depiction is far less elaborate, and what non-combat work they do is more aggressive than the legionaries': they slaughter prisoners and burn Dacian villages. The column strikingly conveys the wildness of Rome's auxiliary soldiers: in several scenes auxiliaries, but never legionaries, are depicted as proudly presenting severed heads to the emperor, and one auxiliary who has taken a head but both of whose hands are occupied in fighting carries the severed head in his teeth, hanging by the hair (see figure, p. 246). At the same time art and archeology reveal changes in legionary equipment that suggest a more specialized role: armor with exaggerated protection for the shoulders and helmets with exaggerated protection for the face and back of the neck, protection against downward blows. Roman legionary armor evolved under the early empire to protect the Roman soldier against attacks from above — exactly the type of attacks he might expect when toiling beneath the walls of Jerusalem; exactly the type of attacks he suffered when assailing Dacian forts. Roman legionaries were used increasingly as combat engineers, and their armor evolved along with the function of its wearers.[20]

Trajan's Column, despite its detail, is a work of art, and it is perhaps unwise to draw from it historical conclusions about the use of soldiers in battle. But certainly Josephus confirms that in his day legionaries did most of the building and auxiliaries displayed most of the bravado. And Agricola's victory at Mons Graupius in Scotland (AD 83), described by Tacitus, reveals the same distinction between legionaries and auxiliaries in battle: the legionaries were left as a reserve outside the rampart of the camp, while the eight thousand auxiliary infantry formed the line of battle, with the cavalry on their wings. Fourteen years before that the Roman general Cerialis had posted his auxiliaries in front of his legions when fighting the Batavians, then in rebellion. These Batavians, restored to loyalty, were to be the best of Agricola's auxiliaries. There are earlier instances too, from AD 16 and 23, of auxiliaries posted to bear the brunt

Auxiliaries fight and legionaries work, Trajan's Column, Rome,
AD 113 (Cichorius pl. cxvi, Museo della Civilta Romana no. 3117.
Photo: akg-images, London).

Auxiliary carrying a severed head in his teeth,
Trajan's Column, Rome, AD 113
(Cichorius pl. xxiv. Photo: Adrian Goldsworthy).

of the fighting. Were the auxiliaries mere cannon fodder? Tacitus explained that Agricola deployed the auxiliaries in front to win, if he could, the glory of a victory without loss of citizen blood, and this motive has also been adduced to explain the positioning of legionaries on Trajan's Column in the back. But the auxiliaries at Mons Graupius won without legionary help, and they usually seem to do so on the column as well. In the chaos of AD 69–70, the Batavian auxiliaries defeated legionaries and regarded themselves as equal or superior to the legions — their sneering at the legionaries produced brawls — and the legionaries regarded the Batavians as one of the strongest forces in the army. Auxiliaries, we now suspect, were paid the same as Roman legionaries. But such was the reputation of the Batavians that an emperor, in time of civil war, might promise them double pay.[21]

This increasing reliance on auxiliaries in battle reflects Roman patterns of recruitment. As the Roman empire piled decade upon decade, the Roman army went farther and farther afield to find soldiers. Legionaries were supposed to be Roman citizens upon enlistment; auxiliaries were not required to be. But to find both, recruiting officers struck out into the wild marches of the empire. By the end of the first century AD, few legionaries were recruited in Italy, and even by the middle of that century the accents of legionaries from the northern borders sounded barbarous to soldiers stationed elsewhere. Such recruiting may have been driven by the reluctance of those in Rome's more civilized dominions to serve or by their greater power to resist conscription, but it was certainly driven also by the sense that men from certain of the empire's less developed areas made excellent soldiers. The Greeks and the Romans were comfortable with the idea that some peoples were simply more warlike than others. Possessed of a vast empire, the Romans naturally recruited heavily from such warlike folk. Of the German tribes living on the Roman side of the Rhine, "the Batavians are outstanding in *virtus*," Tacitus says, and so are "set aside for use in battle, like missiles and arms reserved for war." Through the third century AD over twenty-five Thracian auxiliary units are known, and in the fourth century the Thracians were still recruited for their special warrior qualities. It was in areas where the most warlike recruits came from — Thrace, Britain, Batavia — that the Romans pushed conscription to the point of inspiring revolts, the Thracians, for example, "refusing to give all their able-bodied men to military service." Over time the army also recruited increasingly from colonies of veterans and the sons of soldiers, from young men, that is, brought up in a martial tradition.[22]

The Roman army of the empire went out of its way to recruit *virtus*. And the army went out of its way to encourage *virtus* in its ranks as well. At Jerusalem Longinus the brave cavalryman had acted, Josephus says, in the hope of attracting the eye of Titus, in the hope of earning a reward. Hardly surprising: compared to the Republic, the Roman empire had regularized and elaborated the spurs to rivalry in *virtus* among individual soldiers. The system of military decorations, which Polybius had pointed out as so powerful a motive force in the Republic, was formalized and graded for rank. Decorations were mentioned in soldiers' epitaphs, sometimes noting that they were given *ob virtutem,* "for *virtus"* — and were carved upon their tombstones (see figure): decorations were of enormous importance to soldiers. The creation and elaboration of a permanent rank-structure for the imperial army also allowed promotion in that structure to be used systematically as another form of motivation, and Josephus says it served that function at Jerusalem. "He was made decurion in the same cavalry wing because he captured Decebalus and carried his head to Ranisstorum," reads a proud soldier's tombstone. And no wonder, for not only did promotion bring honor and easier duty, but the pay structure of the Roman army was severely hierarchical — a centurion was paid fifteen times what a common legionary earned. The decision of some soldiers, including a few never promoted to centurion, to lay out in their epitaphs each posting in their entire career, shows how powerful a motivator of soldiers rank was.[23]

Still, despite Longinus's expectation, Titus was not entirely delighted by him and his emulators: he issued an order telling them to prove their bravery without running such risks. Given Titus's own behavior, his soldiers must have chortled; they certainly do not seem to have paid him much attention.[24]

Five days after the capture of the first wall the Romans penetrated the second, were thrown back — Titus and the tribune who had accompanied him over the wall at Jotapata shot arrows to cover the retreat — and four days later pushed their way in again. The siege had now reached its climax: two walls had fallen, and the last wall stretched from the Temple Mount itself.[25]

After giving the besieged in the city a respite to surrender, Titus set each of his four legions to build great ramps of wood and earth at opposite ends of the last wall. Two ramps were raised against the massif of the Antonia fortress, which rose from the corner of the Temple mount: built as King Herod's high castle, it had afterward been the sheer eyrie of the city's Roman garrison. As the Temple dominated the city of Jerusalem, so the Antonia fortress dominated the Temple, and unless the Temple were taken, the city could not be held.[26]

Centurion wearing his decorations. Grave relief of Marcus Caelius,
who vanished in the Varian disaster of AD 9
(Bonn, Rheinisches Landesmuseum. Photo: akg-images, London).

Once again the besieged harassed the builders with raids, missiles, and projectiles from captured Roman engines. For seventeen days the Romans toiled, but underneath them, the defenders tunneled out from the Antonia and propped up the Roman works with timbers. When the timbers were set alight, the ramps collapsed with a tremendous crash. A fierce Jewish sally destroyed the earthworks at the other end of the wall, where the Romans had already brought up their rams, and drove the Romans back to their camps, which they defended from the entrenchments. Once again Titus and his guard charged the attackers in the flank, and the Jews were driven back within the walls. But the Roman attack had been resoundingly defeated. The Romans were despondent. Perhaps Jerusalem could not be taken by assault. Perhaps it would have to be starved out.[27]

Titus decided to postpone his next attack until a wall had been drawn about Jerusalem. He wanted to stop the smuggling of provisions into the city, so that famine would press even harder upon the defenders. They might even surrender. Building a circuit of entrenchments around the whole great city — nearly four and a half miles, with thirteen attached forts — took the Romans only three days, a striking credit to their training. But the achievement reveals something else about the Roman army. Josephus, to whom it seemed the soldiers labored as if possessed, was astonished by the speed of the work, and he reveals how they were motivated: each section of the circuit was assigned to a legion, each portion of a legionary span to a cohort, each cohort's share was split between centurions, each centurion's share split between his subordinates. So at every level soldiers, units, and officers competed with their neighbors under the watchful eye of their superiors, and Titus, the supreme commander, toured the works and was umpire over all.[28]

If the fighting of the Roman imperial army was competitive, so too was Roman military building. "When I was assigning shares of the work, so that each would know what part of the tunneling was his, I arranged for competition between the soldiers of the fleet and the infantry, and thus they cooperated in drilling through the mountain together," records a Roman military engineer from the second century AD. At Lambaesis, Hadrian praised in detail the fort-building demonstration of one of the units displaying its excellence before him: they were expected to be proud of their achievement. Competition seems to have been the usual method by which the Roman army carried out large projects, like Hadrian's Wall and the Antonine Wall in Britain. Suddenly the long stretches of Trajan's Column devoted to legionary building make sense. These are not merely a robotic transfer of material from a written account to sculpture but illustrate the competitive excellence of the legionaries. *Labor* was the Latin word for such excellence in hard work, and along with *patientia* (endurance) *labor* formed part of the wider concept of *disciplina*. What seems so puzzling — the unheroic activities of legionaries on the column, in contrast with the fighting of the auxiliaries — is less so if the legionaries' work is understood to manifest *disciplina*, one of the two fundamental military values of the Romans.[29]

Another meaning of the Latin word *disciplina* was training. Like the training of Greek and Hellenistic armies, Roman training too was fiercely competitive. A particularly successful soldier recorded his triumphs in training on his tombstone:

> Once I was most renowned on the Pannonian shore
> amidst a thousand Batavians the strongest.
> With Hadrian watching I swam the huge waters
> of Danube's deep in full arms.
> While a bolt from my bow hung in the air —
> while it fell — I hit and shattered it with another arrow.
> Neither Roman nor barbarian, no soldier with his javelin,
> no Parthian with his bow, could defeat me.
> Here I lie. I have entrusted my deeds to the memory of this
>   stone.
> Whether another after me will emulate my deeds has yet to
>   be seen.
> I am the first who did such things: I emulated myself.

Swimming, archery, javelin throwing: this paragon excelled in all. An extended description of auxiliary cavalry drill survives: beneath standards and writhing serpent-banners, the cavalry competed in riding and charging, wheeling and circling, in casting blunted javelins at one another and spears at targets. Hadrian's address at Lambaesis, so proudly inscribed in all its details by the addressees, presupposes an acute competitiveness on the part of the soldiers he was reviewing. Some had not done very well, and Hadrian, as in the prize giving at a cringingly sensitive modern school, nevertheless had to stretch to find something good to say about each of them: "You were not boring, despite the heat."[30]

The Latin *disciplina* was a much broader term than the English discipline. Existing in counterpoint to the concept of *virtus*, it came to include not merely obedience and punishment, but nearly every military excellence that was not encompassed under *virtus*, including training and building. Roman *disciplina* was at once something imposed upon Roman soldiers from above and something soldiers were expected to feel in their hearts. As such *disciplina* was, like *virtus*, competitive. "Where is the glory of the old *disciplina*?" Tacitus has a general ask mutineers. "Where once the soldiers had vied in *virtus* and obedience [*modestia*], now their contest was in insolence and impudence," he groans. *Disciplina* was a source of honor, something on which soldiers prided themselves. When they failed in *disciplina*, soldiers sometimes felt crippling shame, just as when they failed in *virtus*. This makes sense of how, as a competitive excellence, *Disciplina* could be worshiped as a divinity, alongside other divinized virtues, including *Virtus* itself. The Roman mind could regard *virtus* and *disciplina* as structurally similar, and soldiers competed in both. And like the parallel Spartan competitions in excellence in combat and in obedience, neither *disciplina* nor *virtus* enjoyed strict precedence in the Roman military mind.[31]

Yet the opposition of *virtus* and *disciplina* did not diminish under the empire, developing instead into a tacit distinction between the legionaries, among whom the stress was upon *disciplina*, and the auxiliaries, among whom the stress was upon *virtus*. It was the exemplars of *virtus* who were increasingly used in battle, and the exemplars of *disciplina* who were increasingly used in construction, to erect the sophisticated engineering works that, as Jerusalem demonstrated, gave the Romans a considerable part of their relative superiority in war. This was a matter of emphasis, not a schism: the auxiliaries were not relieved of drill and building, and the army did not cease to recruit and encourage *virtus* in the legions. But the differing roles of soldiers at Jerusalem and on Trajan's Column betrays a degree of matter-of-fact specialization, specialization built upon the primeval faultline of the Roman army, the opposition between *virtus* and *disciplina*.

After the wall around Jerusalem was complete, Titus ordered four new ramps, larger than the old ones, to be raised against the Antonia; presumably each ramp was assigned to a legion, as the previous ramps had been. In twenty-one days they were complete. A badly coordinated attack on the ramps by the besieged was thrown back, and rams were brought up against the walls. The defenders cast down stones, fire, and missiles, but the Romans held their positions at the bottom of the walls, the rams did their work, and legionaries even pried out four great stones by hand. In the night, when fighting was suspended, the Roman efforts were rewarded when the wall of the Antonia, undermined by the countermines dug beneath the first ramps and weakened by the rams, collapsed. But behind it loomed another wall, erected in haste by the defenders against just such a development. Now Titus appealed with promises of reward and promotion for volunteers to lead the ascent up the rubble to this new wall. Twelve volunteers were found, led by a singularly hideous Syrian auxiliary named Sabinus. He led on bravely but tripped at the top of the wall; he was overwhelmed, and the assault failed.[32]

Two nights later the Romans captured the Antonia, and in an unexpected way. Twenty legionaries on sentry duty banded together and decided, apparently without informing their officers, to make an attempt upon the wall in the dark. They recruited for their adventure a standard-bearer of the Fifth Legion (presumably their own), a trumpeter, and two auxiliary cavalrymen. The first Titus knew of the assault was when the Roman trumpet sang out from the top of the wall, the attackers having climbed and killed the sentries by stealth. The general called the sleeping Romans to arms and hastened with his bodyguard and staff to reinforce the lodgment: he found the Antonia empty of enemies, the defenders having heard the same trumpet blast as he and having fled in panic into the neighboring Temple, thinking the Romans inside the Antonia in force.[33]

The fact that there were no forces held in readiness to exploit the ascent of the wall indicates that, like the undermining of the tower at Gamala, the taking of the Antonia was the independent project of common soldiers who drew a more senior man, the standard-bearer, in with them. That so great an event should hang on the private initiative of private soldiers would be surprising in any army. But it is especially so in the Roman army, which had for centuries in principle doomed to death sentries who left their posts, a custom upon which Josephus remarks. To attack the wall unordered was to risk death at the hands of both Jews and Romans. Why did the Roman sentries attempt it?[34]

The oddest detail of the ascent turns out to be the key. Why, on a night so dark as to allow climbing of the wall unseen, take a legionary standard? For the soldiers to take a trumpeter up the wall made sense, because they used the trumpet to signal their success from the top. But no one would be able to see the standard of the Fifth Legion atop the Antonia. Yet the awkward object was carried up the wall because, seen or unseen, it symbolized the unit of the soldiers engaged in the perilous ascent. Later in the siege standards were carried up the Temple wall in the heat of the fighting — and lost, in a Jewish counterattack. Taking the standard suggests that the soldiers' brave, punishable, valuable act of initiative was a product of the ferocious competition between units in the Roman imperial army.[35]

By Caesar's day soldiers like those of Caesar's famous Tenth Legion had served together long enough to develop a sense of common identity and pride. Some of Caesar's legions survived undissolved into the empire, and Augustus made legions and auxiliary units into formations that were, in principle, permanent. Units began to have long histories and preserved the memories of fighting in many campaigns, under many generals. As old as Roman soldiers' sense of the proud differentness of their units was commanders' exploitation of that feeling to motivate their troops: Caesar appealed to his Tenth Legion as being better than his other units. Under the empire, such appeals were institutionalized: emperors granted legions and auxiliary units titles of honor — Swift, Strong, Claudian, Loyal and True — and auxiliary units were also given decorations which became part of their titles, like the Cavalry Wing of Silius, Twice Decorated with Torques and Arm-rings. By the fourth century AD (and likely earlier) there was a formal system of precedence for units and elaborate heraldry, each unit having its own design painted on its shields, or so it appears from a surviving table of precedence, the *Notitia Dignitatum*.[36]

The rivalry between units of the Roman army was powerful. In time of mutiny, three legions could agree to amalgamate, but unit pride prevented them from extinguishing their identity in another unit, so the standards of all had to be planted together. In time of civil war, rivalry could lead to fighting between units and influence which rival leaders units chose to follow. It was particularly unit rivalry Romans relied upon to push forward military building projects, like the wall around Jerusalem. Later in the siege, when the Romans were trying to push from the Antonia to the Temple, and the access was narrow, rather than simply assign the task to a limited number of units, Titus selected thirty of the best men from each century, so that the goad of unit rivalry would not be lost and the Roman soldiers would "vie man with man and unit with unit."[37]

It is tempting to associate the rivalry between Roman military units with the bonds of soldierly cohesion so valued and encouraged in contemporary armies. No doubt many years of living and fighting together did produce connections of friendship and mutual loyalty among small groups of Roman soldiers, and no doubt those bonds did contribute, to a degree, to the effectiveness of the Roman army in action. But ancient authors stress far more frequently the fierce rivalry between individual Roman soldiers. The religious dedications and tombstones of Roman soldiers, moreover, do not suggest especially warm attachment between soldiers of the smallest and most intimate military groups — they show, rather, stronger attachment between soldiers of the same rank or specialty across units. And there are striking examples too of the lack of close bonds between soldiers. In the subsequent fighting for the Temple at Jerusalem, a group of Roman soldiers who had advanced, inevitably, without orders found themselves isolated on a portico under a burning roof. Their only escape was a long jump down. No friends or comrades came forward to cushion their fall. "I will make you heir to my property if you come and catch me," shouted a smoldering legionary to the watchers beneath. A greedy soldier ran up as bidden — and died when the jumper crushed him and walked away unscathed.[38]

The rivalry between units in the Roman army, then, should perhaps be understood as a form of outward-looking solidarity, rather than inward-looking solidarity arising from internal bonds of friendly sentiment. A Roman unit was less like a modern family, and more like a modern professional sports team, whose members come together to compete against other teams, but whose members' feelings toward teammates are often more rivalrous than affectionate. But whatever the origins of rivalry between soldiers and units, both forms of rivalry were systematically encouraged and exploited by their commanders. Soldiers competed as individuals in *virtus* and *disciplina,* and this competition was nourished and tended by those who commanded the army. But leaders encouraged collective competition in *virtus* and *disciplina* as well. And, if the speeches historians place in the mouths of generals have even a generic relationship to reality, they did so especially by appealing to the history of the unit and the unit's particular pride in that history.[39]

The taking of the Antonia fortress was the decisive moment in the siege of Jerusalem, for now there was no question that the city would fall. Yet there was much more savage fighting — for the Temple, which was burned, and for what lay beyond — and on the Roman side the fighting followed the same pattern as earlier in the siege: brave acts by individual centurions and common soldiers; Roman masses advancing without orders and suffering for it; Titus charging with his cavalry or wanting to fight but being restrained by his staff. But as final victory came closer the Roman soldiers became increasingly uncontrollable, and when Titus finally gave them permission to sack and burn the city, he was merely giving his official imprimatur to what was going to happen anyway. When, after the destruction of the city, Titus paraded his army, decorating and promoting and rewarding with booty those who had distinguished themselves and thanking his soldiers in general for their courage and obedience, we may suspect that some detected more than a slight note of irony at the latter.[40]

When the last resistance in the city failed, the Romans slaughtered until their arms grew weary: now devouring fire and quenching blood fought their own battle for control of the streets. The total Josephus gives for the dead in the siege — one million, one hundred thousand, or nearly half the Jews in Judaea — may be somewhat less unlikely than most such stratospheric figures that survive from antiquity: the siege of Jerusalem was probably the greatest single slaughter in ancient history. Not only was the city sacked and burned, but Titus gave directions that what remained should be wholly demolished, except for a stretch of wall and some high towers which were left as a symbol to the world of Roman strength and as a warning to anyone who might again defy the fury of the Romans.[41]

Bedazzled by the contrasts between the Romans, the chaotic Galileans he commanded, and the Judaeans whose fighting and infighting he witnessed during the Jewish war, Josephus pointed to discipline and training as the key qualities that set the Roman army apart. Josephus's own narrative, however, shows that his formulation was far too simple. Roman soldiers of the empire remained highly volatile, not only subject to panic (like all armies, in all generations) but also to disobedience born of individual and mass aggression. The balance of power between commander and troops, between *disciplina* and *virtus*—which had tilted toward commanders in the last century BC—had retained that tilt but tilted no further. Titus's theoretical authority to plan for battle was unquestioned, as Caesar's had been; it was wrong for soldiers to disobey but still expected, natural, and frequent. Generals could preach and rail against the heedless boldness of their troops, but they did not execute them for it, knowing full well that the success of their soldiers in battle depended on the qualities of spirit that produced that disobedience and being happy to profit from the initiative that spirit produced, as when soldiers without orders undermined the tower at Gamala or made their night ascent up the Antonia. Titus understood exactly what Caesar had: victory depended on maintaining a careful balance between undisciplined *virtus* and competitive *disciplina*.

The Romans saw no contradiction between their training and discipline on the one hand and recruiting and using in battle men not brought up in Roman ways on the other. They did not worry (as many modern commentators have) about the increasing use of barbarian soldiers in the Roman army. To the contrary, the army actively sought out wild soldiers, confident that *disciplina* was easier to teach than *virtus*, which came in the blood or had to be inculcated from birth and could only be evoked, not created, by leadership. A professional, long-service army needed to recruit wilder soldiers to preserve the balance of *disciplina* and *virtus* upon which victory depended. The army of the empire did not try to resolve the tension between the two competing drives but rather placed more weight on both sides of the balance: systematic training but at the same time wilder soldiers, and institutional encouragements to competition between soldiers, both as individuals and units, in both *virtus* and in *disciplina*. The Romans exploited the variations in degree of *virtus* and *disciplina* that their recruiting and training produced, the legions coming to be valued and used especially for their competitive *disciplina,* the auxiliaries for their competitive *virtus.*[42]

To anticipate, these were trends that continued for at least two centuries after the fall of Jerusalem. If in the army of the fourth century AD more of the soldiers were barbarian born — and that is controversial — it was by Roman design. The Romans had been delighted, for centuries, to recruit barbarians for their *virtus,* and in the fourth century barbarians were found especially in élite units, indicating how highly they were valued.[43]

Nevertheless, it is very hard to show that by the mid–fourth century the balance between *virtus* and *disciplina* had finally shifted back toward wild bravery. The late Roman army had spectacular moments of disobedience, but the army's record of disobedience in earlier times was rich as well. Late-antique authors complained about a decline of military training and discipline, but Roman authors always had: the grumbling sounds down the centuries, Tacitus picking up the refrain of Cato, and Vegetius that of Tacitus. Romans nearly always thought their morals were getting worse, and the lapse of *disciplina* was part of that decay. In the context of a Roman defeat, the fourth-century Greek orator Libanius erupts at the predictable explanations: "Don't anyone then tell me about cowardice or softness or lack of training! . . . The spirits of the soldiers and their officers were just as good as they were in the old days, and in skill and training they were in no way worse!" Perhaps, given the strong predisposition of ancient people always to see decline, including Libanius himself when it suited him, Libanius should be believed when he denies it. Later Roman authors were transfixed, just as so many moderns have been, by a false vision of the earlier Roman army as perfectly disciplined.[44]

Rivalry between soldiers of the fourth-century army was still strong: at a siege, fighting under the eyes of the emperor Constantius, Roman soldiers left off their helmets so they could be recognized, and many were shot down with arrows. Common soldiers still took the initiative. Rivalry between units was still strong as well. On the other hand, if sometimes fourth-century soldiers could not be controlled, in more cases they could be, if with difficulty. And the very same soldiers might display both disobedient aggression and high training. At the siege of Amida (AD 359), two units from Gaul could not be restrained from making sallies from the city, even threatening their officers if they were not allowed to attack. But when their attack failed, they withdrew within the walls in perfect step, "as if to music." The fourth-century historian Ammianus Marcellinus could still make the hackneyed contrast between Roman discipline and barbarian size and strength, and the speeches the historian writes for Julian to deliver to his soldiers could be right out of Josephus or Caesar, still trying to strike that winning balance between courage and obedience, between *virtus* and *disciplina*. The evidence is anecdotal and mixed and mushy: if by the mid–fourth century *virtus* had advanced at the expense of *disciplina,* the shift was hardly emphatic. And if shift there was, it is probable that Roman commanders intended it, by their eager recruitment of brave barbarians.[45]

What had changed between Caesar's day and Titus's was the behavior of the supreme commander: unlike Caesar, and unlike most Roman generals of old, Titus fought in a heroic mode, not avoiding—indeed seeking out—opportunities to fight with his own hands. Josephus's accounts of the bravery of Titus must be treated carefully: he was much in debt to Titus, who had begged for his life when Josephus was captured at Jotapata, who had urged his rehabilitation, who had employed him in the Roman service, protected him from subsequent Roman anger, given him lands after the war, and taken him to Italy. Still, writing for a contemporary audience constrained Josephus to embellish rather than invent, and even if we chip away the eulogistic decoration it is quite clear that Titus, whether as Vespasian's subordinate or as supreme commander, was willing, even eager, to fight with his own hands. His behavior is perplexing because heroic generalship had played no great part in Roman fighting for at least three hundred years and was not even very prominent in Roman myths of earlier times. Once upon a time young Roman aristocrats had sought out single combat, but when they grew up to command armies they rarely continued the practice: the treasured *spolia opima,* the dedication made by a supreme commander for killing the opposing general with his own hands, had been won only three times in Roman history, and only once, by Marcellus in 222 BC, in a nonmythical era. There had always been a few fighting army commanders—Marius, for example, had fought in the forefront of his army and led cavalry charges in Africa—but they emphasize the rarity of the phenomenon. More usual was the transition made by the same Marius, who fought a single combat in his youth but jeeringly refused a challenge when consul. An angry Greek could compare the passivity of a Roman general of the early second century BC to the more aggressive Greek tradition of command: "When had he done the duty of a commander? He'd appeared in battle taking auspices and sacrificing and pronouncing vows like a sacrificing seer." By Caesar's day even younger aristocrats seem to have become less eager to risk themselves, and a general—like Caesar—had become no bolder, coming into harm's way chiefly to lead or to rally his troops in a crisis. A scattering of instances reveals that Titus was not unique in his aggression under the early empire: a general cut down an opposing commander in 29 BC, and some thought he deserved the *spolia opima*. But such exceptions serve mostly to emphasize the norm, which was that of Caesar and which was unchanged more than a century later when Vespasian (and other generals in the civil wars of AD 68–70) behaved in much the same way Caesar had and when those around Titus urged him to retreat in the face of the enemy and not risk his valuable person in combat.[46]

Yet however odd he might have been in his own day, Titus stands at the beginning of a growing habit of heroic leadership in the Roman army. Useful, then, to consider what models he may have had for his behavior, and how prevalent such models may have been. This leads us into the realm of imperial nostalgia for the military past, especially for the Greek military past. For an examination of the outlook of Titus's generation creates good reason to suspect that in leading his cavalry in person again and again, in fighting with his own hands, Titus was fighting not in a Roman but in a Greek heroic mode, riding in the hallowed dust of Alexander the Great.

XII

SHIELD WALL AND MASK

THE MILITARY PAST
IN THE ROMAN EMPIRE

I t was in the days of Marius that the nations of the Germans first opposed themselves to Roman arms, at the turn of the last century BC. After Julius Caesar's conquest of Gaul, Rome's dominion bordered their misty realm. In AD 9, the ambition of the emperor Augustus to bring the Germans under Roman rule was shattered by the slaughter of Varus's three legions: from then on the Rhine would be the boundary between the Roman order and the wild. For centuries the Germans raided across the Rhine, and for centuries the Romans sent armies to punish them. In the 350s the powerful German confederacy of the Alamanni, which in the previous century had ravaged Gaul and erupted into Italy, had once again been sacking, even settling, over the river. The emperor Constantius was fully occupied in the East with Persian wars and private cruelty: his cousin, Julian, held the command. The Romans and the Germans met near Strasbourg. The German host had its back to the Rhine.

THE SHIELD WALL AT STRASBOURG, AD 357

"The rays of the sun were already growing red, and the trumpets screamed together, when the forces of footmen were led out at a slow march," writes the late-Roman historian Ammianus Marcellinus, in the fine, purple style of his generation. Cavalry guarded the flanks, some armed with bows, others, both man and horse, clad in heavy armor — the imposing cataphracts. The approach to the enemy from the Roman base was a long one, and Julian wanted to go into camp at the end of it, but his soldiers struck their spears upon their shields, ground their teeth, and demanded battle. Their desire was seconded by Julian's high officers: Florentius the Praetorian Prefect urged that the united enemy not be allowed to scatter. If the enemy slipped away, he said, the Roman soldiers would become entirely uncontrollable in their rage. Julian lectured and pleaded but was contradicted by the shouts of a standard-bearer, and the army moved forward to fight the Germans against the will of its commander. Aemilius Paullus, Julius Caesar, and Titus had all experienced similar defeats.[1]

Cresting a gentle hill covered with standing grain, the Romans caught sight of the Germans by the river beyond. The Roman infantry formed in a tight mass, "like an unbreachable wall." On the right flank of the infantry was the Roman cavalry, including the heavily armored cataphracts and horse archers. To oppose the Roman horse the Germans mixed light infantry among their cavalry: their own horsemen, they thought, were unequal to the cataphracts, but infantrymen could bring down the horses. On the German right, infantry were hidden in a swampy riverbed.[2]

The Roman left approached the riverbed, descried the troops hidden in it, and stopped. Julian reformed the ranks of the infantry in the center, rebuking those calling for an instant attack. Then trumpets on both sides gave the signal, and the Germans charged the Romans, their hair streaming behind them and madness in their eyes. In the center the infantry met head to head, and the Roman infantry locked shields: now a pushing match developed, and "shield-boss pressed against shield boss," as the Germans "tried to push the enemy back with the pressure of their knees," recalling the *othismos,* or push, of the Greek phalanx. The Roman left advanced, expelled the Germans from the riverbed, and put the German right to flight. But against expectation the German cavalry defeated the Roman, and the cataphracts fled. The Roman infantry would have been trampled in the rout had they not raised their shield wall against their own cavalry. Julian left the line to rally the horse, but neither Roman horse nor German played any further role in the battle.[3]

Cheered by the flight of the Roman horse, the German infantry in the center renewed their attack. Javelins flew and the Romans sheltered behind their shield wall, raising the Roman war cry, the *barritus,* "which begins as a faint murmur, and slowly increasing it grows like waves crashing against crags." Roman units came up to reinforce those under pressure, and now the kings and nobles of the Germans joined the assault and pushed their way through the Roman lines. They were stopped by a Roman unit in a tight formation, "in closer order and with the arrays crowded, the soldiers standing fast like towers," presumably another shield wall. The Germans made a supreme effort to "make gaps in the structure of the battle line," but to no avail. Finally, with their attack thwarted, the Germans began to flag, and suddenly they were in flight, and the Romans in merciless pursuit. Despairing Germans plunged into the Rhine: Julian and his officers had to restrain their blood-mad troops from following them. And so the Romans shot the Germans down from the banks. "At last, foaming with barbarian gore," Ammianus writes, "the stained river was astounded at this untoward addition to its flow."[4]

The surprise at Strasbourg is the way the Roman infantry fought, not with the ancestral *pilum* and shortsword, but by forming a wall of interlocked shields. The shield wall had become the standard array of Roman infantry by the mid–fourth century AD. And it was to have a long life: the shield wall is described in a sixth-century tactical manual which reveals that the back of the formation was formed by light-armed missile troops, who threw javelins or shot arrows over the heavy infantry in front of them — creating, for example, the storms of javelins during the infantry combat at Strasbourg. The new Roman shield was round or oval, smaller, now, than the old legionary *scutum* because the soldier did not fight in an independent, dueling style and now had comrades close to defend him with their shields. The men in the front lines might now carry the longsword, the *spatha,* which had mostly replaced the short *gladius,* but especially they carried a thrusting spear — essentially the old Roman *hasta,* or hoplite spear, although called by other names. From a hundred yards — from far enough that small differences in gear could not be noticed — a Roman infantry unit of the fourth century AD must have looked very similar to a Greek phalanx of the fifth century BC (see figures).[5]

This change of fighting style is more striking than the change from maniples to the exclusive use of cohorts. For earlier, even when the array of the Roman infantry had shifted, the fighting technique of the individual Roman infantryman had not: maniple or cohort, he still fought with his

What the late Roman shield wall
may have looked like.
Bronze roundel, third century AD (?)
(SeungJung Kim after drawing
by J. Casey).

pilum, scutum, and shortsword. For century after century, from victory
to victory, from the defeat of Hannibal to Trajan's Dacian Wars, that is
how the Romans fought, but now they had abandoned the gear and technique that had won, and held, their empire.

It is very tempting to root this change in the exigencies of military
crisis, for Rome had indeed endured a military crisis that had crested in
the middle years of the third century AD. The second century AD was the
high-water mark of Roman power: the Romans advanced over the Danube, and the empire briefly extended as far as the Persian Gulf. Detailed
contemporary military narratives are lacking for this age — we read of
wars, but rarely of the battles — and we must resort instead to a handful
of technical military works, a mass of inscriptions on stone, and archeological and artistic remains, especially Trajan's Column. We discern enough
to judge that in these years Rome was often at peace, and when at war,
victorious: perhaps this century was the zenith of the Roman army. Yet
the rooks of defeat began to gather in the reign of Marcus Aurelius
(AD 161–80), with fighting against the Parthians from 161 to 166 and cam-

What the late Roman shield wall may have looked like, mid–third century AD
(detail of Y99, marching soldiers in the Exodus fresco,
Dura-Europos Synagogue Panel WA3, Dura Europos Collection,
Yale University Art Gallery).

paigns against the barbarians on the Danube in 167–75 and 177–80, long
wars and hard ones. The wars continued under emperors more practical
if less admirable than the philosophic Marcus, and by the mid–third century the Roman borders had collapsed, and with them the unity of the
realm. To the misery of barbarian incursion was added that of civil war
between a multitude of claimants for the purple. Extents of the empire
— Gaul, the East — even split off for a time, the better to protect themselves against the attacks from without. This was a singularly embattled
period, but also a singularly badly reported one. At the end of the third
century the heroic efforts of Aurelian (AD 270–75) and Diocletian (AD
284–305) put the empire back together, cast the invaders back over the
borders, and restored imperial authority — but the critical month-to-
month and hour-to-hour details of how they did it are lost in the maw
of time. The ground still surrenders battered military equipment, but in
the third century even inscriptions and sculpture become scarce, reflecting
the poverty of the times or changing fashion.

When the Roman army reappears into the light of the fourth century

— in the pages of Ammianus and in the *Notitia Dignitatum,* which lists units of the late fourth and early fifth centuries under their commanders — there have been profound changes. Military units were smaller than the legions of the high empire. There was more cavalry. There were more specialist units — heavy cavalry and archers and javelin throwers and ballista shooters — and units were gathered into new categories — Legions of the Palace, Vexillations of the Companionship, Auxiliaries of the Palace. The names of weapons had changed. Ranks and titles of officers had changed or changed their meanings, with some old ranks, like the venerable rank of centurion, which had survived more than seven hundred years from the days of the Roman phalanx, giving way to new ranks in units of recent foundation. The rate of change in every aspect of the Roman army was faster between the second and fourth centuries than in any earlier recoverable period. And the demands of this chaotic and dark time seem to explain the rapid rate of change — even while the chaos and darkness make it impossible to trace the changes as they happen or even date most of them with confidence. But even if the needs of men in a crisis drove the changes, the direction of the changes must still be traced and explained.[6]

At Strasbourg it is the shield wall that draws the eye. Ammianus Marcellinus, himself a soldier, casually calls this formation a *testudo,* or tortoise. But it is not the classical Roman *testudo,* as depicted on Trajan's Column: a body of men with a roof of shields over them and shields all around to protect them from missiles, usually during attacks on fortifications. These the Romans still formed in the fourth century and still called them by the same name. The fourth-century shield wall emerges from a different tradition. The Romans had long used phalanx-like arrays as a variation on their normal tactics — they had used one, disastrously, at Cannae, in fact — and had for a long time called such an interlocking-shield arrangement *testudo* as well. At Gamala in Judaea the Romans had formed a shield wall; so too in the fight for the temple at Jerusalem. The best surviving description of such an arrangement — also the only surviving literary description of a Roman army drawn up for action in the second century AD — is Arrian's *Deployment Against the Alans.*[7]

In the reign of the emperor Hadrian, a barbarian tribe, the Alans, made a foray into the unquiet regions beyond Rome's eastern frontier.

In AD 135 the Alans brushed by the Roman borders of the provinces of Armenia and Cappadocia. Flavius Arrianus, the imperial governor of Cappadocia, led his forces out to meet them and left a description of how he intended to array his army. This is the same Arrian who wrote the *Anabasis of Alexander,* the best surviving account of the campaigns of Alexander the Great. Arrian's minor works, his *Deployment,* his *Art of Tactics,* and others, presumably survive because of his prominence as a man of letters, but literary accomplishment was hardly unusual for a second-century AD Roman governor and general.

The world of the *Deployment* is different from that of Trajan's Column, which depicts events thirty years before. The style of the document, first, is curious. Arrian refers to himself as Xenophon, as if he were the mercenary and historian from Classical Greece. Much of the technical vocabulary, which clangs oddly with the Latin names of Roman units, is taken from old Greek and Macedonian military usage. But the savor of fustian extends beyond the style to the military arrangements. The Roman legions are described in Arrian's Greek as phalanxes, and they are drawn up in a close formation eight men deep, a conventional Classical Greek depth. The first four ranks of Arrian's legions are perhaps armed not with the ancestral Roman javelin, but with long thrusting spears: several ranks are to project their spears in front of the formation just as in a Macedonian phalanx. At the same time the *Deployment* prefigures the fourth-century shield wall. If the Alan cavalry approach, the Roman infantry are to interlock their shields as closely as possible and resist their pressure with their shoulders. The last four ranks of Arrian's formation are armed with javelins and are to provide missile fire.[8]

It is possible to interpret Arrian's *Deployment,* according to taste, as a literary fantasy, as the product of a single general's idiosyncratic fixation with Greek and Macedonian tactics, as a one-time ad hoc arrangement against the armored cavalry of the Alans, or as an armywide adaptation of Roman doctrine (either under the influence of Hellenistic tactics or independent of them) to face the cavalry the Romans increasingly faced on their Danube and eastern frontiers. In fact the hard-trained Roman army had long been able to form a phalanx when the circumstances called for one; such tactical flexibility was a reward of Roman professionalism. An early third-century AD tombstone names a Roman soldier as a "phalanx trainee": the phalanx was something the Romans trained in. So the *Deploy-ment* described an array that was probably not a one-time brainstorm in the second century, but an option, an option that had evolved into the normal way of fighting by the mid–fourth century. Just as the manipu-lar array gave way slowly to the cohort, which began as a variation upon it for special circumstances, so, over several centuries, the tactics of *pilum*-shortsword-and-*scutum* gave way to the shield wall, which began as a variation on it.[9]

Yet however practiced Roman soldiers were in forming phalanx-like arrangements, it is nevertheless significant that Arrian chose to depict his *Deployment* as a return to Greek and Macedonian methods of war — and that on the soldier's Latin gravestone, the Greek term "phalanx" — rather than *testudo,* for example — was used to express the role the soldier was training for. If Arrian had an eccentric interest in Greek methods of war-fare, it was an eccentricity that many others in his era shared. A striking artifact offers a route into this world of Greek revival and suggests how widely it extended throughout the Roman army of the second century AD.

THE MASK

Eyes of fathomless sadness stare out from a mangled face: the jagged edges make the gaze seem imprisoned, desperate. Here, as with the Venus de Milo, time's blind assault on an ancient sculpture has accidentally adapted it to the modern taste, making it strangely moving to the viewer (figure A).

Where exactly in the Roman empire this face was found is not known: it now adorns a private collection. But it was probably dug up near the Rhine or Danube, the rivers that formed Rome's northern border. For this face is not the ornament of a Roman house, nor does it thank a civic bene-factor for generosity in a Roman market. Faces such as this are nearly al-ways found in military contexts. They were masks worn by Roman soldiers.

As luck would have it, a description of the use of these masks sur-vives in another work of the very Arrian who left the *Deployment Against the Alans.* Such masks were not used in battle but in equestrian military displays. Wearing them in the display was a mark of rank or excellence in horsemanship. In an appendix to his *Art of Tactics,* Arrian describes a

A. Cavalry sports helmet fragment, bronze alloy, second century AD.

whole display outfit — for man and horse — used on these occasions: yellow plumes, light, elaborately painted shields, colored tunics, tight trousers, and decorative armor for the forehead of the horse. Archeology has turned up many of these objects, especially the helmets and finely worked metal horse-head armor, as well as others that Arrian did not mention, elaborate breastplates and greaves for the men and beautifully carved metal disks for the sides of the horse (figure B).[10]

B. Auxiliary cavalryman equipped for equestrian military display,
reconstruction (SeungJung Kim after photo by B. Merz).

But the mask has not yet yielded up its most surprising secret. Turn
it over, and more surface is revealed, for the right side of the head was
bent back when the mask was crushed (figure C). And the side now revealed sports a luxuriant mass of corkscrew curls: the mask depicts the
face of a woman. Such female masks are not rare. Of the surviving masks
— over a hundred—catalogued through 1996 nearly a fifth are female: they
have been found from Scotland to the Balkans. Other masks are "mixed"
—they have male sideburns but female hair. One female mask, an especially
plump-cheeked, feminine version it seems to us, was so valued that two
different Roman soldiers carved their names and units on it.[11]

Why did Roman soldiers wear female masks? Later, certainly, Roman soldiers did not relish dressing up as women. In the fourth century
AD the emperor Julian punished a unit that had fled in battle by dressing
it in women's clothes, "deeming this punishment worse than death for

C. Back of cavalry sports helmet fragment
depicted in figure A,
bronze alloy, second century AD
(Sammlung Axel Guttmann 709;
SeungJung Kim after photo by K. Göken).

manly soldiers." Any taint of effeminacy was scorned in the army: when
the soldiers rebelled against Severus Alexander they jeered him as a "stingy
girly-man." The root meaning of *virtus* — "manliness" — always remained
strong in the Roman army.[12]

Another mask may provide the beginnings of an answer (figure D).
Snakes coil in the metal hair. The female this mask represents is taken
from Greek myth: Medusa. And the closer one examines second-century
masks, both female and male, the more they seem to call upon a Greek
literary and artistic tradition. The single most common type of male mask
is characterized by a mass of curls above the brow, a mass of curls that
often looks very like the hairstyle popularized in Greek art by depictions
of Alexander the Great (figure E). Other worked pieces of sports armor
— greaves and parade armor and horse-head ornaments — also depict
scenes from myth, some rather obscure, like the story of Ganymede.[13]

Arrian refers to the participants in the cavalry games dividing into

D. Fragment of a cavalry sports helmet, bronze,
Weissenburg, second century AD (Archäologische
Staatssammlung München, Museum für
Vor- und Frühgeschichte. Photo: M. Eberlein).

two teams, and at Straubing two sets of masks were found—one set male,
the other female, the latter with hair standing up in a cone as if forming
a Persian tiara or Phrygian cap (figure F). Perhaps the female masks represent the Amazons against whom the Greeks fought in myth, the cavalry
forming into "Greek" and "Amazon" teams for their drill (compare figure
G). And perhaps this is confirmed by an elaborately decorated shield—
almost certainly used for the same displays—that depicts a battle of Greeks
and Amazons. If so, other masks with exaggerated "eastern" features may
represent not the contemporary Parthians from beyond Rome's border
but the Persians of Themistocles' day or Alexander's, or even Trojans. But
whatever the ultimate identifications of the subjects of the masks, the drill

E. Cavalry sports helmet, bronze, second
century AD, Strass-Moos bei Neuburg a. d. Donau
(Archäologische Staatssammlung München,
Museum für Vor- und Frühgeschichte.
Photo: M. Eberlein).

performances of the second-century auxiliary cavalry seem to have been
antiquarian pageants, spectacles that drew upon Greek history and myth.[14]

It was not only cavalry parade equipment that had this antiquarian
bent, but other equipment as well. Some auxiliary cavalrymen seem to
have worn into actual combat helmets that modern students term pseudo-
Attic, peaked and crested helmets that look like old Greek helmets in art
(compare figure H to I). Some of these are elaborately carved with classical scenes, like the sports helmets, but they are heavier (to provide real
protection in battle) and lack the face mask. If reliefs from the city of
Rome can be trusted, the Praetorian Guard sometimes wore similar classicizing pseudo-Attic helmets (figure J), also elaborately decorated. The
tradition of such gear was very old in Rome, Attic-style helmets having

F. Cavalry sports helmet, bronze, Straubing,
third century AD (Stadt Straubing
Gäubodenmuseum).

been present in Italy for centuries. So it is impossible to know whether
those wearing them under the empire thought them specifically Greek
or merely old-fashioned Roman. But all they had to do was look around
at the simple functional helmets the rest of the army wore to understand
that they were wearing something odd and old (see figure, p. 246).[15]

Whether the female cavalry masks allude to antiquarian Greek and
Amazon pageants, or whether the masks of individuals singled out for
rank and excellence — as Arrian describes the mask wearers — merely drew
heavily upon Greek artistic tradition, they hardly represented the taste

G. Battle of Greeks and Amazons wearing Phrygian caps, volute krater,
Apulian, fourth century BC (Staatliche Antikensammlungen und
Glyptothek München. Photo: Koppermann).

of the auxiliary cavalrymen themselves. In the west, such lore was the
province of educated men, and the themes must have been the inspiration
of aristocratic officers, men with the education in rhetoric and the classics
that was the badge of their rank. By dressing cavalry and Praetorians like
figures from the past, and cavalry for their displays like figures from Greek
history and myth, officers were expressing their own taste, because the
members of the Roman army who most consistently dressed in an antiquarian style were the officers themselves. Since the late Republic at least,
Roman officers had dressed like figures from the Greek past: in art, officers
appear wearing the Hellenistic Greek molded muscle cuirass and pseudo-
Attic helmets with spectacular crests (see figure, p. 227). It is perfectly
possible that Roman aristocratic officers had simply never altered their
costume from a much earlier day when such attire was up-to-date. But
by the empire, the equipment of a Roman officer will have appeared to
contemporaries as no less strangely archaic than the wig and gown of an
English barrister appear to us.[16]

H. Pseudo-Attic Roman cavalry helmet,
Theilenhofen, late second century AD
(Archäologische Staatssammlung München,
Museum für Vor- und Frühgeschichte.
Photo: M. Eberlein).

The antiquarianism of aristocratic officers was not necessarily received
by their troops with horror. A small body of literary work by Roman soldiers and centurions survives, in the form of poems inscribed on stone.
The soldier-poets vary widely in competence and indeed in their mastery
of Latin or Greek: some write admirable verse, a reminder of the diverse
social origins of centurions. The struggles of others with language and
meter can be heartbreaking. But the ambition of those without education
to express themselves in difficult high-culture forms suggests that whatever
their deficiencies they nevertheless revered literary culture, admired the

I. Greek soldier in Attic helmet, Attic stamnos, Achilles Painter,
c. 440 BC (ARV² 992.65; drawing from E. Pfuhl, *Malerei und Zeichnung
der Griechen* vol. 3 [Munich, 1923] fig. 524).

culture of their superiors. So the aristocratic officer—the exemplar of that
culture in their world—whom we imagine (with some wonder) introducing Greeks and Amazons to a border camp in Scotland, may have
been listened to with respect, and the female masks may have been esteemed as artifacts of that admired high culture, rather than despised as
insults to the *virtus* of their wearers.

This Greek revival was not confined to details of costume. While the
Romans were erecting their earthworks against the last wall at Jerusalem,
Antiochus, a young allied prince—the son of the king of Commagene
—asked to be allowed to attack the wall. Titus allowed him, and he rushed
the wall with his guard of "Macedonians," armed and trained in the old
Macedonian way. He failed, and many were killed. But organizing a
Macedonian unit was not unique to Commagene in the East: Nero too

J. Roman soldier (left), possibly a Praetorian, in a pseudo-Attic helmet,
second century AD (Louvre; Réunion des Museés Nationaux / Art Resource.
Photo: R. G. Ojeda).

had organized a "phalanx of Alexander the Great." The experiment was
not a success, but the unit had a long life as a conventional Roman legion,
I Italica. These experiments are the first traces of a growing practical interest in reviving Greek ways of fighting. And they are exactly in the
generation of Titus, whose heroic generalship stood apart from Roman
tradition. Titus seems to have led at least six cavalry charges at the siege
of Jerusalem alone. He used his own guard as a fast reaction force, when
nothing prevented him from assigning that role to another cavalry unit
or sending his guard on without him. Perhaps he too was following the
fashion of his day and looking back to the heroic cavalry charges of Alexan-

der, a figure who is reported to have inspired emulation (if not necessarily of his tactics) in Romans generals before — in Caesar, Pompey, and Germanicus. Titus composed poetry and wrote tragedies in Greek. Alexander rarely wore his armor — and Titus too rode out unarmored to reconnoiter Jerusalem.[17]

In the same generation as Arrian's *Deployment* — in the reign of Hadrian (AD 117–38) — the cavalry masks that resemble Alexander the Great got their start. In that same generation too the Romans built great walls to defend their empire — Hadrian's Wall is only the most famous — and this too may revive a Greek tradition: in a land of mountains and peninsulas the Greeks had built a number of such fortifications. Perhaps the most famous was the wall built on the Isthmus of Corinth to keep the Persians out of the Peloponnese, the wall the Greek victory at Salamis made unnecessary.[18]

In a later time Caracalla (AD 211–17) also organized a phalanx on the Hellenistic model and called its officers after the names of Alexander's generals. He also had a "Spartan" unit, which he called the *Pitanate lochos* in a piece of bravura antiquarianism: Thucydides had sharply corrected Herodotus for claiming that such a unit existed. Nero, Caracalla's predecessor in such experiments, was mad, of course, and Caracalla had an obsession with Alexander. But when cracked weathervanes point in the same direction, there is a strong wind blowing. An admiring — and almost certainly invented — tradition attributes yet another program of Macedonian re-creation to Severus Alexander (AD 222–35): experimenting with Macedonian methods of fighting was unsurprising in an emperor and so could easily find its way into a fictional biography.[19]

Arrian's own *Art of Tactics,* written in the year after the Alan incursion, concerns itself mostly with the arrangements and formations of an idealized Macedonian army, but digressions on Roman and contemporary barbarian practices show that he considered the material he was presenting to be of contemporary relevance. He appended his discussion of Roman cavalry display. Aelian's *Theory of Tactics,* similar to Arrian's *Art* but without the Roman material, was dedicated to Trajan (AD 98–117). Aelian wrote that he was inspired to compose it after discussions with the distinguished Roman officer Frontinus (c. AD 35–103) — author of a lost Roman tactical manual and of a surviving Latin volume of stratagems (many from

Greek sources) — who had encouraged him by expressing a keen interest in Greek tactics, despite their having been superseded by Roman. Half a century earlier Onasander had dedicated his own more general summary of Greek military knowledge and applied philosophy to another Roman general, Quintus Veranius; half a century later Polyaenus dedicated his massive collection of *Stratagems* to the emperors Marcus Aurelius and Lucius Verus: it contains seven books of mostly Greek material, only one of mostly Roman. Another half century later, Greek stratagems formed part of the eccentric work of Julius Africanus, perhaps intended to help Severus Alexander (AD 222–35) in his Persian War. We have no idea how these works were received, but Polyaenus praises his dedicatees for reading works such as his, and the continued writing of them implies that an audience was imagined; what survives may be only a small fraction of the writing on old Greek ways of war that was produced under the Roman empire. And Tacitus, at least, could casually point out a Greek stratagem used by a Roman general in the Batavian war (AD 70) — not ravaging the enemy leader's property, in order to create suspicion in his countrymen — as a "well-known device of generals."[20]

MINDS LIKE THAT OF VEGETIUS

The military antiquarianism of Arrian's day was the product of the common education and intellectual dispositions of the class of men who became high officers in the Roman army of the second century AD. Rome's legions and auxiliary units were commanded by her aristocracy, by equestrians and senators, men who underwent no systematic military education. Long gone were the days of the middle Republic when Roman aristocrats spent their twenties in the army. Senators, who held the highest commands, often commanded a legion on the basis of a single year of military experience — as a "laticlave," or senatorial, military tribune — years before. Imperial self-protection discouraged long military careers for senators during which they might build up a following among the soldiers. Although a few equestrian commanders were promoted centurions and had learned long in the camps, nearly all equestrian and all senatorial officers had the usual education of their class: the education in literature and rhetoric that was so important a social marker in the empire. And to whatever they did, men educated in this fashion took with them the habits of mind that this education produced. The mental worlds of literary men and decision makers were thus nearly identical (indeed, they were often the same men): Rome was an empire without special academies for soldiers or statesmen, without a general staff to mold a distinctive military mindset, and the common education in rhetoric stocked the minds of all. In government this produced a tendency to see all problems in moral terms; in foreign affairs Rome's neighbors might be conceived in terms of long out-of-date stereotypes derived from reading in the classics. Arrian shows traces of this second tendency in the *Deployment* when he (like many others under the empire) refers to the Alans as Scythians, just as Herodotus might have half a millennium before.[21]

If Arrian's *Deployment* seems odd as a military document, as a product of its time the *Deployment* was nearly inevitable. Hadrian reigned in the full flood of the literary and cultural movement called the Second Sophistic. The Greek sophists themselves, spectacular show orators who moved from town to town amidst the adulation we reserve for athletes and operatic tenors, were merely the most public face of this refocusing of the Greek and Latin ruling classes ever more fixedly upon the past. The sophists were the leaders of Atticism, the affectation of using no word that could not be attested in Athenian authors of the fifth or fourth century BC, and pretended such indifference as they could to any events after the death of Alexander. But Atticism, in stronger or weaker strains, spread far beyond professional orators into the speech and writing of the Greek ruling class in general. In the Latin West the counterpart of Atticism was the style of Aulus Gellius (born AD 125–28) or of Apuleius (born c. AD 123), author of the *Golden Ass,* a style which consisted of ransacking the oldest Latin texts they could get their hands on for the ripest archaic words they could find, and sprinkling them like delightful chunks of Stilton all over their writings. The East saw a revival in giving children names from Greek myth—Menelaus and Jason and Nestor (a baby Nestor—imagine!); a revival in using venerable Greek dialects like the muscular Doric of Sparta on inscriptions; and with that a revival of old lettering styles. Studied archaism in architecture and art—making buildings or sculpture to mimic older styles (so well done modern experts are sometimes fooled), for centuries a minor strain in ancient art, increased in popularity and became more careful and exacting. The *Deployment* reflected the tastes and habits of its time.[22]

There were two main intellectual consequences of rhetorical education in the military realm. First was a tendency to conceive the past as exemplary: to the educated, the Greco-Roman past offered not merely a treasury of experience to be called upon when useful, but also a canon of excellent actions that demanded to be imitated or surpassed. And, second, this education encouraged a conception of the past that was peculiarly flat and unarticulated, a conception of the past (shared with most premodern peoples) with what seems to us a deficient sense that men did things differently in different eras of the past in response to different needs — a tendency in extreme cases to view everything that happened in the past as happening at much the same time.

It is in Vegetius's late fourth-century *Epitome of Military Science* that the results of this education applied to military affairs flower most luxuriantly. Vegetius was no soldier, but an educated man living in a time of renewed military crisis. The first book of the *Epitome* was offered to the emperor as an earnest recipe for the reform of military training and was well enough received that Vegetius was commanded to extend his summarizing of earlier authorities into three other books on other areas of military endeavor. Evidently those in charge of military affairs thought the project worthwhile, just as Frontinus had encouraged Aelian two centuries before.[23]

Vegetius was not a blind admirer of the past. He recognized that in some areas — cavalry and the military use of boats on rivers — any advice old authorities might supply had been superseded by contemporary practice, and of those realms he did not treat. But within his purview — infantry in particular — Vegetius's program of reform is almost entirely reactionary. It never strikes him that the Romans might do well to imitate their contemporary enemies, nor does Vegetius regularly invent schemes of his own or discuss those of men of his own generation. Instead, what the Romans must do is re-create the military methods and regimens of their own past, lightly adapted to present conditions. There is no systematic argument (usually no argument at all) about why older techniques are better than contemporary ones: it is simply assumed. The reader's conviction is secured not by compelling logic, but by establishing the author's authority in terms of the literary culture that author and reader are assumed to share. So Vegetius quotes from poetry and drags in Vergil wherever he can: he illustrates a discussion of the qualities to be sought in recruits by a passage on bees from the *Georgics*. To an educated Roman, such quotations compel: they signal that the author has the élite education that commanded confidence in the Roman world. Such display of education is ubiquitous in written products of the common aristocratic literary culture, from a courtroom speech—Apuleius's *Apology*—to Columella's treatise on farming.[24]

As well as establishing his general credibility by literary quotation, Vegetius often makes his case with examples: not apposite contemporary examples, but old, admirable examples that compel attention and imitation, not mere examples but *exempla*. Why should soldiers be recruited from the country rather than the city? Did not Rome call Cincinnatus from his plow? Why use archers? Did not Scipio Aemilianus use archers at Numantia? Why train the army? Did not Gaius Marius train his army to overcome the Cimbri? A reader who shares Vegetius's education was brought up to find such examples far more persuasive than incidents from recent campaigns. Even perfectly good military logic is usefully bolstered by an appeal to antiquity. Why keep a reserve in battle? To reinforce weak points and have troops available for maneuver, naturally. But Vegetius notes also that "the Spartans first discovered this, the Carthaginians imitated it, and the Romans have subsequently used it everywhere." A long and honorable pedigree makes even a good tactic far more appealing. Again, there is nothing at all unusual about this logic. Appeal to—and reverence for—*exempla* was taught to every Roman child whose parents could afford teaching. Volumes of potted *exempla* were published for the use of orators.[25]

Vegetius's work is mostly the product of cutting and pasting from previous Roman military manuals, including that of Frontinus, but—and this is the most puzzling quality of the work—although he knows that what he prescribes is different from the practices of his own day, he shows virtually no awareness that methods of Roman infantry fighting had changed over the course of the past. Romans from the second century BC to the reign of Diocletian (AD 284–305) are all collectively *antiqui*, "the ancients." And the "ancient legion" to which Vegetius exhorts the

Romans to return is an impossible amalgam of (at least) the manipular legion—known to him from Cato's handbook, directly or indirectly—the legion of cohorts, and legions as they were armed and fought under Diocletian. In his blindness to change over time, Vegetius once again was merely a product of his education, for an awareness that methods of doing things changed over time is hard to find in ancient authors, even in the historians, or for that matter in depictions of the past in art. History was not systematically taught: rhetorical education proceeded by snippets and gobbets, either to be imitated in style or mined for an *exemplum*. Knowledge of the past came far more from handbooks of excerpts than from reading continuous history. So *exempla* hung in the air without chronological markers. Scipio was an exemplary man, and so was Cato. What does it matter who came first? The past was past and the past was good, but the past was a single delicious stew rather than a banquet of many successive courses.[26]

So alien are the assumptions and logic of Vegetius's work that it is natural for a modern reader to dismiss him as a meddling crank: he was, by his own admission, no soldier. Surely, we think, the hard men in charge of the army could not have thought in such bizarre terms? But in the early third century there appears an *Ala Celerum,* an auxiliary cavalry unit of *Celeres,* "the Swift." And *Celeres* had been the name of the very first cavalry the Romans ever had, in myth the bodyguard of Romulus himself, now revived after a thousand years. In the late third century the term *triarii*—the term for the last echelon of the manipular legion, a term out of use for centuries—appears in inscriptions. In the fourth century, snuggled in among units with storied histories and boastful new formations—the Thundering Moors, the Armsbearing Defenders, the Junior Tramplers—are units of Latins and Sabines, new units with names plucked from early Roman history. And when Diocletian established two new legions, he established them at a strength of 6,000 men, close to the strength of legions of the high empire, rather than the much smaller strength of contemporary military units. So an inclination to recreate the Roman military past was not confined to Vegetius.[27]

The mindset of Vegetius is that of Arrian. Arrian was a Greek in culture, living in a time—the reign of Hadrian—when fashionable regard for Greek antiquity was at its height: while Vegetius yearned to recreate the Roman past, Arrian yearned to recreate the Greek. When placed in charge of a Roman army, Arrian developed a plan to do just that, a plan which, whether or not he ever put it into action, he was proud enough to publish. Neither the plan nor the way he described it, then, will have struck his contemporaries as irresponsible or odd: his contemporaries shared Arrian's education, just as, later, Vegetius's contemporaries shared his. They all had in common an attitude toward the past that encouraged speculation about and experimentation with older ways of fighting, whether Roman or Greek.

When the Romans formed a shield wall at Strasbourg, they were following what had become their usual drill. Roman soldiers had long formed a phalanx-like shield wall, called the *testudo,* when circumstances required it. But this way of fighting became usual rather than exceptional by the mid–fourth century; it became standard rather than an option. The question is, Why? There is no direct evidence, but Julius Africanus, in the early third century, may provide a clue to the logic: "I've often wondered about the reason for the upshot of military contests, and why the Greeks were defeated by the Romans, and the Persians by the Greeks, but the Persians have not yet been defeated by the Romans." Victory is a question of equipment and tactical system, he concludes: so the Romans simply need to revert to the weapons and tactics of the Greeks. Faced with a military problem, the natural resort was to look back into history. The peculiarities of this logic — among them the assumption that the Persians are fighting in the same way as the Persians more than five hundred years before — were the natural result of the education of the men whose logic it was. Perhaps the Romans reached back into Greek military practice in response to a particular crisis, now lost to all but modern imagination. Certainly the mid–third century AD was rich in military crises, a time when wars barbarian and civil fed upon each other like two sharks twisted in a circle. Or perhaps the deep-seated antiquarianism of Roman commanders of the age of the Second Sophistic was powerful enough by itself to propel a slow move back to the phalanx. In any event, the predominance of the shield wall is likely to have been the consequence of the recollection of the Greco-Macedonian phalanx by men with a profound reverence for an oddly understood past. By the Byzantine period the

Macedonian lineage of contemporary infantry phalanx tactics was taken for granted, and the tradition of Greek tactical treatises — Asclepiodotus, Aelian, Arrian — could be seamlessly integrated into a treatise on contemporary tactics.[28]

Why, ultimately, did the Romans decide to re-create old Greek military practice rather than Roman? Probably because in the age of crisis, the mid–third century AD, the Romans saw little difference between how they were fighting and how the Romans had always fought. Vegetius distinguishes the "ancient legion" from his own time, but he lived after the hinge of the age, the late third and early fourth centuries, when so much had changed. And, as has been noted, he had a great deal of difficulty distinguishing the Roman fighting of Cato's day from that of Diocletian's. To an observer in the 230s AD, change over time in Roman fighting was invisible: to him they always appeared to have fought in the Roman style (as opposed to the Greek or Macedonian). The sharp distinction we make between the age of maniples and the age of cohorts is never made by an ancient author, and an author who treated of both periods — Livy — cheerfully projected cohorts into early times. Perhaps a few learned men knew that the Romans had once fought in the phalanx (so fighting in the phalanx could, at some level, be thought of as a return to the Roman past), but the period after the Roman phalanx was unarticulated in Roman minds and for a long time not distinguished from the Roman present. Greek methods of fighting, by contrast, were unquestionably things of a sharp-edged past. In a time of unusual reverence for the past, and when circumstances seemed to suggest a need to apply to the past for succor and inspiration, the Greek past was the only clearly different military past the Romans had available.[29]

A parallel to the revival of the phalanx is the Romans' rediscovery, at much the same time, of the Hellenistic Greek art of fortification. After a long period of being behind their eastern neighbors in fortification and siegecraft, the Greeks leaped forward in the fourth century BC. The Hellenistic world knew fortifications of enormous sophistication, carefully thought out to resist siege machinery and to allow the most effective use of catapults by the defenders. A Hellenistic treatise, that of Philo from the third century BC, survives and explains that walls should be thick, towers should project from walls (to allow flanking fire) and be round or polygonal (to make ramming more difficult), and that they should have windows for throwing engines. The Romans were aware of these techniques and the theory behind them. In the first century AD, Vitruvius gives instructions similar to those of Philo, and those instructions are echoed by Vegetius in the fourth century. These precepts the Romans employed — but only here and there, inconsistently. In the first two centuries AD there was, instead, a powerful countercurrent in Roman fortification simply to reproduce in stone the earth and wood fortifications of Roman camps, with thin walls and few towers, and those square and rarely projecting much beyond the walls. Yet the invasions and wars of the third century sparked a great upsurge in town fortification and fort construction, a spate that continued from the late third century AD into the fourth. And these new fortifications for the first time systematically applied Hellenistic methods, with thick walls, many more towers (and those projecting and more frequently round or polygonal), and greater attention to windows and angles for missiles and engines. These fortifications were, however, greatly diverse in design. A central brain was not ordaining Hellenistic-style plans; rather, under the pressure of crisis, individual engineers all over the empire were adapting Hellenistic doctrine (perhaps from Roman manuals) in local ways to local needs. The turn to the Greek past, then, was not that of a few, but of many, all over the empire.[30]

The re-creation of the phalanx was never complete: the Romans did not revert to the enormous Macedonian *sarissa,* and Roman javelin throwing was preserved, if shifted to the back of the formation. The Roman army had its own powerful traditions that demanded respect, and Vegetius is their monument. Devotion to the past was not, for the most part, sentimental or doctrinaire: the past was a guide to doing things in the most efficient way because the men of old had, by and large, been better and wiser than the men of the present. But there was nothing in their respect for the past that compelled the Romans to arm the rear ranks of their phalanx with long spears (which could not reach the enemy) rather than javelins (which could). "What use are spears in the middle of the phalanx?" a Byzantine tactical author asked.[31]

Re-creation of the past is hardly the whole story of the Roman army in the fourth century AD. There were influences from the Germans, although perhaps these did not go far beyond dress and the late Roman battle cry, the eerie *barritus,* which the troops let forth at Strasbourg. From the east came horse archers and from the east or beyond the Danube the cataphracts, the heavily armored lancers who fled at Strasbourg. These the Romans had experimented with since the second century and had come up with their own name for them, *clibanarii* ("oven-men"), a joking term that passed into general usage. And the Romans, of course, could come up with ideas of their own, as the anonymous fourth-century *de Rebus Bellicis* (*On Military Affairs*) with its wonderfully impractical inventions reveals (a warship powered by oxen-driven paddle wheels!). But even in the fantasy world of the *de Rebus Bellicis* the past intrudes: the revival of the scythed chariot is urged, albeit with refinements like automatic whips to flog the horses on. And one wonders about the provenance of the cataphracts as well. Were they imported directly from beyond the Roman borders because they were useful? Or did someone read that they had been used in Hellenistic armies and conclude from that that they might be useful? The first cataphract unit appears under Hadrian, commanded by a protégé of the emperor's, right at the height of enthusiasm for the Greek past, right when Arrian was writing. And cataphracts are just one example of the specialist units that were common in the fourth century: once upon a time Hellenistic armies too were made up of many differently armed specialist units. In the fourth century cavalry formed a somewhat larger proportion of the army than they had in the second. Was it because more cavalry were needed? Or had someone been reading about Alexander? Or did someone's reading about Alexander suggest a solution to a tactical quandary? There is no contradiction between military evolution in the face of new pressures and military antiquarianism: in the ancient world practical evolutionary pressures were more likely to push an army back than forward.[32]

The shield wall worked well enough at Strasbourg. Perhaps Arrian's antiquarianism threw up tactics appropriate to face the Alans: we will never know because we do not know whether Arrian's *Deployment* was ever put into action or how it fared if it was. And masks are harmless enough. But the larger question is what happens when men with the mindset that produced the shield wall, the *Deployment,* the mask, and Vegetius's odd handbook — men with the common education of the

Greco-Roman ruling class—found themselves in charge of great campaigns in critical and straitened times. To understand the consequences of placing leaders with this outlook in charge of an army it is necessary to go forward six years from Strasbourg.

XIII

JULIAN IN PERSIA, AD 363

TRIUMPH OF THE GHOSTS

Julian, the victor of Strasbourg, had a horse by the name of Babylonian. Soon after Julian commenced his fatal campaign east into the realm of the Persians, as he prepared to mount Babylonian, the horse collapsed writhing in sickness to the ground, casting off its gold and jeweled adornment. Julian cried out in joy at the omened success of his expedition: "Babylon had fallen to the ground despoiled of her ornaments!" But the emperor's rapture was itself a darker omen. Babylon of the Hanging Gardens had been a windy ruin for centuries. Julian appears not to know whether he was marching against the contemporary Persians or against other Persians from long ago, when Babylon was more than a forbidding set of crumbling walls. Strange, dangerous auspices for so tremendous an invasion.[1]

In AD 360 Julian had revolted against his cousin, the emperor Constantius. In the next year Constantius's adventitious death made Julian supreme without a long and bloody civil war. The empire faced many dangers, and Julian was urged especially to campaign against the Goths in the North. He replied that he was seeking a "better" enemy and prepared instead, against widespread opposition, to invade Persia. The Persians were a better enemy in the same sense that the fall of Julian's horse was an omen of the Persians' destruction: they were better because they were the ancient enemy, the enemy hallowed by tradition as the ancestral foe of Greek civilization. They were better because they had once threatened Greece and had been thrown back by better men; they were better because

Julian's Campaign Against the Persians, AD 363

they had been conquered by Alexander, the best of all, and more recently again by Trajan, best of the Roman emperors.[2]

The rivers Tigris and Euphrates were the twin highways from the dominion of the Romans into the heart of the Persian empire. Having assembled his host, Julian feinted toward the farther river, the Tigris, to confound the plans of his adversary, King Sapor. But he marched down the closer Euphrates, conveying his army's supplies and siege engines and baggage on a flotilla of a thousand riverboats. Crossing into Persian territory, Julian disposed his army in a very long column in order to make it look larger than it was: a device, the historian Ammianus tells us, of

King Pyrrhus of Epirus, that revered Hellenistic master of stratagems and author of a military manual. Earlier, in revolt against Constantius, Julian had made his army appear larger by having it advance in several columns: a stratagem of Alexander, Ammianus informs us, imitated by other skillful generals after him.[3]

Down the Euphrates the army marched, past Dura, an old Roman stronghold against the East, its ruins now nibbled by herds of deer: the Romans devoured the deer in their turn. A Persian fortress surrendered, whirlwinds rent some tents, and boats were lost in a rising of the river. Foraging parties stripped the land around to preserve the supplies carried on the boats; then the fields were fired to deny provision to the enemy. A drunken soldier swam the Euphrates and was slain by the enemy on the other side for his achievement.[4]

The next two Persian fortresses on the river were judged impregnable and so were bypassed. An abandoned town was put to the torch. Finally a Persian force appeared but was driven off after a brisk skirmish. Now the Romans had come to the heavily irrigated part of the Euphrates bank, and they had some difficulty crossing the canals against Persian resistance, despite special bridging boats brought along for the purpose.[5]

The next major obstacle the Romans faced was the fortified city of Pirisabora, set by the river. Negotiations proved fruitless, as did shooting missiles at those on the wall. But by night a Roman ram pierced a tower, and when the defenders also saw the trenches protecting the wall being filled up they retired to the broad citadel of the town. Advancing into the city, the Romans traded arrows, thrown rocks, and volleys from engines with the defenders.[6]

The next day the emperor took action. Surrounding himself with a body of men, their shields tight-knit to protect them against arrows— in the venerable siege *testudo*—Julian advanced upon an ironbound gate of the citadel and cheered on his men as they strove to break it down. The defenders, no doubt astonished at their good fortune, poured down arrows, sling-bullets, and rocks. After a period of futile beating at the gate, and as the volume of enemy fire grew, Julian withdrew defeated, some of his men wounded, himself unhurt.

No military necessity compelled Julian to lead the attack on the gate in person or to attack the gate at all in so venturesome a way. He did it, as Ammianus reveals, because "he had read that Scipio Aemilianus, along with Polybius the historian . . . and thirty men, had undermined a gate of Carthage with a similar attack." Julian's assault on the gate was intended to equal a feat from the Third Punic War, five hundred years before — and not only equal it, but surpass it. For the gate the younger Scipio had attacked had an overhanging arch, and Scipio and his men had labored beneath its stone protection. But there was no such arch at Pirisabora, and Julian had to withdraw, ashamed — blushing — not before his soldiers, who had been wounded in his foolish attack, but before the shade of Scipio Aemilianus, whom he had failed to excel.[7]

Julian's assault on the gate at Pirisabora was an act quite different in kind from his borrowing of stratagems from Pyrrhus and Alexander. The application of the latter, of useful tricks from history or from culled collections, had for centuries been part of the art of the conscientious general. And Julian was especially well qualified to do so because of his formidable education: he was indeed a "leader trained by experience and learning."[8] In his obituary upon Julian, Ammianus writes of him, "Many notable deeds displayed his knowledge of military affairs: sieges of cities and fortresses amidst extreme dangers, battle lines drawn up in various shapes, camps laid out with an eye to safety and health, guards and country outposts intelligently stationed."[9] Julian was a master, in short, of all the parts of warfare covered by ancient military writing; he may indeed have been the author of a lost work on siege engines. Books accompanied Julian on campaign — as many as possible — and were put to good use: he learned from them about an old canal in Babylonia, which he later cleared and employed, and when it was proposed to strike inland from the banks of the Euphrates — when the going was slow because the enemy had broken the dikes and inundated the fields — Julian produced a volume and read to his officers the cautionary tale of Crassus's disaster at Carrhae.[10]

But Julian's action at Pirisabora also reveals a different and disquieting aspect of his education. In a surviving speech Julian says that when he marched to war he always took along "as a commissary, as it were, a description of a campaign [in that region, presumably] composed by an eyewitness long ago," not only for the information and advice it could provide, but also because in such a book a general might find "a paradigm for noble character, if he understands how to set the best men and words and deeds before him, like a craftsman setting a model before himself, and to mold his character upon them, and copy their words."[11]

So being "knowledgeable about ancient things," as Ammianus has Julian describe himself (and as Julian's own surviving writings, which are treacled with ancient lore, amply confirm), did not merely mean that Julian had a library of military techniques to draw upon when he needed them, but also meant that Julian had sets of famous deeds to emulate whether he needed to or not. To someone with Julian's education, as to Vegetius, the contents of the old books had an active, prescriptive force. "For leaders in war, knowledge of deeds is the best instructor of what is needful to emulate the conquerors of old," wrote Polyaenus in his second-century collection of stratagems. "How you may emulate the virtues and victories of the ancients, these stratagems will show." Deeds of old, as at Pirisabora, called out to be imitated or bettered. And so the march of a commander "knowledgeable about ancient things" might take on something of the aspect of the tour of a historical re-creation society. Even small details of Julian's daily life on campaign might be modeled on an exemplary predecessor. In his oaths he imitated Trajan, who had also fought successfully in these parts. "As I hope to make Dacia into a province!" Trajan had sworn. So Julian swore, "as I hope to send the Persians under the yoke!" Even the idea of taking a book to war as a moral guide was itself an imitation: the book was to be an *ephodion*, literally supplies for a trip (so "commissary" above). Once upon a time another had taken a book along to war and used the same strained metaphor of the *ephodion* to describe it: the *Iliad* had been the *ephodion* of Alexander the Great.[12]

The attack on the gate at Pirisabora having failed, Julian settled down for a conventional siege. But rather than build a number of siege towers (as Titus, for example, had at Jerusalem) he ordered the construction of a single gigantic tower, a "vast mass," higher than the towers of the citadel. Ammianus terms this a *helepolis*, a "city-taker," and likens it to the two *helepoleis* that the Hellenistic warlord Demetrius Poliorcetes had built in the late third century BC — other than the Trojan horse the most famous pieces of siege machinery in the ancient world. And the association is likely right, for although the term *helepolis* was also used in the Roman period to describe a low covered ram (and indeed Ammianus depicts the *helepolis* as this humbler engine in his earlier excursus on siege engines), the height of the structure at Pirisabora distinguishes it from the low Roman *helepolis* and suggests that Julian did intend to emulate the famous *helepoleis* of Demetrius. In any event, the *helepolis* was successful even before it was finished: seeing it rise so discouraged the defenders that they surrendered on terms. Where recollection of the Roman past had proved wanting to capture the town, recollection of the Greek past had succeeded. A great supply of grain from the city's magazines was loaded on to the Roman ships, and Pirisabora was burned.[13]

Even before the embers had turned to ash and before the army had uncoiled itself from the ruins, the Persians had ambushed three units of cavalry scouts, killed a few troopers, slain a commander, and seized a standard. Julian rushed out with a force and drove them off, cashiered the two surviving commanders, and of those troopers who had fled, executed ten. Ammianus assures us this was "in accord with the ancient laws," but here Julian's enthusiasm for recreating the past outran his historical knowledge. For Julian was evidently trying to revive the ancient practice of decimation, out of use for more than three centuries: but so dusty was the custom that neither Julian nor his historian realized that decimation involved killing not ten soldiers total, but one out of ten.[14]

The army left Pirisabora and marched on through the irrigated region. After fourteen miles the Roman advance was stopped by inundated fields: the Persians had broken down the dikes. But bridges were contrived over the mires, and the Romans slogged on, harassed by archers. Soon after, the Romans seem to have left the main stream of the Euphrates and struck east into the irrigated heart of Mesopotamia between the Euphrates and the Tigris, marching directly for the Persian capital at Ctesiphon. Their boats followed them on a canal. An abandoned city was burned.[15]

The next walled place to offer resistance to the Romans was Maozamalcha. Julian reconnoitered the city on foot and was set upon by ten Persians who emerged from a hidden postern gate. Two attacked the emperor, who caught their blows upon his shield. His guards cut down one attacker, and, Ammianus says, Julian thrust his sword into the side of the other. As the remaining ambushers fled, the emperor stripped the bodies and carried the spoils in triumph back to the Roman camp. Ammianus waxes antiquarian in his praise of this deed, comparing it to the feats of Valerius Corvus and Manlius Torquatus: with little cause, for this was no solemn duel of champions by challenge, but a desperate affray arising out of an ambush. If Julian was recalling the past it was only in stripping the bodies and glorying over the spoils, vaunting his deeds like a hero of old. But Ammianus's story is unsettling because Zosimus, the other main source for the expedition, knows nothing of Julian's killing an enemy soldier with his own hands. Julian boasts of his imitation of great men of old in his own writings, and other authors confirm that to do so was his habit. But did Ammianus make up *this* particular story to allow him to compare Julian to early Roman heroes? If so, when Ammianus elsewhere says that Julian is imitating a feat from the past, might Ammianus merely be making the comparison after the fact to show off his *own* antiquarian knowledge? In many cases, yes. For Ammianus was a true heir to the fashions of the second century in his relentless display of ancient lore, his use of historical comparisons to praise his heroes and condemn his villains, and his excavation of strange old words from the most antique books he could find.[16]

Yet we are not systematically mistaking literary affectation for historical fact: some of Julian's imitations of the past recorded by Ammianus — the misunderstood decimation, the Trajan-like oaths — must have been well-known public facts, impossible for Ammianus to invent (because he was writing for a contemporary audience, some of whom had been present) and impossible to interpret other than as imitation. And sometimes Ammianus relates a deed of Julian's which we suspect to be an imitation, but which Ammianus (for all his lore) fails to identify as such. Later in the campaign, to restore the confidence of his troops, Julian displayed to them some starving Persian prisoners. This was an old stratagem — the great Spartan general Agesilaus was its most famous practitioner — reported in the collections of both Frontinus and Polyaenus and still reproduced in books in the sixth century AD. But Ammianus, although this would be an admirable opportunity to flaunt his erudition, does not mention the stratagem's proud history. Ammianus does not record at all the equestrian games Julian held near Ctesiphon, which are likely to have been held in imitation of Alexander the Great, who frequently gave games on campaign. In presenting Julian as moved by *exempla,* Ammianus was hardly imposing his own way of thinking on another who thought quite otherwise. Rather, the emperor and his historian shared — and shared with Vegetius, and shared with most educated men of their generation — a common way of thinking about the proper application of the past to the present. This is significant because it suggests that Julian, despite his philosophical interests, his eccentricity in religion, and his unfashionable pointed beard, was not, in his conception of leadership in war, much out of tune with the thinking of his generation.[17]

An assault on the walls having failed, Julian laid Maozamalcha under siege. Engines were brought up, and the trenches before the walls filled. Ballistas were discharged with a screech. Roman units advanced protected by the *testudo:* they attacked with a will because they had heard that the road to Ctesiphon was open if they could take this town. For two days the Romans attacked — and Roman rams had success — but the Romans could not get into the city. Late in the night of the second day it was reported to Julian that a mine under the walls was near completion: Julian ordered an attack upon the walls as a diversion and to provide cover for the noise of digging, and the tunnel was completed. First to emerge from the hole into a private house was Exsuperius, a soldier of the Victores regiment: he cut down a slave girl who was about to give the alarm. Then came Magnus, a tribune, or regimental commander; then Jovian, the chief of the bureau of shorthand writers. Those from the tunnel rushed the wall from the rear, and the city was taken.[18]

In a moment of magnificent literary antiquarianism, Ammianus Marcellinus compares this attack (without suggesting it was an imitation) to the attack of C. Fabricius Luscinus on a Lucanian camp during the Pyrrhic war of the early third century BC, an episode so delightfully obscure that we can be serenely confident it was not on the minds of the men crawling down the fetid tunnel in Babylonia. But Julian, minded like Ammianus, did not let the success pass without his own antiquarian mark: after the city was taken, he summoned the heroes of the siege, and "having praised them before an assembly of the army, in the ancient fashion," he presented them with siege crowns, a type of decoration last seen more than four centuries earlier during the Social War of the early first century BC.[19]

Maozamalcha was bloodily sacked and burned, and many slaves were made from the captives. Julian refused to take any of the women as his share of the plunder — refused even to look at them. Ammianus says that in this he was imitating the continence of Alexander the Great and Scipio Aemilianus, a link that would be easy to dismiss as Ammianus's except for the detail, which Ammianus does not connect with Alexander, that the emperor did accept as booty a boy actor. Although he treated Darius's women with self-denying respect, Alexander famously did later accept as a gift the youthful eunuch Bagoas.[20]

Onward to Ctesiphon! The army marched on past a palace built in Roman style and the Persian king's game preserve, whose wild inhabitants the Roman cavalry slaughtered. Julian rested his army for two days, while the emperor himself detoured to see the site of a city destroyed by the emperor Carus (AD 282–83) during his march upon Ctesiphon. Such tourism was exactly appropriate for an emperor with so close a relationship to the past; in Julian's own account of his trip from Antioch toward the Euphrates to begin the campaign (which survives in a letter) the emperor showed an acute interest in the antiquities he passed. But this visit in Babylonia turned grisly: the ruined city was a place of execution, and Julian found crucified there, as a warning to others, the kinsmen of the Persian officer who had surrendered Pirisabora to the Romans.[21]

Persian marauders began to harass the Romans, killing baggage animals and foragers: in driving them off, Julian was nearly shot down by an engine on the wall of a Persian fortress, which he then spent two days besieging. Julian directed the attack from the front, placing himself once again in peril, and the fortress was taken. But raiders kept ambushing the Roman troops. The Roman camp was more carefully fortified, and Julian gave his army another day of rest.[22]

The fleet of Roman supply boats had been accompanying the army up a canal that had emerged from the Euphrates and now ran parallel to the Tigris. This canal was connected to the Tigris above Ctesiphon by a dry cross-canal, which Julian had read about in his books: Trajan had tried to use it, and Severus had used it. The Roman army dug out the blockage, and the Roman boats sailed into the Tigris. But Ctesiphon was on the other side of the river, and the Persians planned to contest the crossing. It may have been now that Julian held his Alexander-like games, in order to distract the Persians from noticing his preparations for crossing. First Julian sent over five ships, which the Persians set on fire. Julian deftly lied to his army that the flames were the agreed-upon signal that a lodgment had been gained on the other side and sent the rest of the fleet over: after hard fighting, the bank was captured.[23]

Now that Julian had defeated all the natural obstacles that separated him from Ctesiphon, the Persians were finally obliged to meet him in battle. The relative passivity of the Persian army during Julian's nearly two-month invasion of their territory is one of the insoluble mysteries of the campaign: even now King Sapor himself had not arrived to command the force defending his winter capital. Perhaps Julian's feint toward the Tigris at the beginning of the war had been successful; perhaps the force Julian had left on the Tigris had distracted the king; or perhaps the Persian royal army took a long time to assemble: Julian had marched out early in the year.[24]

Here before Ctesiphon, finally, were the formidable Persian cataphracts, "blinding the eyes of onlookers with their gleam." Here were the Persian infantry, with their long shields. Here were the Persian elephants, "looking like hills on the march, the motion of their gigantic bodies threatening doom to any who came near." Julian arrayed his Roman army in three lines, with the weakest troops in the second: this, as Ammianus points out, was the well-known "Homeric array," so called after Nestor's disposition of his troops in the *Iliad* just before he gave the order that his contingent should fight as a mass rather than as individuals. This disposition had been alluded to in Classical Greece, and Pyrrhus had picked it up from Homer and used it, although he interpreted it as a matter of left, right, and center rather than front, middle, and back. (So well known was this ruse that the term was used in rhetoric to denote a speech with a weak middle section.) Julian, the better philologist, corrected Pyrrhus: by Julian's day it was important to get such things right.[25]

The armies approached each other, javelins were thrown, and a cloud of dust swirled up. Then, with battle cries and a blast of trumpets, the lines met in hand-to-hand combat. The Persians began to waver, and wavering became flight: the Romans pursued the enemy up to the very walls of Ctesiphon, but a Roman officer managed to restrain them from pressing into the gates behind the Persians. Twenty-five hundred Persians fell,

Ammianus says, and only seventy Romans. As after the taking of Maozamalcha, Julian rewarded the brave with crowns, again reviving a practice
a long time dead.[26]

At last, Julian stood beneath the walls of Ctesiphon, his objective,
the walls that Trajan, Avidius Cassius, Severus, and Carus had pierced
before him. All that remained was to capture the great city. But now Julian went into council with his officers, and that council produced an astonishing decision: Ctesiphon would not be attacked. The council was
urged that Ctesiphon was "impregnable by its site alone" and that the
army of King Sapor was approaching. The force of this logic, or any logic
to the same end, is difficult to comprehend: four Roman marshals had
found Ctesiphon perfectly pregnable before. And why, other than to besiege Ctesiphon, had Julian carried such formidable siege equipment in
his fleet — such an equipage that none of his previous assaults on strong
places had taken him longer than four days? And can Julian really have
expected to capture Ctesiphon without having to fight the King's army?
This baffling decision was, moreover, related to another, equally perplexing. Julian did not accept the offers of a treaty of peace which may have
been made by Sapor at this time. But the Roman army was neither to
stay before Ctesiphon and await Sapor, nor retreat into Roman territory
up the convenient Tigris, nor withdraw by way of the Euphrates. Instead,
it was to strike north away from the river into the interior. This, in turn,
occasioned another fateful decision: the fleet of boats that carried the
supplies and the siege machinery was to be burned.[27]

The orator Libanius, Julian's panegyrist, was the first to try to justify
this decision. Had the boats not been burned, he said, they would have
fallen into the hands of the enemy, or it would have taken too many men
to pull them back into Roman territory against the current. These and
other justifications have been offered by modern students as well. But
Libanius admits that the decision was denounced at the time; Ammianus thought it dire; the army in Babylonia was horrified; and indeed
the emperor came to regret it, and the order was soon countermanded
— but too late to save the burning boats.[28]

The twin decisions not to attack Ctesiphon and to march north can
be explained if they are combined with a detail provided by Libanius:
Julian was moving to seek out the army of Sapor, which was in fact march-

ing from the north. There was still a considerable Persian force in Ctesiphon, and Julian no doubt preferred to fight the two Persian armies separately, rather than united. Perhaps he feared being attacked from the rear
by Sapor while besieging the Persian capital. It may well be that Julian
expected to return to attack Ctesiphon once Sapor had been driven away.
Or perhaps he expected Ctesiphon to yield without a fight when the
Great King was vanquished — as some of the forts Julian had bypassed
had promised to do. But these considerations merely make the burning
of the boats more perplexing: if Julian had intended to return to the
Tigris, why did he not simply protect the boats with a garrison or tow
them out of harm's way, perhaps to one of the strong places he had captured on his march?[29]

In burning the boats, Julian claimed a place for himself in a high tradition. Alexander had dismissed his fleet when he turned inland in Asia
Minor, an act so famous that it had received the compliment of explicit
imitation by Agathocles of Sicily, when he landed in North Africa to fight
the Carthaginians (310 BC). It was Agathocles who added the refinement
that the fleet should be burned to deny his soldiers any hope of retreat,
and Agathocles' act entered the tradition of stratagems, and perhaps the
literary tradition as well, where it may have encouraged Vergil to give space
in the *Aeneid* to the old legend that Aeneas's wanderings were delayed
(or halted) by the wayfarers' women burning the Trojan ships. In burning
his boats, Julian was behaving as he had at Pirisabora and all through his
campaign: emulating the past. And this instance of emulation was not a
fantasy of Ammianus's: dumbfounded at the folly of the decision, the
historian failed to make the connection to Alexander and Agathocles.[30]

Upon leaving the Tigris, Julian's expedition almost immediately came
to grief. King Sapor's army was in the area — Persian cavalry harassed the
Romans, and Persian cataphracts were seen — but the Persian host would
not fight the Romans, preferring to starve them. The Persians fired the
crops along the Roman line of march, and so great was the conflagration
that the Romans had to camp while it died down. It was now, in order
to reassure his troops, that Julian employed the venerable stratagem of
presenting starving enemy captives to them naked, to show how feeble
the enemy were. In vain: the army was becoming unmanageable, and
the soldiers took advantage of the assembly to cry out that they should

return the way they had come. There was nothing to eat back there, the emperor and his officers replied: all that territory had been wasted. The route of march was left up to the gods, whose opinion was solicited by sacrifice — but the gods were asked only about routes of retreat (and refused to endorse any): Sapor's unwillingness to fight and the army's perilous supply situation had now doomed Julian's expedition. The army turned west, crossed the Dyala (a tributary of the Tigris), and trudged back toward the great river. The Persians had burnt all the crops. A sandstorm came up, and Julian sent his army into camp to prevent a panic (was the King's host approaching?). The Roman army was now thoroughly unnerved.[31]

Dawn, and with it so large a force of cataphracts that the King himself must be nearby. But although gathering in larger bodies, the Persians would still not commit to a pitched battle, merely to demonstrations and harassment and delaying actions to run down the Roman supplies. In a skirmish, Macameus, a Roman unit commander, killed four foes; then the Persians swarmed him and he was mortally wounded. His brother Maurus avenged him by slaying the man who had struck him down, and although shot through the shoulder with an arrow, terrified those who approached, and got Macameus's body away with the last traces of life still in it. This episode of frontline fighting by senior officers was one of many: Julian placed himself repeatedly in peril, and the unit commander was the second man out of the tunnel at Maozamalcha. More broadly, it appears that in the fourth century heroic leadership had become usual among higher officers to a degree never before seen in the Roman tradition: what had been a (possibly eccentric) choice in the time of Titus was now common behavior. While in Julius Caesar losses were listed in men and centurions, in Ammianus they are listed in men and tribunes — who commanded regiments at least six times as large as the centuries of Caesar's centurions. Where an estimate is possible, the tribunes of Julian's army, like the centurions of Caesar's, had a much higher chance of being killed than the soldiers they led. The emperor Constantius himself practiced with all sorts of weapons and was especially good at infantry hand-to-hand combat drill. This habit of heroic command was to last into the sixth century, where it flowered again into a tradition of combat by challenge between the lines before battle. One of Justinian's generals, although over seventy and fat, was the first up the ladder during an attack on a town: he fell from the top of the ladder and crashed to the ground. The enemy all turned their missiles upon him, and his guards had to cover him over with their shields and drag him away by the foot. But when he was towed out of range and had been set upon his feet again, the tough old warrior went right back up the ladder.[32]

A sign of the power of this heroic code in the fourth century is the way its influence spread from army officers proper into civilian officialdom. If the tribune was the second man out of the hole at Maozamalcha, that is far less surprising than the fact that he was immediately followed by the exalted chief of the civilian bureau of shorthand writers. Later in the retreat Anatolius, the Master of the Offices (another civilian), was killed in the fighting; the government traveled with the emperor and thus many high civil officials were carried into Persia with Julian. Secundus Salutius, the elderly Praetorian Prefect (a civilian), was also endangered; he had to be rescued by one of his assessors, yet another civilian official.[33]

It is impossible to be certain of the origins of this habit of high officers leading from the front and fighting with their own hands, but it is likely they shared the culture of Julian and Ammianus and were partners in their resurrection of the full Hellenistic vision of command, exemplified by Alexander and the Homeric heroes he had imitated in his turn: the commander as arrayer, trickster, and fighter, all at the same time. If so, the triumph of heroic leadership provides welcome confirmation for something we have already come to suspect: that antiquarian leadership, as exemplified by Julian, was not confined to that peculiar emperor or to like-minded intellectuals such as Ammianus and Vegetius, but pervaded the culture of the fourth-century Roman officer corps as a whole. When a civilian official sent a secret message about the Persians to Roman military officers, he could use archaic Latin and abstruse historical allusions as a code to convey the message that Sapor was preparing to attack the empire: "That ancient king, not content with Hellespont, having bridged Granicus and Rhyndacus, comes invading Asia with a multitude of races . . . 'tis done and lamented, lest Greece beware." The officers who received it puzzled over the message, but, educated in the same tradition as the author, they figured out the meaning. The average officer may have been unconscious of the weight of the past upon him, merely having a sense that a commander *should* be aggressive and charge at the front of his men (without any real understanding of the historical origins of that sense). But even so unconscious an outlook might, if widespread, have real consequences for the Roman army.[34]

On the day Macameus and Maurus proved themselves heroes, the Romans drove off the Persian attacks. Soon the Romans arrived at the Tigris but found the bridge burnt by the Persians. Since nearly all their bridging equipment had been destroyed with the fleet, the Romans would have to make their way home up the east bank of the river. But the Romans did find an unplundered estate, and there rested for two days. On the first day of their renewed march up the river the Persians attacked the rear of the marching column. In the fighting a Persian satrap was killed, and the Roman who killed him stripped his body and presented the arms to Julian for a reward: another glimpse of the revival (or survival) of the rituals of single combat. The Romans marched on through the ravaged landscape, their supplies steadily dwindling: now a Persian force tried to block their passage with cataphracts, horse archers, and elephants. Julian drew up his army in a crescent, with wings curving forward, and ordered a fast advance to deprive the Persians of a chance to use their arrows. Ammianus does not make the connection, but the combination of these two tactics suggests that Julian was emulating Miltiades' famous plan for the Athenians at the battle of Marathon in 490 BC. The Persians were driven back, but the Romans did not hold the field and returned to their tents after the battle. Such was the hurt of the Romans that they had to agree to a three-day truce, which they could ill afford because of their scarcity of food: the Roman beasts were now so worn out that they could not carry even what food the Romans had left.[35]

Julian was now seeing ominous visions by night, and a falling star added to his foreboding. When the Romans set out after the truce expired, the Persians pressed them hard from ambuscade. The rear guard was attacked: Julian flew to its aid without his armor. Then report came that the van was threatened as well. Now the center was assailed, and from somewhere came flying a spear and took Julian through the body. The emperor was dying. But he would die as he had lived, forever racing with the admired ancients. As he lay in his tent he held a discussion about the immortality of the soul, as dying men with philosophical pretensions had done for centuries, on the model of the immortal Socrates. By midnight, Julian was dead.[36]

The army of the Romans now lacked both food and a leader. The second deficiency, at least, could be made good: Jovian, an officer of the bodyguard, was hurriedly made emperor by the soldiers. Julian's death and the succession were soon reported to Sapor by a deserter, and the King bade the harrying of the Romans continue. The army reeled north again, along the bank of the river, attacked by elephants, cavalry, and missiles and followed by taunts that Julian had been murdered by his own men. Three tribunes were killed fighting bravely. Now the Persians were becoming bold enough to attack the Roman marching camps. Finally, half a month after the beginning of the retreat, the Romans could go no further: for four days they tried to march on but turned back in the face of Persian resistance. The soldiers demanded to be allowed to cross the Tigris to the safety of the west bank, and some Gauls and Germans, powerful swimmers, managed to get over by forging through the torrents, but the rest waited vainly, hungrily, for rafts to be contrived from the hides of the last pack animals.[37]

It was at this point that Sapor offered Jovian an unequal peace, requiring him to surrender Roman land and border fortresses, including the great Roman bastion of Nisibis, which the King had attacked three times in vain. To extract the army, which starved even as the negotiations dragged on, and to escape the east before a rival to his power might arise, Jovian was compelled to accept Sapor's terms. Now the Romans were no longer attacked by the Persian army, but many soldiers were still lost in the march back to Roman territory — starved, drowned, or taken as slaves by marauding Persians and Saracens. And so it was the remnants of Julian's expedition came home.[38]

THE BATTLE OF ADRIANOPLE
AND THE ROMAN ARMY OF THE FOURTH CENTURY AD

Julian's campaign in Persia was a disaster, a disaster that only diplomacy prevented from becoming a catastrophe. Fifteen years later the emperor Valens led his army to destruction at the battle of Adrianople against the Goths (AD 378). Again diplomacy was called in where arms had failed, and the Goths were allowed to settle or wander, vassals in law but as independent chiefdoms in fact, inside the empire: a dark precedent with darker consequences. There were many battles after, but in the next century the Roman empire in the West was overrun.

The pivotal Adrianople campaign is not as insightfully reported as Julian's eastern expedition—Ammianus was not a participant, not privy, as a staff officer (as he had been with Julian), to the councils of the emperor. But the familiar theme of aggression in command leaps out. The Goths were rampaging in Thrace, having rebelled against Valens, who had allowed them to settle south of the Danube. A battle against them was lost; a second, although bloody, was inconclusive. The Goths would not easily be overcome. Yet there was no need to meet them in the field at all. The Goths were inexperienced in siegecraft, and so properly defended Roman cities were safe: the Goths could be walled up in defiles and starved, harried by cavalry and ambushes, and channeled and chivvied from place to place. Eventually, insisted Sebastianus, the general Valens placed in charge of dealing with them, the Goths would have to surrender or withdraw over the Danube. The war could be won without another risky pitched battle.[39]

It was not to be. Valens, envying (we are told) the successes of Sebastianus and of his own cousin Gratian, who had been campaigning victoriously in the west, decided to bring the Goths to battle. He had summoned Gratian to assist him with his formidable army from Gaul, and Gratian was marching hard toward him. But Valens decided to fight the battle before Gratian arrived, so that he would not have to share the glory of victory with him. We can think what we want of the motives the historians attribute to Valens: he died in the resulting cataclysm. But there is no doubt that, although at least two safer options were available to him—harrying rather than fighting or waiting for Gratian and his army—Valens chose the most aggressive and dangerous strategy. And if the motives that the tradition attributes to Valens are to be believed, he was an analogue to the Roman general who marched to disaster at Trebia in the Second Punic War (218 BC)—the general who sought battle in winter because he dreaded being superseded by the next year's consuls, or his wounded colleague's recovering enough to share his glory.[40]

Even at the last moment the fighting at Adrianople might have been averted — a prominent Roman hostage rode toward the Gothic wagons as a preliminary to talks. But two Roman officers, burning for action, led their units to the attack without orders and were thrown back. The hostage reined his horse; the Gothic cavalry charged; the battle was joined. Such was the slaughter that the body of the emperor Valens was never found.[41]

The Romans had a tradition of highly aggressive, impatient strategy in war — a tradition visible in the Second Punic War, in Caesar's campaigns, and in Titus's insistence upon assailing the walls of Jerusalem rather than starving the city out. "Time would accomplish anything," Josephus had Titus say, "but for glory, speed was necessary." Even commanders who were cautious in their selection of occasions for battle, careful in their arraying, and masters of trickery — Paullus, Caesar — nevertheless moved very quickly to fight the enemy. Celerity was a powerful old Roman military excellence, and powerfully emphasized by Paullus's army's complaining when it took him a mere fifteen days to bring Perseus to battle after the consul's arrival with the army. In battle, a Roman general might be cautious or bold. But caution outside battle — strategic caution — was far rarer: the strategy of Fabius Maximus, following Hannibal around rather than attacking him, was rejected by the Romans at the time and found few emulators later in Roman history, however much wise heads might advocate it. In the realm of war strategy the impatient commands of *virtus* were never seriously challenged.[42]

In the days of the Second Punic War, when aggression brought defeat, the Romans could raise another, larger army the next year, and when that was destroyed, a larger still, and even after Hannibal reaped that third army at Cannae, the Romans could raise yet more men and fight on until Carthage was finally defeated. At one time the Romans had possessed an enviable reputation for losing and coming back with more troops the next year: Roman manpower gushed like a fountain, said a Greek. But in the fourth century there was no question of quickly replacing the troops lost at Adrianople. The late Roman army had difficulty recovering from defeat. Counting soldiers brought to battle — rather than meaningless "paper strength" — the fourth-century Roman army was small, expensive, and fragile. Julian met the Germans at the battle of Strasbourg with only thirteen thousand men. To put down the dangerous rebellion of Firmus in North Africa, Theodosius had only thirty-five hundred; perhaps twenty thousand rode to destruction with Valens at Adrianople. The number that survives for the army Julian led into Persia, sixty-five thousand, is so unusually large for its period as to inspire suspicion: if it is right at all it represents perhaps the whole force of the Roman army on the Syrian border. The Romans had often assembled larger armies in the Republic and perhaps under the early empire as well.[43]

The reasons the mid–fourth century Roman army was small and difficult to replenish probably include a weakened economy, a rickety tax system, a woefully inefficient army pay and supply system (all made worse by rampant corruption), the reluctance of many potential soldiers from within the empire to serve (resulting in clumsily administered conscription), the reluctance of soldiers from one area of the empire to be transferred elsewhere, and the frequent desertion that followed from many of these other deficits. In the face of such obstacles the Romans still managed, at least until Adrianople, to field a professional army, soldier by soldier not demonstrably inferior in any respect — discipline, training, bravery, equipment — to the Roman army of the earlier empire, and in some respects — in cavalry, fortifications, and perhaps siegecraft — superior. In straitened times, whether by decision or default, numbers on the battlefield and usable reserves had been sacrificed to quality.[44]

There were men who knew how to lead an army like this, men like Valens's general Sebastianus, men like those who had pleaded with Julian not to march east into the realm of the Persians. The army of the fourth century needed to be treasured, to be commanded with care and circumspection, not risked unnecessarily. It needed to be wielded with calculated finesse, like a rapier: its tragedy was to be commanded by men like Julian and Valens, men who used it like a mace, as Roman commanders always had. Julian used it so because of his conscious relationship with an admired past. Valens and other aggressive late-antique commanders were also lashed on by history, even though they may have been less conscious of it. What commanders knew (and were told by those around them) is that leading their armies boldly at the enemy was expected and admired behavior: they might be more or less aware that those expectations were the legacy of Roman *virtus* mingled with the Greek legacy of Alexander. There was, in short, a dangerous mismatch between the capabilities of the Roman army of the fourth century and the culture of its commanders, visibly or invisibly guided by the tradition in which they fought. This mismatch led the Roman army to defeats from which it could not recover. In the end, the soldiers did not overcome the ghosts of the past. In the end, it was the ghosts who won.

THE ROMANS

CONCLUSION

Procopius of Caesarea wrote of the wars that Justinian, Emperor of the Romans, fought against the barbarians." So the great historian of the sixth century AD, opening his work in imitation of Thucydides, who wrote nearly a thousand years before. Thucydides compared his war, the Peloponnesian War, to the Trojan War to illustrate its magnitude: so does Procopius. But the mention of Homer kindles anger, the elegant mantle of literary allusion slips, and suddenly, bizarrely, Procopius is extolling the archers of his day by contrast to those in the *Iliad*. The archers of Justinian were mounted, wore armor, and carried spears, shields, and swords. The wretched archers in Homer had none of these things but hid behind other warriors and slunk about stealing. They did not even draw their bowstrings back to the ear: no wonder their arrows wrought so little. This outburst was brought on by thoughts of contemporaries who compared present methods unfavorably to those in Homer, sneering at archery and advocating the hand-to-hand fighting of the *Iliad*. Even in the sixth century AD, men still appealed to Homer as a model of how to fight. The modern reader sympathizes instinctively with Procopius's preference for the improved methods of his own day but also realizes that Procopius's fury is not that of a man serenely confident that everybody agreed with him.[1]

Suppose that the logic of Procopius, the familiar logic of technological advance, had ruled the evolution of Roman fighting on land. In that case the Romans adopted the Greek phalanx because it was more effective than how they fought before — and that may indeed be so, since we do not know when the phalanx was adopted or what threats Rome then faced. When a military challenge arose to which the phalanx was unequal, there should (by this logic) have been a crisp change to a new, more appropriate way of fighting, to the manipular legion. Yet in fact the manipular legion shows in it traces of a long struggle with the phalanx, which survived in the form of the *triarii* and in the form of the subunits (centuries and centurions, their commanders) of which the manipular array was assembled. In the heyday of the manipular array the Romans did in fact face forms of enemy fighting to which the array was sometimes unequal, especially the Hellenistic phalanx, especially when wielded by generals like Hannibal. Then, by technological logic, the Romans should have changed the way they fought, but then they did not. It was only when the Romans had conquered most of the Mediterranean littoral with the manipular array — when they should not, in this logic, have changed their successful ways — that the Romans did, in fact, finally discard the array of maniples for the array of cohorts.

If the legion of cohorts had replaced the legion of maniples because it was decisively more effective in battle, the change should have been rapid. Instead it was slow, taking at least forty years and perhaps centuries. The two arrays long coexisted, as options; but eventually one option squeezed out the other. And there was a third option as well, a close-packed phalanx-like array. If under the empire the threats to Rome changed in ways that made a phalanx evidently superior to the old *pilum-scutum*-and-*gladius* fighting of the Romans, a rapid change to the phalanx might again have been expected. Yet, once again, the two methods long coexisted as options. By the fourth century the infantry phalanx had finally displaced the *pilum-scutum*-and-*gladius* array, just as the cohort finally displaced the maniple. But it is hard to see how it could ever be more effective in any generation to eliminate options, even if only gradually. If the Romans valued their phalanx especially to resist horsemen, they should have kept their *pilum-scutum*-and-*gladius* style of fighting to defeat infantry, a role it had played admirably for perhaps six hundred years. But the Romans faced German infantry at Strasbourg in the phalanx: the choices available to a Roman general of the early empire had vanished. A confident advance from worse to better military technology and method describes the military history of the Romans no better than it does that of the Greeks.

As in Greek warfare, many factors combined to determine how Roman ways of fighting on land changed over time. There were economic and social forces at play—seen in the declining wealth required to join the Roman army of the Republic, the powerlessness of the Roman soldiers of the late Republic, which allowed the legion of cohorts to prevail, and the eagerness of non-Romans to join the army under the empire. Politics came into it too: at Rome politics was always closely bound to war. There was pressure from military crises—especially in the third century AD. And, as in the Greek case, there was the power of culture.

Four cultural features were most powerful. First was the Roman habit of single combat and the associated moral quality, *virtus,* aggressive courage. Because *virtus* was so admired in all generations of Roman fighting, it nudged the way Romans fought to allow them to display it in battle. This might promote change—inspire the modification of the phalanx into the manipular legion—but it might also slow change, retard the move away from that same array and frustrate generals who wished to profit from Greek military science.

Opposed to *virtus* was *disciplina,* in origin the ethos of the Roman phalanx and the other founding ideal of the Roman martial code. It was this ethic of restraint that allowed commanders control over their soldiers—soldiers whom the cult of *virtus* often made ungovernable. *Disciplina* was something imposed, but also something felt: as a military excellence *disciplina* and its elements—obedience, training, laboring—were no less competitive than *virtus.* The secret of the success of the Roman army lay not its array, nor in its training and *disciplina* alone, but exactly in the mix of *virtus* and *disciplina.* Much of the story of the Roman army under the empire is that of recruiting and reinforcing both *virtus* and *disciplina,* of undergirding and strengthening both, but of trying to maintain the balance.

It was especially the influence of Greece that set *virtus* and *disciplina* in conflict in the Roman army of the Republic. Greek influence over Rome was pervasive, but in the military sphere it took the particular form of Greek ideals and techniques of generalship. These were increasingly powerful among Roman leaders over time and were often resisted by

Roman soldiers. The triumph of Greek influence was marked by the eventual transition from the legion of maniples to the legion of cohorts, the latter more convenient for the commander but less appealing to the soldiers than the old manipular array that had grown up, like a vine caressing an oak, around Roman military values.

Finally, there was the Romans' profound love of the past, influential in their military history in every generation. In the Republic this love slowed and guided change — even the legion of cohorts was organized by centuries, which went back to the Roman phalanx. Under the empire, when combined with admiration for Greek military methods and molded by the archaizing culture of the Second Sophistic, love of the past produced military antiquarianism: commanders who behaved like Alexander, who revived the Greek phalanx, and who struggled to re-create the deeds of exemplary ancients.

Both Greek and Roman soldiers fought under the spell of the past. But the way Greeks and Romans understood their past was different and had different consequences. To the Greeks the epic past was an inspiration and a guide — but as a rule they did not re-create the past merely for re-creation's sake. The Roman past of time-hallowed ethics and ancient ways of doing things, and the Roman deathgrip upon that past, offered different advantages, but also different dangers. The Roman ability to preserve into the fourth century AD the archaic value system of *virtus* and *disciplina* was fundamental to their military success. Yet, ultimately, when they turned under the empire to re-creating rather than merely preserving the past, they did so more naïvely than the Greeks had done. In the end the Greek relationship with the military past made Greek armies better, but in Rome's later centuries the Roman relationship with the military past made the Roman army worse.

The story of the evolution of ground warfare in antiquity resembles the evolution of ancient literature. Unlike modern literature (which relentlessly seeks after the new) ancient literature changed over time by the process of *aemulatio,* competitive emulation: contemporary writers read their revered elders and exercised their creativity in doing the same thing better. When a literary problem had to be solved, the first resort of the artist was to look to the tradition for a solution, rather than to his own unfettered imagination. What was genuinely new in literature (and there was much) often arose from the triumphant solving of literary problems that had stumped previous generations or from combining and reconciling different traditions (in Latin literature especially). An ancient poet or prose writer always had one eye cocked back to the past, and sometimes both, because also characteristic of this literary culture were whole-scale leaps back into the past, as in the second century AD. As unlikely as it may seem, literary *aemulatio* offers a more robust model than technological progress for understanding the change in ancient methods of fighting.[2]

Aemulatio harnessed the power of competition to literary achievement: and so literary achievement was driven by a tremendous force, sovereign in war as well. The Greeks knew that competition could be both good and ill for man. "There are two kinds of Strife on the earth," sang the old poet Hesiod, "not one,"

> One is praised by those who know her, the other blamed,
> for they have completely different spirits.
> The one compels war and ill and battle — she is cruel.
> No man loves her, but by necessity
> and the deathless gods' will men honor this hard Strife.
> But the other Strife gloomy Night bore, as an elder daughter,
> and the high-throned son of Chronos who dwells above
> rooted her in the earth, and she is better towards men by far.
> Even the lazy she stirs to labor
> for any man yearns to work when he sees another
> rich, and who speeds to plow and husband and order his
>   household;
> neighbor strives with neighbor as he hastens to riches.
> This Strife is good for mortal men. Potter is jealous of potter,
>   and craftsman of craftsman; beggar envies beggar and
>   bard envies bard.[3]

The ancients knew that one way to prevail in hard and warlike strife was to cultivate with loving care her elder sister, kindly strife. The best ancient armies recruited soldiers from societies with strong competitive traditions and encouraged ferocious competition at every rank and every organizational level. The best ancient leaders — Alexander or Julius Caesar — knew how to call upon that competition to get their soldiers to perform at their best. But to be fruitful, the competition of soldiers had to be controlled and directed. The armies of Sparta, Macedonia, and Rome came to be trained, and contemporaries pointed to the unusually harsh discipline of the Roman army and of Spartan society. But to look only at training and discipline as the keys to victory is to worship the waning moon and not to know that it forms a crescent because a greater shadow covers it — the shadow of rivalry. For if the best ancient armies were trained and disciplined, it was because the best ancient armies had a special need for training and discipline: it was the singular and ungovernable competitiveness of the best ancient soldiers that made such training and discipline necessary.[4]

The best ancient armies were not those that set themselves against the manners of their age. The best ancient armies were those that found ways to exaggerate and exploit the yearnings of their individual soldiers. The best ancient generals did not stand athwart the stream of their time but were carried along by its deepest currents. Perhaps that is true in any generation of warriors. And perhaps it will always be true, or will be true at least until that unimaginable millennium when the nature of man changes, when men become kind, and when there is need no longer for

> War-Cry, the daughter of War
> prelude to spears, to whom
> men are sacrificed in holy death for the city.
> (Pindar, fr. 78 Maehler)

AUTHOR'S NOTE AND

ACKNOWLEDGMENTS

This is a history of methods of fighting on land from the age of Homer through the fourth century AD, intended to be readable by and — the author hopes — enjoyable to the interested reader who knows nothing about the subject, the casually knowledgeable, and the adept. It is the book of a historian of the classical world led to a military subject by curiosity about how practical methods of doing anything at all might change over many centuries in a world with very limited technological progress. This curiosity demanded a case study offering a considerable number of stages of evolution, with stages well enough attested that the differences between them could be discerned and the reasons for them guessed. I also sought an activity important to the ancients and upon which the screw of necessity pressed: while I might have traced changes in the style of sculpture, say, such changes might have as their causes no more than flighty shifts in fashion. Fighting on land meets all these criteria, while few other practical arts can be traced in such detail, stage by stage, over the millennium from early Greece to late Rome. Having settled upon the evolution to be traced, the book sticks quite close to its story: even other arenas of ancient warfare — fighting at sea, fortification and siegecraft, and logistics — appear mostly for the purposes of comparison.

The theme of this book is change over time and its causes. Those familiar with ancient military history will discover little new in the realm of What? and When? Readers will find little novel in the accounts of battles, and they will discover venerable controversies dodged or merely noted in passing, and the argument molded to accommodate competing views. For this is rather a book about Why? — about why change occurs at all, its causes when it does occur and reasons when it does not, and why it happens when it does and not earlier or later. And in relentlessly asking Why? one finds other historical questions arising: Where did the Greek phalanx come from? Why was the army of Alexander so successful? Where did Roman discipline come from? Where did the Roman legion come from? Why was the Roman army so successful? Why did the Roman army's fortunes decline in late antiquity? What did the most victorious armies of antiquity have in common? What are the sources of military excellence in the ancient world, or in any human society?

A historian enters a new subfield as if venturing into a rustling cage in a darkened zoo: will the denizens be savage leopards or cuddly lambs? frisky monkeys or somnolent sloths? As it turned out, meeting so many military historians of antiquity was one of the special joys of writing this book. The manuscript was read through with invaluable comments by A. Goldsworthy, P. Rance, N. V. Sekunda, M. P. Speidel, and H. van Wees. E. Wheeler answered a host of queries. Acute readers will recognize that my debt to the work of van Wees and Wheeler is more profound than notes can convey. To most of the above as well as to H. Elton and the editors of the *Cambridge History of Greek and Roman Warfare* (and to Michael Sharp at Cambridge University Press) I am grateful for permission to cite writings in advance of publication.

This book would have been cold and sad had it not been written in the happy proximity of E. A. Meyer's intellectual furnace: she was a constant source of sparkling ideas, she cheerfully hewed wood, and she ruthlessly hauled away to the ash heap what was overdone.

The manuscript was also read and improved by E. C. Kiesling, H. C. E. Midelfort, M. and D. Lendon, and J. Campbell. I learned a great deal about plain writing from R. McQuilkin and L. Heimert.

M. Powers graciously double-checked the references and drafted the index. The immense task of assembling the illustrations was carried out with admirable zeal and good humor by S. McGowen. I am grateful to B. Nelson for the maps, and to S. Kim for the drawings. Generous contributions were made to the costs of illustrations by Yale University Press, by the Dean of the College of Arts and Sciences and the Vice President for Research and Graduate Studies at the University of Virginia, and, alas, by the author. The skill of L. Purifoy and his interlibrary loan staff at UVA's Alderman library never ceases to delight, nor does the library's wisdom in providing its incomparable *Library Delivery Service*.

I have benefited from enjoyable discussions with, or help from, R. Alston, J. Bedell, E. Borza, S. Buckley, D. B. Campbell, J. S. Clay, D. Cohen, J. Dillery, G. Gallagher, J. Gibert, G. Hays, S. Holcomb, P. Hunt, J. Marincola, B. Meissner, C. Mileta, C. Olmsted, D. Ralston, P. Sabin, R. Saller, T. J. Smith, O. Stoll, R. Tannenbaum, A. J. Woodman, and D. Yates.

The Greek chapters of this book were drafted at the Center for Hellenic Studies, under the friendly eyes of K. Raaflaub and D. Boedeker, while I enjoyed leave support from the University of Virginia, and the book has progressed during summers spent at MIT through the gracious hospitality of H. Ritvo, P. Perdue, and P. Khoury.

L. Heimert of Yale University Press has been a vigorous and charming editor, admirably assisted by K. Condon and M. Egland. L. Kenney ably copyedited the manuscript. Translations are mine except when indicated otherwise, but they cannot fail in many cases to echo the work of previous translators. To those I may have slighted I offer my grateful acknowledgments here.

CHRONOLOGY

The outline chronology is closely linked to the particular interests of this book. For a more detailed chronology of ancient battles (up to 31 BC) and supplying the main ancient references, see J. D. Montagu, *Battles of the Greek and Roman World* (London, 2000); for a more detailed chronology of Roman military history, see A. Goldworthy, *Roman Warfare* (London, 2000) pp. 10–15.

Greek Warfare

BC

c. 1400–1200	Height of Mycenean civilization
c. 1200	Traditional date of the Trojan War
c. 1150	Final destruction of Mycenae
776	First Olympiad
c. 725	First appearance of hoplite equipment in Greece
c. 700	Date of *Iliad* (?)
c. 700 and after	Lelantine War between Chalcis and Eretria
c. 650	Mass production of hoplite figurines begins at Sparta
c. 650–640	Hoplite vase paintings of Chigi/Macmillan painter
c. 640–600	Tyrtaeus, war poet of Sparta
c. 550	Battle of Champions at Thyrea (Sparta vs. Argos)

520	Establishment of *hoplitodromos* (race in hoplite armor) as an Olympic event
499–494	Ionian Revolt (vs. Persia)
490	First Persian invasion of Greece
490	Battle of Marathon (Athens defeats Persians)
480–479	Xerxes' invasion of Greece
480	Battle of Artemisium (Greeks vs. Persian at sea; indecisive)
480	Battle of Thermopylae (Persians defeat Greeks; stand of three hundred Spartans under King Leonidas)
480	Battle of Salamis (Greeks defeat Persian fleet)
479	Battle of Plataea (Greeks under Pausanias defeat Persians under Mardonius)
479	Battle of Mycale (Greeks defeat Persians by land and sea)
477	Formation of Athens's Delian League
431–404	Peloponnesian War between Sparta and Athens
430	Plague at Athens
425	Athenian light troops capture Spartan hoplites on Sphacteria
425/4	Spartans establish cavalry
424	Battle of Delium (Boeotians defeat Athenians)
418	Battle of Mantinea (Sparta and allies defeat Argos and allies)
415–413	Athenian expedition to Syracuse, Athenians defeated
413	Spartans establish fort at Decelea in Attica
410	Battle of Cyzicus (Athenians defeat Peloponnesian fleet)

406	Battle of Arginusae (Athenians defeat Peloponnesian fleet)
405	Battle of Aegospotami (Peloponnesians destroy Athenian fleet)
404	Surrender of Athens
401	March of the Ten Thousand to Cunaxa and then escape to the Black Sea
395–387/6	Corinthian War (Sparta and allies vs. Thebes, Athens, and allies)
390	Victory of Athenian peltasts over Spartan hoplites at Lechaeum
371	Battle of Leuctra (Boeotians defeat Spartans and allies)
370	Death of Jason of Pherae
362	Second Battle of Mantinea (Boeotians vs. Spartans, indecisive)
348	Philip II of Macedon captures Olynthus, an ally of Athens
338	Battle of Chaeronea (Philip II of Macedon defeats Greek allies and conquers Greece)
336	Murder of Philip II of Macedon; accession of Alexander
335	Alexander campaigns in Thrace and Illyria, destroys rebellious Thebes
c. 335	Establishment of *ephebeia* at Athens (two years of compulsory military training and service)
334–323	Alexander's Asian Campaign
334	Battle of Granicus River (Alexander defeats satraps)
334	Alexander's siege of Halicarnassus
333	Battle of Issus (Alexander defeats Darius III)
332	Alexander's siege of Tyre

332	Alexander's conquest of Egypt
331	Battle of Gaugamela (Alexander defeats Darius III)
326	Battle of Hydaspes River (Alexander defeats Porus)
324	Mutiny of Macedonians at Opis; Alexander must turn back
323	Death of Alexander at Babylon
323–322	Greece revolts: Lamian War (Antipater defeats Greeks)
317	Battle of Paraetacene (Antigonus the One-Eyed vs. Eumenes, indecisive)
317/6 (Winter)	Battle of Gabiene (Antigonus the One-Eyed defeats Eumenes)
312	Battle of Gaza (Ptolemy I defeats Demetrius Poliorcetes)
305–304	Demetrius Poliorcetes' siege of Rhodes
301	Battle of Ipsus (Antigonus the One-Eyed killed)
c. 300	Invention of chain mail
222	Battle of Sellasia (Achaean League and Macedonia defeat Cleomenes of Sparta)
217	Battle of Raphia (Ptolemy IV defeats Antiochus III)

Roman Warfare
BC

753	Traditional date for the founding of Rome
578–535	Traditional date of King Servius Tullius (and the "Servian census" indicating Roman use of hoplite arms)
509	Traditional date for the expulsion of the kings: Rome becomes a Republic

496	Traditional date for the Battle of Lake Regillus (Rome defeats the Latins, becomes head of the Latin League)
407	Traditional date of outbreak of war with Veii
406	Traditional date for the beginning of Roman military pay
390	Traditional date for the sack of Rome by the Gauls
361	Traditional date for the single combat of Manlius Torquatus with the Gaul
349	Traditional date for the single combat of Valerius Corvus with the Gaul
343–341	First Samnite War
340–338	The Latin War (Rome gains final control of Latium)
340	Traditional date of Manlius Torquatus's execution of his son
326–304	Second Samnite War
298–290	Third Samnite War
280–274	Pyrrhus campaigns in Italy and Sicily
280	Battle of Heraclea (Pyrrhus defeats the Romans)
279	Battle of Asculum (Pyrrhus defeats the Romans)
275	Battle of Beneventum (Romans defeat Pyrrhus)
264–241	First Punic War (Rome vs. Carthage)
260	Battle of Mylae (Romans defeat Carthaginian fleet)
256	Battle of Ecnomus (Romans defeat Carthaginian fleet)
255	Battle of Bagradas River (Carthaginians defeat Romans in Africa)
250	Battle of Drepanum (Carthaginian fleet defeats Romans)

242	Battle of Aegates Islands (Romans defeat Carthaginian fleet)
225	Battle of Telamon (Romans defeat Gauls)
218–201	Second Punic War (Rome vs. Carthage)
218	Battle of Trebia (Hannibal defeats Romans)
217	Battle of Lake Trasimene (Hannibal defeats Romans)
217	Q. Fabius Maximus *dictator*
216	Battle of Cannae (Hannibal defeats Romans)
207	Battle of Metaurus (Romans defeat Hasdrubal, preventing the reinforcement of Hannibal)
206	Battle of Ilipa (Scipio defeats Carthaginians in Spain)
202	Battle of Zama (Scipio defeats Hannibal in Africa)
215–205	First Macedonian War (Rome and allies vs. Philip V of Macedon)
200–196	Second Macedonian War (Rome vs. Philip V of Macedon)
198	Siege of Atrax (Macedonian phalanx resists Romans)
197	Battle of Cynoscephalae (Flamininus defeats Philip V)
195	Battle of Emporiae (victory of M. Porcius Cato in Spain)
192–189	War against Antiochus (King of Seleucid Empire)
190	Battle of Magnesia (Romans and allies defeat Antiochus)
171–168	Third Macedonian War (Romans vs. Perseus, King of Macedon)
171	Battle of Callinicus (Perseus defeats Romans)
168	Battle of Pydna (Aemilius Paullus defeats Perseus)

167	Livy's manuscript breaks off (little military detail until 58 BC)
149–146	Third Punic War (Rome destroys Carthage)
143–133	War of Numantia (in Spain)
111–105	War against Jugurtha (in North Africa)
108	Battle of Muthul river (Romans defeat Jugurtha)
113–101	War against the Cimbri and Teutones
105	Battle of Arausio (Cimbri and Teutones defeat Romans)
c. 104	Posited military reforms of Marius
102	Battle of Aquae Sextiae (Marius defeats the Teutones)
101	Battle of Vercellae (Marius defeats the Cimbri)
after 102	Roman citizen cavalry abolished, along with ten-year military service prerequisite for political office
90–88	Social War (Rome against many of her Italian allies)
89–85	First Mithridatic War
83–82	Second Mithridatic War
74–63	Third Mithridatic War
67	Battle of Zela (Mithridates defeats the Romans)
73–71	Revolt of Spartacus
58–51	Julius Caesar's conquest of Gaul
57	Battle of the Sambre (Caesar defeats the Nervii)
52	Battle of Gergovia (Vercingetorix defeats Caesar)
52	Siege of Alesia (Caesar defeats and captures Vercingetorix)
53	Battle of Carrhae (Parthians defeat and kill Crassus)
49–45	Civil war between Caesar, Pompey, and Pompey's followers

49	Battle of Ilerda (Caesar defeats Pompeians in Spain)
48	Siege of Dyrrachium (Caesar besieges Pompey but withdraws)
48	Battle of Pharsalus (Caesar defeats Pompey; Pompey murdered in Egypt)
46	Battle of Thapsus (Caesar defeats the Pompeians in North Africa)
45	Battle of Munda (Caesar again defeats the Pompeians in Spain)
44	Murder of Julius Caesar
42	Battle of Philippi (Octavian and Antony defeat the murderers of Caesar)
31	Battle of Actium (Octavian defeats the fleet of Antony and Cleopatra)
27	Traditional date of the establishment of the Roman empire; Octavian takes the name Augustus
27 BC–AD 14	Reign of Augustus; Romans conquer to the Danube

AD

9	Varian *clades* (Arminius ambushes and destroys three legions under Quinctilius Varus beyond the Rhine)
14	Rhine and Danube legions mutiny on the death of Augustus
14–37	Reign of Tiberius
14–17	Campaigns of Germanicus in Germany
37–41	Reign of Gaius Caligula
41–54	Reign of Claudius
43	Conquest of southern Britain
54–68	Reign of Nero

66–70	The Jewish War
70	Siege of Jerusalem
68–70	Emperors Galba, then Otho, then Vitellius, then Vespasian: Civil War
68	Battle of Bedriacum (Vitellius defeats Otho)
69	Battle of Cremona (Vespasian's generals defeat Vitellius)
69–70	Batavian revolt
70–79	Reign of Vespasian
79–81	Reign of Titus
81–96	Reign of Domitian
83	Battle of Mons Graupius (Agricola victorious in Scotland)
96–98	Reign of Nerva
98–117	Reign of Trajan
101–102	First Dacian War (against King Decebalus)
105–106	Second Dacian War
114–117	Parthian War (Trajan captures Ctesiphon)
117–138	Reign of Hadrian
122	Construction of Hadrian's Wall begins
128	Hadrian reviews the troops at Lambaesis, and his remarks are recorded on stone
132–136	Bar Kochba rebellion (Judaea)
135	Incursion of the Alans, date of Arrian's *Deployment Against the Alans*
138–161	Reign of Antoninus Pius
161–180	Reign of Marcus Aurelius
161–66	Parthian War
167–75, 177–80	Wars on the Danube
180–192	Reign of Commodus

193	Civil War
193–211	Reign of Septimius Severus
198	Severus invades Parthia and sacks Ctesiphon
211–217	Reign of Caracalla
222–235	Reign of Severus Alexander
235–284	So-called Crisis of the Third Century: many invasions, civil wars, and emperors, all very badly reported
260–268	Reign of Gallienus, traditionally credited with increasing the Roman emphasis on cavalry
270–275	Reign of Aurelian, who recovers Gaul and the East
284–305	Reign of Diocletian, who restores the borders
312	Battle of Milvian Bridge (Constantine defeats Maxentius)
324–337	Constantine sole ruler
337–361	Reign of Constantius
357	Battle of Strasbourg (Julian defeats the Alamanni)
359	Persian capture of Amida
360–363	Reign of Julian
363	Julian's invasion of Persia; death of Julian
363–364	Reign of Jovian
364	Accession of Valentinian and Valens (Valentinian dies 375)
378	Battle of Adrianople (Visigoths defeat and kill Valens)
379–395	Reign of Theodosius
380–382	Settlement of the Visigoths in the empire
394	Battle of Frigidus River (Theodosius defeats his rivals)
410	Visigoths capture and sack Rome

ABBREVIATIONS

Standard abbreviations are used for ancient authors and works, from the *Oxford Classical Dictionary* (3d ed.) where possible and sometimes expanded for clarity's sake. I have used the following abbreviations for modern reference books, collections of inscriptions, papyri, literary fragments, and other *variorum* assemblages of ancient material:

AE	*L'Année épigraphique*, various editors (Paris, 1888–).
Bosworth *Comm.*	A. B. Bosworth, *A Historical Commentary on Arrian's History of Alexander*, 2 vols. (Oxford, 1980–95).
Broughton *MRR*	T. R. S. Broughton, *The Magistrates of the Roman Republic* vol. 1 (New York, 1951).
CIL	*Corpus inscriptionum latinarum*, various editors (Berlin, 1883–).
den Boeft *Comm. XXIII*	J. den Boeft et al., *Philological and Historical Commentary on Ammianus Marcellinus XXIII* (Groningen, 1998).
den Boeft *Comm. XXIV*	J. den Boeft et al., *Philological and Historical Commentary on Ammianus Marcellinus XXIV* (Leiden, 2002).
FGH	F. Jacoby (ed.), *Die Fragmente der griechischen Historiker* (Leiden, 1923–58).
IG	*Inscriptiones graecae*, various editors (Berlin, 1873–).

ILS	*Inscriptiones latinae selectae,* 3 vols., H. Dessau (ed.) (Berlin, 1892–1916).
Janko *Comm.* 4	R. Janko, *The Iliad: A Commentary, Vol. iv: Books 13–16* (Cambridge, 1992).
Kirk *Comm.* 1	G. Kirk, *The Iliad: A Commentary, Vol. i: Books 1–4* (Cambridge, 1985).
Kirk Comm. 2	G. Kirk, *The Iliad: A Commentary, Vol. ii: Books 5–8* (Cambridge, 1990).
LIMC	*Lexicon iconographicum mythologiae classicae,* H. C. Ackermann and J.-R. Gisler (eds.) (Zürich, 1971–).
ML	R. Meiggs and D. Lewis (eds.), *A Selection of Greek Historical Inscriptions to the End of the Fifth Century* BC, rev. ed. (Oxford 1988[1969]).
Oakley *Comm.*	S. P. Oakley, *A Commentary on Livy Books VI–X* vol. 2 (Oxford, 1988).
Pritchett, *GSAW*	W. K. Pritchett, *The Greek State at War,* 5 vols. (Berkeley and Los Angeles, 1971–91).
P. Oxy.	*The Oxyrhynchus Papyri,* various editors (Oxford, 1898–).
RE	*Real-Encyclopädie der classischen Altertumswissenschaft,* A. F. von Pauly et al. (eds.) (Stuttgart, 1894–).
ROL	*Remains of Old Latin,* 4 vols., E. H. Warmington (ed.) (Cambridge, Mass., 1935–40).
SIG³	*Sylloge inscriptionum graecarum,* 3d ed., W. Dittenberger (ed.) (Leipzig, 1915–24).
Smallwood *Nerva*	E. M. Smallwood (ed.), *Documents Illustrating the Principates of Nerva, Trajan and Hadrian* (Cambridge, 1966).

Tod *GHI*   M. N. Tod (ed.), *A Selection of Greek*
Historical Inscriptions, 2 vols. (Oxford,
1933–48).

NOTES

---◆◆---

More expansive bibliographical notes to each chapter are collected following the glossary.

Prologue

1. K. W. Nolan, *Operation Buffalo* (New York, 1991), quoted pp. 269, 276; withdrawal 284–6 (quoted 285). On this battle see also the official Marine history, G. L. Telfer, L. Rogers, and V. K. Fleming, *U.S. Marines in Vietnam, Fighting the North Vietnamese, 1967* (Washington, D.C., 1984) pp. 95–104. For this narrative I am wholly dependent upon secondary accounts: the dialogue in particular seems to be based on decades-old recall and should be treated with appropriate suspicion.

2. Objective, Nolan, *Operation Buffalo* pp. 244, 249, 253, 344. Thirty-one bodies, 322 (but listed as thirty-four at p. 172); need to recover new bodies, 298, doing so, 302; casualties in I Co., 299–303, quoted 301. 5 July, 321–2, 325–9.

3. Quoted, Nolan, *Operation Buffalo* p. 250. For drive to recover cf. 35–6, 110, S. Zaffiri, *Hamburger Hill* (Novato, Calif., 2000[1988]) pp. 162, 227–8 (268 on using bodies as bait). After-action report, Nolan, *Operation Buffalo* quoted p. 249. On Somalia, M. Bowden, *Black Hawk Down* (New York, 1999).

4. Pledge, M. J. Jacques and B. H. Norton, *Sergeant Major, U.S. Marines* (New York, 1995) p. 272 (on Vietnam): "The incredible extremes taken to recover Staff Sergeant Hall's body served well to remind every Marine in the company of the efforts that would be made to bring back the body of any dead Marine." Quoted, Nolan, *Operation Buffalo* p. 357, cf. 458. Bodies damaged by U.S. fire, p. 302.

5. Greeks vs. Romans, contrast Pritchett, *GSAW* vol. 4 (=W. K. Pritchett, *The Greek State at War* vol. 4 [Berkeley and Los Angeles, 1985]) pp. 94–259 with C. M. Gilliver, *The Roman Art of War* (Stroud, 1999) p. 123; and cf. the ancient Germans, Tac. *Germ.*

6. War in the Pacific, E. Bergerud, *Touched with Fire: The Land War in the South*

Pacific (New York, 1996) pp. 403–25; J. A. Lynn, *Battle: A History of Combat and Culture* (Boulder, Colo., 2003) pp. 219–80; cf. E. B. Sledge, *With the Old Breed* (New York, 1990[1981]) p. 34.

Introduction

1. B. Cunliffe (ed.), *The Temple of Sulis Minerva at Bath. Volume 2: The Finds from the Sacred Spring* (Oxford, 1988). Quoted curse tablet nr. 10 (pp. 122–3), trans. R. S. O. Tomlin (adapted). For the seal-stones, pp. 27–33 (it cannot be shown conclusively that they were deposited at one time, but seems highly likely), and for the catapult washer, pp. 8–9.

2. On ancient catapult design, E. W. Marsden, *Greek and Roman Artillery: Historical Development* (Oxford, 1969) and *Greek and Roman Artillery: Technical Treatises* (Oxford, 1971), brought up to date by D. Baatz, *Bauten und Katapulte des römischen Heeres* (Stuttgart, 1994) pp. 113–283. Both nomenclature, which seems to have been inconsistent and to have changed over time, and design are controversial.

3. Quoted, Frontin. *Strat.* 3.*pr.*; cf. Tac. *Hist.* 3.84, 5.13 for the sense that there was nothing more to learn about siege technology. On Roman advances in catapults, Marsden, *Historical Development* pp. 174–206.

4. H. Sides, *Ghost Soldiers* (New York, 2001) pp. 275–6; cf. 247–8 and 267 for the prisoners' amazement at an up-to-date U.S. plane, the P-61: "at first they thought it was German, or possibly Russian . . . a 'black barn swallow,' a '*War of the Worlds* rocket.'"

5. Greek two-handled shield, or *aspis*, A. M. Snodgrass, *Arms and Armor of the Greeks* (Ithaca, N.Y., 1967) pp. 53–5. *Sarissa*, P. Connolly, "Experiments with the *Sarissa*—The Macedonian Pike and Cavalry Lance—A Functional View," *Journal of Roman Military Equipment Studies* 11 (2000) pp. 103–112, and N. V. Sekunda, "The *Sarissa*," *Acta Universitatis Lodziensis, Folia Archeologica* 23 (2001) pp. 13–41 summarize the long controversy about how this weapon was made. For the Roman heavy javelin, the *pilum*, and its long life (from the Republic into the fourth century AD), M. C. Bishop and J. C. Coulston, *Roman Military Equipment* (London, 1993) pp. 48–50, 65–7, 109, 123, 160.

6. Chain mail, Varro *Ling.* 5.116; H. R. Robinson, *The Armour of Imperial Rome* (New York, 1975) p. 164; P. Connolly, *Greece and Rome at War*² (London, 1998) p. 124. Helmet, Robinson, *Armour* pp. 13–61; M. Junkelmann, *Römische Helme* (Mainz, 2000) pp. 45–87; saddle, M. C. Bishop, "Cavalry Equipment of the Roman Army in the First Century AD," in J. C. Coulston (ed.), *Military Equipment and the Identity of Roman Soldiers* (BAR Int. Ser. 394; Oxford,

1988) pp. 67–195 at 116. Bow, J. C. Coulston, "Roman Archery Equipment," in M. C. Bishop (ed.), *The Production and Distribution of Roman Military Equipment* (BAR Int. Ser. 275; Oxford, 1985) pp. 220–366.

7. *Lorica segmentata,* M. C. Bishop, *Lorica Segmentata* vol. 1 (Duns, 2002) p. 91. Artillery on the battlefield, Marsden, *Historical Development* pp. 164–98. Elephants, H. H. Scullard, *The Elephant in the Greek and Roman World* (Ithaca, N.Y., 1974); cataphracts, M. Mielczarek, Cataphracti *and* Clibanarii (Lodz, 1993) pp. 67–85.

8. Sling-dart, Polyb. 27.11; anti-elephant corps in 168 BC, Cass. Dio (Zonar.) 9.22; cf. Livy 44.41.4; Polyaenus, *Strat.* 4.21; chariot, Anon. *de Reb. Bel. pr.* 13, 14.1; squirt-gun and wolf bones, Jul. Afr. *Kest.* 2.4, 1.11 (Viellefond).

9. Veg. *Mil.* 3.26.34; cf. 4.46; Arr. *Tact.* 19; Syr. Mag. *Strat.* 14.20–1 (Dennis).

10. Some ways of fighting have advantage over others, e.g. Hdt. 9.62, Polyb. 18.28–32; Jul. Afr. *Kest.* 1.1 (Viellefond); adapted to circumstances, e.g. Polyb. 1.30.7–11, 4.11.7–9; adopted in response to threats, e.g. Xen. *Hell.* 3.3.7–11; Polyb. 2.33; Caes. *B Civ.* 1.44; *B Afr.* 71–2. Samnites, in response to threat, and copying a Roman trait: the *Ineditum Vaticanum* (*FGH* 839 F 1) trans. T. J. Cornell, *The Beginnings of Rome* (London, 1995) p. 170; Diod. Sic. 23.2.1; Athen. *Deip.* 273F. Sword, F. Quesada Sanz, "*Gladius hispaniensis:* An Archeological View from Iberia," *Journal of Roman Military Equipment Studies* 8 (1997) pp. 251–70 gathers the references (p. 253); cavalry equipment, Polyb. 6.25.3–10; copying a Roman trait 6.25.11; for this *topos* F. Walbank, *A Historical Commentary on Polybius* vol. 1 (Oxford, 1957) p. 75 *ad loc.* 1.20.15. Still in the second century AD, Arr. *Tact.* 33.1–3, 44.1. Foreign peoples could also be thought to copy Roman methods, Herodian 3.4.8.

11. Quoted, Thuc. 1.71.3; quoted, Pliny *HN* 7.200; cf. Vitr. 10.13.1–3.

12. Diod. Sic. 15.44.1–4, trans. C. L. Sherman (adapted); cf. Nepos 11.1. The details of Iphicrates' reforms (not reproduced here) are one of the great controversies of Greek military history: see below pp. 96–97. Catapults, see Hero's *Belopoeica* (late first century AD; text in Marsden, *Technical Treatises* pp. 18–60) with S. Cuomo, "The Machine and the City: Hero of Alexandria's *Belopoeica,*" in C. J. Tuplin and T. E. Rihll (eds.), *Science and Mathematics in Ancient Greek Culture* (Oxford, 2002) pp. 165–77 at 168–70.

13. Philip II, Diod. Sic. 16.3.2, and see below pp. 121–24 for full discussion of this reform. On Vegetius, pp. 282–84. For backward-looking military writing I allude to the stratagem collections of Polyaenus, Frontinus, and Julius Africanus, Onasander's *On Generalship,* the tactical treatises of Asclepiodotus, Aelian, and Arrian, and the artillery treatises gathered by Marsden, *Technical Treatises,* of which the fuller are historical in orientation. Only Aeneas Tacticus's fourth-century BC fragment on defending fortified cities (although

it contains historical examples), Xenophon's *Hipparchicus,* and the anonymous fourth-century AD *de Rebus Bellicis* are not primarily backward looking.

14. Inherited idea, Livy 4.48.6. Quoted, O. Murray, "Gnosis and Tradition," in J. P. Arnason and P. Murphy (eds.), Agon, Logos, Polis: *The Greek Achievement and its Aftermath* (Stuttgart, 2001) pp. 15–28 at 19.

15. Past as brake to progress: so it is primarily to J. Keegan, *A History of Warfare* (New York, 1993) pp. 23–46.

The Greeks

1. The war, Thuc. 1.15.3; Hdt. 5.99; prohibition of missiles, Strabo 10.1.12; cf. Polyb. 13.3.2–4; poem, quoted Archilochus 3 (West).

2. The women of Colias, quoted Hdt. 8.96.

Chapter I. Fighting in the *Iliad*

1. Killing of Patroclus, Homer, *Iliad* (=*Il.*) 16.787–828; Hector's vaunt, quoted, *Il.* 16.834–5; retort, 16.849–54 (cf. 18.454–6).

2. Claim of Euphorbos, quoted, 17.14–16 (trans. Lattimore, adapted); Zeus, 17.205–6.

3. Quoted, *Il.* 4.473–83 (trans. Lattimore; but here and elsewhere I adjust Lattimore's phonetic spellings of some Homeric names to the more recognizable Latin versions).

4. Threats, quoted *Il.* 21.588; defiances, quoted 13.824; cf. 20.244–55; genealogy, e.g. 20.206–41. Poplar, quoted, *Il.* 4.482–4 (trans. Lattimore).

5. Vaunting, quoted *Il.* 11.453–4; formal duels, 3.67–380, 7.67–312; cf. 22.254–9; Achilles and Hector, 22.131–366.

6. Quoted, *Il.* 16.692–6 (trans. Lattimore); cf. 11.299–303.

7. *Il.* 5.12–26, 5.244–310, 5.565–89.

8. Quoted, "always," *Il.* 6.208 = 11.784; Thersites, quoted 2.248–9; Kalchas, quoted 1.69; for ranking cf. 2.201–2, 2.768–9, 12.269–71; battle, 4.225 etc.

9. Quoted, *Il.* 10.109–10 (trans. Lattimore).

10. Achilles, *Il.* 19.216–19; Odysseus, 3.202.

11. First to kill, *Il.* 8.256–7; running out, 5.85–6, 6.445, 22.458–9; cf. 2.701–2; as competitive, 8.253–5, 11.216–7; reviling as competitive, 20.251–2; cf. 1.304; boasted of, 20.432–3; quoted, 23.483. Numerical score, 16.785, 16.810; compared, 13.446–7.

12. Bravery, *Il.* 6.444–6; strength and skill, 7.197–289, 22.320–7; a god, quoted, 17.631–2; Achilles, quoted, 20.99–100 (trans. Lattimore). Idomeneus, quoted *Il.* 16.345–50 (trans. Lattimore). "The gory detail . . . is there to illustrate the

superior force of the ideal warrior," H. van Wees, "Heroes, Knights, and Nutters: Warrior Mentality in Homer," in A. B. Lloyd (ed.), *Battle in Antiquity* (London, 1996) pp. 1–86 at 39.

13. Fleetness of foot, *Il.* 6.228, 21.564–605, 22.137–230; quoted, 14.520–2 (trans. Lattimore); the especially swift hero, 20.407–18.

14. Strength, *Il.* 10.479; bravery, 1.226–8, 10.41, 10.307, 13.276–87; fleetness, 10.316–64; cunning, 7.142, 10.247–579; compete in meetings, 2.370, 3.221–3, 9.54; quoted, 15.284, with Janko *Comm.* 4 p. 259 (=R. Janko, *The Iliad: A Commentary, Vol. iv: Books 13–16* [Cambridge, 1992]), 9.441, and 1.490.

15. Hector and Periphetes, *Il.* 15.638–52; Deiphobos, 13.402–17. Instances of killing without heroic performance are gathered by van Wees, "Heroes, Knights, and Nutters" pp. 36–8. *Euxos*, e.g. *Il.* 5.285, 5.654, and esp. Sarpedon's famous encapsulation of the heroic essence of battle (12.328), "Let us go and either yield a *euxos* to someone, or someone will yield one to us." Hector, quoted, *Il.* 22.393–4 (trans. Lattimore, adapted); cf. 7.89–91. Son of Kopreus, quoted, *Il.* 15.638–44 (trans. Lattimore, adapted); cf. 14.470–4. The poem can also have heroes introduce themselves, e.g. *Il.* 21.153–60.

16. Quoted, *Il.* 11.431–2; quoted, *Il.* 20.389–92 (trans. Lattimore).

17. Quoted, *Il.* 16.808–11 (l. 810, trans. Lattimore, adapted).

18. First blow, *Il.* 7.232; Hector, quoted, 7.237–43 (trans. Lattimore) with Kirk *Comm.* 2 pp. 267–8 (=G. Kirk, *The Iliad: A Commentary, Vol. ii: Books 5–8* [Cambridge, 1990]; the meaning of ll. 238–40 is somewhat obscure), cf. 5.253–4.

19. *Il.* 4.293–308 (trans. Lattimore, adapted) with Kirk *Comm.* 1 pp. 360–62 (=G. Kirk, *The Iliad: A Commentary, Vol. i: Books 1–4* [Cambridge, 1985]).

20. Throw from chariot, *Il.* 5.15; thrust, 17.463–5. On chariots in the *Iliad*, defending the poem's depiction of their use as historically plausible, H. van Wees, "The Homeric Way of War: The *Iliad* and the Hoplite Phalanx (I)," *Greece and Rome* 41 (1994) pp. 1–18 at 9–13.

21. Ajax, *Il.* 17.354–9; Poulydamas, 12.61–107.

22. Quoted, *Il.* 16.212–17 (trans. Lattimore); cf. 13.125–35 (13.131–3=16.215–7) with Janko *Comm.* 4 pp. 60–2 (the exact meaning of 13.132=16.216 is obscure). Five companies, 16.169–99.

23. Catalogue of ships, *Il.* 2.484–877. Lack of consequence of arraying: the insight is that of A. Andrewes, "Phratries in Homer," *Hermes* 89 (1961) pp. 129–140 at 129–30, picked up by H. van Wees, "Leaders of Men? Military Organization in the *Iliad*," *Classical Quarterly* 36 (1986) pp. 285–303, and esp. 300: "Contingents are brought on stage for one reason only: they are needed to provide each of the major heroes with something to draw up." Like wasps, *Il.* 16.259–65.

24. Protect archer, *Il.* 4.112–15; wounded, 11.586–94, 14.427–32; throw back, 11.215, 13.145–8; prevent despoiling, 4.532–5, 5.621–6, 13.487–95; holding ground alone, 11.409–20, 11.473–84; break a mass, 15.615–38, 17.281–5, 20.362.

25. Menestheus, quoted, *Il.* 2.553–5 (trans. Lattimore); for Nestor, cf. 7.325, and Kirk *Comm.* 1 pp. 153–4 lists his tactical suggestions. Achilles, quoted 16.199. Poulydamas's array, 12.61–109; his wisdom, 12.210–29, 18.249–52, 18.31–3; memory of his divisions, 12.196–8, 290–3 and bk. 13 *passim*. Ajax, quoted *Il.* 17.360–5 (trans. Lattimore); cf. 17.356.

26. Quoted, *Il.* 2.362–6 (trans. Lattimore, adapted).

27. Achilles' claim, *Il.* 1.163–71; Nestor, quoted, 1.277–81 (trans. Lattimore).

28. Quoted, *Il.* 11.380, 11.385–90 (trans. Lattimore).

29. Abuse, *Il.* 4.242; praising epithet, 2.604, 8.173 = 13.150; grounds for pride, 13.262–3.

30. Quoted, *Il.* 5.171–3 (trans. Lattimore).

31. Teucer, quoted, *Il.* 13.313–14; shoots down many, 8.266–334; his glory, cf. 15.462; funeral games, 23.850–83. Odysseus in the *Odyssey* (= *Od.*) 8.215–28, 22.1–118; stringing his bow, *Od.* 19.572–87, 21.1–423; Menelaus, quoted, *Il.* 4.196–7 = 4.206–7 (trans. Lattimore, adapted).

32. *Il.* 11.407–10 (trans. Lattimore, adapted).

33. Diomedes, *Il.* 5.251–6, 8.93–6; cf. Hector's flight, 22.136–201; Achilles' inability to catch Hector, 22.201; Achilles' speed, e.g. 21.564; Agamemnon, 14.80; cf. 17.91–101; Odysseus, 14.83–102.

34. Nestor appalled, *Il.* 8.139–44; Diomedes fears mockery, 8.146–50; quoted, 8.152–55 (trans. Lattimore).

35. The references to Homer and Greek education are gathered by K. Robb, *Literacy and Paideia in Ancient Greece* (New York, 1994), esp. pp. 159–82; "teacher of Greece," quoted Pl. *Resp.* 606E; by heart, Xen. *Symp.* 3.5. For Homer as a teaching text in Greek-speaking Hellenistic and Roman Egypt, R. Cribiore, *Gymnastics of the Mind: Greek Education in Hellenistic and Roman Egypt* (Princeton, 2001) pp. 140–2, 194–7 (the *Iliad* more than the *Odyssey*), 204–5, 226.

36. Quoted, Pl. *Resp.* 606E. Admirable and imitated, Pl. *Prt.* 326A.

37. Crafts, quoted Pl. *Resp.* 598C–D. "Encyclopedia," the image is E. Havelock's, *Preface to Plato* (Cambridge, Mass., 1963) pp. 61–86.

Chapter II. The Last Hoplite

1. The earliest and most detailed account is Herodotus (= Hdt.) 1.82 (to be read with J. Dillery, "Reconfiguring the Past: Thyrea, Thermopylae and Narrative Patterns in Herodotus," *American Journal of Philology* 117 [1996] pp. 217–54

at 218–37). The trophy is added, and that Othryades lay unnoticed is stated or implied, by Plut. *Mor.* 306A–B (quoting Chrysermus and suggesting that the terms of the conflict were set by the Delphic Amphictyons), Theseus in Stobaeus *Flor.* 3.7.68 (=*FGH* 453 F 2; cf. 287 F 2b), *Suda s.v.* Othryades, and other later authors (see bibliographical note). Poem, quoted *Anth. Pal.* 7.430 *ll.* 1–9 (trans. draws on Paton). *Anth. Pal.* 7.431 picks up the detail that the soldiers died in place, "never turning our necks, and where we first planted our feet, there we died." For Spartan claims to heirship of Agamemnon, Hdt. 1.67–9. 7.159; Argive, Thuc. 5.69.1.

2. Died after inscribing trophy, Theseus and *Suda;* suicide, Herodotus (see previous note), *Anth. Pal.* 7.526. Argive statue, Paus. 2.20.7.

3. In jeopardy, Eur. *HF* 191–4; cf. Plut. *Mor.* 220A. Skill at arms unimportant for hoplites, Pl. *Lach.* 182A–B; cf. Eur. *El.* 388–90 (condemned by most editors); Xen. *Cyr.* 2.3.9–11. The skill of warriors of other types is praised, as against the simple physical fitness of hoplites: Xen. *Hell.* 3.4.16; *Oec.* 21.7.

4. See bibliographical note for discussion of the formality of hoplite battle. For "fair and open," quoted, Xen. *Hell.* 6.5.16; cf. Dem. *Or.* 9.48, "rulebound and open"; Polyb. 13.3.2–5 (both retrospective and likely idealizing). Delay before battle, Pritchett, *GSAW* vol. 2 pp. 147–55 gathers the evidence. For fighting "when both sides were ready," Thuc. 3.107.4; cf. 7.5.1–2. Formal challenges to battle are attested (Diod. Sic. 13.73.1 [408 BC], 15.32.6 [378 BC], 15.65.4, 15.68.4 [369/8 BC]) but not in contemporary authors: Diodorus may be retrojecting a Hellenistic practice (Hellenistic instances are gathered by Pritchett, *GSAW* vol. 2 pp. 147–8). Rules agreed, cf. Thuc. 5.41.2, 5.76.3 and see below, n. 11. Sacred truces, Pritchett, *GSAW* vol. 1 pp. 116–26 gathers the evidence. Array, esp. Hdt. 9.26–28, and Pritchett, *GSAW* vol. 2 pp. 194–9 tabulates the evidence, showing that the left wing was not always second in honor (as he implies, p. 192): e.g. Thuc. 5.67, 6.67; Xen. *Hell.* 4.2.18, instances in which the center seems to have been more honorable than the left. Sacrifice, Pritchett, *GSAW* vol. 1 pp. 109–15 and vol. 3 pp. 83–90 and M. H. Jameson, "Sacrifice before Battle," in V. D. Hanson (ed.), *Hoplites: The Classical Greek Battle Experience* (London, 1991) pp. 197–227 gather the evidence. Spartans, Xen. *Lac.* 13.8; Plut. *Lyc.* 22.1–3. Paean, Pritchett, *GSAW* vol. 1 pp. 105–8 gathers the evidence; Spartan pursuit, Hdt. 9.77; Thuc. 5.73.4; Plut. *Lyc.* 22.5=*Mor.* 458E; recovering the dead, Pritchett, *GSAW* vol. 4 pp. 153–235, 246–9 gathers the evidence; trophy, Pritchett, *GSAW* vol. 2 pp. 246–75 gathers the evidence; built while garlanded, Xen. *Hell.* 4.3.21. Herodotus, quoted 7.9.

5. Tyrtaeus fr. 11, 19, 23a (West). My interpretation of Tyrtaeus follows H. van Wees, "The Development of the Hoplite Phalanx," in id. (ed.), *War and*

Violence in Ancient Greece (London, 2000) pp. 125–66 at 146–54, who gathers the iconographic evidence.

6. For sixth-century aristocrats riding to battle but fighting as hoplites, see P. A. L. Greenhalgh, *Early Greek Warfare: Horsemen and Chariots in the Homeric and Archaic Ages* (Cambridge, 1973). For grand Athenians serving as hoplites, G. R. Bugh, *The Horsemen of Athens* (Princeton, 1988) pp. 10–11. Pericles' helmet, Plut. *Per.* 3.2. On the Spartan "cavalry," J. F. Lazenby, *The Spartan Army* (Warminster, 1985) pp. 10–12 gathers the evidence. Spartan kings and victors, Plut. *Lyc.* 22.4.

7. Arist. *Pol.* 1297B; cf. 1289B.

8. Oath, quoted, Tod *GHI* 2.204, with P. Siewert, "The Ephebic Oath in Fifth-Century Athens," *Journal of Hellenic Studies* 97 (1977) pp. 102–111. Cf. Eur. *Phoen.* 1073–4. *Paraspistes*, Eur. *El.* 886; *Ion* 1528; *Phoen.* 1435; cf. Soph. *OC* 379. War poetry: Tyrtaeus, Callinus, Alcaeus, and Mimnernus (all trad. seventh century BC), and Simonides (c. 556–468 BC), of whom a new fragment, about the battle of Plataea and couched in highly Homeric terms, was published in 1992 (see D. Boedeker and D. Sider [eds.], *The New Simonides* [New York, 2001]). For the praise of warriors in epic terms in funerary inscriptions, W. Peek, *Griechische Vers-Inschriften* vol. 1 (Berlin, 1955) nrs. 11, 20, 1224 for *promachoi;* 73, 321 for *aristos* (and cf. Xen. *An.* 6.5.24). For hoplites in Greek vase painting, in the absence of a formal corpus see the assemblages of F. Lissarrague in *L'Autre guerrier: Archers, peltastes, cavaliers dans l'imagerie attique* (Rome, 1990), P. Ducrey, *Warfare in Ancient Greece* (New York, 1986, trans. J. Lloyd, from *Guerre et guerriers dans la Grèce antique* [Paris, 1985]), and M. Recke, *Gewalt und Leid. Das Bild des Krieges bei den Athenern im 6. und 5. Jh. v. Chr.* (Istanbul, 2002). H. L. Lorimer, "The Hoplite Phalanx with Special Reference to the Poems of Archilochus and Tyrtaeus," *Annual of the British School at Athens* 42 (1947) pp. 76–138 gathers the (rare) vase images of hoplites fighting in the phalanx. For hoplites on gravestones see C. W. Clairmont, *Classical Attic Tombstones* (Kilchberg, 1993) e.g. 1.194, 1.361, 1.460, 1.192, 2.217 (all illustrated in the plates vol.). Sixth-century revival of bronze, A. M. Snodgrass, *Early Greek Armour and Weapons* (Edinburgh, 1964) p. 134; id., *Arms and Armor of the Greeks* (Ithaca, N.Y., 1967) pp. 96–7 with p. 36 on the advantages of iron.

9. Quoted, Hdt. 7.226–7. On Greek military awards for bravery, Pritchett, *GSAW* vol. 2 pp. 276–90 collects the references (recorded on tombstones, p. 279); see the bibliographical note for controversy. Alcibiades and Socrates, Pl. *Symp.* 220D–E; Plut. *Alc.* 7.3. For competitive ethos among hoplites, cf. Thuc. 6.31.3; Plut. *Ages.* 18.3; *Pel.* 19.4.

10. Quoted, *Il.* 9.318–9 (trans. Lattimore, adapted).

11. Lelantine war rule, Strabo 10.1.12; Polyb. 13.3.4; cf. Archilochus fr. 3 (West), all to be read with E. L. Wheeler, "Ephorus and the Prohibition of Missiles," *Transactions of the American Philological Association* 117 (1987) pp. 157–82 (who does not believe that the agreement was historical). Spartan, Thucydides 4.40.2 with S. Hornblower, *A Commentary on Thucydides* vol. 2 (Oxford, 1996) pp. 195–6. U.S. Civil War, quoted G. W. Gallagher (ed.), *Fighting for the Confederacy: The Personal Recollections of General Edward Porter Alexander* (Chapel Hill, 1989) p. 118.

12. Quoted, Eur. *HF* 162; safer, 188–203; cf. Soph. *Aj.* 1120–3, where scornful surprise is expressed at an archer's pride, and where archery is defended as an effective craft, *techne,* rather than a heroic way of fighting. Patroclus's funeral games, *Il.* 23.850–83. Callicrates, quoted, Hdt. 9.72 (trans. Grene, adapted); cf. Plut. *Mor.* 234E. Deprecation of the bow at the expense of close-combat weapons is already visible in the seventh-century Archilochus fr. 3 (West).

13. Survival of missiles in the phalanx into late sixth and early fifth century, H. van Wees, *Greek Warfare: Myths and Realities* (London, 2004) pp. 50–2, 176–7. And hoplites do not scorn to throw stones under special circumstances even later, Thuc. 4.43.3 (425 BC).

14. Polydoros, *Il.* 20.407–18.

15. Quoted, Tyrtaeus 12.1–9 and 13–14 (West; trans. Lattimore, adapted).

16. Quoted, *Vit. Aesch.* 11 (trans. Lattimore); two sea battles, Paus. 1.14.5.

17. *Iliad,* quoted 11.409–10; disgraceful in lyric, Tyrtaeus 10.16–31, 11.15–20, 12.17 (West); Callinus 1.14–19 (West). Quoted, Tyrtaeus 12.16–20, 11.29–30 (cf. 11.4), and 10.31–2=11.21–2 (West). Archilochus (fr. 5 [West]) and Alcaeus (fr. 428a [L-P]) have poems expressing indifference to having thrown away their shields in flight: but the poems startle only if doing so was thought shameful.

18. Quoted, Eur. *HF* 163–4; cf. Xen. *An.* 6.5.17; Plut. *Mor.* 234E; Plut. *Phoc.* 23.2. Quoted, Pl. *Lach.* 190E; cf. *Leg.* 706C; Arist. *Eth. Nic.* 1116B. Herodotus's account of Othryades' suicide has puzzled readers since Plutarch (*Mor.* 858C–D). But cf. Cass. Dio 64[63Loeb].11 for a Roman soldier committing suicide to prove his bravery.

19. Aristodemus, quoted Hdt. 9.71; cf. Plut. *Phoc.* 25.2; Sophanes, Hdt. 9.74.

20. Eur. *Supp.* 846–56 (trans. Kovacs); cf. *El.* 377–8 (condemned by many editors).

21. Grid, Aristophanes fr. 72 (K-A). Failure to keep time, Plut. *Mor.* 210F-211A; Aul. Gell. 1.11.1–5; fled before decided, Lys. *Or.* 14.5; rise again and first to die, Xen. *Hell.* 5.4.33; first to flee, Ar. *Pax* 1177; Thuc. 5.10.9; fled early, Lys. *Or.* 16.15; hung on longest, Lys. *Or.* 16.18. Died in place, Xen. *Hell.* 4.5.10, 4.8.38–9; Dem. *Or.* 60.19; fought free, Xen. *Hell.* 7.4.24.

22. Spartan mother, quoted Plut. *Mor.* 241F. On the Athenian legal offense of

leaving one's place (*lipotaxion*), D. Hamel, "Coming to Terms with *lipotaxion*," *Greek, Roman, and Byzantine Studies* 39 (1998) pp. 361–405; abandoning one's shield (*rhipsaspia*), T. Schwertfeger, "Der Schild des Archilochus," *Chiron* 12 (1982) pp. 253–79 at 264–73. Cleonymus, van Wees, *Greek Warfare* pp. 193–4 gathers the references. Trembling, Tyrtaeus 11.14 (West); "tremblers," Hdt. 7.231; Plut. *Ages.* 30.2; jostling, Thuc. 5.10.7; teeth, Polyaenus, *Strat.* 3.9.7; shaking, *P.Oxy.* 2317 = *Adespota Iambica* 38 (West); fouling, Ar. *Pax* 241. On the physical symptoms of fear in the phalanx, V. D. Hanson, *The Western Way of War* (New York, 1989) pp. 100–3. Changing color, quoted *Il.* 13. 279. N. Loraux, "The Warrior's Fear and Trembling," in id., *The Experiences of Tiresias* (Princeton, 1995 [trans. P. Wissing, from *Les Expériences de Tirésias* (Paris, 1989)]) pp. 75–87 at 77 gathers references to how fear appears on the face in Homer, and at 87 discusses how appearing fearful, acceptable in Homer, is not so in the phalanx. For the Corinthian helmet as perhaps concealing fear I am indebted to E. C. Kiesling.

23. Brasidas, quoted Thuc. 4.126.5; cf. Pl. *Leg.* 706C. "Slave to his arms," quoted Eur. *HF* 190–3 (trans. Kovacs, adapted). Tyrtaeus 10.1–2, 27–30, 11.19–20, 12.23–42 (West). Demosthenes, quoted *Or.* 60.19. Lechaeum, quoted Xen. *Hell.* 4.5.10; cf. 6.4.16; Plut. *Ages.* 29.4–5.

24. Volunteer for cavalry, in Athens, Lys. *Or.* 14–16, esp. 14.7, 16.13; Sparta, Xen. *Hell.* 6.4.11; given the opportunity, they would dismount to fight, Xen. *Hell.* 4.4.10. Lame Spartan, Plut. *Mor.* 210F.

25. For the *hoplitodromos* and *apobates* (certainly fifth century, perhaps earlier), N. B. Reed, *More than Just a Game: The Military Nature of Greek Athletic Contests* (Chicago, 1998) pp. 9–19, 42–55, who notes (pp. 3–4, 53) how they contradict hoplite ethics and practice and that the latter was nearly a "historical re-enactment." Homeric fighting styles, of course, do not begin to explain all Greek athletic events or the whole phenomenon of Greek sports. Against hoplites running, Pl. *Leg.* 706C-D (see below, p. 87). Note that chariots appear on sixth-century pots in hoplite battle scenes (van Wees, *Greek Warfare* pp. 176–7), so the chariot may not have been fully expelled from hoplite fighting until c. 500 BC. For the pyrrhic dance, the evidence is gathered by P. Ceccarelli, *La pirrica nell'antichità greco romano* (Pisa, 1998). For pride in manipulating a shield in Homer, *Il.* 7.238–9.

26. Press of bodies, Asclep. *Tact.* 5.2; Aelian, *Tact.* 14.6 (but describing the closer-formed Macedonian phalanx); terror of battle affects all, Eur. *Bacch.* 303–5; posted to the front, Lys. *Or.* 16.15, 16.18. Duels, *Il.* 3.67–380, 7.67–312; contest in funeral games, *Il.* 23.798–825. Later single combats, see p. 84; for Alexander pp. 133–38; in Hellenistic times p. 148.

Chapter III. Two Stubborn Spartans

1. Herodotus (=Hdt.) 7.41, 61–80; the horse heads belong to the so-called Eastern Ethiopians (7.70; cf. 3.94), who live near India, or so Herodotus imagines. There is much fantasy in Herodotus's catalogue of peoples.

2. Hdt. 7.108, 118–120, 127.

3. League, Hdt. 7.145; Athens, 7.161, 8.2–3; Argos, 7.148–52; Thessaly, 7.172–4.

4. Logic of defending Thermopylae, Hdt. 7.175–7; events at sea, 7.188–92, 8.8–13.

5. Forces at Thermopylae, Hdt. 7.202–3, 206; see J. F. Lazenby, *The Defence of Greece 490–479 BC* (Warminster, 1993) pp. 134–5 for the difficulties with Herodotus's figures. For the Olympics, cf. 8.26; Leonidas, 7.207.

6. Hdt. 7.210–20, quoted, 7.220.

7. Hdt. 7.104; cf. 9.48.

8. Quoted, Hdt. 9.53; *taxis,* 9.57, an episode discussed further below. Quoted, Eur. *Heracl.* 840; cf. 828–9. For parallel of city and warrior, cf. Hdt. 9.27, Thuc. 5.101; Xen. *Hiero* 2.15.

9. Delphic oracle, H. W. Parke, *The Delphic Oracle* vol. 2 (Oxford, 1956) nr. 1=J. Fontenrose, *The Delphic Oracle* (Berkeley and Los Angeles, 1978) nr. Q26. The historicity of this oracle does not concern us: merely the mode of thinking it reveals.

10. Reliable or not, Lys. *Or.* 25.31; just or unjust, Dem. *Or.* 2.8–10; *hybris,* Xen. *Hell.* 5.3.13; self-control, Thuc. 1.68.1. Quoted, Thuc. 3.82.2; cf. 3.57.1, 3.64.4. Anger, Xen. *Hell.* 3.2.21, 3.5.5; fear, Thuc. 1.75.3; longing, *IG* I³ 1179. Greek city apes aristocrat, e.g. Hdt. 9.26–7; Thuc. 2.61–4; Dem. *Or.* 18.66, 22.76. For anthropomorphic ways cities deal with each other and for Athens as an aristocrat, see bibliographical note.

11. Spartan *sophrosyne,* Thuc. 1.68.1, 1.84.3; Critias *Lac. Pol.* 88 B6 *l.* 22 (D–K); break into run, esp. Xen. *Hell.* 4.3.17 and V. D. Hanson, *Western Way of War* (New York, 1989) pp. 135–47 gathers the references. Spartans and pipe players, Thuc. 5.70; anger, quoted Plut. *Mor.* 458E; cf. Aul. Gell. 1.11.1–5; "without a gap," quoted, Plut. *Lyc.* 22.3. *Pilos* helmet, N. V. Sekunda, "Classical Warfare," in J. Boardman (ed.), *The Cambridge Ancient History*² *Plates to Volumes V and VI* (Cambridge, 1994) pp. 167–94 at 175–8; for its spread, P. Dintsis, *Hellenistische Helme* vol. 1 (Rome, 1986) pp. 57–73 with *Karte* 5.

12. War between cities equal in power can be envisioned as "a contest of bravery [*andragathia*], with shame as the penalty," Thuc. 5.101; cf. Eur. *Supp.* 778–81. For the city conceived as a phalanx, cf. Pl. *Menex.* 246B. Prizes for cities, e.g. Hdt. 9.105; and Pritchett *GSAW* vol. 2 pp. 283–6 gathers the references, to which D. Hamel, *Athenian Generals* (Leiden, 1998) p. 65 n. 26 adds.

13. For the date of the mature phalanx, see above p. 48 and below pp. 400–401. Grave markers, the data are from I. Morris, *Death-Ritual and Social Structure in Classical Antiquity* (Cambridge, 1992) pp. 128–55.

14. Hdt. 7.223–5, quoted, 228, 225. For the Spartans fighting at the last like Homeric heroes, the insight is that of N. Loraux, "The Spartans' 'Beautiful Death,'" in id., *The Experiences of Tiresias,* trans. P. Wissing (Princeton 1995) pp. 63–74 at pp. 71–73 (= "La 'belle mort' Spartiate," *Ktema* 2 [1977] pp. 105–120). For tragedy, D. M. Pritchard, "'The Fractured Imaginary': Popular Thinking on Military Matters in Fifth-Century Athens," *Ancient History* 28 (1998) pp. 38–61 at 45–6, 48–51 gathers the references. For pots, see the collections of hoplite images listed p. 342 n. 8. For the *apobates,* see above p. 56. Cf. Hdt. 8.38–9. Quoted, *Il.* 13.131–3=16.215–7 (trans. Lattimore), recalled in Xen. *Mem.* 3.1.7; *Cyr.* 6.3.25; Polyb. 18.29.6; Eust. *Il.* ad loc. 13.128–33 (449.2–5 [Van der Valk]).

15. Artemisium, Hdt. 8.9–18, 21; Athenians, Greek plans, 8.40–1.

16. Greek arguments and Themistocles, Hdt. 8.49, 56–64, 74–5, 78–82; Battle of Salamis, 8.83–96; Diod. Sic. 11.18–19.3; Aesch. *Pers.* 353–471; quoted 418–28.

17. Hdt. 8.97–114, 133; Greek plans, 8.144, 9.6; Hyacinthia, 9.7–11; Mardonius, 9.12–15.

18. Cithaeron, Hdt. 9.19; Masistius, 9.20–5.

19. Hdt. 9.26–7; cf. 7.159, 161. Tendency to move right, Thuc. 5.71.

20. Greek array, numbers, Hdt. 9.28–30; Persian array, 9.31–2.

21. Sacrifices, Hdt. 9.36–7; Mardonius, 9.38–43. I reject, with most commentators (e.g. Lazenby, *Defence of Greece* p. 231) the story that the Spartans traded places with the Athenians and then traded back: Hdt. 9.46–7. Persian cavalry, spring, 9.49.

22. Hdt. 9.50–1.

23. Hdt. 9.52–5.

24. Hdt. 9.56–7.

25. Hdt. 9.59–63.

26. Hdt. 9.65–6, 68, 70, 89.

27. Barrows, 9.85; those honored, 9.71; Pausanias on Amompharetus, Hdt. 9.55; officers cashiered, Thuc. 5.72.1; death, Xen. *Hell.* 5.4.23–4 (for the expectation, even if thwarted in this instance); *An.* 2.6.4.

28. Spartan obedience, Xen. *Lac.* 2.14; *Hell.* 7.1.8; Plut. *Ages.* 1.2; the Spartan army, Thuc. 5.66.

29. Quoted, Hdt. 8.59. I thank E. C. Kiesling for pointing out the significance of this passage to me.

30. Punished, purified, Xen. *An.* 5.7.34–5.

31. Trial, Xen. *An.* 5.8.1; muleteer, 5.8.2–12; plunder, 5.8.13; fallen, 5.8.14–17; for their own good, 5.8.19.

32. *Eutaxia,* Xen. *An.* 5.8.13; quoted, 5.8.14; cf. 3.1.38, 3.2.29–31. Spartan officers, quoted, Thuc. 5.66.4; five levels, Xen. *Lac.* 11.4–5; Thuc. 5.66.3 lists the same top four but leaves out the lowest, the file leaders. On Athenian officers, H. van Wees, *Greek Warfare: Myths and Realities* (London, 2004) p. 99. Generals and captains of Ten Thousand, higher pay, Xen. *An.* 7.2.36, 7.6.1; cf. 7.3.10; lower officers appointed ad hoc when needed for complicated maneuvers, Xen. *An.* 3.4.21–2; cf. 4.3.26; higher ones serve *vice* generals and command special units, see G. B. Nussbaum, *The Ten Thousand* (Leiden, 1967) p. 32 nn. 2–3; cf. p. 15 n. 3. Vote, Xen. *An.* 3.2.30–2.

33. Advantageous, Xen. *Eq. Mag.* 1.24; *Mem.* 3.3.10; cf. *Oec.* 13.9; kindness, *Eq. Mag.* 6.1–3; superiority, 6.4–6; reward and punishment, *Cyr.* 1.6.20; cf. *Oec.* 5.14.15; willing obedience, *Cyr.* 1.6.21–5; cf. *Mem.* 3.3.9–10, 3.5.21–3. *Il.* 12.310–28 (the speech of Sarpedon to Glaucus) is the classic Iliadic expression of the need to justify privileges by martial excellence, and Xenophon echoes it at *An.* 3.1.37; but see *Oec.* 21.7 for a different view. Oath, Tod, *GHI* 2.204; cf. Soph. *Ant.* 666–7.

34. Obedience at Sparta, quoted Xen. *Lac.* 8.2; Clearchus, quoted Xen. *An.* 1.3.15; cf. Thuc. 2.11.9, 5.9.9. Thermopylae, Hdt. 7.228.

35. Inferiority, Xen. *Mem.* 3.3.14, 3.5.15–19; cf. Plut. *Phoc.* 25. Competition, Xen. *Cyr.* 2.1.22–4; also, *Oec.* 21.4–8.

36. Slaves, Xen. *Lac.* 8.2 (above); Pausanias, Plut. *Arist.* 23.2 (with Thuc. 1.95.1); Clearchus, Xen. *An.* 2.6.9–15; cf. 1.5.11–12, 2.3.11; Thuc. 8.84.2; Xen. *Hell.* 6.2.19; Diod. Sic. 14.7.6–7.

37. *Kala,* Xen. *Lac.* 4.4. Quoted, Plut. *Mor.* 236E; supreme, Hdt. 7.104, 9.48; Xen. *Hell.* 1.6.32, 4.8.38; Diod. Sic. 15.64.3–5.

38. Hamel, *Athenian Generals* p. 62, with a list of sixty-four prosecutions of Athenian generals (pp. 140–57).

Chapter IV. The Guile of Delium

1. Thucydides (=Thuc.) 4.76.
2. Thuc. 4.89–93.1.
3. Thuc. 4.93.2–94.1.
4. Thuc. 4.94.2–96.4; Eur. *Supp.* 855–6 (see above p. 52); for the association of the *Supplices* with Delium, S. Hornblower, *A Commentary on Thucydides* vol. 2 (Oxford 1996) p. 309 gathers the discussions.
5. Thuc. 4.96.4–6.
6. Thuc. 4.96.8–101.2; Socrates, Pl. *Symp.* 221A–C.

7. Cleomenes tricks the Argives, Hdt. 6.77–80; Argive losses, 7.148; King Soüs, Plut. *Lyc.* 2.1–2; Thermopylae, Hdt. 7.211 and Diod. Sic. 11.9.4–10.4; Pericles, Thuc. 2.39.1; cf. Hdt. 9.54; Eur. *Andr.* 445–9; Lysander, Plut. *Lys.* 7.4. For military deceit, P. Krentz, "Deception in Archaic and Classical Greek Warfare," in H. van Wees (ed.), *War and Violence in Ancient Greece* (London, 2000) pp. 167–200 at 183–199 offers a formidable list of instances.

8. Possibly naïve later statements of the formality of Greek warfare, Dem. *Or.* 9.48; Polyb. 13.3.2–6. Herodotus, 7.9. Tactics at Marathon, Hdt. 6.111–13. Replay of Thyrea, Thuc. 5.41.2–3 (the Spartans first dismissed the proposal as ridiculous: but they agreed). The Greeks saw the contrast between fighting "openly" and trickery: E. Heza, "Ruse de guerre — trait caractéristique d'une tactique nouvelle dans l'oeuvre de Thucydide," *Eos* 62 (1974) pp. 227–44 at n. 10 gathers the references.

9. Herodotus on Aristodemus, 9.71; Sophanes, Hdt. 6.92, 9.74–5. For the Greek tradition of one-on-one fighting, Pritchett, *GSAW* vol. 4 pp. 16–21 and *id., Studies in Ancient Greek Topography* vol. 7 (Amsterdam, 1991) p. 186 collects the references. Add Plut. *Nic.* 18.2 (414 BC); Paus. 6.3.2 (360s BC), and cf. Plut. *Pel.* 17.3; Xen. *Hiero* 2.15.

10. Theban memorial, Tod *GHI* 2.130. For competition among generals, cf. Xen. *Hell.* 4.7.5 (with the athletic metaphor); 7.2.20, 7.5.19; *An.* 3.1.24, 4.7.12, 5.2.11; Plut. *Arist.* 8.3–5; *Pel.* 16.1; Polyaenus, *Strat.* 3.11.15. Generals in the phalanx, E. L. Wheeler, "The General as Hoplite," in V. D. Hanson (ed.), *Hoplites: The Greek Battle Experience* (London, 1991) pp. 121–70 gathers the references; for generals dying in battle, W. K. Pritchett, "The General on the Battlefield," in id., *Essays in Greek History* (Amsterdam, 1994) pp. 111–44 at 127–9 gathers the references. Eion poem, quoted, Aeschin. *In Ctes.* 185 = Plut. *Cim.* 7.5; cf. Hdt. 7.161.

11. Menestheus, *Il.* 2.553–5; Homer as practical guide, Ar. *Ran.* 1034–6; Xen. *Symp.* 4.6. *Iliad* comes up, e.g. Pl. *Lach.* 191B-C; *Resp.* 404B-C; Xen. *Mem.* 3.1.4, 3.1.8, 3.2.1–2; Arist. *Eth. Nic.* 1116A; Plut. *Mor.* 223A and for the long tradition of referring to *Il.* 13.131–3 = 16.215–7, "shield leaned on shield," see above p. 346 n. 14. Rhapsode, Pl. *Ion* 541B (Socrates gently mocks his pretension to be the best general in Greece by virtue of being the best rhapsode). "Charioteers," *heniochoi* and *parabatai* at Delium, Diod. Sic. 12.70.1.

12. Hermocrates, quoted Xen. *Hell.* 1.1.31; cf. Hdt. 8.83; quoted, Ar. *Av.* 363; Brasidas, quoted Thuc. 5.9.4–5 (trans. Crawley); cf. 3.30.4; Xen. *Hell.* 5.1.4; *Hiero* 2.16. Chabrias, Nepos, 12.2–3; Polyaenus, *Strat.* 2.1.2; Diod. Sic. 15.32.5–6, with J. K. Anderson, "The Statue of Chabrias," *American Journal of Archaeology* 67 (1963) pp. 411–13.

13. Themistocles, Hdt. 8.124; bull and rooster, Plut. *Mor.* 238F = *Marc.* 22.5; Spar-

tan kings' portion, Xen. *Lac.* 15.2–3; Pl. *Resp.* 547D–8A; Agesilaus, Xen. *Ages.* 1.17; Dercylidas, Xen. *Hell.* 3.1.8 (cf. *Il.* 6.153).

14. Xenophon defensive, *Eq. Mag.* 5.9–11; *Cyr.* 1.6.27. Plutarch, quoted Plut. *Lys.* 7.4; expressions of distaste, Hdt. 1.212; Thuc. 2.39.1; Soph. *Phil.* 88–95; Eur. *Rhes.* 510–17 with Pritchett *GSAW* vol. 2 pp. 174–6. "Stealing," Xen. *An.* 4.6.11–16, with D. Whitehead, *"Klope polemou:* 'Theft' in Ancient Greek Warfare," *Classica et Mediaevalia* 39 (1988) pp. 43–53 at p. 46. Agesilaus, Xen. *Hell.* 6.5.16; Alexander, Arr. *Anab.* 3.10.2; Curt. 4.13.8–10.

15. Raids, Xen. *Eq. Mag.* 5.12; quoted, Pl. *Leg.* 706C–D.

16. Practical efficacy, Thuc. 3.30.4, 5.9.4–5; Xen. *Eq. Mag.* 5.9–11; *Cyr.* 1.6.27–41. Mantinea, Thuc. 5.71–2. Spartan King, quoted Thuc. 2.11.9.

17. Dishonorable, e.g. Soph. *Phil.* 88–95; Eur. *Rhes.* 510–17. Sphacteria, quoted, Paus. 1.13.5.

18. Demosthenes, quoted *Or.* 60.21; Brasidas, Thuc. 4.126.5. Not real defeat, cf. Plut. *Pel.* 15.4–5; *Pyrrh.* 18.1; Polyb. 13.3.3; Arr. *Anab.* 3.10.3. For the ranking of Greek cities, see above p. 62.

19. Tactics not met by tactics, e.g. Xen. *Hell.* 4.3.15–21, 7.5.20–25. Obedience to Spartan kings, e.g. Thuc. 5.60.2. Pagondas, Thuc. 4.91–3. For the age of Pausanias, see M. E. White, "Some Agiad Dates: Pausanias and His Sons," *Journal of Hellenic Studies* 84 (1964) pp. 140–52 at 151. Commanders' deaths in battle, see above n. 10. Even a tactically minded general like Xenophon would dismount and fight with his hoplites, Xen. *An.* 7.3.45. Mantinea, Thuc. 5.59.4–60.6, 65.5–6; disadvantage, Thuc. 5.65.2.

Chapter V. The Arts of War

1. Mantinea, Thuc. 5.66–74.

2. Spartan cavalry, Thuc. 4.55.2; Argive hoplites, Thuc. 5.67.2, with Pritchett *GSAW* vol. 2 pp. 221–4.

3. Balanced force, quoted Plut. *Pel.* 2.1; cf. Xen. *Hell.* 3.4.23, 4.1.21, 4.3.15, 6.1.8–9, 6.1.19; *An.* 7.6.25–30; Arist. *Pol.* 1321A, all with J. G. P. Best, *Thracian Peltasts and their Influence on Greek Warfare* (Groningen, 1969) pp. 75–7, 124–5; anticipated in Thuc. 7.5.3. Combined arms, J. K. Anderson, *Military Theory and Practice in the Age of Xenophon* (Berkeley and Los Angeles, 1970) pp. 116–19.

4. Xen. *Hell.* 4.5.10–17.

5. For Masistius, see above p. 69; outbreak of war, Thuc. 2.13.8; archers, 3.98.1, 3.107.1. For Athenian archers, A. Plassart, "Les Archers d'Athènes," *Revue des études grecques* 26 (1913) pp. 151–213 at 195–204 collects the references.

6. For the use of peltasts before and in the Peloponnesian War, Best, *Thracian Peltasts* pp. 3–35; not much by the Athenians, R. Osborne, "An Other View:

An Essay in Political History," in B. Cohen (ed.), *Not the Classical Ideal: Athens and the Construction of the Other in Greek Art* (Leiden, 2000) pp. 23–42 at 33–40. Lack of range dangerous: in Xenophon's *Anabasis* the Greeks find their javelin-men and few Cretan archers out-ranged by the Persians, and so must draft a unit of slingers from other duties (Xen. *An.* 3.3.7–20; cf. 3.4.15). For slingers in classical Greek warfare, Pritchett *GSAW* vol. 5 pp. 6–14 gathers the references.

7. Thrusting spear, Best, *Thracian Peltasts* pp. 7, 103–4, citing depictions on pots—and, of course, carrying the *pelte* shield strongly implies that peltasts expected close combat. Stones, Xen. *Hell.* 4.6.7, 5.1.12. Rushing and massing, Thuc. 7.30.2. Shield over back, Xen. *An.* 7.4.17 (cf. *Il.* 11.545); dance, 6.1.5. For the mix of spear throwing and thrusting in the *Iliad,* see H. van Wees, "The Homeric Way of War: The *Iliad* and the Hoplite Phalanx (II)," *Greece and Rome* 41 (1994) pp. 131–55 at p. 145. For stone throwing in the *Iliad,* Pritchett, *GSAW* vol. 5 pp. 3–5 gathers the references. Slings in epic: alluded to only at *Il.* 13.600 and 716.

8. Diod. Sic. 15.44.1–4; Nepos 11.3–4; and see the bibliographical note to this chapter. For equipment in the *Iliad,* see H. van Wees, "The Homeric Way of War: The *Iliad* and the Hoplite Phalanx (II)," *Greece and Rome* 41 (1994) pp. 131–55 at 132–3.

9. Running in combat viewed as a contest, cf. Xen. *An.* 3.4.44–9, 4.3.29. Spartan hoplites catch and kill peltasts, Xen. *Hell.* 4.4.16.

10. Greek square or rectangle, Asclepiodotus, *Techne Taktike* (=Asclep. *Tact.*) 7.4; Aelian, *Taktike Theoria* (=Aelian, *Tact.*) 18.4–9; Arrian, *Techne Taktike* (=Arr. *Tact.*) 16.9–14; wedge, Asclep. *Tact.* 7.3 (quoted, cranes); Aelian, *Tact.* 18.4; Arr. *Tact.* 16.6–7. Rhombus, Asclep. *Tact.* 7.2, 7.5–9; Aelian, *Tact.* 18.2–3, 19.1–13; Arr. *Tact.* 16.3–5, 17.1–2 (strictly, the tacticians call it a rhomboid, and Arrian 16.3 doubts that Jason invented it, believing he used an older invention). For the maneuverability of Thessalian cavalry (but with no mention of the rhombus), Xen. *Hell.* 4.3.6–7; Diod. Sic. 17.21.4; Curt. 3.11.15. For Thessalian horsemanship, see Xen. *Hell.* 7.5.16.

11. Close order (perhaps) is the array "both by rank and by file," Asclep. *Tact.* 7.6; Aelian, *Tact.* 19.3–4. Elongated front and back is "by rank but not by file," Asclep. *Tact.* 7.7; Aelian, *Tact.* 19.3; elongated left and right is "by file but not by rank," Asclep. *Tact.* 7.8; Aelian, *Tact.* 19.11 (also useful for wheeling the formation left or right because each trooper has another in front of him to follow, Aelian, *Tact.* 19.12; cf. Xen. *Cyr.* 2.2.8); open order is "neither by rank nor by file," Asclep. *Tact.* 7.9; Aelian, *Tact.* 19.6–9 (who explains its purpose).

12. Quoted, Aelian, *Tact.* 21.2. Too close together, Asclep. *Tact.* 7.4; Aelian, *Tact.*

18.8, 19.2 (savage); Arr. *Tact.* 16.14; cf. Syr. Mag. *Strat.* 17 (Dennis); Athenian cavalryman, Xen. *Oec.* 11.17; square formation easier, Asclep. *Tact.* 7.4;
Aelian, *Tact.* 18.5; Arr. *Tact.* 16.10. Irresistible, Polyb. 4.8.10.

13. Jason trains his mercenaries, Xen. *Hell.* 6.1.6, 6.4.28. For a Thessalian mock
battle (at the tomb of Achilles, on Alexander's campaign), Philostr. *Her.* 53.16
(de Lannoy). Flying, Xen. *Eq. Mag.* 8.5–6; new maneuvers, 3.5; cf. *Mem.*
3.5.19.

14. Orator, quoted Isocrates *Ep.* 2.20; cf. *Or.* 8.118; for Greek views of the character of the Thessalians, H. D. Westlake, *Thessaly in the Fourth Century BC*
(London, 1935) pp. 40–1 gathers the references; dragging murderer, Arist.
fr. 166 (Rose). Even leaving aside mercenaries, not all Thessalian cavalry will
have been aristocrats: we hear of one Meno of Pharsalus who could mount
three hundred (Dem. *Or.* 23.199) or two hundred ([Dem.] *Or.* 13.23) of his
own serfs for the Greek campaign against Eion in 476–5 BC, but Westlake
(*Thessaly* p. 36) is right to consider this unusual: in Xenophon's depiction,
the serfs of Jason's Thessaly can only be imagined as rowers (*Hell.* 6.1.11).
Achilles, Westlake, *Thessaly* p. 43. Athenian cavalry training, at the latest by
360s (when Xenophon's *Hipparchichus* was written), although probably much
older, and hoplites, not until the 330s (see below, p. 415).

15. *Anthippasia,* Xen. *Eq. Mag.* 3.10–13 (riding right through an enemy formation is a maneuver for which Aelian *Tact.* 19.6 notes that the rhombus in
loose order is particularly suited). On the contest, D. G. Kyle, *Athletics in
Ancient Athens* (Leiden, 1987) pp. 189–90. For the (proposed) *Anthippasia*
on the Parthenon, J. J. Pollitt, "The Meaning of the Parthenon Frieze," in
D. Buitron-Oliver (ed.), *The Interpretation of Architectural Sculpture in Greece
and Rome* (Hanover NH, 1997) pp. 51–65 at 57. Rivalry, quoted, Xen. *Eq.
Mag.* 1.26; mercenaries, 9.3–4; two horsemen, *Eq.* 8.10–11.

16. Agesilaus, Xen. *Hell.* 3.4.16 [=*Ages.* 1.25]; cf. 4.2.5–7. Thessalian pride in
horsemanship, Xen. *Hell.* 4.3.9. Philopoemen, quoted Plut. *Phil.* 7.3 (cf.
Polyb. 10.22.9) and Plut. *Phil.* 7.4–5 (trans. adapted from Perrin).

17. Thessalian cavalry, bravery and maneuver, Diod. Sic. 17.21.4 (cf. Curt. 3.11.15);
bravery and skill, 17.33.2; bravery and horsemanship, 17.57.4. Cavalry riding
considered as a learned skill, Xen. *Cyr.* 4.3.10–12. Horsemanship in epic, *Il.*
4.303, 16.809, 23.289 (with the chariot race 23.272–533).

18. Agesilaus, Xen. *Hell.* 3.4.16 [=*Ages.* 1.25]; for light-armed skill, cf. Xen. *Oec.*
21.7, Polyaenus, *Strat.* 3.9.31; Pl. *Leg.* 830E, 833E–834C. Archer, quoted Soph.
Aj. 1121 (rendering *banausos* as "working class"). At sea, quoted Thuc. 7.70.3
(trans. Crawley, adapted), literally "that what happened on deck not be left
behind by one of the other *technai*," cf. 7.70.7–8.

19. Quoted, Nepos 11.2.1–2.

20. There are traces of a sense of competition between peltasts and hoplites, with peltasts charging forward without orders to attack before friendly hoplites can come to grips, Xen. *An.* 4.4.20, 6.5.26; cf. 4.3.34.

21. Boeotians wavering, Xen. *Hell.* 6.4.9; Polyaenus, *Strat.* 2.3.3; Paus. 9.13.8. Argument between boeotarchs, Diod. Sic. 15.53.3; Plut. *Pel.* 20.2; Paus. 9.13.6–7. Oracles and prodigies, Xen. *Hell.* 6.4.7; Diod. Sic. 15.53.4–54.4; Polyaenus, *Strat.* 2.3.8, 12; Plut. *Pel.* 21–22; perhaps to counter-act a set of bad prodigies, Diod. Sic. 15.52.3–7.

22. Xen. *Hell.* 6.4.9–13.

23. Evolution half completed, Plut. *Pel.* 23.2; Theban depth and deployment, Xen. *Hell.* 6.4.12–13; Diod. Sic. 15.55.1–2. Serpent, Polyaenus, *Strat.* 2.3.15. Right wing to hang back, Diod. Sic. 15.55.2, but see V. D. Hanson, "Epameinondas, the Battle of Leuktra (371 BC), and the 'Revolution' in Greek Battle Tactics," *Classical Antiquity* 7 (1988) 190–207 at pp. 197–9, who doubts it; tactics not new, Hanson, "Epameinondas" pp. 192–4 gathers the references.

24. Fight and consequences, Xen. *Hell.* 6.4.13–16; cf. Diod. Sic. 15.55.2–56.4; quoted, Xen. *Hell.* 6.4.16. One step, quoted Polyaenus, *Strat.* 2.3.2. Thyrea wreaths, N. Robertson, *Festivals and Legends: The Formation of Greek Cities in Light of Public Ritual* (Toronto, 1992) pp. 161–4 gathers the references.

25. Quoted, Xen. *Hell.* 6.4.14. Sacred band, Plut. *Pel.* 23.2–4, who appear as the "picked men," *epilektoi*, in Diodorus's account (15.55.2–56.2).

26. Spartan drill, Arist. *Pol.* 1338B; cf. Xen. *Lac.* 11.5–10 (quoted 11.8); Plut. *Pel.* 23.3. Syracuse, Thuc. 6.72.4; Argos, Thuc. 5.67.2; cf. Diod. Sic. 12.75.6, 12.79.4; coup, Diod. Sic. 12.80.2–3. For trained corps in Greek warfare, Pritchett *GSAW* vol. 2 pp. 221–4 and L. Tritle, "*Epilektoi* at Athens," *Ancient History Bulletin* 3 (1989) pp. 54–9 gather the references. After Leuctra, the Boeotians may have established mass training (Xen. *Hell.* 6.5.23; Plut. *Mor.* 788A), but the evidence is equivocal. Pericles, Thuc. 2.39; training worthless, Pl. *Lach.* 182E–184C; cf. Xen. *Cyr.* 2.3.9–11. Even physical training was rare, Xen. *Hell.* 6.1.5. Xenophon's view, *Cyr.* 2.1.22–29, 2.3.17–22, 3.3.50–56, 6.4.14; *Mem.* 3.12.5. Athenian training (see bibliographical note), Arist. *Ath. Pol.* 42.3 with 42.4 for the spear and shield; and for the rise in prestige of light infantry weapons, note the implications of Arist. *Pol.* 1321A; Theophr. *Char.* 27.3, 13.

27. Sacred Band, Plut. *Pel.* 18–19 (for martial competition of lovers, cf. Pl. *Symp.* 178E–9A; Spartan lovers usually stand side by side, Xen. *Symp.* 8.35; Eros, Athen. *Deip.* 561E. For both see D. Ogden, "Homosexuality and Warfare in Ancient Greece," in A. B. Lloyd (ed.), *Battle in Antiquity* (London, 1996) pp. 107–68, with pp. 111–115 on Thebes and pp. 117–119 on Sparta.

28. Artisans of war, quoted Xen. *Lac.* 13.5; cf. Thuc. 6.72.3; Plut. *Pel.* 23.3; teaching hoplite skills newfangled at Athens, Pl. *Lach.* 182A–B; *Euthyd.* 271D–72A.

Hoplite fighting as a *techne,* Pl. *Resp.* 374B–D; cf. Thuc. 4.33.2. For pride in technique, ML 51. Competition, Pl. *Leg.* 833E–34A; Spartan spell, e.g. Xen. *Mem.* 3.5.15–16.

29. References to helot soldiers are gathered by C. Hamilton, "Social Tensions in Classical Sparta," *Ktema* 12 (1987) pp. 31–41 at 34–6. Spartan king, quoted Thuc. 1.84.4. Courage a function of experience, Thuc. 2.87–92; mix of experience and inborn, Xen. *Cyr.* 3.3.5, 3.3.55; *Mem.* 3.9.2; function of knowledge, Arist. *Eth. Nic.* 1116B; Pl. *Lach.* 193–9; *Prt.* 349–50, 359–60; mercenary bravery and good technique, Arist. *Eth. Nic.* 1116B; better than citizens, Xen. *Hell.* 6.1.5–6; *Eq. Mag.* 9.4.

30. Agesilaus, Plut. *Ages.* 26.4–5 = Polyaenus, *Strat.* 2.1.7; cf. Xen. *Lac.* 7.1–2; Plut. *Lyc.* 24.2–4.

31. Spartan education, Xen. *Lac.* 2.1–11, 3.1–5 (at 2.1–2 and 3.1 Xenophon observes that these practices were unique). Make brave, Thuc. 2.39.1; Arist. *Pol.* 1338B. Athenian admirer, quoted Critias 88 B9 (D–K).

32. Boys stealing, Xen. *Lac.* 2.6–9; cf. Plut. *Lyc.* 17.3–4, 18.1; *krypteia,* Plut. *Lyc.* 28.1–4; husbands, Xen. *Lac.* 1.5; cf. Plut. *Lyc.* 15.3–4. Ban on foreigners (*xenelasia*) to protect secrets, Thuc. 2.39.1. Old rule — indeed a *rhetra,* according to Plutarch — Plut. *Lyc.* 13.5–6 = *Ages.* 26.2–3. For *metis* as a craftsmanly intelligence, the insight is that of H. Jeanmaire, "La Naissance d'Athéna et la royauté magique de Zeus," *Revue archéologique* 48 (1956) pp. 12–39, who gathers the references. "*Mêtis* implies the manipulation of, and gaining power over, nature by means of technical tools," S. von Reden, *Exchange in Ancient Greece* (London, 1995) p. 61.

33. Banausic vs. noble *technai,* J. W. Humphrey, J. P. Oleson, and A. N. Sherwood, *Greek and Roman Technology: A Sourcebook* (London, 1998) pp. 580–4 conveniently gathers the ancient authors. Training by contest, Xen. *Cyr.* 1.6.18, 2.1.22, 2.3.21–4, 3.3.10 (for cavalry, see above); Pl. *Leg.* 829B–34D. *Techne* of generalship, Pl. *Ion* 540D–41A; *Euthyd.* 290B–D, 291C; *Leg.* 921D; Xen. *Cyr.* 1.6.13.

Chapter VI. Alexander the Great

1. Sacrifice, Arrian, *The* Anabasis *of Alexander* (= Arr. *Anab.*) 1.11.5; for the trees, Pliny *HN* 16.238; Philostr. *Her.* 9.1–3 (de Lannoy; specifying elms); *Anth. Pal.* 7.141, 385.

2. Arr. *Anab.* 1.11.6–7 with Bosworth *Comm. ad loc.* (= A. B. Bosworth, *A Historical Commentary on Arrian's History of Alexander,* 2 vols. [Oxford, 1980–95]).

3. Sacrificed, Arr. *Anab.* 1.11.7–8 (with Bosworth *Comm. ad loc.*). Genealogy, Plutarch, *Alexander the Great* (= Plut. *Alex.*) 2.1; offerings, Diodorus (= Diod.

Sic.) 17.17.3; Just. *Epit.* 11.5.12; Alexander and Hephaestion, Arr. *Anab.* 1.12.1; the Hephaestion detail is doubtful (Bosworth *Comm. ad loc.*). Race, Plut. *Alex.* 15.4–5. In general, on the trip to Troy, Plut. *Mor.* 331D.

4. Tutor, Plut. *Alex.* 5.5. Alexander remained quite devoted to this tutor, Lysimachus by name, who, despite his age, accompanied the king on his Asian campaign. Hephaestion, Arr. *Anab.* 7.14.2–10, quoted 7.14.4. Human sacrifice, Plut. *Alex.* 72.3; dragged, Quintus Curtius Rufus, *History of Alexander the Great of Macedon* (= Curt.) 4.6.29 and *FGH* 142 F 5 (both likely legends). Cf. Curt. 8.4.26, Diod. Sic. 17.97.3 for other alleged imitations of Achilles.

5. Arr. *Anab.* 1.12.8–13.2 with Bosworth *Comm. ad loc.;* Diod. Sic. 17.18.2–4.

6. Fight, Arr. *Anab.* 1.15.6–8. Diod. Sic. 17.20.1–7 and Plut. *Alex.* 16.4–5 give different versions of this fight, but no matter: it is the fact of Alexander's combat that is important. Panic, Arr. *Anab.* 1.16.1; Diod. Sic. 17.21.4.

7. Attributes, Diod. Sic. 17.21.4; advised, Arr. *Anab.* 1.13.3–7; Plut. *Alex.* 16.1–3.

8. Worn, Diod. Sic. 17.18.1, 21.2; carried, Arr. *Anab.* 1.11.8 with Bosworth *Comm. ad loc.;* cf. 6.9.3.

9. Fleet, Arr. *Anab.* 1.20.1; Diod. Sic. 17.22.5–23.3.

10. Arr. *Anab.* 1.21.1–3; cf. Diod. Sic. 17.25.5. For competition, cf. Arr. *Anab.* 2.27.6.

11. *FGH* 148, 44 col. 2 (= *P. Oxy.* 1798), author unknown.

12. Deployment, Arr. *Anab.* 2.7.1–8.4; cf. Curt. 3.9.7–8. Unfolding, Polyb. 12.19.6; cf. Curt. 3.9.12.

13. Offset, Polyb. 18.29–30; Balkan foes, Arr. *Anab.* 1.6.1–4; cf. for Macedonian drill, Arr. *Anab.* 1.1.9, 1.2.4, 1.4.2, 1.6.6, 1.6.10, 3.13.6; Curt. 3.2.13–14.

14. Pammenes as host, Plut. *Pel.* 26.5; cunning, Polyaenus, *Strat.* 5.16; lessons, also Just. *Epit.* 6.9.7, 7.5.1–3.

15. *Il.* 13.130–3 = 16.215–7, trans. Lattimore. For other Greek recollections of this passage, see above p. 346 n. 14. Diod. Sic. 16.3.2 makes the connection to Homer, and Polyb. 18.29.6 quotes *Il.* 13.131–3 of the Macedonian phalanx (but without naming Philip); cf. Polyb. 12.21.3; Livy 33.8.14; Curt. 3.2.13.

16. Another tradition traced the Macedonian phalanx to the *Iliad,* via Charidemus, the fourth-century BC mercenary commander (Eust. *Il. ad loc.* 13.128–33 [449.2–5 {van der Valk}]), making no mention of Philip (but see Diod. Sic. 17.30.2 for the connection).

17. *Il.* 12.400–2, trans. Lattimore, adapted; cf. 5.795–8, 14.404–5. For the Macedonian strap, Plut. *Aem.* 19.1; *Cleom.* 11.2 (but both passages are equivocal); cf. Hdt. 1.171. For this reconstruction of the shields Macedonians used with the *sarissa* see bibliographical note.

18. Descent, Plut. *Alex.* 2.1; Pammenes, Plut. *Pel.* 18.2.

19. Similar arrays at Granicus River: Arr. *Anab.* 1.14.6–7; Issus: Arr. *Anab.* 2.10.3; Gaugamela: Arr. *Anab.* 3.14.2 (phalanx array, Arr. *Anab.* 3.11.9–10; Diod. Sic. 17.57.2–3); Hydaspes: Arr. *Anab.* 5.16.2, 4; cf. 5.22.7. Not in normal position, Arr. *Anab.* 1.28.3, 5.13.4 (with Bosworth *Comm. ad loc.*). In these two emergencies Alexander's array was in part dictated by the fact that, like the mercenaries in Xenophon's *Anabasis* (4.7.8) and the Romans (Polyb. 6.40.9; Joseph. *BJ* 3.97), the Macedonian order of march rotated day by day (marching first being more pleasant). When time to set up the regular ranked array was lacking, this rotation imposed a different order of battle. In a battle in which the units were conventionally arrayed, the unit possessing the day's rotating right to march first, the *hegemonia*, "leadership," might attack first (Arr. *Anab.* 1.14.6) but without being in a special position in the line (Arr. *Anab.* 1.14.1).

20. Hypaspists (Shield Bearers), W. Heckel, *The Marshals of Alexander's Empire* (London, 1992) p. 247, making sense of Theopompus (*FGH* 115 F 348); and cf. Diod. Sic. 17.57.2. *Asthetairoi,* Arr. *Anab.* 2.23.2 with G. T. Griffith, in *id.* and N. G. L. Hammond, *A History of Macedonia* vol. 2 (Oxford, 1979) pp. 709–12. This interpretation of *asthetairoi* is controversial: M. B. Hatzopoulos, *L'Organisation de l'armée macédonienne sous les Antigonides* (Athens, 2001) p. 72 n. 7 gathers the literature and (weakly) endorses Griffith. *Atakton,* Diod. Sic. 17.80.4; Curt. 7.2.35–8.

21. Infantry *agema* ("leader" or "vanguard"), Arr. *Anab.* 3.11.9; Heckel, *Marshals* pp. 244–52. Social standing of cavalry, Anaximenes *FGH* 72 F 4; Curt. 6.9.21, 10.7.20; Griffith *History of Macedonia* vol. 2, p. 706. King and cavalry *agema,* Arr. *Anab.* 5.22.6, 3.11.9 with Curt. 4.13.26 and Diod. Sic. 17.57.1. Order of cavalry squadrons, Arr. *Anab.* 3.11.8 with Curt. 4.13.26 and Diod. Sic. 17.57.1. Order of hipparchies, quoted Diod. Sic. 18.3.4.

22. Philip from the left, combining Diod. Sic. 16.86 with Plut. *Alex.* 9.2; this seems to be the modern consensus (Griffith, *History of Macedonia* vol. 2 pp. 596–603) but the information on Chaeronea is dreadful. Philip commands phalanx, Diod. Sic. 16.4.5; Polyaenus, *Strat.* 4.2.2. Spartans, Xen. *Lac.* 11.8–10, with J. K. Anderson, *Military Theory and Practice in the Age of Xenophon* (Berkeley and Los Angeles, 1970) pp. 104–8 on this difficult passage. But the Spartan battalion of the Sciritai traditionally held the left wing (Thuc. 5.67.1). Athenians, Hdt. 6.111 for the norm (with A. Raubitschek, "The Gates in the Agora," *American Journal of Archaeology* 60 [1956] pp. 279–82 and N. V. Sekunda, *Marathon 490 BC* [Oxford, 2002] pp. 54–8), although it may not have been followed at Marathon, the battle for which Herodotus describes it: Plut. *Arist.* 5.3; *Mor.* 628D. Alternatively, the tribes' relative positions may have been settled by lot: W. K. Pritchett, *Marathon* (Berkeley and Los Angeles,

1960) pp. 145–9. But Alexander's system resembles neither of the Athenian possibilities. Thebans, Plut. *Mor.* 282E.

23. Plataea, Hdt. 9.26–8 (see above, pp. 69–70). Balkans, Arr. *Anab.* 1.1.11–2.6. The luxury of placing the Macedonian cavalry on the right wing also depended upon having allied cavalry to protect the left: in Alexander's battle against the Triballi, in the absence of allies (Arr. *Anab.* 1.2.5–6) the Macedonian cavalry was necessarily split up (cf. Arr. *Anab.* 5.22.6).

24. Quoted, Arr. *Anab.* 7.5.4–6; cf. *Ind.* 42.9. Shield taken from Troy, *Anab.* 6.9.3.

25. Quoted, Curt. 5.2.2–5 (cf. Arr. *Anab.* 3.16.11 for a parallel reform of the cavalry; Diod. Sic. 17.65.2–3). There is a textual problem—a "new" prize? or "nine" prizes?—which I have elided: see J. E. Atkinson, "The Infantry Commissions Awarded by Alexander at the End of 331 BC (Curtius Rufus V.2.2–5)," in W. Will (ed.), *Zu Alexander dem Grossen, Festschrift G. Wirth* (Amsterdam, 1988) pp. 413–35 and M. B. Hatzopoulos, *Macedonian Institutions under the Kings* vol. 1 (Athens, 1996) pp. 443–52 for this and other discussion. This is a very Homeric scene: a rank ordering is established by reputation, and even the judging itself conceived as competitive, as on the shield of Achilles (*Il.* 18.507–8).

26. First through third prizes, Hdt. 9.71. On the practice, see above pp. 45–6. Funeral games, *Il.* 23.262–70.

27. Prizes, Arr. *Anab.* 4.18.7=Curt. 7.11.12 (with ranking); watched, Arr. *Anab.* 2.23.4; wounded, Arr. *Anab.* 1.16.5; cf. 2.12.1.

28. Recited, Arr. *Anab.* 2.7.7, 2.12.1; honored, Arr. *Anab.* 1.16.5, 7.10.3–4; Plut. *Alex.* 39.1–2; Diod. Sic. 17.46.6, 17.89.3. Lysippus, Arr. *Anab.* 1.16.4. Quoted, Diod. Sic. 17.21.6.

29. Duel, Curt. 9.7.16–22; Diod. Sic. 17.100–101; cf. Plut. *Alex.* 31.1–3; and at royal funerals, Diyllos *FGH* 73 F 1. Halter, Arist. *Pol.* 1324B (presumably around his waist; cf. wounded Amazon statue type, e.g. J. Boardman, *The Archaeology of Nostalgia* [London, 2002] pp. 170–1). Boar, Athen. *Deip.* 18A. Hunting, Arr. *Anab.* 4.13.1–2; Curt. 8.1.13–16; Plut. *Alex.* 40.1; birds and foxes, Plut. *Alex.* 23.3; weasel, Plut. *Alex.* 41.3. Ball games, Plut. *Alex.* 73.3; Athen. *Deip.* 19A. Drinking competitions, Plut. *Alex.* 70.1. Formal games, A. B. Lloyd, "Philip II and Alexander the Great: The Moulding of Macedon's Army," in *id.* (ed.), *Battle in Antiquity* (London, 1996) pp. 169–198 at n. 19 gathers the references. Greek stars imported, Arr. *Anab.* 3.1.4, 7.14.10 (three thousand for Hephaestion's funeral games deep in Asia—the cost is unimaginable); Curt. 9.7.16. Alexander as *apobates,* Plut. *Alex.* 23.2. Cf. Alexander's companions: Plut. *Alex.* 40.1; Athen. *Deip.* 539C. Curtius gets in the spirit by reporting remarkable individuals: Catanes the archer (7.5.41–3), and Philip, a remarkable runner in armor (8.2.35–6).

30. Gangs, Plut. *Alex.* 31.1–2; Clitus, Arr. *Anab.* 4.8.6–8 = Curt. 8.1.22–52 = Just. *Epit.* 12.6.1–4. Philip training with competition, Diod. Sic. 16.3.1; Alexander, Diod. Sic. 17.2.3; cf. Arr. *Anab.* 7.23.5.

31. Competition between units, cf. Curt. 7.6.26. *Iliad* as *ephodion,* supplies for traveling, Plut. *Alex.* 8.2; memorized, Dio. Chrys. *Or.* 4.39; casket, Plut. *Alex.* 26.1–2; Pliny *HN* 7.107–8; wounded, Plut. *Alex.* 28.2; Alexandria, Plut. *Alex.* 26.3–7. Textual editing, Strabo 13.1.27; cf. Plut. *Alex.* 8.2. Pre-onset sacrifice, see R. Parker, "Sacrifice and Battle," in H. van Wees (ed.), *War and Violence in Ancient Greece* (London, 2000) pp. 299–314. Clean-shaven heroes: beards are known in the *Iliad* (A. Mau, "Bart," *RE* 3.1 [1897] cols. 30–4 at 30 gathers the references) but on old men, *Il.* 22.74, 24.516, and as a sign of the coming of manhood, *Il.* 24.348; cf. *Od.* 10.278–9, 11.319–20. The razor was known, and only once in epic is a hero of fighting age said to wear a beard, *Od.* 16.175–6: but this is Odysseus when being transformed from a beggar. Alexander, Polyaenus, *Strat.* 4.3.2; Plut. *Thes.* 5.4 = *Mor.* 180B (but the tradition places a practical interpretation on this order), and judging by artistic representations, this order seems to have been obeyed. For Alexander and Homer see also Plut. *Mor.* 331C–D.

32. Thersites, *Il.* 2.248–9.

33. Nestor, *Il.* 2.362–6; trans. Lattimore, adapted (see above p. 32); Hector, *Il.* 12.88–90 = 197, trans. Lattimore, adapted; cf. 13.128–9.

34. Halts, Arr. *Anab.* 2.10.1, 3; Polyb. 12.20.1–7; cf. Curt. 3.10.3, Just. *Epit.* 11.9.7. Thessalians, Arr. *Anab.* 2.9.1; flanking force, quoted Arr. *Anab.* 2.9.2; further right wing, Arr. *Anab.* 2.9.3–4.

35. A unit of archers, with no consistent position in the line (Arr. *Anab.* 1.14.1, 2.9.2) may have been Macedonian (Arr. *Anab.* 3.12.2), but perhaps not (Bosworth *Comm. ad loc.*). Similarly the mysterious cavalry *prodromoi* or *sarissophoroi* (Arr. *Anab.* 1.14.1, 6, 2.9.2, 3.12.3) may have been Macedonian light cavalry, but perhaps not (Bosworth *Comm. ad loc.* 1.12.7). At the Hydaspes too some of the companion cavalry may have been sent outside the main line, although the details are obscure (Arr. *Anab.* 5.16.3; Curt. 8.14.15–17). At Granicus River some non-Macedonian troops were deployed among the Macedonian units in the array (Arr. *Anab.* 1.14.1).

36. Appeals by name; Arr. *Anab.* 2.10.2; trumpets, Diod. Sic. 17.33.4; cf. Curt. 3.10.1–2.

37. Right wing, Arr. *Anab.* 2.10.3; cf. Diod. Sic. 17.33.3; left wing, Arr. *Anab.* 2.11.2.

38. Phalanx, Arr. *Anab.* 2.10.5–7, quoted Arr. *Anab.* 2.10.6; cf. 3.15.3. Alexander wounded, Curt. 7.6.8; echoing the rotating order of march, see above n. 19. After death, Curt. 10.7.20–8.23; Diod. Sic. 18.2.2.

39. Arr. *Anab.* 2.11.1–3.

40. Quoted, Arr. *Anab.* 2.10.4; cf. 1.1.9; Plut. *Alex.* 20.4. Led from right, see above n. 19; Gaugamela, Arr. *Anab.* 3.14.2–3; Curt. 4.15.23–30. Attempted single combat at Issus, Polyb. 12.22.2; Diod. Sic. 17.33.5; Curt. 3.11.7.

41. Diod. Sic. 17.33.5–34.7 (quoting 34.4); Curt. 3.11.7–12 (for the building metaphor, 9); cf. Polyb. 12.22.2–3; Plut. *Alex.* 20.4–5 (Darius wounds Alexander, not to be believed). Cf. the traditions of Alexander's single combat with the son of Porus (Arr. *Anab.* 5.14.4) and with Porus himself at the battle of the Hydaspes (Just. *Epit.* 12.8.3–4).

42. Darius, Plut. *Alex.* 21.3; also Porus, Arr. *Anab.* 5.19.1. Olympics, Plut. *Alex.* 4.5.

43. Plut. *Mor.* 327A–B, trans. Babbitt.

44. Fight in person, Arr. *Anab.* 1.8.1–3, 2.23.4–5; Curt. 4.9.25, 7.7.35–7, 8.11.14–16, 8.13.13–15; Diod. Sic. 17.34.1; single combat, Arr. *Anab.* 3.28.3 = Curt. 7.4.33–40; casualties, Arr. *Anab.* 1.22.7, 2.10.7, 3.15.2, 4.3.3, 4.23.3.

45. "Most kingly," quoted, Plut. *Demetr.* 44.5. Quoted *Il.* 12.318–21 (trans. Lattimore).

46. Cf. R. Lane Fox, *Alexander the Great* (London, 1973) pp. 64–5. And, perhaps, earned the favor of Zeus, Plut. *Alex.* 27.5–6.

47. Rivalry, Arr. *Anab.* 2.10.6; praising self, Arr. *Anab.* 2.7.7; Curt. 8.1.22–26; Just. *Epit.* 12.6.2. No Homer, Arr. *Anab.* 1.12.1; Plut. *Alex.* 15.4–5.

48. Swords, Thuc. 1.6.1.

49. Arr. *Anab.* 7.1.4.

50. "To the strongest," Arr. *Anab.* 7.26.3; Diod. Sic. 17.117.4; the alternate tradition, "to the best" (Diod. Sic. 18.1.4; Curt. 10.5.5) is even more Homeric.

Chapter VII. Hellenistic Warfare

1. *SIG³* 1061, with N. B. Crowther, "*Euexia, Eutaxia, Philoponia:* Three Contests of the Greek Gymnasium," *Zeitschrift für Papyrologie und Epigraphik* 85 (1991) pp. 301–4, who gathers other references to those contests (about which we know nearly nothing other than their names). For the mysterious *lithobolos,* Pritchett *GSAW* vol. 5 p. 1 n. 1 implies that the stones were thrown by hand, M. Launey, *Recherches sur les armées hellénistiques* vol. 2 (Paris, 1950) pp. 830, 832–3, thinks that a species of catapult was involved.

2. For the set of Samian inscriptions, E. Preuner, "Griechische Siegerlisten," *Mitteilungen des kaiserlich deutschen archäologischen Instituts, Athenische Abteilung* 28 (1903) pp. 338–82 at 353–70.

3. For the text of the gymnasiarchal law of Beroea, Ph. Gauthier and M. B. Hatzopoulos, *La Loi gymnasiarchique de Beroia* (Athens, 1993): banned,

B.27–29; javelin and bow, B.10–12 (for an English translation, M. M. Austin, *The Hellenistic World from Alexander to the Roman Conquest* [Cambridge, 1981] pp. 203–7). Public instructors, Launey, *Recherches* pp. 815–35 gathers the evidence, and see P. Roesch, "Une loi fédérale béotienne sur la préparation militaire," *Études Béotiennes* (Paris, 1982) pp. 307–54, esp. 347–9 for discussion of trainers who instructed boys and men in "archery, the javelin, and deploying themselves in the formations of war" (*ll.* 12–16). Roesch also (p. 349) gathers evidence of *taktikoi,* trainers in formations, in royal employ. Philopoemen, quoted, Plut. *Phil.* 9.7, 11.1.

4. *Eutaxia, SIG³* 1061 *l.* 17. Roman discipline, Polyb. 6.37–8. For Hellenistic Greek discipline, the essential epigraphical documents are gathered by M. B. Hatzopoulos, *L'Organisation de l'armée macédonienne sous les Antigonides* (Athens, 2001) pp. 151–67, discussed pp. 141–5 (the most important document is translated by M. M. Austin *The Hellenistic World from Alexander to the Roman Conquest* [Cambridge, 1981] pp. 136–8). For being asleep on watch a soldier of Philip V was fined one drachma, a Roman soldier (at least in theory) executed (Polyb. 6.37).

5. Philip's training, Diod. Sic. 16.3.1; Polyaenus, *Strat.* 4.2.10; at Chaeronea (Polyaenus, *Strat.* 4.2.2) Philip had his phalanx withdraw in good order under enemy pressure, a maneuver that required training. Phalanx of twenty thousand at Chaeronea (an estimate), G. T. Griffith in *id.* and N. G. L. Hammond, *A History of Macedonia* vol. 2 (Oxford, 1979) p. 599 n. 4.

6. Friendship, Plut. *Eum.* 10.3; Antigonus, Plut. *Demetr.* 19.3–5, 28.4; *Eum.* 15.2; "Cyclops," Plut. *Mor.* 11B; Eumenes, Plut. *Eum.* 11.2; Nepos 18.5 with J. Hornblower, *Hieronymus of Cardia* (Oxford, 1981) p. 212 on the contrast the sources draw between the two figures, and pp. 196–223 for how they are characterized. Conference at the siege of Nora, Plut. *Eum.* 10.2–4.

7. Diod. Sic. 19.25–26.8; quoted, 19.26.9.

8. Diod. Sic. 19.27.2–28.4 with A. M. Devine, "Diodorus' Account of the Battle of Paraitacene (317 BC)," *The Ancient World* 12 (1985) pp. 75–86 at 76–9: there is confusion in the details of Diodorus's account. On the cavalry units formed of pages (correcting Devine), see N. G. L. Hammond, "Royal Pages, Personal Pages, and Boys Trained in the Macedonian Manner During the Period of the Temenid Monarchy," *Historia* 39 (1990) pp. 261–90 at 271.

9. Array of Antigonus, Diod. Sic. 19.29. Tarentines, 19.29.2 (on whom see G. T. Griffith, *The Mercenaries of the Hellenistic World* [Cambridge, 1935] pp. 246–50 and N. V. Sekunda, "Classical Warfare," in J. Boardman [ed.], *The Cambridge Ancient History² Plates to Volumes V and VI* [Cambridge, 1994] pp. 167–94 at 178–9). The contrast between Alexander and his successors should not be over-stated: especially later in his campaign Alexander had used Asian troops

fighting in their own style in his army and had experimented with training Asians to fight in the Macedonian manner: Hammond, "Royal Pages" pp. 275–80 gathers the evidence and that of his successors elaborating his example (pp. 280–4). Vying, quoted, Diod. Sic. 19.27.1.

10. Competitive *techne*, Polyb. 9.20.9; rank order, Polyb. 5.68.5; Diod. Sic. 19.81.5, 29.19.1; cf. Polyb. 2.66.4; debate, Plut. *Pyrrh.* 8.2. Quoted, Diod. Sic. 18.34.5.

11. Quoted, Plut. *Phil.* 14.5 and Polyb. 9.12.2; "outgeneral," Diod. Sic. 19.4.7, 19.26.5, 19.39.1; Plut. *Eum.* 15.7; cf. 6.3–4; boxers, Polyb. 1.57.1–4; good and bad, Polyb. 4.8.3–5.

12. "From history," quoted Polyb. 1.57.5; cf. 9.12.2. Ways of learning listed, Polyb. 11.8.1–2; experience, Polyb. 5.50.4, 5.63.13, 7.15.2, 9.14.4, 15.15.3; cf. Diod. Sic. 23.15.10, 30.22.1; "athletes," Polyb. 15.9.4; Plut. *Demetr.* 5.2; common soldier, Polyb. 1.84.6; checkers, Polyb. 1.84.7.

13. Tactical manual, Aelian, *Tact.* 1.1 (Roman period but drawing on a Hellenistic original). Homeric *tactica*, Aelian, *Tact.* 1.2, Eust. *Il. ad loc.* 8.325 (588.15–20 [van der Valk]); 13.128–33 (449.2–5; I am indebted to N. V. Sekunda for these references). Stratagem manual, Polyaenus, *Strat.* 1.pr.4–13 (Roman period but drawing on Hellenistic practice); cf. Paus. 4.28.7–8; Strabo 1.2.3–5. Astronomy and geometry, Polyb. 9.12–20.5; Odysseus, Polyb. 9.16.1; cf. 15.16.3. On the Hellenistic "Bronze Age revival," see the bibliographical note.

14. Philopoemen, Plut. *Phil.* 4.4–6; Crete, 13.3, 6; Eumenes, Plut. *Eum.* 14.4–5; Phocion, quoted, Plut. *Phoc.* 25.1; Xen. *Hiero* 2.16; cheered, Polyb. 1.32.7.

15. Diod. Sic. 19.30.1–4.

16. Skill at arms, Polyb. 21.9.3; cf. Diod. Sic. 24.5.2; training, Plut. *Phil.* 13.3; Polyb. 22.3.8–9; fight in person, Plut. *Pyrrh.* 7.4–5, 22.6; Polyb. 7.17.3. Eumenes, quoted, Diod. Sic. 18.31.1; cf. Plut. *Eum.* 7.4–7.

17. Commanders' monomachy, Plut. *Pyrrh.* 7.4–5; Plut. *Phil.* 7.6, 10.4–7; Polyb. 11.18.4. Quoted, Plut. *Phil.* 7.7; cf. Polyb. 1.64.6. Command and fight, Plut. *Phil.* 10.8; *Eum.* 8.1; ranked, Plut. *Pyrrh.* 26.1; Polyb. 3.47.7; "cleverness and courage," Polyb. 8.34.10; Diod. Sic. 20.23.6, 30.20.1. At risk, Polyb. 10.32.7–33.3, 11.2.5–11; but admiration, Polyb. 10.49.9, 14, and see A. Eckstein, *Moral Vision in the Histories of Polybius* (Berkeley and Los Angeles, 1995) pp. 28–55 on this theme; Pyrrhus, quoted Plut. *Pyrrh.* 16.7–8.

18. Emulation of Alexander, see esp. Plut. *Pyrrh.* 8.1; *Phil.* 4.4–5; cf. Polyb. 5.10.10. Pyrrhus, quoted Diod. Sic. 22.11.1 = Plut. *Pyrrh.* 26.5 = *Anth. Pal.* 6.130; cf. Plut. *Pyrrh.* 7.4. For Pyrrhus's descent and name, Plut. *Pyrrh.* 1; for coins, W. Ameling, "Alexander und Achilleus. Eine Bestandsaufnahme," in W. Will (ed.), *Zu Alexander dem Grossen, Festschrift G. Wirth* (Amsterdam, 1988) pp. 657–92 at 689. Strip off armor, Plut. *Eum.* 7.7.

19. Silver shields, quoted, Diod. Sic. 19.30.6; cf. 19.41.2, 19.43.1; Plut. *Eum.*

16.3–4. The Silver Shields are reported to have been all at least sixty years old (Diod. Sic. 19.41.2; Plut. *Eum.* 16.4), but men who left Macedonia with Alexander in 334 BC could be as young as thirty-six, so fast had history moved. Slingers, quoted Diod. Sic. 19.109.2. Weapons training, Polyb. 5.64.3; mercenaries, Polyb. 11.13.3, 15.13.1. Alexander's phalanx, quoted, Curt. 3.2.13–14.

20. Courage trainable, Polyb. 6.11a.11 (Buettner-Wobst), 6.48.3, 6.52.10; Frontin. *Strat.* 4.1.3. Training makes better, Polyb. 10.22.7; training wins battles, Polyb. 1.9.7–8. "Athletes of war," J. Hornblower, *Hieronymus of Cardia* p. 193 n. 42 gathers the references (add Polyb. 2.20.9; Plut. *Eum.* 16.4). Experience makes formidable, Polyb. 3.35.8, 3.89.5; Diod. Sic. 18.7.2, 19.16.1, 20.3.3, 20.62.4, 25.9.1. For classical Greek discussions, see above, p. 352 n. 29.

21. Diod. Sic. 19.30.7–31.1 (quoted 19.31.1); for the idea of parallel competition of general and soldier, Polyb. 3.81.2–3; Diod. Sic. 19.24.3; Plut. *Pyrrh.* 7.4; cf. Polyb. 1.45.9.

22. Competition with judge, Polyb. 1.40.11, 2.69.4–5; Diod. Sic. 19.83.5.

23. Already knowing, Diod. Sic. 19.29.2. Leaders compete in drilling, Polyb. 5.65. Training competitive, cf. Plut. *Phil.* 7.4–5, 9.7; Diod. Sic. 19.3.2. For the *hoplitodromos,* etc., see p. 56; for Alexander, see p. 128.

24. Diod. Sic. 19.31.2–32.2; Polyaenus, *Strat.* 4.6.10. Devine, "Paraitacene" p. 86 suspects that Antigonus's losses are exaggerated.

25. Diod. Sic. 19.34.8, 37–39 ("out-generalled," 39.1); Plut. *Eum.* 15.3–7 ("out-generalled," 15.7); Nepos 18.8–9; Polyaenus, *Strat.* 4.6.11, 4.8.4. Tent, quoted Plut. *Mor.* 182D.

26. Diod. Sic. 19.40–43 (Eumenes' quest for single combat, 42.5; deployment on the left, 19.40.2, 42.4–5); Polyaenus, *Strat.* 4.6.13; Put. *Eum.* 16–18.1 (*polytropos,* 16.3).

27. Diod. Sic. 19.44.1–2; Nepos 18.10–13; Plut. *Eum.* 18.2–19 (Antigonus clearminded, 16.5); quoted, *Eum.* 19.2.

28. Arginusae, Xen. *Hell.* 1.6.24; Philip V, Polyb. 5.2.4–5.

29. For Tarentines, see above p. 145. *Thureophoroi,* Polyb. 5.53.8, 10.29.6, with N. V. Sekunda, "Military Forces in the Hellenistic World and the Roman Republic," in P. Sabin, H. van Wees and M. Whitby (eds.), *Cambridge History of Greek and Roman Warfare* (Cambridge, forthcoming). Neo-Cretans, Polyb. 5.3.1, 5.65.7, 5.79.10; cf. Livy 42.55.10 (but the interpretation of Neo-Cretans is controversial, E. Foulon, "Contribution à une taxinomie des corps d'infanterie des armées hellénistiques (II)," *Les Études classiques* 64 [1996] pp. 317–38 at 334). Ethnic names, Griffith, *Mercenaries* pp. 241–251. Ptolemy IV's Egyptian phalanx, Polyb. 5.79.4. Ptolemy IV's generals, quoted Polyb. 5.64.1.

30. Boeotia, Roesch, "Une loi fédérale," pp. 352–4; Sparta, Plut. *Cleom.* 11.2,

23.1; Achaean league, Plut. *Phil.* 9.1–3; Polyaenus, *Strat.* 6.4.3; Paus. 8.50.1 (but some Achaeans had been so equipped before: Polyb. 2.65.3, 4.69.4–5, 5.91.6–8, with Sekunda, "Military Forces." Hannibal, Polyb. 3.87.3, 3.114.1, 18.28.9–10; 160s BC, N. V. Sekunda, *Hellenistic Infantry Reform in the 160's BC* (Lodz, 2001) esp. pp. 117–124 and 176–9.

The Greeks, Conclusion

1. Strife (*Eris*) and Oath, Hes. *Op.* 804; *Theog.* 226, 231.
2. Polyb. 18.29.
3. For Greek chariots, A. K. Nefedkin, *Chariotry of the Ancient Greeks (16th–1st centuries BC)* (St. Petersburg, 2001) gathers the evidence (in Russian, with English summary). Chariots in the tactical tradition, Asclep. *Tact.* 8; Aelian, *Tact.* 22; Arr. *Tact.* 2.5, 19; Xenophon, Xen. *Cyr.* 6.1.27–30. "Not naturally suited," Asclep. *Tact.* 1.3. Pammenes, quoted Plut. *Pel.* 18.2.
4. For Assyrian siegecraft, see Y. Yadin, *The Art of Warfare in Biblical Lands* vol. 2 (Jerusalem, 1963) pp. 313–17. Paphos (besieged 498 BC), the siege-mound itself never properly published, but see J. H. Iliffe, "Excavations at Aphrodite's Sanctuary of Paphos (1951)," *Liverpool Libraries, Museums, and Arts Committee Bulletin* 2 (1952) pp. 29–66 at 53–6; F. G. Maier, "Ausgrabungen in Alt-Paphos, 1950–1971," *Chiron* 2 (1972) pp. 17–35 at 25–7; or more briefly id., *Alt-Paphos auf Cypern. Ausgrabungen zur Geschichte von Stadt und Heiligtum 1966–1984* (Mainz, 1984) p. 22, but with full bibliography of the excavations at pp. 30–2. Economically on Eastern siegecraft and its route to Greece, see A. Ferrill, *The Origins of War* (Boulder, Colo., 1997) pp. 74–6, 170–4. On Greek siege-craft in general, Y. Garlan, *Recherches de poliorcétique grecque* (Athens, 1974).
5. Siegecraft in the *Iliad:* when the Trojans attack the walled Achaean camp, Sarpedon pulls the wall down with his hands (*Il.* 12.397–9), and Hector (with the help of Zeus) shatters the gate with a great stone (12.445–62). Patroclus tries to climb the wall of Troy (16.702–4) but is prevented by Apollo.
6. On the hierarchical social structure of the Athenian fleet, H. van Wees, *Greek Warfare: Myths and Realities* (London, 2004) pp. 209–13, 230–1, but obedience was still a problem, 219–20. Artemisium, Hdt. 8.11. For tactical fighting on land inspired by fighting at sea, see p. 410. Hoplite battle on deck, Thuc. 1.49.

The Romans

1. Hydra, Plut. *Pyrrh.* 19.5.
2. Polyb. 6.37–39; Joseph. *BJ* 2.577, 3.70–107, 5.482–83; Veg. *Mil.* 1.1.

3. Polybius's evaluation of Romans vs. Macedonians, A. M. Eckstein, *Moral Vision in the Histories of Polybius* (Berkeley and Los Angeles, 1995) pp. 170–72. Formation, Polyb. 18.28–32.

Chapter VIII. Early Roman Warfare

1. Aul. Gell. 9.11.5–9 preserves the account, perhaps lightly adapted, of an unnamed annalist (=Claud. Quad. fr. 12 [Peter], but the identification as Claudius Quadrigarius is controversial), at least two centuries after the event. In that version the cognomen is given as Corvinus, "of the Raven," rather than Corvus. Other major accounts are Livy 7.26 (with Oakley *Comm.* [=S. P. Oakley, *A Commentary on Livy Books VI–X* vol. 2 (Oxford, 1998)] pp. 237–47, with pp. 30–32 on the name variation and pp. 230–32 on the sources), and Dion. Hal. 15.1. See Broughton *MRR* vol. 1 (=T. R. S. Broughton, *The Magistrates of the Roman Republic* vol. 1 [New York, 1951]) p. 129 for a full list of testimonia. Swept from the field, Livy 7.26.7–9.

2. Helmet, cf. Dion. Hal. 15.1; auspicious bird, Livy 7.26.3–5.

3. Aul. Gell. 9.13 (=Claudius Quadrigarius fr. 10 [Peter]) (quoted), and Livy 7.9.7–10.14 (with Oakley *Comm.* pp. 113–48) are the main accounts; see Broughton *MRR* vol. 1 p. 119 for a full list of testimonia.

4. Romulus, Val. Max. 3.2.3; Livy 1.10.4–7; Curatii, Livy 1.24–6; Dion. Hal. 3.12–21 gives slightly different details.

5. Marcellus, Plut. *Marc.* 2.1; Servilius, Plut. *Aem.* 31.2; Servilius's boast, Livy 45.39.16; witnesses, quoted Polyb. 6.39.10; cf. 6.39.3–4; law, Pliny *HN* 35.7; Senate, Livy 23.23.6; *provocatoria,* Aul. Gell. 2.11.4; characteristic, Polyb. 6.54.4; Aemilianus, Polyb. 35.5.1–2; Livy, *Per.* 47; F. W. Walbank, *A Historical Commentary on Polybius* vol. 3 (Oxford, 1979) p. 648 gathers other passages. Meteoric, Plut. *Marc.* 2.2.

6. Celts, Polyb. 3.62.5; Diod. Sic. 5.29.2–3; for the Greeks, see above, pp. 84, 133–38, 148; cf. also the Persians, Diod. Sic. 17.6.1; and the Carthaginians, Polyb. 9.24.5. Pyrrhus, single combats, Plut. *Pyrrh.* 7.4, 24.2–3; hands over equipment, 16.7–17.3; cf. Dion. Hal. 19.12; horned helmet, Plut. *Pyrrh.* 11.5; Roman multiple duelists: also Siccius Dentatus, with eight or nine duels (Dion. Hal. 10.37.3; Val. Max. 3.2.24).

7. *Amph.* 648–53; long recognized as a Plautine addition to his Greek original, J. Genzmer, *Der 'Amphitruo' des Plautus und sein griechisches Original* (Kiel, 1956) pp. 123–25.

8. "Dark night," quoted Ennius, *Phoenix* 311 (*ROL*); rings, Pliny *HN* 33.9; rival in *virtus,* quoted Accius 106–8 (*ROL*).

9. Livy 7.26.2.

10. Younger Torquatus, 340 BC; full version in Livy 8.6–8; quoted Livy 8.7.15–19, with Oakley *Comm.* pp. 436–51; see Broughton *MRR* vol. 1 pp. 136–37 for a full list of testimonia. Forbidding challenges, cf. Livy 5.19.9. Oakley *Comm.* p. 131 gathers more cases of commanders forbidding fighting without explicit orders and also traces the convention of asking permission for single combat.

11. Quoted, Sall. *Cat.* 9.4.

12. Polyb. 6.21.7–23.16. Polybius's account is fleshed out by scattered references in later authors, especially Livy 8.8.3–14, a famously confused and difficult passage, to be read with Oakley *Comm.* pp. 451–75. For *velites*, cf. Livy 26.4.4, 38.21.13.

13. *Velites* without officers or standards, Polyb. 6.24.1–4; sent on expeditions, Polyb. 11.22.10; cf. Polyb. 3.65.3–7, 3.69.8, 3.72.2, 3.101.6, 3.104.5, 10.39.1, 11.32.2 = Livy 28.33.3–5; Polyb. 18.19.9, 18.21.1; Livy 26.4.4–10, 28.16.4, 30.11.9–10. As skirmishers, Polyb. 1.40.6, 2.30.1–6. On the large number of javelins *velites* carry, Livy 26.4.4; Lucilius 7.323 [*ROL*]. *Velites* fighting hand to hand, Livy 31.35.4–6, 38.21.12–13, 44.35.19; cf. Polyb. 29.14.4. *Hastati* and *principes* maneuvering, Polyb. 18.30.7–8; throw *pila*, Livy 28.2.5–6; cf. 9.13.2–5, 9.35.4–6; continued missile throwing, A. Zhmodikov, "Roman Republican Heavy Infantrymen in Battle (IV–II Centuries BC)," *Historia* 49 (2000) pp. 67–78 gathers the references.

14. Gaps, Polyb. 11.22.10; covering, Polyb. 15.9.7. *Velites*, Polyb. 11.22.9–10, 15.9.9, 18.24.10; their fighting long, Polyb. 3.73.3, 11.22.9, and for ebb and flow, cf. Frontin. *Strat.* 2.3.20. Falling back, Livy 8.8.9 and quoted 8.8.12; a phalanx, Polyb. 15.14.5.

15. Concern for "open" side, e.g., Caes. *B Gall.* 7.50; centuries, Polyb. 6.24.3–8 (who sees only the commanders, the centurions, not the centuries themselves); soldier's frontage, Polyb. 18.30.6–9 (six feet, with F. W. Walbank, *A Historical Commentary on Polybius* vol. 2 [Oxford, 1967] pp. 588–89) vs. Veg. *Mil.* 3.14, 15 (three feet). Polybius seems to imply that each maniple had two standards, 6.24.6, but Varro (*Ling.* 5.88), one. For passages implying a shapeless mob rather than a drilled rectangle, Polyb. 15.15.7, 18.30.7.

16. "Peculiar," quoted Polyb. 2.33.7. Dangers of withdrawal, tactician, Asclep. *Tact.* 10.13; flight, e.g., Xen. *Hell.* 6.2.21; Polyb. 1.19.9–11.

17. Census classes, Livy 1.43.1–2; Dion. Hal. 4.16–18; cf. Festus 48L s.v. *classes clipeatas* (but the lower census classes may have been added subsequently, D. Rathbone, "The *Census* Qualifications of the *Assidui* and the *Prima Classis*," in H. Sancisi-Weerdenburg et al. [eds.], De Agricultura. *In Memoriam P. W. de Neeve* [Amsterdam, 1993] pp. 121–52). Hoplite equipment in Etruria, P. F. Stary, "Foreign Elements in Etruscan Arms and Armour: 8th to 3rd Centuries BC," *Proceedings of the Prehistoric Society* 45 (1979) pp. 179–206 at 191–97. Etruscan orgins of Roman phalanx, Diod. Sic. 23.2.1; Athen. *Deip.*

273F; the *Ined. Vat.* (*FGH* 839 F 1), trans. T. J. Cornell, *The Beginnings of Rome* (London, 1995) p. 170 with comments as to reliability.

18. 270s, Dion. Hal. 20.11.2 (a two-handed spear, indeed, which may imply that the Romans were influenced at one point by the Macedonian array); cf. Livy 8.8.3. *Hastati:* unless *hasta* meant a javelin at some early time, Ennius *Ann.* fr. 281 [*ROL*] and Livy 26.4.4. "Come to the *triarii,*" quoted Livy 8.8.11; *pyknosis,* Polyb. 15.14.4.

19. Veii, Livy 8.8.3; cf. Livy 4.59.11–60.8; Diod. Sic. 14.16.5. Gauls, Plut. *Cam.* 40.3–4; Dion. Hal. 14.9–10; Samnites, *Ined. Vat.* (*FGH* 839 F 1); cf. Athen. *Deip.* 273F; Sall. *Cat.* 51.38. For a summary of the whole debate, Oakley *Comm.* pp. 455–57. Reason tactical, H. Delbrück, *Geschichte der Kriegskunst in Rahmen der politischen Geschichte³* vol. 1 (Berlin, 1920) p. 280 (= *Warfare in Antiquity,* trans. W. J. Renfroe [Lincoln, Neb., 1990] p. 272).

20. Polyb. 6.20; Polybius's description of the enrollment of the legions is highly problematic, as P. A. Brunt, *Italian Manpower 225 BC–AD 14* (Oxford, 1971) pp. 625–34 shows; but we are interested in the principle, not the details.

21. T. B. Macaulay, *The History of England from the Accession of James the Second,* vol. 6 (New York, 1898 [London, 1848–61]) pp. 27–28. The Polybian system may have evolved from one in which Romans *did* go to war in their civic microcommunities: the Roman phalanx was assembled of centuries, which were also voting units in the *comitia centuriata* (Livy 1.43; Dion. Hal. 4.16–21), and these centuries may have been assembled on the basis of some preexisting association between the members (but perhaps not: Cornell, *Beginnings of Rome* pp. 190–97 gathers the scholarship and argues no).

22. Greek preservation of microcommunities, see H. van Wees, *Greek Warfare: Myths and Realities* (London, 2004) pp. 97–100, 103; comparison to schoolyard games, H. M. D. Parker, *The Roman Legions* (Oxford, 1928) p. 13. For Roman soldiers viewed atomistically, cf. Livy 28.19.9.

23. Quoted, Sall. *Cat.* 7.6; spear, Livy 34.15.4; cf. 35.5.2.

24. Animal standards, Pliny *NH* 10.16; wolfskins, Polyb. 6.22.3; cavalry half naked, Polyb. 6.25.3–4 with A. Alföldi, *Der frührömische Reiteradel und seine Ehrenabzeichen* (Rome, 1979) pp. 49–53.

25. Tubertus, Diod. Sic. 12.64.3; Livy 4.29.5–6; Val. Max. 2.7.6; Aul. Gell. 17.21.17.

26. *Velites,* Polyb. 6.21.7; coat of mail, 6.23.15.

27. Parallels: the Spartans sent the youngest soldiers out from the phalanx on missions requiring speed, Xen. *Hell.* 2.4.32, 4.5.14–16, 4.6.10. Headgear, Polyb. 6.22.3. Decorations, quoted Polyb. 6.39.3–4.

28. *Velites* skirmishing, Polyb. 1.40.7, 11.32.2–3 = Livy 28.33.2–3; Polyb. 10.32.2–3, 18.19.9–12, 18.21; extended, Polyb. 1.18.6, 1.19.6, 1.56–57, 3.106.4–107.1, 3.112.6, 11.21.7, 14.8.4; Livy 23.29.1, 27.2.11, 27.26.3; vs. foragers, Polyb. 3.102.2;

expected, Livy 23.16.4; cf. 8.6.16. Forbidden, see above, n. 10. In a confused passage Livy (26.4.4–7, 9) seems to date the introduction of the *velites* to 211 BC. But this cannot be right (see recently G. Daly, *Cannae: The Experience of Battle in the Second Punic War* [London, 2002] pp. 71–73).

29. Cavalry single combatants, J. B. McCall, *The Cavalry of the Roman Republic* (London, 2002) p. 84; dismount, Polyb. 6.25.4; cf. 3.65.9, 11.21.4; see McCall, *Cavalry* p. 69; man to man on foot, Polyb. 3.115.3; among the *velites,* Livy 31.35.5.

30. Equal in *virtus,* quoted Accius fr. 123 (*ROL*). Sons duplicate, see esp. Cic. *Rab. Post.* 2. Oakley *Comm.* pp. 132–33 discusses this Roman habit. Spartans, [Plut.] *Mor.* 238A–B, and the Spartans too seem to have tried to give their younger men more opportunity to excel in war (J. F. Lazenby, *The Spartan Army* [Warminster, 1985] p. 12).

31. *Seniores* and *iuniores,* Livy 1.43.2; Dion. Hal. 4.16.2. "Veterans," quoted, Livy 8.8.8; and Livy calls the *rorarii,* which may be an old name for the *velites,* "minus roboris aetate factisque," "weaker in age and deeds," that is, young and yet to prove themselves. Oath, quoted Livy 22.38.4.

32. Twelve tables, Tab. 10.6–7 (Crawford). Old men were expected still to be eager for glory and to envy young up-and-comers, Livy 28.40.8.

33. Polybius on the legion, 18.28, 31–32. He would, of course, interpret Roman success in this way. Polybius was a professional Greek officer, and professional Greek officers were educated to consider certain factors — like formation — decisive in war: see J. E. Lendon, "The Rhetoric of Combat: Greek Military Theory and Roman Culture in Julius Caesar's Battle Descriptions," *Classical Antiquity* 18 (1999) pp. 273–329 at 282–85, 290–95, and 304–6. Most Greeks think phalanx better, Polyb. 18.28, 18.32.13. Greek armies convert, N. V. Sekunda, *Hellenistic Infantry Reform in the 160's BC* (Lodz, 2001); Hannibal, Polyb. 18.28.9.

34. Auctions, Livy 2.14.1–4; Plut. *Pub.* 19.6; animals, Aul. Gell. 11.1.2–4; prayer, e.g., the Arval hymn, *ILS* 5039; on the Roman preservation of archaic language, E. A. Meyer, *Legitimacy and Law in the Roman World* (Cambridge, 2004) pp. 59–62.

35. Names of centuries and centurions' titles, M. P. Speidel, "The Names of Legionary *Centuriae,*" *Arctos* 24 (1990) pp. 135–37.

Chapter IX. The Wrath of Pydna

1. Enrollment, Livy 42.31–35.2; escort, Livy 42.49.
2. Auxiliaries, Livy 42.35.6–7; Crete, cf. Livy 43.7.1–4; lies, Livy 42.43.1–3; ancestors, quoted Livy 42.47.5; cf. Diod. Sic. 30.7.1.
3. Perseus descends, Livy 42.53–57; Callinicus, Livy 42.57–60.2; cf. Plutarch,

Life of Aemilius Paullus (= Plut. *Aem.*) 9.2; Cass. Dio (Zonar.) 9.22.1; rest of year, Livy 42.60.3–67.

4. Fighting, Plut. *Aem.* 9.3; investigation, Livy 43.4.5–13, 43.7.5–8.10, 43.9.4–10.8, 43.11.1–2, 9–11; Cretans, Livy 43.7.1–4; Dardanians, Plut. *Aem.* 9.3.

5. New consul, Livy 43.12.3–9, 44.1.1–2.3; passes, Livy 44.2.9–5.13; Dium, Livy 44.6–8, 44.10.1–4; cf. Cass. Dio (Zonar.) 9.22.1; Diod. Sic. 30.10–11; Romans, Livy 44.8.8–9.11, 44.10.5–13.14, 44.16.1–2.

6. Livy 44.22.2–15; Plut. *Aem.* 11.1–3; cf. Polyb. 29.1.

7. Paullus vs. C. Manlius, Livy 38.44.9–49.1; cf. 35.6.9–10, 8.4–9; tribune, Livy 39.4.1–5.6.

8. Livy 44.21, 44.22.17.

9. Wells, Plut. *Aem.* 14; Livy 44.33.1–4; Cass. Dio (Zonar.) 9.23; changes, Livy 44.33.5–11; Plut. *Aem.* 13.5; rebuke, Plut. *Aem.* 13.4; Livy 44.34.1–5; quoted, Livy 44.34.5.

10. Elpeus, Livy 44.8.5–6; fortified, Livy 44.32.10–11, 44.35.8–9; Plut. *Aem.* 13.3; cf. Cass. Dio (Zonar.) 9.23; council, Livy 44.35.6–8; Paullus's plan, Livy 44.35.8–15; Plut. *Aem.* 15; cf. Cass. Dio (Zonar.) 9.23; *velites* and distraction, Livy 44.35.16–24; cf. Polyb. 29.14.4. Roman vs. Greek light infantry, Livy 31.35.5–7, and see above, pp. 187–88.

11. Flank march, Polyb. 29.15; Livy 44.35.8–24; Plut. *Aem.* 16.1–2; location of the battle, Strabo 7 fr. 22; Plut. *Aem.* 16.3; Cass. Dio (Zonar.) 9.23 with N. G. L. Hammond, "The Battle of Pydna," *Journal of Hellenic Studies* 104 (1984) pp. 31–47 at 33; Paullus's trick, Plut. *Aem.* 16.3–17.3; Livy 44.36.1–37.4: the praise of Paullus's maneuver must come from Polybius, the common source of Plutarch and Livy, himself the author of a tactical manual.

12. Eclipse, Livy 44.37.5–8; Cass. Dio (Zonar.) 9.23; Frontin. *Strat.* 1.12.8. In another tradition Gallus explained it after the fact, Cic. *Rep.* 1.23; Val. Max. 8.11.1. Paullus and Macedonians, Plut. *Aem.* 17.4–5; cf. Polyb. 29.16.

13. Plut. *Aem.* 17.6; Livy 44.37.10–40.1 (Livy writes Paullus a speech defending his decision).

14. Length of Pydna campaign, Livy 45.41.3–5; Plut. *Aem.* 36.3; App. *Mac.* 19.

15. Paullus vs. Varro, Livy 22.38–43; broken ground, Polyb. 3.110.2, 112.2; no delay, Polyb. 3.110.3–4, 112.4–5.

16. Message to Fabius, Livy 22.49.10; Trebia, Polyb. 3.70.7–8; Trasimene, Polyb. 3.80.4; Fabius, Polyb. 3.89.3, 3.94.8; Minucius, Polyb. 3.90.6; all want battle, Polyb. 3.92.4; codictator, Polyb. 3.103.4; saved by Fabius, Polyb. 3.105; instructions, Polyb. 3.108.1–2.

17. Attacks on Hannibal, Livy 27.1.8–15, 27.12.11–17; centurion, Livy 25.19.9–17; Senate, Livy 27.33.9–11; cf. 27.40.9; disobeyed, Livy 25.14.3–13; Fulvius's army, Livy 25.21.5–7; Gauls, quoted Strabo 4.4.2; cf. [Caes.] *B Afr.* 73.

18. Stories of the start of the battle, Plut. *Aem.* 17.6–18.2; Livy 44.40.2–10; Cass. Dio (Zonar.) 9.23. Array, Frontin. *Strat.* 2.3.20, "triplicem aciem cuneis instruxit, inter quos velites subinde emisit" "he formed the triple array [i.e., the usual manipular formation] with his units and frequently sent out his *velites* between them." *Cuneus,* literally, "wedge," here (as usually in Roman military parlance) means no more than "unit," i.e., maniple; cf. P. Fraccaro, *Opuscula IV: Della guerra presso i Romani* (Pavia, 1975) p. 47; *pace* Hammond, "The Battle of Pydna" p. 42. And Hammond (pp. 42–43) oddly supposes that Frontinus is describing the day before the battle.

19. Quoted, Plut. *Aem.* 19.1–2; cf. Polyb. 29.17.

20. Plut. *Aem.* 20.1–3.

21. Paullus aware, Plut. *Aem.* 17.2; Atrax, Livy 32.17.7–15; cf. Livy 36.18.2–5; App. *Syr.* 35; quoted, Polyb. 18.29.1; Perseus chooses the field, Plut. *Aem.* 16.5.

22. Spain, Plut. *Aem.* 4.2; Ligurians, Livy 40.27.1–7; dinners, Polyb. 30.14 = Plut. *Aem.* 28.5; on Paullus as a commander, cf. Diod. Sic. 30.20; Plut. *Aem.* 12.1. It is hardly surprising, then, that one tradition interpreted Paullus's being pushed back by the Macedonians as a plan of the consul's, Frontin. *Strat.* 2.3.20. To son, quoted Sempronius Asellio fr. 5 (Peter) = Aul. Gell. 13.3.6.

23. Horatii, see above, p. 175; Bagradas, Polyb. 1.33.9. See Livy 10.14.14–21 and 10.29.13 for earlier, third-century examples of tactics, but their value is unclear. Also Polyb. 2.33. Varying array, Polyb. 15.9.7; deepening, Polyb. 1.33.9, 3.113.3; wheeling, Polyb. 11.22.11–23.6; independent lines, Polyb. 14.8.11, 15.14.4; Livy 33.1, 34.15.6; detached maniples, Polyb. 18.26.1–4; legions in reserve, Livy 27.12.14, 29.2.9, 29.36.8, 30.18.2; approaching in the *agmen quadratum,* or "square column," Livy 31.37.1, 35.3.2, 39.30.9; cf. App. *Ib.* 86. The invention of the cohort is also part of this tactical tradition, see below, pp. 224–30. Cavalry, J. B. McCall, *The Cavalry of the Roman Republic* (London, 2002) pp. 55–62; *velites,* see above, n. 10 and chap. 8 n. 13. Emporiae, Livy 34.14–16.2.

24. Scipio, Cic. *Q. Fr.* 1.1.23; *Tusc.* 2.62; cavalry equipment, Polyb. 6.25.3–11 with McCall, *Cavalry* pp. 26–52; Greek troops, see above, n. 2; cf. Livy 38.29.3–7; and note Flamininus's Cretans in 197 BC, Livy 33.3.10; elephants, Polyb. 18.23.7, 18.25.5–7. Elephants were first used by the Romans in 200 BC (Livy 31.36.4) although the Romans had been fighting against elephants since Pyrrhus's day. Stratagem, Livy 36.10.11; path, Plut. *Cat. Mai.* 13.1. Competition, Livy 35.14.5–12; App. *Syr.* 10; Plut. *Flam.* 21.3–4: the famous tale of the discussion between Scipio Africanus and Hannibal at Ephesus, usually dismissed as apocryphal, but no matter for our purposes so long as it is old.

25. Scipio: Livy 29.19.12; Plut. *Cat. Mai.* 3.7; H. H. Scullard, *Scipio Africanus* (Ithaca, 1970) pp. 237–38; Paullus, Plut. *Aem.* 6.4–5; in Greece, Polyb.

30.10.3–6; Plut. *Aem.* 28; Livy 45.27.5–28.6, 45.32.8–11; library, Plut. *Aem.* 28.6; dog, Plut. *Aem.* 10.3–4; cf. Cic. *Div.* 1.103–4. Natural science in Greek military thinking, cf. Polyb. 9.14–20; Onasander, *Strat.* 39.

26. Quoted, Polyb. 13.3.7; cf. 36.9.9; Livy 42.47.8; quoted, Livy 24.14.6; cf. 34.19.6, 35.4.7; prosecutions, N. Rosenstein, Imperatores Victi: *Military Defeat and Aristocratic Competition in the Middle and Late Republic* (Berkeley and Los Angeles, 1990) pp. 114–40 gathers the references; Varro, Livy 22.61.14.

27. Ticinus, Polyb. 10.3.3–7; Livy 21.46.7–10 (but some denied this story); Cannae, Livy 22.53; aggression, Frontin. *Strat.* 4.7.4; slowly, Livy 29.19.13; spoil, Livy 29.19.3–4; Plut. *Cat. Mai.* 3.5–8; gods, Polyb. 10.2.9–12, 10.11.7; Livy 26.19.4.

28. Varro at Cannae, Polyb. 3.113.3; Paullus, quoted Livy 44.34.4.

29. Advance against orders, see above, pp. 200–203 and cf. Livy 34.47.6–7. Perseus's reluctance to advance, cf. Livy 44.37.11.

30. Plut. *Aem.* 21.1–2; *Cato Mai.* 20.7; Frontin. *Strat.* 4.5.17; Just. *Epit.* 33.2.1–4.

31. Turn of the tide, Plut. *Aem.* 20.4–5; Livy 44.41.6–9; cf. Polyb. 18.32.3–4; elephants disrupt, Livy 44.41.3–5; casualties, Plut. *Aem.* 21.3 (more than twenty-five thousand); Livy 44.42.7 (about twenty thousand).

32. Scipio Aemilianus, Plut. *Aem.* 22; Livy 44.44.1–3.

33. Surrender, Livy 44.45.5, 13; Plut. *Aem.* 23–24.1; division of Macedonia, Livy 45.18.6, 29.5–10; Diod. Sic. 31.8.8–9. Paullus angry, Plut. *Aem.* 26.5–6; lecture, Polyb. 29.20 = Livy 45.7.4–8.9 and Plut. *Aem.* 27; Diod. Sic. 30.23.1.

34. Livy 45.34.1–6; Plut. *Aem.* 29; App. *Ill.* 9.

35. Troops unhappy, Livy 45.34.7, 35.6, 37.10; Plut. *Aem.* 29.3, 30.2; enemy's proposal, Livy 45.35.5–36.8; Plut. *Aem.* 30.3–31.2; Servilius, Livy 45.36.9–39.19; Plut. *Aem.* 31.2–32.1; both Livy and Plutarch write him speeches, no doubt drawing on a lost speech in Polybius.

Chapter X. Caesar's Centurions and the Legion of Cohorts

1. Simply counting in J. D. Montagu, *Battles of the Greek and Roman Worlds* (London, 2000).

2. Caesar, *Gallic War* (= Caes. *B Gall.*) 7.6–17; explain, 7.19; capture of Avaricum, 7.28.

3. To Gergovia, Caes. *B Gall.* 7.34; river, 7.35; for the stratagem, cf. Amm. Marc. 21.8.3. For another famous Greek tactic used by a late-Republican Roman, App. *Mith.* 42 (cf. Arr. *Anab.* 3.13.6).

4. Caes. *B Gall.* 7.36.

5. Leader of Aedui, Caes. *B Gall.* 7.32–33; march, Caes. *B Gall.* 7.37–41.

6. Caes. *B Gall.* 7.42–43.

7. Fear, Caes. *B Gall.* 7.43; plan, 7.44–46.

8. Caes. *B Gall.* 7.45.

9. Caes. *B Gall.* 7.46–7, 50.

10. Caes. *B Gall.* 7.47–51.

11. Pharsalus, Caesar, *Civil War* (= Caes. *B Civ.*) 3.99; the Sambre, quoted Caes. *B Gall.* 2.25; cf. 6.40; *B Civ.* 1.46, 3.53, 3.64, 3.67.

12. Crastinus, Caes. *B Civ.* 3.91, 99; cf. 2.35; *B Gall.* 5.35, 6.38, 6.40; *B Afr.* 45; *B Hisp.* 23; Vorenus and Pullo, quoted *B Gall.* 5.44; cf. App. *Mith.* 89.

13. Brave, e.g., Livy 26.5.12–17, 26.48.6; disobedient, e.g., Livy 25.14.7; phlegmatic, quoted, Polyb. 6.24.9.

14. Tactics-minded officers, Caes. *B Gall.* 1.52, 2.20, 2.25–26, 7.45, 7.62, 7.81, 7.86–87; heroic officers of old, cf. Livy 25.14–15, 27.14.8; bravery of late Republican commanders a function of leadership, *B Gall.* 2.25, 5.33, 5.35, 6.40, 7.87–88 (8.48 is an exception); cf. Plut. *Mar.* 20.6; *Sull.* 29.5; *Luc.* 28; App. *Ill.* 20; *Mith.* 49–50, 85. In a general catastrophe, as at Zela in 67 BC, tribunes could still die in large numbers (Plut. *Luc.* 35.1; App. *Mithr.* 89), but Caesar mentions only a single death of a tribune in combat in his whole account of the Gallic War (*B Gall.* 5.15). Duel before Munda, *B Hisp.* 25.

15. Citizen cavalry abolished, J. B. McCall, *The Cavalry of the Roman Republic* (London, 2002) pp. 100–113 (last attested in Val. Max. 5.8.4); *contubernales,* McCall, *Cavalry* p. 112; ten campaigns rule lapses, pp. 111, 116–17; social standing declines, J. Suolahti, *The Junior Officers of the Roman Army in the Republican Period* (Helsinki, 1955), esp. pp. 297–98; five years as a ranker, Polyb. 6.19.1–5; Pharsalus, Plut. *Pomp.* 67–68.1; Caes. *B Civ.* 3.82. For other exchanges of views, cf. *B Civ.* 1.67, 1.71–72, 2.30–31; *B Gall.* 3.5, 5.28–30; *B Afr.* 82. Marius, Plut. *Mar.* 3.2; cf. Plut. *Ant.* 62. Pompey, Plut. *Pomp.* 7.2, 19.2, 35.3. Panic, quoted, Caes. *B Gall.* 1.39; but not always, *B Gall.* 5.52.

16. Quoted, Caes. *B Gall.* 7.52.

17. Standard-bearers, *B Gall.* 4.25, 5.37; *B Civ.* 3.64; elephant, *B Afr.* 84. *Virtus* in Caesar, J. E. Lendon, "The Rhetoric of Combat: Greek Military Theory and Roman Culture in Julius Caesar's Battle Descriptions," *Classical Antiquity* 18 (1999) pp. 273–329 at 306–16.

18. Thapsus, *B Afr.* 82–83; Forum Gallorum, Cic. *Fam.* 10.30.2; held back, Caes. *B Gall.* 7.19; *B Civ.* 3.37; *B Hisp.* 30; cf. Plut. *Mar.* 16.1, 18.4–19.1; compelled, *B Civ.* 1.82, 3.37; jeered, *B Gall.* 3.17; cf. 3.24; Plut. *Mar.* 16.3–4.

19. Caesar withdraws, Caes. *B Gall.* 7.53; what follows, 7.54–89.

20. Caes. *B Civ.* 1.38–42.

21. Caes. *B Civ.* 1.43–44, quoted: "ordines suos non magnopere serverent, rari dispersique pugnarent. . . . ipsi autem suos ordines servare."

22. Caes. *B Civ.* 1.45.

23. Caes. *B Civ.* 1.45–6.

24. Cohorts in the *triplex acies,* Caes. *B Civ.* 1.83. *Antesignani,* Caes. *B Civ.* 3.84 "adulescentes atque expeditos ex antesignanis electis" may imply that the *antesignani* were younger than the rest of the legionaries. The *antesignani* had been the *hastati* of the manipular legion; what the term meant in Caesar's day is unclear, but *antesignani* were used for special missions (cf. *B Civ.* 1.57) and might be mixed with cavalry (*B Civ.* 3.75, 3.84), rather like the *velites* of old; so perhaps a trace of the age divisions did survive. See N. V. Sekunda, *Republican Roman Army 200–104 BC* (London, 1996) pp. 32–34; A. von Domaszewski, "Antesignani," *RE* 1.2 (1894) cols. 2355–56.

25. One line, *B Afr.* 13; two, Caes. *B Gall.* 3.24; *B Civ.* 1.83; empire, Veg. *Mil.* 2.6, 2.15; line relief, cf. Caes. *B Gall.* 1.52; *B Civ.* 3.94; flank guard, *B Civ.* 3.89; five and five, *B Afr.* 81; third line detached, *B Afr.* 60.

26. Ilerda, Caes. *B Civ.* 1.45; Dyrrachium, *B Civ.* 3.62–67; city, *B Civ.* 3.111; encircle, *B Civ.* 3.93; detached, *B Alex.* 31; surprise, *B Gall.* 7.87–88; support, *B Gall.* 7.86–87; *B Civ.* 3.64–65; sallies from circle, *B Gall.* 5.33–35; cf. *B Alex.* 40; in sequence, *B Civ.* 2.41; face either direction, *B Afr.* 17; outside battle, *B Gall.* 3.11; *B Civ.* 1.18; *B Alex.* 57; forage, *B Gall.* 6.36.

27. Ilipa, Polyb. 11.23.1; surprise attack, 11.33.1–2; Muthul River, Sall. *Jug.* 49.6 and 51.3.

28. On this change, see the bibliographical note. Minimum forty years' transition: from c. 147 BC for the publication of books 1–15 of Polybius (see F. W. Walbank, *Polybius* [Berkeley and Los Angeles, 1972] p. 21 [the cohort is glossed at Polyb. 11.23.1]) to 108 BC, the dramatic date of the Battle of Muthul River, in which both maniples and cohorts appear: in principle the manipular array could have vanished immediately thereafter.

29. From reading, Cic. *Luc.* 2; *Balb.* 47; Diod. Sic. 39.9; treatises, Cic. *Fam.* 9.25.1; boasting, Sall. *Jug.* 85.12; cf. Cic. *Man.* 28; *Font.* 43; Brutus, Plut. *Brut.* 4.4; Plut. *Ant.* 45.6. Caesar, J. E. Lendon, "The Rhetoric of Combat" pp. 281–304.

30. For the property qualification, see bibliographical note. For the farm that the qualification implies, N. Rosenstein, "Marriage and Manpower in the Hannibalic War: *Assidui, Proletarii* and Livy 24.18.7–8," *Historia* 51 (2002) pp. 163–91 at 190–91; by the mid–second century BC the state was supplying equipment to recruits: Rosenstein gathers the evidence at p. 176 n. 40.

31. Disobedience of soldiers, e.g., Plut. *Luc. passim; Pomp.* 11.3–4.

32. No legionary cohort officers, standards, B. Isaac, "Hierarchy and Command-Structure in the Roman Army," *The Near East under Roman Rule* (Leiden, 1998) pp. 388–402 at pp. 392–98 (reprinted from Y. Le Bohec [ed.], *La Hiérarchie [Rangordnung] de l'armée romaine sous le Haut-Empire* [Paris, 1995] pp.

23–31). Centuries and centurions, M. P. Speidel, "The Names of Legionary Centuriae," *Arctos* 24 (1990) pp. 135–37. No *genius,* M. P. Speidel and A. Dimitrova-Milčeva, "The Cult of the *Genii* in the Roman Army and a New Military Deity," in M. P. Speidel, *Roman Army Studies* vol. 1 (Amsterdam, 1984) pp. 353–68 at 355 (reprinted from *Aufstieg und Niedergang der römischen Welt* 2.16.2 [1978] pp. 1542–55).

Chapter XI. Scenes from the Jewish War AD 67–70

1. Josephus, *Jewish War* (=*BJ, Bellum Judaicum*) 3.64–69.
2. Training Galileans, *BJ* 2.577–82; their flight, 3.129–30. Roman training, quoted 3.72–75; cf. 3.102–7.
3. Training, Veg. *Mil.* 1.9–19, 1.26–27, 2.23; cf. Tert. *ad Mart.* 3; every day, Veg. *Mil.* 2.23; for archeological traces, see bibliographical note. Lambaesis, *ILS* 2487+9133–35 = Smallwood *Nerva* 328; translated in B. Campbell, *The Roman Army, 31 BC–AD 337. A Sourcebook* (London, 1994) pp. 18–20.
4. Quoted, *BJ* 2.577, 3.74, 3.86; cf. 1.22, 1.142, 2.529, 3.467, 5.79, 5.122, 5.353; for Josephus's admiring description of the Roman army, 3.70–109. For his rebuke of his own soldiers by comparing them to Romans, *BJ* 2.580.
5. Gabara, *BJ* 3.132–34; Jotapata, siege, *BJ* 3.141–339; length, 3.316; Titus, 3.324; dead, 3.337; Josephus 3.340–408. Large numbers in Josephus (see J. J. Price, *Jerusalem Under Siege: The Collapse of the Jewish State 66–70 CE* [Leiden, 1992] pp. 205–9), as in any ancient historian, are to be regarded with extreme suspicion: but since no divisor has the backing of logic or evidence, I reproduce Josephus's numbers with this warning.
6. Vespasian's campaign, *BJ* 3.409–69; Tiberias, cf. Joseph. *Vit.* 352; Tarichaeae, Titus's charge, *BJ* 3.470–91 (Josephus writes a harangue for him); horse killed: Suet. *Tit.* 4.3 may refer to this battle; town captured, *BJ* 3.492–502.
7. *BJ* 4.2–35; without orders, 4.44–45; Vespasian 4.31–35. For the topography of Gamala and the archeology of this site (which confirms Josephus's account), D. Syon, "Gamla: Portrait of a Rebellion," *Biblical Archeology Review* 18 (1992) pp. 20–37: a vast number of missiles have been recovered, including over a thousand stones shot from throwing engines.
8. Vespasian, *BJ* 3.236; cf. Suet. *Vesp.* 4.6 for the injury. And cf. *BJ* 4.372–3 for Josephus's presentation of Vespasian's attitude: better to win by intellect than by fighting; also Tac. *Hist.* 2.5. On the oddity of the appointment of a son as his father's subordinate, B. W. Jones, "Titus in Judaea, AD 67," *Latomus* 48 (1989) pp. 127–34 at 127–28.
9. Gamala, setback and speech, *BJ* 4.36–48; taken, 4.62–83; Gischala, 4.84–120.
10. Peraea, *BJ* 4.410–39; Idumaea and Samaria, 4.443–50; Dead Sea, 4.476–77.

11. Nero and what followed, *BJ* 4.491–502; Tac. *Hist.* 5.10; June, *BJ* 4.545–55; Vespasian emperor, *BJ* 4.585–5.1.

12. *BJ* 5.40–66.

13. *BJ* 5.69–97. For Caesar, above pp. 218–20; cf. Onasander, *Strat.* 33.

14. *BJ* 5.106–20, 130–35.

15. *BJ* 5.121–29, quoted 125. Titus did punish breaches of discipline, and with death: *BJ* 6.155 (cf. 6.362) — but not acts of aggression.

16. *BJ* 5.258–95. Cass. Dio 66(65 Loeb).5.1 records Titus's being hit in the shoulder with a stone at somewhere around this point. On the proverb, E. L. Wheeler, "*Polla Kena tou Polemou:* The History of a Greek Proverb," *Greek, Roman, and Byzantine Studies* 29 (1988) pp. 153–84.

17. Romans penetrate the wall, *BJ* 5.296–302. The exact topography of Jerusalem and the location of the walls — especially the "second" wall — are notorious puzzles (see Price, *Jerusalem Under Siege* pp. 290–92) but of no importance here. Skirmishing, *BJ* 5.303–8; Longinus, 5.312–14; Pudens, 6.169–76.

18. Other rash auxiliaries at Jerusalem, *BJ* 6.54–68, 6.81–90; by the ankle, 6.161–63. Trajan's Column adapts literary account, e.g., F. Coarelli, *The Column of Trajan,* trans. C. Rockwell (Rome, 2000) pp. 11–14.

19. Standard scene, Cichorius (ed.) pls. xxiv, lxii, lxvi, lxix–lxx, cvi. Attack on wall, pls. cxvi–cxvii (illustrated). All the more surprising, because on a patriotic monument, we would expect the citizen legionaries' contribution to be exaggerated rather than diminished.

20. Legionaries work, e.g., Cichorius (ed.) pls. iv, xxiv, xcviii, ci, cxxii; auxiliary sentries, pls. xi–xii, cxxvii–cxxix; detail of fatigues, e.g., pls. xi–xx; legionaries fight, pls. xl, lxxi, xcvi, cxiii; nonlegionary fatigues, pls. xxxiii, xxxv, cvii; massacre, pls. xxix; burn, pls. lvii, lix, cliii. Auxiliaries wilder, e.g., Tac. *Hist.* 2.22. Presenting heads, pls. xxiv, lxxii; in his teeth, xxiv (illustrated); cf. cxiii. The sculptural convention of the column made a sharp distinction between the equipment of legionary troops and that of auxiliary infantry (probably far sharper than existed in reality) — the former with rectangular shields and banded-mail cuirasses and the latter with oval shields and unarticulated cuirasses: all six soldiers with severed heads are auxiliaries. But the artist was being overfastidious: citizen soldiers too were great takers of heads, see bibliographical note. Changes in Roman armor and helmets, see M. C. Bishop and J. C. Coulston, *Roman Military Equipment* (London, 1993) pp. 85–96 and A. Goldsworthy, *The Roman Army at War 100 BC–AD 200* (Oxford, 1996) pp. 213–16, 220–21 (with other explanations of the trend).

21. Mons Graupius, Tac. *Agr.* 35; Cerialis, Tac. *Hist.* 5.16; Batavians at Mons Graupius, Tac. *Agr.* 36. AD 16 and 23, Tac. *Ann.* 2.16, 4.73. Without citizen blood, Tac. *Agr.* 35. Defeated legionaries, Tac. *Hist.* 4.20; regarded as excellent,

Tac. *Hist.* 2.27–28; cf. 2.69, 4.12. Auxiliary pay, R. Alston, "Roman Military Pay from Caesar to Diocletian," *Journal of Roman Studies* 84 (1994) pp. 113–23, but attacked by M. A. Speidel, "Sold und Wirtschaftslage der römischen Soldaten," in G. Alföldy, B. Dobson, and W. Eck (eds.), *Kaiser, Heer, und Gesellschaft in der römischen Kaiserzeit* (Stuttgart, 2000) pp. 65–94 who argues for a 5/6 ratio. Double pay, Tac. *Hist.* 4.19. In this paragraph I depend heavily upon C. M. Gilliver, "Mons Graupius and the Role of Auxiliaries in Battle," *Greece and Rome* 43 (1996) pp. 54–67.

22. For recruiting patterns, see bibliographical note; sound barbarous, Tac. *Hist.* 2.74; cf. *ILS* 2671; Batavians, Tac. *Germ.* 29; Thracian units, combining the counts of J. Spaul, *Ala²* (Andover, 1994) pp. 221–35 and *Cohors²* (Oxford, 2000) pp. 341–42, 353–54; and Thracian soldiers are increasingly found in other units as well, J. C. Mann, *Legionary Recruitment and Veteran Settlement during the Principate* (London, 1983) p. 66. Fourth century, [Anon.] *Expositio Totius Mundi* 50 (Rougé); cf. Amm. Marc. 26.7.5. Resistance, quoted Tac. *Ann.* 4.46; cf. *Hist.* 4.14; *Agr.* 15, 31 with P. Brunt, "Conscription and Volunteering in the Roman Imperial Army," *Roman Imperial Themes* (Oxford, 1990) pp. 188–214 at pp. 204–5.

23. Longinus, *BJ* 5.312–14; decorations, Polyb. 6.39.1–10; under empire, V. A. Maxfield, *The Military Decorations of the Roman Army* (Berkeley and Los Angeles, 1981) pp. 145–217 gathers the references. Promotion at Jerusalem, *BJ* 6.53, 142, cf. 7.14–15; captor of Decebalus, *AE* 1969/1970.583, economizing somewhat with the truth, for Decabalus committed suicide, Cass. Dio 68.14.4; see M. P. Speidel, "The Captor of Decebalus: A New Inscription from Philippi," *Journal of Roman Studies* 60 (1970) pp. 142–53. For promotion, cf. *ILS* 7178. Centurion's pay, M. A. Speidel, "Sold und Wirtschaftslage" pp. 83–84; beneath centurions there were soldiers who received 1.5 times or double normal pay (pp. 69–70). Ranks beneath centurion, e.g., *ILS* 2117, cf. 2658. It is especially soldiers who commission their own gravestones who lay out their careers at such length: G. Forni, "L'anagraphia del soldato e del veterano," in D. M. Pippidi (ed.), *Actes du VIIe congrès international d'épigraphie grecque et Latine* (Bucharest and Paris, 1979) pp. 205–28 at p. 227 (reprinted in G. Forni, *Esercito e marina di Roma antica* [Stuttgart, 1992] pp. 180–205).

24. Titus's order, *BJ* 5.316.

25. *BJ* 5.331–47; cf. Cass. Dio 66(65Loeb).6.1. On Titus's archery, Suet. *Tit.* 5.2 may apply here.

26. *BJ* 5.238–45; cf. Tac. *Hist.* 5.11.

27. Harassed, *BJ* 5.358; collapsed, 5.466–71; sally, 5.473–90.

28. *BJ* 5.491–511; competition, 5.502–3.

29. Engineer, quoted *ILS* 5795; Lambaesis, *ILS* 2487+9133–35 (=Smallwood

Nerva nr. 328); cf. Tac. *Hist.* 3.27. Walls, D. J. Breeze and B. Dobson, *Hadrian's Wall*[3] (London, 1987) pp. 70–83, 95–96, 110–11. *Disciplina, labor,* and *patientia,* G. Horsmann, *Untersuchungen zur militärischen Ausbildung im republikanischen und kaiserzeitlichen Rom* (Boppard am Rheim, 1991) pp. 187–97.

30. *Disciplina* as training, O. Mauch, *Der lateinische Begriff Disciplina. Eine Wortuntersuchung* (Freiburg, 1941) p. 78 gathers the references. Epitaph, *ILS* 2558 = Smallwood *Nerva* 336, with M. P. Speidel, "Swimming the Danube under Hadrian's Eyes," *Ancient Society* 22 (1991) pp. 277–82. Auxiliary cavalry, Arr. *Tact.* 34–36, 38.5, 40.10–11, 42.4–5. Lambaesis, see above, n. 29. Training competitive, cf. Veg. *Mil.* 1.9.

31. Quoted, Tac. *Ann.* 1.35, "ubi veteris disciplinae decus?" Quoted, Tac. *Hist.* 3.11, "virtutis modestiaeque . . . certamen"; cf. 1.64; ashamed, J. E. Lendon, *Empire of Honour* (Oxford, 1997) pp. 248–49 gathers the references; compare the shame from failure in *virtus,* id., "The Rhetoric of Combat: Greek Military Theory and Roman Culture in Julius Caesar's Battle Descriptions," *Classical Antiquity* 18 (1999) pp. 273–329 at 310–12. *Virtus* and *Disciplina* as divinities, A. von Domaszewski, *Die Religion des römischen Heeres* (Trier, 1895) pp. 40–41, 44–45, gathers the evidence. On the cult of *Disciplina,* add E. Birley, "The Religion of the Roman Army: 1895–1977," *Aufstieg und Niedergang der römischen Welt* 2.16.2 (1978) pp. 1506–41 at 1513–15.

32. New ramps, *BJ* 5.522–23; cf. 6.150–51, 6.220; twenty-one days, 6.5; fighting, 6.15–67.

33. *BJ* 6.68–71.

34. Independent project, cf. A. Goldsworthy, "Community under Pressure: The Roman Army at the Siege of Jerusalem," in id. and I. Haynes (eds.), *The Roman Army as a Community* (Portsmouth, R.I., 1999) pp. 197–210 at p. 208. Josephus would hardly have failed to credit Titus with this plan if he could have. Death for sentries, *BJ* 5.482–83; cf. Polyb. 6.36–37. Initiative, e.g., *BJ* 5.79; in contrast to *BJ* 5.121–22, 6.17.

35. Later in siege, *BJ* 6.225–26; cf. 6.403; see Goldsworthy, "Community under Pressure" p. 204 on this episode.

36. Tenth Legion, *B Afr.* 16. Unit identity, e.g., Tac. *Hist.* 2.11, 3.24, 5.16. Appeal to Tenth, Caes. *B Gall.* 1.40–41. Livy 41.3.7 reports an appeal to legionary rivalry in 178 BC, but its reliability is unclear. Unit decorations, Maxfield, *Decorations* pp. 218–35; quoted, *AE* 1930.92. For unit titles, decorations, and precedence, Lendon, *Empire of Honour* pp. 262–64.

37. Standards, Tac. *Ann.* 1.18; cf. 1.23, 1.28; fighting, Tac. *Hist.* 2.68, 88; claimants, Tac. *Hist.* 2.74; see Lendon, *Empire of Honour* p. 250. Temple, quoted, *BJ* 6.142; cf. Tac. *Hist.* 3.27.

38. For cohesion, see esp. Tac. *Ann.* 1.21; cf. Caes. *B Civ.* 2.41; *B Alex.* 16; Tac.

Hist. 4.46. Dedications and tombstones, J. E. Lendon, "The Roman Army Now," *The Classical Journal* 99 (2004) pp. 441–49 at 445–46. Jumper, *BJ* 6.177–89, trans. Thackery, adapted.

39. Speeches, Tac. *Hist.* 3.24, 5.16.

40. Brave acts, *BJ* 6.81–90, 6.161–63, 6.172–74, 6.186–87; without orders, 6.179–89, 6.257–66; Titus with cavalry, 6.246–47; restrained, 6.132–34; cf. 6.89. And anecdotes suggest this pattern was not confined to the special circumstances of the siege of Jerusalem: cf. Tac. *Ann.* 13.36; Tac. *Hist.* 1.62, 2.18, 3.3, 3.19–20, 3.22–23, 3.26, 4.34; Joseph. *BJ* 7.199. There is a controversy about whether Titus wanted the temple saved (as Josephus insists, *BJ* 6.236–43) or ordered its destruction, see Price, *Jerusalem Under Siege* p. 170. Uncontrollable, *BJ* 6.284; permission, 6.353; parade, 7.5–16.

41. *BJ* 6.403–7.4; Tac. *Hist.* 5.13 gives six hundred thousand besieged in the city.

42. On *virtus* conceived as inborn, J. E. Lendon, "War and Society in the Hellenistic World and the Roman Republic," in P. Sabin, H. van Wees, and M. Whitby (eds.), *Cambridge History of Greek and Roman Warfare* (Cambridge, forthcoming).

43. Barbarians especially in elite units, M. J. Nicasie, *Twilight of Empire: The Roman Army from the Reign of Diocletian until the Battle of Adrianople* (Amsterdam, 1998) p. 53; J. H. W. G. Liebeschuetz, *Barbarians and Bishops* (Oxford, 1990) pp. 15–16. For the controversy about increasing use of barbarians in the Roman army, see bibliographical note.

44. Complaints about discipline, P. Southern and K. R. Dixon, *The Late Roman Army* (New Haven, 1996) pp. 170–78 collect the references. Quoted, Lib. *Or.* 24.5; cf. 24.3; but contrast Libanius complaining about discipline, *Or.* 11.38.

45. Rivalry between soldiers, Amm. Marc. 20.11.12; initiative, 31.16.6; rivalry between units, 29.6.13; for unit loyalty, cf. Procop. *Bell.* 5.12.18. For attacking without orders, cf. Amm. Marc. 28.5.6, 31.12.16, but mostly the soldiers are held back: 14.2.15, 14.2.17, 24.4.11–14, 25.1.2, 27.10.9–10, 31.7.10. Holding back the troops was still a problem in the sixth century: Maurice, *Strat.* 1.8, 2.18, 3.5, 3.11, 12.B14; Procop. *Bell.* 1.18.16–25. Gauls, Amm. Marc. 19.5.2–3 and 19.6.3–12 (quoted 19.6.9). Contrast, Amm. Marc. 16.12.47; speeches, Amm. Marc. 16.12.9–12, 16.12.33, 23.5.21, 24.3.6.

46. Josephus and Titus, *BJ* 3.396–97, 3.408, 4.628–29; Josephus, Joseph. *Vit.* 416–29; and see Z. Yavetz, "Reflections on Titus and Josephus," *Greek, Roman, and Byzantine Studies* 16 (1975) pp. 411–32. Josephus's audience for the *Bellum Judaicum,* Joseph. *BJ* 1.30; *Vit.* 361–67; *Ap.* 1.50–52. Marius fights, Plut. *Mar.* 20.6; Sall. *Jug.* 98.1; cf. Livy 39.31.6–9. Marius one-on-one, Plut. *Mar.* 3.2 vs. Frontin. *Strat.* 4.7.5. Second century BC, quoted Livy 35.48.13. 29 BC, Cass. Dio 51.24.4 with J. W. Rich, "Augustus and the *Spolia Opima,*"

Chiron 26 (1996) pp. 85–127. According to Suetonius, Germanicus (*Calig.* 3.2) had killed an enemy in hand-to-hand combat, and Drusus (*Claud.* 1.4) had sought it out; cf. Plut. *Pomp.* 19.2, 35.3; but see also Goldsworthy, *Roman Army at War* pp. 154–56 on the rarity of the phenomenon. AD 68–70, cf. Tac. *Hist.* 3.17, 4.77, 5.21; but see Tac. *Agr.* 37.

Chapter XII. Shield Wall and Mask

1. Quoted, Ammianus Marcellinus (=Amm. Marc.) 16.12.7; what follows, Amm. Marc. 16.12.8–15 (the historian writes Julian a speech urging his troops to go into camp), 18–19.

2. Wall, quoted Amm. Marc. 16.12.20. Right flank, Amm. Marc. 16.12.7, 21–22; hidden, Amm. Marc. 16.12.23, 27; Lib. *Or.* 18.56.

3. Amm. Marc. 16.12.27–41; Lib. *Or.* 18.56–59. Pushing, quoted Amm. Marc. 16.12.37, "artissimis conserens parmis"; cf. 31.13.2.

4. Germans charge, Amm. Marc. 16.12.42–45; shield wall (16.12.44), "nexamque scutorum compagem"; *barritus,* quoted 16.12.43; Roman formation, quoted 16.12.49, "densior et ordinibus frequens" (the exact sense here cannot be recovered, but soldiers in close order are clearly meant); 16.12.50, "temptabant agminis nostri laxare compagem." On these formations, see E. L. Wheeler, "The Legion as Phalanx," *Chiron* 9 (1979) pp. 303–18 at 315. Rout, quoted Amm. Marc. 16.12.57.

5. Shield wall, cf. Amm. Marc. 14.2.10, 29.5.48, 31.7.12. Sixth century, Maurice, *Strat.* 12.B.16; cf. Procop. *Bell.* 1.18.46; Syr. Mag. *de Strat.* 16 (Dennis). Archers and javelin-men in the back, Maurice, *Strat.* 12.A.7, B.12; cf. Syr. Mag. *de Strat.* 16, 35 (Dennis). For javelins thrown before the lines came together, Amm. Marc. 31.7.12; after contact, Amm. Marc. 16.12.43, 46. Vegetius (see below) describes a similar arrangement (3.14), but it is not clear to what period it applies or whether it is a mixture of different periods. Equipment, I. P. Stephenson, *Roman Infantry Equipment: The Later Empire* (Stroud, 1999) pp. 15–24, 52–75 (concentrating on the third century); P. Southern and K. R. Dixon, *The Late Roman Army* (New Haven, 1996) pp. 99–115. The archeological evidence is equivocal for the date of the change from *pilum* to thrusting spear (or, more exactly, the permanent division of Roman infantry into specialist spearmen and specialist javelineers, *lanciarii*). But Julius Africanus, *Kestoi* 1.1.55–56, 84 (Viellefond), criticizes the Romans for using their short javelin rather than the longer Greek spear, so the general change does not appear to have happened by his day (AD 231?).

6. Changes, M. J. Nicasie, *Twilight of Empire: The Roman Army from the Reign of Diocletian until the Battle of Adrianople* (Amsterdam, 1998) pp. 14–22,

43–74; names of weapons, Veg. *Mil.* 2.15; of ranks, A. H. M. Jones, *The Later Roman Empire* vol. 1 (Oxford, 1964) pp. 633–40.

7. *Testudo* as shield wall, Amm. Marc. 16.12.44, 29.5.48, 31.7.12; siege *testudo*, Amm. Marc. 20.11.8, 24.4.15; Cannae, Polyb. 3.113.3; *testudo*, Arr. *Tact.* 11.4–6. For this usage, see Wheeler, "Legion as Phalanx" p. 307. Shield wall in Jewish War, Joseph. *BJ* 4.33, 6.245.

8. Xenophon, Arr. *Ektaxis* 10, 22; terminology, A. B. Bosworth, "Arrian and Rome: The Minor Works," *Aufstieg und Niedergang der römischen Welt* 2.34.1 (1993) pp. 226–75 at 267; array and armament, Arr. *Ektaxis* 5–6, 15–17. The details of the array are obscure: see bibliographical note.

9. For interpretations of the *Deployment,* see the bibliographical note. *Discens phalang(arium)*, J. Ch. Balty, "Apamea in Syria in the Second and Third Centuries AD," *Journal of Roman Studies* 78 (1988) pp. 91–104 at 101. The phalangite is attested along with a *lanciarius,* a javelineer (J. Ch. Balty and W. Van Rengen, *Apamea in Syria. The Winter Quarters of Legio II Parthica,* trans. W. E. H. Cockle [Brussels, 1993] p. 25) and a *discens lanchiari(um),* a trainee javelineer (p. 26), who together with the phalanx trainee suggests the division of the infantry into front ranks of spearmen and rear ranks of javelin-throwers that appears in Arrian and the sixth-century Maurice (M. P. Speidel, "The Framework of an Imperial Legion," in R. J. Brewer [ed.], *The Second Augustan Legion and the Roman Military Machine* [Cardiff, 2002] pp. 125–43 at 130–32).

10. Arr. *Tact.* 34–44, with the costume described at 34.

11. J. Garbsch, *Römische Paraderüstungen* (Munich, 1978) nr. O40; cf. R. Mac-Mullen, "Inscriptions on Armor and the Supply of Arms in the Roman Empire," *American Journal of Archaeology* 64 (1960) pp. 23–40 at 36.

12. Julian, Zos. 3.3.5; Severus Alexander, Herodian 6.9.5. On attitudes toward effeminacy in the Roman army, see J. E. Lendon, *Empire of Honour* (Oxford, 1997) pp. 241–42.

13. Garbsch, *Paraderüstungen* nr. B21.

14. Arr. *Tact.* 36–38. Straubing, J. Keim and H. Klumback, *Der römische Schatzfund von Straubing* (Munich 1951). Greeks and Amazons, H. R. Robinson, *The Armour of Imperial Rome* (New York, 1975) pp. 108, 124 (this is controversial: see bibliographical note). Dura shield, C. Hopkins, F. E. Brown, R. J. Gettens, "The Painted Shields," in M. I. Rostovtzeff, F. E. Brown, and C. B. Welles (eds.), *The Excavations at Dura-Europos: Preliminary Report of the Seventh and Eighth Seasons of Work 1933–1934 and 1934–1935* (New Haven, 1939) pp. 326–69 at 349–63 with pls. xliv–v; the connection between the shield and the Straubing masks is made by M. Simkins, *The Roman Army from Hadrian to Constantine* (Oxford, 1979) p. 29.

15. Pseudo-Attic cavalry helmets, M. Junkelmann, *Römische Helme* (Mainz, 2000) esp. pp. 9–15, 87–90. Praetorian Guard, Robinson, *Armour* pp. 64–65. This is controversial: see bibliographical note.

16. Officers, Robinson, *Armour* pp. 136–39, 143, 147–52; G. Waurick, "Untersuchungen zur historisierenden Rüstung in der römischen Kunst," *Jahrbuch des römisch-germanischen Zentralmuseums Mainz* 30 (1983) pp. 265–301 at 277, 287–88, 300; M. Junkelmann, *Die Legionen des Augustus* (Mainz, 1986) p. 120.

17. Antiochus's "Macedonians," Joseph. *BJ* 5.460–65; "phalanx of Alexander," Suet. *Nero* 19.2; cf. Cass. Dio 55.24.2. For the history of the legion, M. Absil, *"Legio I Italica,"* in Y. Le Bohec (ed.), *Les Légions de Rome sous le Haut-Empire* vol. 1 (Lyon, 2000) pp. 227–38. Titus's cavalry changes: agreeing with J. J. Price, *Jerusalem Under Siege: The Collapse of the Jewish State 66–70 CE* (Leiden, 1992) p. 129 that, like his others, Titus's charges at Joseph. *BJ* 5.82, 5.90 and 5.486 will have been on horseback, although Josephus does not specify. Titus's Greek poetry and tragedy, *Suda* s.v. *Titos;* unarmored, compare Joseph. *BJ* 5.61 to Curt. 3.13.25 (the connection to Alexander is made by B. W. Jones, "The Reckless Titus," in C. Deroux [ed.], *Studies in Latin Literature and Roman History VI* [Brussels, 1992] pp. 408–20 at 414).

18. Alexander masks, Garbsch, *Paraderüstungen* pp. 23–24; M. Junkelmann, *Reiter wie Statuen aus Erz* (Mainz, 1996) pp. 38–41. For Hadrian's Wall as Greek revival, J. G. Crow, "The Function of Hadrian's Wall and the Comparative Evidence of Late Roman Long Walls," in [no ed.], *Studien zu den Militärgrenzen Roms III* (Stuttgart, 1986) pp. 724–29 at p. 725; for Greek walls, H. van Wees, *Greek Warfare: Myths and Realities* (London, 2004) p. 129; Isthmus wall, Hdt. 8.71, 9.8–9.

19. Caracalla, Cass. Dio 77(78 Loeb).7.1–2, 18.1; Herodian 4.8.2–3, 4.9.4–5; cf. Thuc.1.20.3; Hdt. 9.53. Severus Alexander, *SHA Alex.* 50.4–5.

20. On the contemporary material in Arrian, P. A. Stadter, "The *Ars Tactica* of Arrian: Tradition and Originality," *Classical Philology* 73 (1978) pp. 117–28 at 123–27. Frontinus, Aelian, *Tact. pr.* 3; Julius Africanus, *Kestoi,* 1.1.50–88 (Viellefond); praise of dedicatees, Polyaenus, *Strat. 5.pr.* Batavian War, Tac. *Hist.* 5.23; cf. Thuc. 2.13.1; Polyaenus, *Strat.* 1.36.2.

21. For modern scholarship, see bibliographical note; Scythians, Arr. *Ektaxis* 26, 31.

22. Names, letter forms, E. L. Bowie, "Greeks and Their Past in the Second Sophistic," *Past and Present* 46 (1970) pp. 3–41 at 31–35; Doric, S. Swain, *Hellenism and Empire* (Oxford, 1996) p. 74.

23. Vegetius, *Epitoma Rei Militaris* (= Veg. *Mil.*) 2.*pr.*, 3.*pr.*

24. Cavalry, Veg. *Mil.* 3.26.34; boats, 4.46; no argument, e.g., Veg. *Mil.* 2.18; *Georgics,* Veg. *Mil.* 1.6; cf. 1.5, 1.19, 2.1.

25. Cincinnatus, Veg. *Mil.* 1.3; cf. 3.*pr.*, 4.9, 4.20, 4.26. Scipio, Veg. *Mil.* 1.15; cf. 3.10, 3.24; Marius, Veg. *Mil.* 3.10; reserve, quoted Veg. *Mil.* 3.17.2.

26. No awareness of change: cf. Jul. Afr. *Kest.* 1.1 (Viellefond), who understands that Classical Greek, Macedonian, and Roman ways of fighting were different but sees no internal evolution in each. "Ancient legion," Veg. *Mil.* 2.15–17.

27. *Ala Celerum,* and discussing the revival of old Latin terms in the military, M. P. Speidel, *"Ala Celerum Philippiana," Tyche* 7 (1992) pp. 217–20; cf. Livy 1.15.8. *Triarii, CIL* 6.37281 and *AE* 1981.777 with Speidel, "Framework" p. 132. For the Latini and Sabini, *Not. Dig.* Oc. V.194–95 (Seeck). For other late-antique archaizing unit names, see M. P. Speidel, "The Four Earliest *Auxilia Palatina," Revue des études militaires anciennes* 1 (2004) pp. 137–50. Diocletian's legions, Veg. *Mil.* 1.17 with H. Elton, "Military Forces in the Later Roman Empire," in P. Sabin, H. van Wees, and M. Whitby (eds.), *Cambridge History of Greek and Roman Warfare* (Cambridge, forthcoming). On the sizes of late Roman military units, Nicasie, *Twilight of Empire* pp. 67–74.

28. Quoted, Jul. Afr. *Kest.* 1.1.1–4 (Viellefond); equipment, 1.1.8–9; revert, 1.1.83–88. Lineage taken for granted, Syr. Mag. *Strat.* 16.37–39 (Dennis); integrated, 15–16; and see C. Zuckerman, "The Military Compendium of Syrianus Magister," *Jahrbuch der österreichischen Byzantinistik* 40 (1990) pp. 209–24 at 217–19. For the sixth-century phalanx in use, Procop. *Bell.* 8.8.31–32, 8.29.17–22.

29. 230s, Jul. Afr. *Kest.* 1.1 (Viellefond). Early cohorts in Livy, M. J. V. Bell, "Tactical Reform in the Roman Republican Army," *Historia* 14 (1965) pp. 404–22 gathers the references. Greek methods past, Aelian, *Tact. pr.;* Arr. *Tact.* 32.2–3.

30. Philo: walls thick, *Bel.* 1.11; flanking fire, 1.3; ramming difficult, 1.2–4; windows, 1.20–21. Roman awareness of Hellenistic science, Vitr. 1.5.2–8; Veg. *Mil.* 4.1–2; Roman fortifications, J. Lander, *Roman Stone Fortifications* (BAR Int. Ser. 206; Oxford, 1984), with a vast number of illustrations, and p. 11 on Greek influence evident on city fortifications under Augustus (which may have been largely ornamental). Late third century and after, S. Johnson, *Late Roman Fortifications* (Totowa, N.J., 1983), wall thickness, p. 37; towers, pp. 38–40; artillery, p. 79; diversity of design, pp. 259–60; for suggestion of Hellenistic origins, p. 10; cf. on late third- and fourth-century towers, Lander, *Roman Stone Fortifications* pp. 198–255; use with artillery, pp. 258–59; diversity of design, pp. 252–57.

31. Syr. Mag. *Strat.* 16.52 (Dennis).

32. Small barbarian influence, Nicasie, *Twilight of Empire* pp. 107–16; decorations too, see chap. 13 n. 19. Beginnings of Roman cataphracts, M. Mielczarek, Cataphracti *and* Clibanarii (Lodz, 1993) p. 32. Warship, [Anon.] *de Rebus Bellicis* 17; cf. 15.1; chariots, 12–14. First known cataphract unit, the *Ala Gal-*

lorum et Pannoniorum Cataphractaria, J. Spaul, *Ala²* (Andover, 1994) pp. 82–84, with *CIL* 11.5632 for the date and commander, with stress on his relationship to the emperor.

Chapter XIII. Julian in Persia, AD 363

1. Amm. Marc. 23.3.6 with den Boeft *Comm. XXIII* (= J. den Boeft et al., *Philological and Historical Commentary on Ammianus Marcellinus XXIII* [Groningen, 1998]) p. 46, with p. 156 on the state of Babylon.

2. "Hostes . . . meliores," Amm. Marc. 22.7.8, cf. 22.12.1–5, 23.5.4–5, 25.4.23. On Julian's attitude toward Persia, Julian. *Or.* 1.17C-18B, 28B-D, 2.63A-B with A. Marcone, "Il significato della spedizione di Giuliano contro la Persia," *Athenaeum* 67 (1979) pp. 334–56 at 338–39.

3. March, Amm. Marc. 23.3.6, 9; cf. Zos. 3.13.2; Julian. *Ep.* 98.402B (Bidez=nr. 58 in Wright's Loeb ed.). Like Pyrrhus, Amm. Marc. 24.1.3 (and Caesar, see p. 214); cf. Amm. Marc. 27.2.5; for the tactical manual, Aelian, *Tact.* 1.2; Cic. *Fam.* 9.25.1; Plut. *Pyrrh.* 8.2; Frontin. *Strat.* 2.6.10. Like Alexander, Amm. Marc. 21.8.3. F. J. Lomas Salmonte, "Lectura helénica de las *Res Gestae Iuliani* de Amiano Marcelino a la sombra de Alejandro Magno," in J. M. Croisille (ed.), *Neronia IV: Alejandro Magno, modelo de los emperadores romanos* (Brussels, 1990) pp. 306–27 at 321–26 collects other possible instances of Julian's imitation of Alexander.

4. Amm. Marc. 24.1.5–16; Zos. 3.14.1–4.

5. Amm. Marc. 24.2.1–8; Zos. 3.15–17.2; bridging boats, cf. Amm. Marc. 23.3.9.

6. Amm. Marc. 24.2.9–14; Zos. 3.17.3–18.2; cf. Lib. *Or.* 18.227–28.

7. Amm. Marc. 24.2.14–17 with den Boeft *Comm. XXIV* (= J. den Boeft et al., *Philological and Historical Commentary on Ammianus Marcellinus XXIV* [Leiden, 2002]) p. 60.

8. Amm. Marc. 24.1.2, "usu et docilitate firmatus," with *Comm. XXIV* p. 5 on *docilitate*. On Julian's education, Lib. *Or.* 18.12–21; Amm. Marc. 16.5.6–7; cf. 17.11.1.

9. Amm. Marc. 25.4.11, "castrensium negotiorum scientiam"; cf. 25.4.1, 25.4.7.

10. Julian as author of manual, Lydus, *Mag.* 47; carries books, Julian. *Or.* 3.124A–D; Lib. *Or.* 18.72; cf. 18.53; canal, 18.245–47; Crassus, 18.233.

11. Quoted Julian. *Or.* 3.124B–C. For Julian on imitation of *exempla*, cf. *Or.* 3.104A–106B; *Epist. ad Them.* 253A–54B; *Caes.* 333C–4D.

12. Quoted, Amm. Marc. 23.5.21, "antiquitatum peritus," in a speech 23.5.16–23 (cf. 24.3.5), in which Ammianus characterizes Julian by having him mention Lucullus, Pompey, Antony, Antony's lieutenant Ventidius, the Curtii, Mucii and Decii, Numantia, Fidenae, Veii, and Falerii. Julian is the only figure in

Ammianus to use ancient *exempla* in his speeches (R. Blockley, "Ammianus Marcellinus's Use of *Exempla*," *Florilegium* 13 [1994] pp. 53–64 at 57). For ancient learning in Julian's own writing, e.g., *Or.* 1–7 *passim,* and for an exhaustive survey, see J. Bouffartigue, *L'Empereur Julien et la culture de son temps* (Paris, 1992). Quoted, Polyaenus, *Strat.* 5.*pr.* Oaths, quoted Amm. Marc. 24.3.9; *ephodion,* Julian. *Or.* 3.124B and Plut. *Alex.* 8.2.

13. Amm. Marc. 24.2.18–19, "molem ingentem, superaturam celsarum turrium minas"; Zos. 3.18.3 also describes the height of Julian's *helepolis.* For the term *helepolis* used to describe a low ram, Joseph. *BJ* 3.121, 3.230–32; Amm. Marc. 23.4.10–13 (the excursus on siege engines, with den Boeft *Comm. XXIII* p. 57, 72–78; but Ammianus also associates this low *helepolis* with Demetrius; den Boeft *Comm. XXIV* p. 63 notes that the Pirisabora *helepolis* does not correspond with the *helepolis* in the excursus). For the *helepoleis* of Demetrius, see Diod. Sic. 20.48, 91; Plut. *Demetr.* 21.1–2; Vitr. 10.16.4 with E. W. Marsden, *Greek and Roman Artillery: Technical Treatises* (Oxford, 1971) pp. 84–90. Surrender, Amm. Marc. 24.2.19–22; Zos. 3.18.3–6.

14. Amm. Marc. 24.3.1–2 with den Boeft *Comm. XXIV* pp. 73–75; cf. Zos. 3.19.1–2; Lib. *Or.* 18.229–30. It is also possible that Julian knew the true meaning of decimation but feared the reaction of his army to his executing so many soldiers. Julian was not the last to try to revive decimation: Maurice, *Strat.* 1.8.17 (for which I thank P. Rance).

15. Amm. Marc. 24.3.3–4.1; Zos. 3.19.3–4; cf. Lib. *Or.* 18.223–27. The problems with the exact route of Julian's march are intractable; I use the reconstruction of den Boeft *Comm. XXIV* pp. 42–46, following J. Matthews, *The Roman Empire of Ammianus* (Baltimore, 1989) pp. 149–51.

16. For the spelling "Maozamalcha," see den Boeft *Comm. XXIV* p. 102. Ambush, Amm. Marc. 24.4.2–4. Compare to Zos. 3.20.2–3; Libanius (*Or.* 18.236) does not know the killing either, but he mentions the episode only in passing. Ammianus's own comparisons, e.g., 16.12.41, 21.9.2, 25.2.3, 25.3.8; cf. 24.6.7, 25.1.15, 29.5.22, 29.5.32. For Ammianus's use of archaic military vocabulary, see, e.g., 24.1.13, 24.6.8–9, the latter with den Boeft *Comm. XXIV* p. 185.

17. Naked, Amm. Marc. 24.8.1 with den Boeft *Comm. XXIV* p. 224; cf. Frontin. *Strat.* 1.11.17; Polyaenus, *Strat.* 2.1.6; Maurice, *Strat.* 7.A.5; cf. Onasander, *Strat.* 14.3. Games, Lib. *Or.* 1.133, 18.249–50, with den Boeft *Comm. XXIV* pp. 174–75. Libanius's misstatement at *Or.* 24.37, that the games were held outside the walls of Babylon, may allude to this Alexander connection: Alexander was planning gigantic funeral games at Babylon for Hephaestion when Alexander died, and the games were given for him instead (Arr. *Anab.* 7.14.10). Julian's beard, Amm. Marc. 25.4.22; Julian. *Mis.* 338B–39A.

18. Assault, Amm. Marc. 24.4.10–20; Zos. 3.21.1–22.2; cf. Lib. *Or.* 18.235–37.

Mine, Amm. Marc. 24.4.21–3 with den Boeft *Comm. XXIV* pp. 130–33. Zos. 3.22.3–4 gives the name of the first soldier to emerge as Superantius. Cf. Lib. *Or.* 18.238–39. Rushed, Zos. 3.22.5–6; Lib. *Or.* 18.239.

19. Amm. Marc. 24.4.24; cf. Val. Max. 1.8.6 for Fabricius. Siege crowns, V. Maxfield, *The Military Decorations of the Roman Army* (Berkeley and Los Angeles, 1981) pp. 68–69, 251. Even as a historical reconstruction, the award was in error (like Julian's misunderstanding of decimation): in the Republic the *corona obsidionalis,* which Julian here presents, correctly went to a general who broke a siege; it was the *corona muralis* that went to the soldier who first mounted a wall (den Boeft *Comm. XXIV* pp. 135–37). The whole system of crowns as decorations had gone out of use by the early third century AD (Maxfield, *Decorations* pp. 248–50), by which time the significance of the crowns had quite changed anyway (p. 64). It was replaced by a new system of "barbarian *chic*" decorations, torques (now worn around the neck, unlike the earlier decorations, which were hung from the cuirass) and wristbands and embroidered clothes (M. P. Speidel, "Late Roman Military Decorations I: Neck- and Wristbands" and "— II: Gold-Embroidered Capes and Tunics," *Antiquité Tardive* 4 [1996] pp. 235–43 and 5 [1997] pp. 231–37), which Julian here passes over, preferring to revive the ancient decorations.

20. Amm. Marc. 24.4.25–27 with den Boeft *Comm. XXIV* pp. 141–42, who gathers the references on Alexander and Scipio. Bagoas, Curt. 6.5.23. On the sack, Zos. 3.22.6–7; Lib. *Or.* 18.240–41.

21. Visit, Amm. Marc. 24.5.1–4; Zos. 3.23.1; cf. Lib. *Or.* 18.243. For Julian's interest in Carus's campaign, Julian. *Or.* 1.18A. The army also noted in passing the tomb of Gordian (Amm. Marc. 23.5.7, 17; Zos. 3.14.2) and the so-called tribunal of Trajan (Amm. Marc. 24.2.3; Zos. 3.15.3). Julian's account, *Ep.* 98 (Bidez=nr. 58 in Wright's Loeb ed.): an old camp, an oddly made road, an acropolis.

22. Amm. Marc. 24.5.5–12; Zos. 3.24.1.

23. Canal, Amm. Marc. 24.6.1–2 with den Boeft *Comm. XXIV* pp. 171–72; Zos. 3.24.2; Lib. *Or.* 18.245–47; Sozom. *Hist. eccl.* 6.1. Games, Lib. *Or.* 18.248–50, with n. 17 above. Landing, Amm. Marc. 24.6.4–7; Zos. 3.25.1–4; cf. Lib. *Or.* 18.250–54.

24. For the chronology, den Boeft *Comm. XXIV* p. xxiii. Libanius remarks on this passivity, *Or.* 18.243, as does Gregory Nazianzus *Or.* 5.9. Success of the Tigris feint: *Epitome* of Magnus in Malalas (*FGH* 225 F 1.9). The force left on the Tigris, Amm. Marc. 23.3.5 (thirty thousand men); Zos. 3.12.4–5 (eighteen thousand); Lib. *Or.* 18.214–15 (twenty thousand); Magnus (*FGH* 225 F 1.3) (sixteen thousand). Long to assemble, Lydus, *Mag.* 3.34; early in year, Lib. *Or.* 18.214; cf. Greg. Naz. *Or.* 5.9; Socrates, *Hist. eccl.* 3.21.

25. Amm. Marc. 24.6.8–9 with den Boeft *Comm. XXIV* pp. 186–87; cf. *Il.* 4.297–300; classical, Xen. *Mem.* 3.1.7–8; Pyrrhus, Frontin. *Strat.* 2.3.21; rhetoric, Quint. *Inst.* 5.12.14. For Julian's close familiarity with the military passages of the *Iliad*, Julian. *Or. 2 passim*.

26. Battle, Amm. Marc. 24.6.10–13; cf. Zos. 3.25.5; Lib. *Or.* 18.254–55. Losses and crowns, Amm. Marc. 24.6.15–16 (with den Boeft *Comm. XXIV* pp. 196–97), and once again Julian was somewhat muddled: the *corona civica,* which the emperor granted, was not properly given by a commander but (even under the empire) by a fellow soldier: Maxfield, *Decorations* p. 64. For the casualties, cf. Zos. 3.25.7.

27. Decision not to attack Ctesiphon, Amm. Marc. 24.7.1–2 (Greg. Naz. *Or.* 5.10 describes the defenses of Ctesiphon). Offers of treaty, Lib. *Or.* 18.257–59; cf. 1.133, 30.41; Socrates *Hist. eccl.* 3.21. Into interior, Amm. Marc. 24.7.3; Zos. 3.26.2 with den Boeft *Comm. XXIV* pp. 208–11. Boats burned, Amm. Marc. 24.7.4; Zos. 3.26.2–3, and den Boeft *Comm. XXIV* pp. 212–13 for other references.

28. Justification, Lib. *Or.* 18.262–63. As later events showed, boats could indeed be towed upstream, albeit slowly, Zos. 3.28.2. There was also a tradition, mostly Christian (but see also Amm. Marc. 24.7.5), that Julian had been tricked into burning the boats by false Persian deserters; den Boeft *Comm. XXIV* p. 212 gathers the references. Alarmed at decision, Amm. Marc. 24.7.4; cf. 24.7.8; Zos. 3.28.3; cf. Greg. Naz. *Or.* 5.12. For modern discussions of the burning of the fleet, den Boeft *Comm. XXIV* pp. 212–15.

29. Lib. *Or.* 18.260 (with den Boeft *Comm. XXIV* p. 208–9); but Libanius's other explanations for the march, that he was marching toward Arbela, the field of Gaugamela, where Alexander had defeated Darius in 331 BC, and that he was touring the Persian empire, are probably not to be credited: one gets to Arbela by marching along the Tigris, not by striking inland. Sapor's army to the north, Amm. Marc. 25.1.1. Forts, Amm. Marc. 24.2.1–2; Zos. 3.15.1–2. There is also the story (Amm. Marc. 23.3.5, 24.7.8, 24.8.6; Zos. 4.4.2; Lib. *Or.* 18.260) that Julian hoped to make a junction with a second Roman force —that which had pinned Sapor in the north—which was supposed to have made a more northerly invasion of the Persian empire, a second thrust that never developed (Lib. *Or.* 18.214–15, 260). I suspect that this is an apologetic tradition intended to place the blame for the failure of the expedition on the commanders of that northern force.

30. Alexander, Arr. *Anab.* 1.20.1; Diod. Sic. 17.22.5; Agathocles, Diod. Sic. 17.23.2–3, 20.7.5; stratagem tradition, Polyaenus, *Strat.* 5.3.5; Verg. *Aen.* 5.604–63; but the legend goes back to Hellanicus (fifth century BC) and was

known to Aristotle: Dion. Hal. 1.72.2–4; Plut. *Mor.* 265B-C. Did that mythical burning inspire Agathocles?

31. On the Persian strategy, Greg. Naz. *Or.* 5.10; fire, Amm. Marc. 24.7.7–8; Julian's stratagem, Amm. Marc. 24.8.1 with den Boeft *Comm. XXIV* pp. 223–24; debate and march, Amm. Marc. 24.8.2–7; Zos. 3.26.3–4.

32. Maurus and Macameus, Amm. Marc. 25.1.1–2; Zos. 3.26.5; heroic leadership, e.g., Amm. Marc. 15.4.10, 21.3.3, 31.8.9–10; cf. 27.10.12. On Julian's aggressive behavior in battle, Amm. Marc. 25.4.10. Men and tribunes, Amm. Marc. 16.12.63; cf. 31.5.9 (for suggestions as to the sizes of fourth-century units, H. Elton, "Military Forces in the Later Roman Empire," in P. Sabin, H. van Wees, and M. Whitby [eds.], *The Cambridge History of Greek and Roman Warfare* [Cambridge, forthcoming]); Constantius, Amm. Marc. 21.16.7; cf. Julian. *Or.* 2.53A–C. Sixth-century single combat by challenge, Procop. *Bell.* 1.13.29–38, 4.13.11–17, 4.24.10–12, 7.4.21–30, 8.31.11–16, 8.35.11; cf. 1.18.31 and esp. 7.23.2; single combat in the course of wider combat, 1.14.45–50, 1.18.38, 2.3.25, 5.18.29, 5.29.20–21, 6.1.20, 6.1.23, 8.8.25–27; heroic leadership in general, 1.15.15–16, 2.26.26–27, 4.11.50–53, 5.7.5, 5.18.4, 5.18.10–15, 6.2.20–24, 6.5.18–19, 6.10.19–20, 7.19.22–6, 7.37.28, 8.8.38, 8.11.57–8, 8.11.64. Justinian's general, 8.11.40–51.

33. Amm. Marc. 25.3.14; Zos. 3.29.3. *Notarii*, shorthand writers, were not mere stenographers but had come to be important officials with varied duties, sometimes including diplomacy and espionage.

34. Julian praises Constantius for his fighting and arraying in explicitly Homeric terms: *Or.* 2.52D–53D. Secret code, quoted Amm. Marc. 18.6.17–19; Granicus, of course, refers to Alexander; Rhyndacus to the war of Lucullus against Mithridates. On this message (and the learned common culture which made it possible), see F. Trombley, "Ammianus Marcellinus and Fourth-Century Warfare," in J. W. Drijvers and D. Hunt (eds.), *The Late Roman World and its Historian* (London, 1999) pp. 17–28 at 21–22. For style, compare a military letter of appointment from Julian. *Ep.* 152 (Bidez=nr. 11 in Wright's Loeb ed.)

35. Amm. Marc. 25.1.3–2.1; Zos. 3.27–28.3; for Marathon, Hdt. 6.111–13, Just. *Epit.* 2.9.11. Running at archers had become a well-known stratagem, Frontin. *Strat.* 2.2.5; Jul. Afr. *Kest.* 1.1.83–86, and cf. Plut. *Luc.* 28.1, and was used elsewhere on Julian's Persian campaign: Amm. Marc. 24.2.5, 24.6.11. For the crescent formation, cf. 16.2.13. And it is hardly impossible that other ancient double envelopments — Cannae and Ilipa — were also inspired by this story of Marathon.

36. Amm. Marc. 25.3.1–7; Zos. 3.28.4–29.1; cf. Lib. *Or.* 18.268–69. Was he

imitating Alexander, again, in not wearing his armor? Cf. Titus (above, p. 279). Soul, Amm. Marc. 25.3.23; cf. Lib. *Or.* 18.272.

37. Amm. Marc. 25.5.1–6.15, 25.7.4; Zos. 3.30.

38. Terms, Amm. Marc. 25.7.5–12; Zos. 3.31; cf. Lib. *Or.* 18.277–78; return, Amm. Marc. 25.7.14–8.7, 15–17; Zos. 3.33.1–2; cf. Lib. *Or.* 18.280.

39. Battle lost, see Amm. Marc. 31.5.9, inconclusive, 31.7.10–16. For the Adrianople campaign, M. J. Nicasie, *Twilight of Empire: The Roman Army from the Reign of Diocletian until the Battle of Adrianople* (Amsterdam, 1998) pp. 233–56. Goths, Amm. Marc. 31.8.1, 4–5, 31.10.21, 31.11.2–5; Zos. 4.22.2–3, 4.23.4–6, 4.24.1; on siegecraft, cf. Amm. Marc. 31.6.4. Sebastianus, Zos. 4.23.6.

40. Valens, Amm. Marc. 31.11.6, 31.12.1, 6–7; Zos. 4.24.2–4; cf. Trebia, Polyb. 3.70.7–8.

41. Amm. Marc. 31.12.14–17, 31.13.12.

42. For Roman strategic aggressiveness, the insight is that of A. Goldsworthy, *The Roman Army at War 100 BC–AD 200* (Oxford, 1996) esp. pp. 114–15 and id., "'Instinctive Genius:' The Depiction of Caesar the General," in K. Welch and A. Powell (eds.), *Julius Caesar as Artful Reporter* (London, 1998) pp. 193–219 at 196–201 (collecting advocates of caution, p. 196). Titus, quoted Joseph. *BJ* 5.498.

43. Fountain, Plut. *Pyrrh.* 21.10; Strasbourg, Amm. Marc. 16.12.2; versus 35,000 Alamanni, itself an exceptionally large number (16.12.26). Firmus, Amm. Marc. 29.5.29; Adrianople (an estimate), Nicasie, *Twilight of Empire* p. 246. Eastern army of Julian, Zos. 3.13.1, and much of it may not have accompanied Julian down the Euphrates, Amm. Marc. 23.3.5. The other very large fourth-century figures also come from Zosimus (AD 312, 98,000 vs. 188,000 [2.15.1–2]; AD 324, 130,000 vs. 165,000 [2.22.1–2]; AD 324, 130,000 [2.26.3]; exception: AD 398, 70,000 [Oros. 7.36.12]; see Nicasie, *Twilight of Empire* pp. 204–5) and should probably be likewise sharply reduced. For army sizes, see bibliographical note.

44. For institutional problems, see bibliographical note. For resistance to moving, Amm. Marc. 20.4.4, 10, 31.7.4. High quality of the mid-fourth-century army: this is the growing consensus of contemporary students, e.g., Nicasie, *Twilight of Empire* pp. 10, 261–64; P. Rance, "Combat in the Later Roman Empire," in P. Sabin, H. van Wees, and M. Whitby (eds.), *Cambridge History of Greek and Roman Warfare* (Cambridge, forthcoming).

The Romans, Conclusion

1. Procop. *Bell.* 1.1.

2. Concisely on *aemulatio*, T. G. Rosenmeyer, "Ancient Literary Genres: A Mi-

rage?" *Yearbook of Comparative and General Literature* 34 (1985) pp. 74–84 at 81–82.

3. Hes. *Op.* 11–25; cf. *Theog.* 224–31.

4. Greeks noticed exceptional Spartan competitiveness, Xen. *Lac.* 4.2; Pl. *Resp.* 545A; Plut. *Lyc.* 25.3; *Ages.* 5.3; unlike the rest of the southern Greeks, young Spartans fought duels, Xen. *An.* 4.8.25; Plut. *Mor.* 233F–4A, 240E–F. On Macedonian dueling, see pp. 128–29.

GLOSSARY

<hr>

Achaeans: Homeric term for the Greeks who came against Troy; also called Argives.

agathos: Homeric status term meaning at once brave, strong, highborn, and rich. Later Greek emphasized the sense of bravery. *Esthlos* is a synonym.

ala: under the Roman empire, a unit of auxiliary cavalry.

andreia: lit. "manliness." Greek for courage, a competitive excellence (*aretē* [see below]).

apobates: lit. "dismounter." Greek sport involving leaping on and off a moving chariot while wearing hoplite armor.

Archaic Greece: period of Greek history from c. 800 to 500 BC.

aretē (pl. *aretai*): Greek competitive excellence. In Homer these include bravery, strength, skill with weapons, fleetness of foot, persuasiveness in council, and *metis*, cunning intelligence. Can also simply mean courage, when used as a synonym for *andreia* (see above).

auxiliaries (*auxilia*): under the Roman empire, soldiers recruited from noncitizens. They formed infantry cohorts or cavalry *alae* rather than legions (which were made up of citizens).

cataphract: heavy cavalryman, both man and horse armored, armed with a long thrusting spear.

century (*centuria*): the elementary subunit of the Roman army, consisting originally (presumably) of 100 men in the day of the Roman phalanx, of c. 60 in the time of the manipular legion, and c. 80 in the time of the legion of cohorts. Commanded by a centurion.

Classical Greece: period of Greek history from c. 500 to 323 BC.

cohort (*cohors*): the major subunit of the late Republican and early imperial legion of cohorts. In Caesar's day, a unit of c. 480 men (made up of six c. 80-man centuries) (see figure, p. 225).

consul: the supreme magistrate of the Roman Republic, whose chief duties were military leadership and cult. Two were elected each year and under the mid-Republic the consuls had charge of Rome's most important wars. A consul's command might be extended past his year of office — as a proconsul.

disciplina: basic military value of the Romans (parallel to and conceived in opposition to *virtus* [see below]). The concept incorporated "discipline" as imposed by leaders, but also competitive self-discipline: competition in obedience, training, and laboring.

ephebe: young Greek male citizen undergoing military training. At Athens c. 335 BC two years of training and service were made compulsory. The institution was called the *ephebeia*.

gladius: sword (more fully, *gladius hispaniensis* — Spanish sword). The Roman legionary shortsword (see figures, pp. 180, 246).

greaves: armor for the lower legs (see figure, p. 54).

hastati: the first formed echelon of the Roman manipular legion: armed with sword, *scutum* (see below), and *pila* (see below) (see figures, pp. 179–80).

Hellenistic: period of Greek history from the death of Alexander (323 BC) to the final Roman conquest of Ptolemaic Egypt (31 BC).

helots: the subservient population of Sparta, sometimes described as serfs or state slaves, who greatly outnumbered their citizen masters.

hoplite: Greek heavy infantryman armed with a spear, large round shield (*aspis,* sometimes wrongly called a *hoplon*), and helmet, often also a breastplate and greaves. See figures, pp. 54, 64. Usually fights in the phalanx (see below).

hoplomachoi: professional teachers of hoplite drill and tactics, who appeared in Greece around the end of the fifth century BC.

horseguard (*agema*): lit. "vanguard." Elite cavalry unit in the army of

Alexander the Great and his successors that rode and fought with the commander.

kakos: Homeric status term meaning at once lowborn, poor, weak, and cowardly: later Greek emphasized the sense of cowardly.

maniple (*manipulus*): the major subunit of the mid-Republican manipular legion, consisting of two centuries (see above) of *hastati* or *principes* (see above and below)(c. 120 men) or two half-strength centuries of *triarii* (see below)(60 men). Maniples formed on the battlefield with gaps between them to allow troops to withdraw or advance (see figure, p. 179).

metis: a form of competitive Greek cunning intelligence. A Homeric *aretē* (see above) also practiced by later Greek commanders.

panoply: a full set of hoplite armor with shield.

peltast: Greek light infantryman, usually armed with a small shield (*pelte*), originally crescent-shaped, and javelins or a longer spear (see figures, pp. 95, 97).

phalanx: a block of hoplites, usually eight or more men deep (see figures, pp. 42–43).

pilum (pl. *pila*): Roman legionary javelin; heavy to maximize impact and used at short range (see figure, p. 180).

principes: the second formed echelon of the Roman manipular legion: armed with sword, *scutum* (see below), and *pila* (see above) (see figures, pp. 179–80).

sarissa: the long Macedonian pike, used two-handed (see figures, pp. 122–23).

scutum: long, convex (sometimes even half-cylindrical) Roman shield: oval under the Republic, and increasingly rectangular as used by legionaries under the empire (see figures, pp. 180, 226).

Shield Bearers (*hypaspists*): elite infantry unit in the phalanx of Alexander the Great and his successors.

sophrosyne: the Greek excellence (*aretē* [see above]) of self-control, a Spartan specialty.

taxis: position of an individual in a hoplite formation (by extension the position of a unit or army on the field — hence "tactics").

techne (pl. *technai*): Greek for a manual craft or (later) an intellectual art. Originally déclassé in contrast to heroic *aretē* (see above).

throwing engine: a general term used in this book for ancient twisted-cord-powered (torsion) artillery, whether employing one torsion coil and an "overhand" motion (sometimes called a catapult by moderns) or projecting a missile from between two coils (sometimes called a ballista by moderns). The ancient terminology—*ballista, catapulta, scorpio, onager, oxybeles,* and others—was used with mischievous inconsistency.

triarii: the third formed echelon of the Roman manipular legion, who formed a phalanx and were armed with sword, *scutum* (see above), and a thrusting spear. The oldest soldiers in the legion (see figures, pp. 179–80).

tribune of the soldiers (or military tribune, *tribunus militum*): Roman aristocratic officer. Six were assigned to each legion. By the fourth century AD tribune had become instead the usual term for a unit commander. Not to be confused with a tribune of the people (*tribunus plebis*), a political office of the Republic and early empire.

trireme: the predominant Greek warship of the fifth century BC. A ramming galley with three banks of oars and c. 170 rowers.

tropē: the mass turning to flight of a phalanx in a hoplite battle, celebrated by the victors by the erection of a trophy.

velites: young or poor warriors who fought in an irregular, dueling style in front of the manipular legion; armed with a small shield, sword, and light javelins. Some wore wolfskins on their heads or other distinguishing marks (see figures, pp. 179–80).

virtus: lit. "manliness." A basic Roman military value (along with *disciplina* [see above]). The aggressive courage that Romans proved by seeking out single combat.

BIBLIOGRAPHICAL NOTES

It has seemed best to confine the numbered endnotes to (a) citations of ancient evidence, (b) modern works that collect bodies of ancient evidence, are necessary to interpret or understand the ancient evidence, or are cited on matters of fact, and (c) modern works quoted in the text and the author's most urgent intellectual debts. Reserved for the bibliographical notes to each chapter are brief general introductions to the relevant ancient sources, guidance as to where the reader can go to follow the various topics further in the modern scholarship, and, where they may be necessary to the argument in the text, more extended discussions of modern writings and scholarly controversies. In both the endnotes and the bibliographical notes the author has been ruthlessly selective (and has tried to cite works in English wherever possible), and has denied himself altogether the academic pleasure of citing items merely because they are obscure.

Introduction

In the "cultural" study of war — grounded in the belief that the ways and ideals of the combatants, rather than a purely internal military logic, often better explain how war is fought — I follow a growing body of work, of which I admire especially R. L. O'Connell, *Sacred Vessels* (Boulder, Colo., 1991), and E. C. Kiesling, *Arming Against Hitler* (Lawrence, Kan., 1996). The recent pace-setter of this movement is J. A. Lynn's *Battle: A History of Combat and Culture* (Boulder, Colo., 2003), with an especially illuminating theoretical appendix (pp. 331–41) on the mutual feedback between cultural ideals and the realities of war.

For general introductions to warfare in both Greek and Roman antiquity, see J. Warry, *Warfare in the Classical World* (Norman, Okla., 1995), and P. Connolly, *Greece and Rome at War*[2] (London, 1998), both lavishly illustrated. Osprey (Oxford, now London) publishes many short volumes on Greek and Roman military topics: those authored by N. V. Sekunda are invaluable. For details of equipment, note also an excellent collection of illustrations of sculpted weapons reliefs, E. Polito, *Fulgentibus Armis: Introduzione allo studio dei fregi d'armi antichi* (Rome, 1998). A useful resource, giving the ancient citations for each battle up to 31 BC, is J. D. Montagu, *Battles of the Greek and Roman Worlds* (London, 2000).

A guide to the great volume of German work on ancient military history in the late nineteenth and early twentieth centuries is J. Kromeyer and G. Veith, *Heerwesen und Kriegführung der Griechen und Römer* (= I. von Müller and W. Otto [eds.], *Handbuch der Altertumswissenschaft* 4.3.2 [Munich, 1928]). Frustratingly perverse but a forefather to the present work in its interest in treating the evolution of tactics as a historical problem, seeking reasons for change, and relating military forms to the wider world of the combatants, is H. Delbrück, *Geschichte der Kriegskunst in Rahmen der politischen Geschichte*[3] vols. 1–2 (Berlin, 1920), translated by W. J. Renfroe as *History of the Art of War*, vol. 1, *Warfare in Antiquity*, and vol. 2, *The Barbarian Invasions* (Lincoln, Neb., 1990). On Delbrück (with insight into his perversity), see G. A. Craig, "Delbrück: The Military Historian," in P. Paret (ed.), *Makers of Modern Strategy* (Princeton, 1986) pp. 326–53.

For a more conventional account of ancient military evolution, stressing internal military logic rather than cultural influences, see G. Brizzi, *Il guerriero, l'oplita, il legionario* (Bologna, 2002), translated into French as *Le Guerrier de l'antiquité classique* (Monaco, 2004). Brizzi's extensive bibliographical notes complement mine and are especially full on non-English scholarship.

For a broader history of Greco-Roman technology, a dip can be taken into J. W. Humphrey, J. P. Oleson, and A. N. Sherwood, *Greek and Roman Technology: A Sourcebook* (London, 1995), or a long bath in B. Meissner, *Die technologische Fachliteratur der Antike* (Berlin, 1999), with M. D. Reeve's notice in *Classical Review* 53 (2003) pp. 331–4, updating the literature.

There was a scholarly controversy through many decades of the nineteenth and twentieth centuries about whether the Greeks and Romans even had a recognizable idea of progress. The Ayes have it (see L. Edelstein, *The Idea of Progress in Classical Antiquity* [Baltimore, 1967], who summarizes the literature, pp. xi–xxxiii). But there was continual conflict in ancient thinking between a forward-looking, technological, improvement-oriented conception of human history and a backward-looking, decline-oriented conception (E. R. Dodds, "The Ancient Concept of Progress," in id., *The Ancient Concept of Progress and Other Essays on Greek Literature and Belief* [Oxford, 1973] pp. 1–25, with more literature; on this conflict in Greek thought, see especially E. A. Havelock, *The Liberal Temper in Greek Politics* [New Haven, 1957] pp. 36–124). In philosophical circles the idea of progress lost ground after the fifth century BC, and in everyday thinking it was always far weaker (especially at Rome) than past-mindedness.

The Greeks

For the evolution of Greek military practice, see the useful narrative of A. Ferrill, *The Origins of War* (Boulder, Colo., 1997), admirable in its interest in the causes of change; the present book may, however, make the reader wonder about Ferrill's tendency to attribute changes in Greek military practice to eastern influence. Beautifully illustrated is V. D. Hanson, *The Wars of the Ancient Greeks* (London, 1999); but the present book may provoke the reader to question Hanson's agrarian theory of the evolution of Greek warfare, most fully presented in *The Other Greeks* (New York, 1995) pp. 221–335 (discussed below, pp. 407–8). Also with good illustrations are P. Ducrey, *Warfare in Ancient Greece* (New York, 1986; trans. J. Lloyd from *Guerre et guerriers dans la Grèce antique* [Paris, 1985]), and N. V. Sekunda, "Classical Warfare," in J. Boardman (ed.), *The Cambridge Ancient History² Plates to Volumes V and VI* (Cambridge, 1994) pp. 167–94, a concise and perceptive account, stressing economic and institutional barriers to Greek military evolution.

On a multitude of detailed points about Greek warfare, W. K. Pritchett, *The Greek State at War*, 5 vols. (Berkeley and Los Angeles, 1971–91) gathers the ancient references. For an up-to-date survey of the scholarship and its controversies, see H. van Wees, *Greek Warfare: Myths and Realities* (London, 2004): I rely heavily on the ideas of van Wees in this book and in the articles that have led up to it. For *catalogues raisonées* of the enormous scholarship about Greek warfare, see R. Lonis, "La Guerre en Grèce. Quinze années de recherche: 1968–1983," *Revue des études grecques* 98 (1985) pp. 321–79, P. Ducrey, "Aspects de l'histoire de la guerre en Grèce ancienne, 1945–96," in P. Brulé and J. Oulhen (eds.), *Esclavage, guerre, économie en Grèce ancienne. Hommages à Yvon Garlan* (Rennes, 1997) pp. 123–38, and K.-J. Hölkeskamp, "La guerra e la pace," in S. Settis et al. (eds.), *I Greci* vol. 2.2 (Turin, 1997) pp. 481–539.

On Mycenean warfare, see R. Drews, *The End of the Bronze Age* (Princeton, 1993). Gathering and discussing the evidence on the Lelantine War is V. Parker, *Untersuchungen zum lelantischen Krieg und verwandten Problemen der frühgriechischen Geschichte* (Stuttgart, 1997). On the archeology of Greek military equipment (by far the most important evidence for early Greek warfare), see A. M. Snodgrass, *Early Greek Armour and Weapons* (Edinburgh, 1964) and *Arms and Armor of the Greeks* (Ithaca, 1967), E. Jarva, Archaiologia *on Archaic Greek Body Armour* (Rovaniemi, 1995), and J. P. Franz, *Krieger, Bauern, Bürger: Untersuchungen zu den Hopliten der archaischen und klassischen Zeit* (Frankfurt, 2002).

Chapter I. Fighting in the *Iliad*

There are many English translations of the *Iliad;* I have always thought that the rolling, grumbling lines of Richmond Lattimore evoke the Greek of the poem best, and the translations of the *Iliad* in this chapter are often Lattimore's or adapt Lattimore's.

The date of the *Iliad* — or, more exactly, of when a purely oral tradition was written down and so achieved relative textual fixity, with or without the intervention of a single "Homer" — has never been in greater dispute than it is now. The traditional date, around 750 BC, is under attack from down-daters who advocate c. 700 BC, or the seventh century, or even the sixth century (the controversy can be traced in the various contributions to *Symbolae Osloenses* 74 [1999]). I have opted for the compromise c. 700 BC out of timidity, not conviction: I find none of the arguments compelling. Only a very late date (after 550 BC, say) would substantially interfere with the argument made here.

The literary or strata-of-composition reasons for the *Iliad*'s use of

Apollo and Euphorbos to detract from Hector's achievement present an old puzzle, assessed by K. Reinhardt, *Die* Ilias *und Ihr Dichter* (Göttingen, 1961) pp. 308–40, S. Farron, "The Character of Hector in the *Iliad*," *Acta Classica* 21 (1978) pp. 39–57 at 48–50, and R. Janko, *The Iliad: A Commentary, Vol. iv: Books 13–16* (Cambridge, 1992) pp. 408–10.

For up-to-date bibliography and able summaries of the many controversies which surround Homeric fighting, see O. Hellmann, *Die Schlachtszenen der* Ilias (Stuttgart, 2000). For the mechanics of one-on-one combat description in the *Iliad*—defiances, killing, introduction of the victim, stripping the body, and vaunting—see M. Mueller, *The Iliad* (London, 1984) pp. 80–95, or H. van Wees "Heroes, Knights, and Nutters: Warrior Mentality in Homer," in A. B. Lloyd (ed.), *Battle in Antiquity* (London, 1996) pp. 1–86, with references (but van Wees does not think Homeric combat as competitive as I and most others do). For the introduction of the victim, see especially G. Strasburger, *Die kleinen Kämpfer der* Ilias (Frankfurt, 1954) pp. 15–36. For a broader discussion of patterns in the depiction of combat, see B. Fenik, *Typical Battle Scenes in the* Iliad (Wiesbaden, 1968).

For a conventional account of Homeric values, see conveniently W. Donlan, *The Aristocratic Ideal in Ancient Greece* (Lawrence, Kan., 1980) pp. 3–25, with references. This conception has been elaborated by many hands from A. Adkins's fundamental *Merit and Responsibility* (Oxford, 1960) pp. 30–60. On martial skill in the *Iliad*, see S. Saïd, "Guerre, intelligence et courage dans les histoires d'Hérodote," *Ancient Society* 11/12 (1980/81) pp. 83–117 at 86–89; but the role of skill in Iliadic fighting is controversial: van Wees "Heroes, Knights, and Nutters" p. 39 n. 101. On the competitive quality of insults and utterances before combat, see R. Martin, *The Language of Heroes* (Ithaca, 1989) pp. 65–77. On the competitive quality of public speaking and giving advice, see M. Schofield, "*Euboulia* in the *Iliad*," *Classical Quarterly* 36 (1986) pp. 6–31.

The discussion of the glory of the kill depending on the excellence of the victim draws upon J. E. Lendon, "Homeric Vengeance and the Outbreak of Greek Wars," in H. van Wees (ed.), *War and Violence in Ancient Greece* (London, 2000) pp. 1–30 at 8–9. Here I question the conventional understanding of the descriptions of those about to be (or just) slain as intended only to arouse pathos in the reader, e.g., S. L. Schein,

The Mortal Hero (Berkeley and Los Angeles, 1984) pp. 72–76. But I do not try to provide a full explanation for all features of Homeric battle: Iliadic battle scenes are a mass of cross-cutting narrative purposes.

It used generally to be taken for granted that combat in the *Iliad* was primarily a matter of duels between heroes. But J. Latacz's *Kampfparänese, Kampfdarstellung und Kampfwirklichkeit in der* Ilias, *bei Kallinos und Tyrtaios* (Munich, 1977), to be read with R. Leimbach's review, *Gnomon* 52 (1980) pp. 418–25, forcefully argued what had been a minority view, that the conflict of masses in formation was in fact decisive. Latacz's view has found supporters, *inter alia* W. K. Pritchett, *The Greek State at War* vol. 4 (Berkeley and Los Angeles, 1985) pp. 7–33. But H. van Wees in "Kings in Combat: Battles and Heroes in the *Iliad*," *Classical Quarterly* 38 (1988) pp. 1–24 and "The Homeric War of War: The *Iliad* and the Hoplite Phalanx (I)" and "(II)," *Greece and Rome* 41 (1994) pp. 1–18 and 131–55, has attacked Latacz's position and proposed a compromise: heroic individuals fighting in front of a loose swarm combined with masses assembled ad hoc and soon dispersing. Van Wees adjusts his stand in "Homeric Warfare," in I. Morris and B. Powell (eds.), *A New Companion to Homer* (Leiden, 1997) pp. 668–93, with references also to previous literature about the relationship between mass and individual fighting (p. 679; which Latacz, *Kampfparänese* also supplies, pp. 68–72) and summarizes his views in his *Greek Warfare: Myths and Realities* (London, 2004) pp. 153–65. Van Wees's is the most convincing attempt to find a historical way of fighting behind the *Iliad*, but I do not think the project possible.

On the conflict of values between Achilles and Agamemnon, M. J. Bennett, *Belted Heroes and Bound Women* (Lanham, Md., 1997) pp. 81–91 offers a good exposition. On the vexed heroic status of archery in the *Iliad*, see B. J. Hijmans, "Archers in the *Iliad*," in [no ed.], *Festoen (Festschrift A. N. Zadoks-Josephus Jitta)* (Groningen, 1976) pp. 343–52. On the status of holding one's ground vs. running away, see T. Schwertfeger, "Der Schild des Archilochus," *Chiron* 12 (1982) pp. 253–80 at 254–57. On the tension between opportunistic and "chivalrous" fighting in Homer, see van Wees, "Heroes, Knights, and Nutters" pp. 36–44.

On the relationship of Classical Greeks to their past, a useful survey is A. Raubitschek, "What the Greeks Thought of their Early History," *Ancient World* 20 (1989) pp. 39–45, and, on their pervasive past-mindedness,

B. A. Van Groningen, *In the Grip of the Past* (Leiden, 1953). Generally on the continuing influence of Homer, K. Robb, *Literacy and Paideia in Ancient Greece* (New York, 1994); in religion, W. Burkert, *Greek Religion* (Cambridge, Mass., 1985) pp. 119–25 (trans. J. Raffan, from *Griechische Religion der archaischen und klassischen Epoche* [Stuttgart, 1977]); in art, D. Castriota, *Myth, Ethos, and Actuality: Official Art in Fifth-Century BC Athens* (Madison, 1992); J. Boardman, *The Archaeology of Nostalgia: How the Greeks Re-Created Their Mythical Past* (London, 2002).

Chapter II. The Last Hoplite

On the Battle of Champions at Thyrea, especially important in a considerable literature are P. Kohlmann, "Othryades: Eine historisch-kritische Untersuchung," *Rheinisches Museum* 29 (1874) pp. 463–80, and L. Moretti, "Sparta alla metà del VI secolo II: La guerra contro Argo per la Tireatide," *Rivista di filologia classica* 76 (1948) pp. 204–22. L. Piccirilli, *Gli arbitrati interstatali greci* vol. 1 (Pisa, 1973) nr. 8, and F. J. Fernandez Nieto, *Los Acuerdos bélicos en la antigua Grecia* vol. 1 (Santiago de Compostela, 1975) nr. 10, gather the ancient references and older scholarship; for newer scholarship, see M. Nafissi, *La Nascita del kosmos: Studi sulla storie e la società di Sparta* (Naples, 1991) p. 157 n. 17. See N. Robertson, *Festivals and Legends: The Formation of Greek Cities in the Light of Public Ritual* (Toronto, 1992) pp. 179–207, for a valiant attempt to make sense of the conflicting traditions and associated Peloponnesian festivals and monuments (with the enjoyably angry rebuttal of W. K. Pritchett, "Aetiology sans Topography," in id., *Thucydides' Pentekontaetia and Other Essays* [Amsterdam, 1995] pp. 205–79 at 228–62, not neglecting abuse of Canada [p. 262]). The Thyrea combat is, of course, a semi-mythical event (at best), but the argument here depends on how ancient authors described it, not on what actually happened. Note the difference between the later versions and the fifth-century BC version of Herodotus (1.82), who knows nothing of the trophy or of the Argives overlooking the wounded Othryades and being surprised in the morning: to Herodotus the battle simply ended (presumably by agreement) at nightfall, and the Argives assumed that the winner would be settled by a head count, not by who held the field. In Herodotus's version only the Spartan interpretation of victory accords with hoplite convention (hardly surprising if in c. 550 those conventions were still coalescing). In the later versions the story has been altered to accord better with the norms of hoplite combat.

On the hoplite battle (my description is conventional), see V. D. Hanson, *The Western Way of War* (New York, 1989), who draws on the method pioneered by J. Keegan in *The Face of Battle* (London, 1976) to offer an evocative account of the hoplite experience of battle. For mechanics of combat and technical vocabulary, W. K. Pritchett, "The Pitched Battle," in *The Greek State at War* vol. 4 (Berkeley and Los Angeles, 1985) pp. 1–93 at 33–93, and E. L. Wheeler, "Land Combat in Archaic and Classical Greece," in P. Sabin, H. van Wees, and M. Whitby (eds.), *Cambridge History of Greek and Roman Warfare* (Cambridge, forthcoming). On controversial details, especially whether the rear ranks pushed on the backs of those in front and how closely hoplites were arrayed, see A. Goldsworthy, "The *Othismos,* Myths and Heresies: The Nature of Hoplite Battle," *War in History* 4 (1997) pp. 1–26 and H. van Wees, "The Development of the Hoplite Phalanx," in *id.* (ed.), *War and Violence in Ancient Greece* (London, 2000) pp. 125–66 at 126–34 for the state of the question. I do not believe that the evidence permits of confident answers.

The date mature phalanx fighting as described here developed is subject to controversy. Different pieces of hoplite equipment appear at different times after 725 BC (A. M. Snodgrass, *Early Greek Armour and Weapons* [Edinburgh 1964]), and so the old scholarship dated a "hoplite revolution" to the late eighth or early seventh century. But since the equipment was useful for other forms of fighting (see L. Rawlings, "Alternative Agonies: Hoplite Martial and Combat Experiences Beyond the Phalanx," in H. van Wees [ed.], *War and Violence in Ancient Greece* [London, 2000] pp. 233–59), the date of their invention tells us little about the coming of the phalanx. Around 650 BC the mass production of hoplite figurines at Sparta begins (A. J. B. Wace, "The Lead Figurines," in R. M. Dawkins [ed.], *The Sanctuary of Artemis Orthia at Sparta* [London, 1929] pp. 249–84 with J. Boardman, "Artemis Orthia and Chronology," *Annual of the British School at Athens* 58 [1963] 1–7). What has traditionally been interpreted as a mature phalanx appears also on a few vases of the Macmillan (or Chigi) painter near the same time, so most now date the mature phalanx around 650 BC. But van Wees ("Development of the Hoplite Phalanx" pp. 134–46), drawing upon the work of others, argues that the pots depict the hoplites carrying two spears (one perhaps for throwing) and a formation of only one rank: not, then, the mature phalanx. In *Greek Warfare: Myths and Realities* (London, 2004) pp. 183–84, van Wees proposes a four-stage evolution: (a) invention of hoplite armor, late eighth century; (b) most hoplites begin to fight hand-to-hand, late seventh century; (c) hoplites, horsemen, and light-armed missile troops begin to cease mingling in battle, c. 500, a trend still incomplete in the Persian Wars; (d) the mature phalanx, seen for the first time in Thucydides' description of the Peloponnesian War (431–404 BC). In this down-dating he draws upon P. Krentz, "Fighting by the Rules: The Invention of the Hoplite Agôn," *Hesperia* 71 (2002) pp. 23–39 at 35–37, who suggests that mature hoplite warfare dates no earlier than the mid–fifth century. E. L. Wheeler, "Land Combat in Archaic and Classical Greece," offers a less radical down-dating and dates the mature phalanx to the sixth century. I am quite agnostic as to whether the mature phalanx should be dated to the seventh, sixth, or early fifth centuries and suspect that the evidence to decide is lacking. What should be learned from this debate is that the process of evolution from an earlier mixed style of warfare was slow and piecemeal, that the nascent phalanx may have become deeper over time, and that the final exclusion of missile weapons from the phalanx may have happened quite late in its development.

The role of light troops in the mature hoplite battle is unclear: they are little mentioned in descriptions of battles, but recently P. Hunt, *Slaves, Warfare, and Ideology in the Greek Historians* (Cambridge, 1998) and H. van Wees, "Politics and the Battlefield: Ideology in Greek Warfare," in A. Powell (ed.), *The Greek World* (London, 1995) pp. 153–78 at 162–65 have argued that there were more present than appears and that they were edited out of battle descriptions to glorify the hoplites at the expense of humbler (Hunt would say often slave) warriors.

On the formality of the classical hoplite battle, see J. Ober, "The Rules of War in Classical Greece," in id., *The Athenian Revolution* (Princeton, 1996) pp. 53–71, W. K. Pritchett, *The Greek State at War* vol. 2 (Berkeley and Los Angeles, 1974) esp. pp. 147–207 and more generally in vols. 1–4 of that work, and W. R. Connor, "Early Greek Land Warfare as Symbolic Expression," *Past and Present* 119 (1988) pp. 3–29. The formality of hoplite warfare has recently been questioned (for a general discussion, see below, pp. 410–11). Van Wees, *Greek Warfare* pp. 134–35 emphasizes the tactical exploitation of ritual features like the delay before battle and challenges: but such use reemphasizes that such features did exist and were taken seriously.

The conventional picture of the dependence of Greek constitutional development upon hoplite fighting was elaborated from Aristotle in a classic article by M. P. Nilsson, "Die Hoplitentaktik und das Staatswesen," *Klio* 22 (1929) pp. 240–49 (conveniently summarized by the author in English in the *Journal of Roman Studies* 19 [1929] pp. 1–3). This thesis propelled influential works, such as A. Andrewes's *The Greek Tyrants* (London, 1956), is deeply embedded in the textbooks, and is noticed outside classical studies: see J. M. Bryant in "Military Technology and Socio-cultural Change in the Ancient Greek City," *The Sociological Review* 38 (1990) pp. 484–516. In this vulgate interpretation the phalanx admitted to political power a middling social stratum, a "hoplite class," of those who could afford hoplite armor but who were excluded by the older aristocratic governments when horses ruled the battlefield: thus archaic oligarchies, where wealth rather than birth commanded political participation, succeeded dark age aristocracies. Although not by nature a Marxist theory, it owes some of its continuing influence to its appeal to Marxists needing to motivate a transition from aristocratic to bourgeois (for that is often what really lies under "hoplite") predominance. But there was never any actual evidence for the theory (Aristotle knew less about the period in question than we do: he had no archeologists to help him); compelling doubts have long been expressed (e.g., J. Salmon, "Political Hoplites?" *Journal of Hellenic Studies* 97 [1977] pp. 84–101 at 93–101), and recent work has dealt it a deathblow: see K. Raaflaub, "Soldiers, Citizens, and the Evolution of the Early Greek *Polis*," in L. G. Mitchell and P. J. Rhodes (eds.), *The Development of the* Polis *in Archaic Greece* (London, 1997) pp. 49–59 at 53–57 and H. van Wees, "Tyrants, Oligarchs and Citizen Militias," in A. Chaniotis and P. Ducrey (eds.), *Army and Power in the Ancient World* (Stuttgart, 2002) pp. 61–82. M. Shanks, *Art and the Greek City State* (Cambridge, 1999) pp. 107–9 gives a fuller summary of the controversy, with references to the scholarship.

It seems to me far more likely that the phalanx, rather than being the invention of the middling, was instead the product of the values of those at the top of Greek society: I follow A. M. Snodgrass, "The Hoplite Reform and History," *Journal of Hellenic Studies* 85 (1965) pp. 110–22 at 114–16, 120–22, H. W. Singor, "*Eni Prôtoisi Machesthai:* Some Remarks on the Iliadic Image of the Battlefield," in J. P. Crielaard (ed.), *Homeric Questions* (Amsterdam, 1995) pp. 183–200 at 198–99 (drawing upon his — alas, Dutch — dissertation), and J. P. Franz, *Krieger, Bauern, Bürger. Untersuchungen zu den Hopliten der archaischen und klassischen Zeit* (Frankfurt, 2002) esp. pp. 116–20. If the phalanx plays a political role in Greece, it is not in the incubation of a middling, cooperative ethos, it is in the diffusion of aristocratic ideals downward in society.

It is nothing new to notice that the formality and ritual of phalanx fighting reflects the competitive — *agonistic* is the term of art — culture of the Greeks. K.-J. Hölkeskamp, "La guerra e la pace," in S. Settis et al. (eds.), *I Greci* vol. 2.2 (Turin, 1997) pp. 481–539 at 494–501 gathers and summarizes the literature. Important formulations include A. Brelich, *Guerre, agoni e culti nella Grecia arcaica* (Bonn, 1961) (with pp. 22–34 on the combat at Thyrea) and R. Lonis, "Victoire et agôn," in id., *Guerre et religion en Grèce a l'époque classique* (Paris, 1979) pp. 25–40. (I discuss this literature further below, p. 407.) The novelty of my approach lies in emphasizing the competition between individuals in the phalanx and understanding this competition as a force for change. For the aristocratic origins of some agonistic aspects of phalanx fighting, see M. Detienne, "La Phalange: problèmes et controverses," in J.-P. Vernant (ed.), *Problèmes de la guerre en Gréce ancienne* (Paris, 1968) pp. 119–42, esp. pp. 123–24. For discussion of other theories of the origin of the phalanx, see below, pp. 407–9.

For Classical Greek warriors conceiving of themselves in Homeric terms, N. Loraux, "*Hebe* et *Andreia:* deux versions de la mort du combattant Athénien," *Ancient Society* 6 (1975) pp. 1–31 esp. 19–25 and E. L. Wheeler, "The Hoplite as General," in V. D. Hanson (ed.), *Hoplites: The Classical Greek Battle Experience* (London, 1991) pp. 121–70 at 122–23 (an important paper to which I am much in debt).

The granting of a formal prize for excellence — called *aristeia* — to a soldier or city contingent in the Persian Wars (480–479 BC) is controversial. D. Hamel, *Athenian Generals* (Leiden, 1998) pp. 64–66 agrees with W. K. Pritchett, *The Greek State at War* vol. 2 (Berkeley and Los Angeles, 1974) pp. 283–86 that they did, but van Wees, *Greek Warfare,* pp. 182–83 with nn. 57 and 61 maintains that the usual way Herodotus describes this, the simple verb *aristeuein,* "to be the best," refers to no formal award, but to public (or Herodotus's) opinion only. Yet in one case (Hdt. 8.11) an individual "receives the *aristeion,*" and the Greeks did give prizes to heroes by vote (Hdt. 8.123–24), so they knew the institution: but how formal the prize was in each instance when Herodotus indicates who "was best," second, and third or even more vaguely "who won renown" (Hdt. 7.227, 9.73) cannot be known. In the text I propose a weak compromise (a formal honor roll, but not a prize). By 432 BC formal first prizes were certainly awarded (Pl. *Symp.* 220D; Plut. *Alc.* 7.3). Plato proposes the award of formal second and third prizes (*Leg.* 943C), but whether he reflects contemporary reality or proposes to change it is unknown.

On the passive courage of the hoplite (and the resulting devaluation of missile troops and cavalry), see esp. I. G. Spence, *The Cavalry of Classical Greece* (Oxford, 1993) pp. 168–71. I have also frequently drawn upon the unpublished Macquarie dissertation of D. M. Pritchard, "The Fractured Imaginary: Popular Thinking on Citizen Soldiers and Warfare in Fifth-Century Athens" (1999), especially his discussions of hoplite courage (pp. 86–99) and the devaluation of missile-armed troops and cavalry (pp. 108–15). Pritchard briefly summarizes his treatment of the status of archers and cavalry in "'The Fractured Imaginary': Popular Thinking on Military Matters in Fifth Century Athens," *Ancient History* 28 (1998) pp. 38–61 at pp. 49–50.

The competitive bravery of immobility has its analogies in the era of the musket: "When a shell passed over a column of the 52nd, the men 'instantly bobbed their heads'; Colborne, the commanding officer, shouted 'for shame, for shame! That must be the second battalion (who were recruits), I am sure.' In an instant every man's head went as straight as an arrow" (quoted Keegan, *The Face of Battle* p. 178).

Chapter III. Two Stubborn Spartans in the Persian War

We see earlier Greek wars like wild and giddy reflections in the shards of a shattered mirror. With the war against the Persians Greek history finds a voice, that of Herodotus, the father of history. Of the many English translations available, I prefer the slightly archaic syntax of D. Grene, as sounding similar to what Herodotus's Greek will have sounded like to his contemporaries. The Persian War books of Herodotus should be read with R. W. Macan, *Herodotus: The Seventh, Eighth, and Ninth Books* (London, 1908) and M. A. Flower and J. Marincola, *Herodotus Histories: Book IX* (Cambridge, 2002). See the latter (pp. 31–35) for a pessimistic evaluation of the chief sources for the Persian Wars other than Herodotus, the first-century AD Plutarch's *Lives* of *Themistocles* and *Aristides,* and the first-century BC Diodorus of Sicily (drawing on the fourth-century BC Ephorus).

On the Persian Wars, strongly recommended is P. Green's lyrical *The Greco-Persian Wars* (Berkeley and Los Angeles, 1996; a revised ed. of his *Xerxes at Salamis* [New York, 1970]). For recent scholarship and controversies, see the sensible treatment of J. F. Lazenby, *The Defence of Greece 490–479 BC* (Warminster, 1993), with pp. 130–48 on Thermopylae and pp. 217–47 on Plataea.

For Herodotus's account of Thermopylae, see J. Dillery, "Reconfiguring the Past: Thyrea, Thermopylae and Narrative Patterns in Herodotus," *American Journal of Philology* 117 (1996) pp. 217–54 at 234–42. For Homeric echoes in his account (often noticed), see M. Flower, "Simonides, Ephorus, and Herodotus on the Battle of Thermopylae," *Classical Quarterly* 48 (1998) pp. 365–79 at 375. On the topography of the battle of Thermopylae (an extremely unsatisfying subject of study because the changing sea level means it is no longer a narrow chokepoint between mountain and sea), the issues can be traced through W. K. Pritchett, "Herodotos and His Critics on Thermopylae," *Studies in Ancient Greek Topography* vol. 4 (Berkeley and Los Angeles, 1982) pp. 176–210.

For Herodotus's information on Plataea, see R. Nyland, "Herodotos' Sources for the Plataiai Campaign," *L'Antiquité classique* 61 (1992) pp. 80–97. For Homeric echoes in Herodotus's account, see D. Boedeker, "Heroic Historiography: Simonides and Herodotus on Plataea," in id. and D. Sider (eds.), *The New Simonides* (New York, 2001) pp. 120–34. For the topography of the Plataea battlefield (many of the important landmarks named in Herodotus cannot be identified, and so controversy will never end), the literature can be traced through W. K. Pritchett, "The Strategy of the Plataiai Campaign," *Studies in Ancient Greek Topography* vol. 5

(Berkeley and Los Angeles, 1985) pp. 92–137. On the (controversial) status of Amompharetus, J. F. Lazenby, *The Spartan Army* (Warminster, 1985) pp. 48–50.

For Persian Wars fighting viewed in Homeric terms, see also the recently discovered Simonides fragment on Plataea, D. Sider, "Fragments 1–22W². Text, *Apparatus Criticus,* and Translation," in D. Boedeker and id. (eds.), *The New Simonides* pp. 13–29, or conveniently in Flower and Marincola, *Herodotus Histories: Book IX* pp. 315–19; for other proposed uses of Homeric analogy in memorializing the Persian Wars, D. Boedeker, "Paths to Heroization at Plataea," in id. and Sider (eds.), *The New Simonides* pp. 148–63 at 154.

About the rise of the *polis* as a political form — why? when? definition? — controversy will never cease. R. Osborne, *Greece in the Making, 1200–479 BC* (London, 1996) summarizes the evidence; but the reader should be aware that the city is often envisioned as arising in opposition to aristocrats and their values (see above, p. 402), rather than from them, as is suggested in this book. On the Greek *polis* conceived as an individual, see N. Loraux, "Mourir devant Troie, tomber pour Athènes. De la gloire du héros à l'idée de la cité," *Social Science Information* 17 (1978) pp. 801–17 esp. 812–14 (reprinted in G. Gnoli and J.-P. Vernant [eds.], *La Mort, les morts dans les sociétés anciennes* [Cambridge, 1982] pp. 27–43). This tendency has been discussed especially in Thucydides, see V. Hunter, "Thucydides and the Sociology of the Crowd," *Classical Journal* 84 (1988) pp. 17–30; J. V. Morrison, "A Key Topos in Thucydides: The Comparison of Cities and Individuals," *American Journal of Philology* 115 (1994) pp. 525–41. For the qualities of a city's character, see K. J. Dover, *Greek Popular Morality in the Time of Plato and Aristotle* (1974) pp. 310–11.

For cities' anthropomorphic ways of dealing with each other — kinship, "friendship," etc. — H. van Wees, *Greek Warfare: Myths and Realities* (London, 2004) pp. 6–18 gathers the references and the modern discussions. Focusing especially on emotions, rivalry over rank, and revenge between cities, is J. E. Lendon's "Homeric Vengeance and the Outbreak of Greek Wars," in H. van Wees (ed.), *War and Violence in Ancient Greece* (London, 2000) pp. 1–30 at 13–22. Broadly, on the tendency to conceive of democratic Athens in terms of aristocratic excellence (although drawing opposite conclusions from mine), see N. Loraux, *The Invention of Athens* (Cambridge, Mass., 1986; trans. A. Sheridan from *L'Invention d'Athènes: Histoire de l'oraison funèbre dans la 'cité classique'* [Paris, 1981]). On the competitive *sophrosyne* of the Spartans, see J. E. Lendon, "Spartan Honor," in C. D. Hamilton and P. Krentz (eds.), Polis *and* Polemos (Claremont, Calif., 1997) pp. 105–26 at 121–23.

For the parallel between civic and individual experience in the phalanx, see J.-P. Vernant, "City-State Warfare," in id., *Myth and Society in Ancient Greece,* trans. J. Lloyd (New York, 1988) pp. 29–53 esp. 38 (translating "Introduction" in id. [ed.], *Problèmes de la guerre en Grèce ancienne* [Paris, 1968] pp. 9–30). I elaborate his insight into a force for change in military method.

Unlike the French cultural approach (adopted here), English-speaking authors have tended to understand the origins of hoplite fighting in economic or political terms. Nearly a century ago G. B. Grundy, in *Thucydides and the History of His Age*[2] vol. 1 (Oxford, 1961 [London, 1911[1]]) pp. 245–49, argued that the paradox of fighting heavily armed in masses in a mountainous land was to be explained by the fact that, in so poor a country, the crops in the plains had to be protected (an argument revived and improved by N. V. Sekunda, "Classical Warfare," in J. Boardman [ed.], *The Cambridge Ancient History*[2] *Plates to Volumes V and VI* [Cambridge, 1994] pp. 167–94 at 167–68). V. D. Hanson, concisely in "The Ideology of Hoplite Battle, Ancient and Modern," in id. (ed.), *Hoplites: The Classical Greek Battle Experience* (London, 1991) pp. 3–11 at 4–6 turns Grundy on his head to argue that the formality of hoplite battle was the result of a "wonderful, absurd conspiracy" (p. 6) among the small farmers who made up the phalanx to reduce the dangers of war to their persons and farms. But the Greeks did not think hoplite fighting reduced casualties (Hdt. 7.9), and, as Grundy noticed, hoplite armies in fact eagerly ravaged each others' crops (why couldn't they conspire to prevent that entirely?) — and how could such an intercity "conspiracy" in reality be reached between the men of rival states and preserved over time? More attractive is the political interpretation of P. Cartledge, in "Hoplites and Heroes: Sparta's Contribution to the Technique of Ancient Warfare," in the *Journal of Hellenic Studies* 97 (1977) pp. 11–27 at 23–24, who argues for another kind of conspiracy, that of hoplites in each city to preserve their political predominance against their inferiors by excluding them from warfare. J.

Ober in "The Rules of War in Classical Greece," in id., *The Athenian Revolution* (Princeton, 1996) pp. 63–71 at 59–60 elaborates this idea: the formality of hoplite warfare, relegating both cavalry and light-armed to subordinate roles, served to protect the political predominance of the hoplite middle against both poor and rich. Although doubting the existence of this "hoplite middle," I think it likely that the higher-ups' desire to exclude the lowest-downs from the privilege of fighting probably did play a role in the evolution and preservation of the mature phalanx.

But neither an economic nor a political explanation accounts for why the Greeks came to fight in this particular way, rather than in other ways which would secure the same economic or political ends — by duels of single champions, for example, which would preserve the crops and farmers (Hanson's economic goal) and, depending on how the champions were chosen, exclude members of unfavored social strata (Cartledge and Ober's political goal). In the old days the villages of the Megarid — it was much later believed — practiced upon each other a bloodless symbolic war of kidnapping, leaving farmers untouched (Plut. *Mor.* 295B-C). This road, rather than the phalanx, is one that economic or political motives might have pushed the Greeks along. To be persuasive, a theory of the origin of the phalanx must offer a mechanism for arriving at the phalanx in particular, not merely an ultimate cause that might have had any number of results — not only a tap is needed, but also a hose-pipe. Hans van Wees's social theory of the origin of the mature phalanx — he connects it to growing late sixth-century/early fifth-century egalitarianism in Greek society at large — has the opposite problem: a pipe but no tap (*Greek Warfare* pp. 195–96). Van Wees attractively argues that the mature phalanx was impossible while "hierarchical personal ties bound men together, as they did in archaic Greek society, [when] horsemen operated alongside their followers on foot, while heavy- and light-armed men fought in unequal pairs." But if the replacement of those old hierarchies with more egalitarian social relations allowed the mature phalanx to form, this social change did not exert any positive pressure toward making that military change happen in the first place.

My argument has attempted to provide both a motive and a mechanism for change, and it does not exclude social, political, or economic influences and enablers (although I much prefer Grundy's economic theory to Hanson's). Yet it should be strongly emphasized that the cultural theory of hoplite origins proposed here rests upon several controversial assumptions, including (1) that the city-state predates the phalanx and so could be an influence upon it; (2) that the *Iliad* does not depict the developed phalanx (as some have argued, see above, p. 398) but that the *Iliad* was complete enough and already enjoyed sufficient cultural authority to influence the development of the phalanx.

On Greek military discipline, W. K. Pritchett, in *The Greek State at War* vol. 2 (Berkeley and Los Angeles, 1974) pp. 232–45 gathers essential references, concluding that "discipline in the army . . . differed little from that of a citizen" (p. 245); see also van Wees, *Greek Warfare,* pp. 109–12 with vivid examples of indiscipline. For Athens (about which we know the most), see D. Hamel, *Athenian Generals* (Leiden, 1998) pp. 59–64.

On the culture of the Ten Thousand and their similarity to a *polis,* see G. B. Nussbaum, *The Ten Thousand* (Leiden, 1967); for discipline among the Ten Thousand conceived as grounded in horizontal rather than vertical bonds, see esp. pp. 19–25. For Xenophon's understanding of military leadership, see H. R. Breitenbach, "Xenophon von Athen," *RE* 9A.2 (1967) cols. 1567–2052 at 1728–32 and, in English, N. Wood, "Xenophon's Theory of Leadership," *Classica et Medievalia* 25 (1964) pp. 33–66 at 51–55. For the competitiveness of obedience at Sparta, see J. E. Lendon, "Spartan Honor," pp. 120–21. For Greek, and especially Spartan, conceptions of the role of beating in military discipline, S. Hornblower, "Sticks, Stones, and Spartans," in H. van Wees (ed.), *War and Violence in Classical Greece* (London, 2000) pp. 57–82. More broadly, on Spartan martial culture, J. Ducat, "La Société spartiate et la guerre," in F. Prost, *Armées et sociétés de la Grèce classique* (Paris, 1999) pp. 35–50.

Chapter IV. The Guile of Delium

The Richard Crawley translation of the historian Thucydides is one of the greatest translations of an ancient author into any modern language, and now it can be read in the helpful Landmark edition, edited by R. Strassler. Thucydides should be read with A. W. Gomme, A. Andrewes, and K. J. Dover, *A Historical Commentary on Thucydides,* 5 vols. (Oxford, 1945–81) and, gathering more recent literature, S. Hornblower, *A*

Commentary on Thucydides, 2 vols. (so far) (Oxford, 1991–). The best English account of the Peloponnesian War is D. Kagan, *The Archidamian War* (Ithaca, 1974), with pp. 279–87 on the Delium campaign, *The Peace of Nicias and the Sicilian Expedition* (Ithaca, 1981), and *The Fall of the Athenian Empire* (Ithaca, 1987), all now abridged as *The Peloponnesian War* (New York, 2003). For the proposed site of the battle of Delium, see J. Beck, "Delion 424 vor Chr.," in J. Kromeyer, *Antike Schlachtfelder* vol. 4 (Berlin, 1924–31) pp. 177–98; W. K. Pritchett, *Studies in Ancient Greek Topography* vol. 2 (Berkeley and Los Angeles, 1969) pp. 24–36, vol. 3 (Berkeley and Los Angeles, 1980) pp. 295–97. For an engaging discussion of the battle and its legacy, V. D. Hanson, *Ripples of Battle* (New York, 2003) pp. 171–243.

It used to be conventional that a period of "primitive" ritualized chivalrous phalanx warfare gave way to more rational "modern" methods of fighting, relying on tactics and trickery. The old position, visible in J. Kromayer and G. Veith, *Heerwesen und Kriegführung der Griechen und Römer* (=I. von Müller and W. Otto [eds.], *Handbuch der Altertumswissenschaft* 4.3.2; Munich, 1928) pp. 93–95, saw Epaminondas's tactical victory at Leuctra (371 BC) as the revolutionary moment of transition. Victor Hanson ("Epameinondas, the Battle of Leuktra (371 BC), and the 'Revolution' in Greek Battle Tactics," *Classical Antiquity* 7 [1988] pp. 190–207) showed that Epaminondas's tactics were not new and that the shift had to be pushed back at least to Delium in 424 BC. Others have argued that it was the Peloponnesian War, beginning in 431 BC, that broke down the old rules (e.g., J. de Romilly, "Guerre et paix entre cités," in J.-P. Vernant [ed.], *Problèmes de la guerre en Grèce ancienne* [Paris, 1968] pp. 207–20 at 215–16). Was it the democratic ethos of Athens that wrecked the old formalism? So J. Ober, "The Rules of War in Classical Greece," in id., *The Athenian Revolution* (Princeton, 1996) pp. 53–71 at 63–68. Was it the example of naval tactics? Thus P. Vidal-Naquet, "The Tradition of the Athenian Hoplite," *The Black Hunter,* trans. A. Szegedy-Maszak (Baltimore, 1986) pp. 85–105 at p. 93 (translating "La Tradition de l'hoplite Athénien," in J.-P. Vernant [ed.], *Problèmes de la guerre en Grèce ancienne* [Paris, 1968] pp. 161–81). But it should have given pause to those who pushed the revolution back to the early years of the Peloponnesian War that they were placing it at the very beginning of the surviving detailed reports of hoplite-against-hoplite battle, which are contained in Thucydides. A black hole in the evidence has been filled by wishful thinking. In fact, scholars (e.g., S. Saïd, "Guerre, intelligence et courage dans les histoires d'Hérodote," *Ancient Society* 11/12 [1980/1] pp. 83–117 at 92–108; P. Krentz, "Deception in Archaic and Classical Greek Warfare," in H. van Wees [ed.], *War and Violence in Ancient Greece* [London, 2000] pp. 167–200) have shown that tricky and tactical generalship can be traced as far back as we have literary accounts of hoplite fighting. Diligent searching has also turned up much light infantry at battles, even before the Peloponnesian War (see above, p. 401). It is possible, therefore, to deny altogether the formal, ritual quality of hoplite warfare: see P. Krentz, "The Strategic Culture of Periclean Athens," in id. and C. Hamilton (eds.), Polis *and* Polemos (Claremont, Calif., 1997) pp. 55–72 at 55–61 (but he adjusts his position in "Fighting by the Rules: The Invention of the Hoplite *Agôn*," *Hesperia* 71 [2002] pp. 23–39), and drawing on Krentz, the measured rejection of H. van Wees, *Greek Warfare: Myths and Realities* (London, 2004) pp. 115–21, 132–38. The controversy is not surprising: as has been argued here, ritual elements and ruthless advantage-taking long coexisted. I have tried to explain how that long coexistence might be possible.

On the Greek intellectual quality of *metis,* cunning intelligence, see the strange and wonderful volume of M. Detienne and J.-P. Vernant, *Cunning Intelligence in Greek Culture and Society,* trans. J. Lloyd (Sussex, 1978, translating *Les Ruses de l'intelligence: la* mètis *des grecs* [Paris, 1974]). Particularly on the Spartan culture of cunning, see A. Powell, "Mendacity and Sparta's Use of the Visual," in id. (ed.), *Classical Sparta: The Techniques Behind her Success* (Norman, Okla., 1989) pp. 173–92. On the opposition between *metis* and hoplite ritual, see P. Vidal-Naquet, "The Black Hunter and the Origin of the Athenian *Ephebeia,*" *The Black Hunter,* trans. A. Szegedy-Maszak (Baltimore, 1986) pp. 106–28 (translating *Le Chasseur noir* [Paris, 1981]), and J. Hesk, *Deception and Democracy in Classical Athens* (Cambridge, 2000). On the continuing tension between rules and trickery, see E. L. Wheeler, "Land Combat in Archaic and Classical Greece," P. Sabin, H. van Wees, and M. Whitby (eds.), *Cambridge History of Greek and Roman Warfare* (Cambridge, forthcoming), who points out that stratagems often work by taking advantage of the expectation that a commander will behave by the rules. On the subject of military guile in general, E. L. Wheeler, *Stratagem and the Vocabulary of Military Trickery* (Leiden, 1988). Wheeler regards the tension between fighting openly — he calls it the "Achilles ethos" — and fighting by trickery — the "Odysseus ethos" — as perennial in Western military culture (pp. xiii–xiv). I am much in debt to this insight.

Chapter V. The Arts of War in the Early Fourth Century BC

For the details of the evolution of Greek land warfare in the fourth century, A. Ferrill, *The Origins of War* (Boulder, Colo., 1997) pp. 149–70 offers an economical survey, arguing in many cases for influence from the East. N. V. Sekunda, "Classical Warfare," in J. Boardman (ed.), *The Cambridge Ancient History² Plates to Volumes V and VI* (Cambridge, 1994) pp. 167–94 argues that the mainland Greek lack of fiscal structures (and simple poverty) explain some patterns of evolution (or lack of it) — I have drawn upon his idea. On the spread of cavalry, see I. G. Spence, *The Cavalry of Classical Greece* (Oxford, 1993) pp. 1–33. On the evolution of Greek military training, see W. K. Pritchett, *The Greek State at War* vol. 2 (Berkeley and Los Angeles, 1974) pp. 208–31; on fourth-century hoplite drill, see J. K. Anderson, *Military Theory and Practice in the Age of Xenophon* (Berkeley and Los Angeles, 1970) pp. 94–110 (also noting the emphasis on the javelin at the expense of bow and sling among light troops, p. 112). On mercenaries in Classical Greece, see H. W. Parke, *Greek Mercenary Soldiers* (Oxford, 1933). On the increased use of mercenaries in the fourth century (a real phenomenon, but often overestimated), see L. A. Burckhardt, *Bürger und Soldaten* (Stuttgart, 1996) pp. 76–153.

On the battle of Lechaeum, see A. Konecny, "*Katekopsen ten moran Iphikrates*. Das Gefecht bei Lechaion im Frühsommer 390 v. Chr.," *Chiron* 31 (2001) pp. 79–127. On peltasts and their use and origins, see J. G. P. Best, *Thracian Peltasts and Their Influence on Greek Warfare* (Groningen, 1969), who points out the similarity of their equipment to that used by the heroes in Homer (pp. 8–15). For depictions of peltasts in art, F. Lissarrague in *L'Autre guerrier: Archers, peltastes, cavaliers dans l'imagerie attique* (Paris, 1990) pp. 151–89. Study of peltasts is complicated by the fact that the Greeks used the term to describe not only light infantry carrying the *pelte*, but also more broadly any light infantry (with *pelte* or without), and also (later) any soldier, however armed, with a shield smaller than the large hoplite *aspis*. So soldiers of the Hellenistic phalanx (who carried a small shield, see below, pp. 417–18) might be described as peltasts.

Iphicrates' equipment reform is controversial because Diodorus's (15.44.4) and Nepos's (11.1) similar accounts (probably drawing on Ephorus) are profoundly muddled. Some body of men, they say, got a smaller, round shield (*pelte*) and a longer spear and sword. Nepos adds that they exchanged their metal armor for linen; Diodorus says that Iphicrates gave them a new kind of boot, named for him, and rather vaguely implies that the changes were based on Iphicrates' campaigning in the East (which Ferrill, *The Origins of War* p. 160 picks up). But did the soldiers subject to this reform start as (a) hoplites, as Diodorus and Nepos seem to think, giving up their large *aspis* shield and still fighting as hoplites but now *called* peltasts (because of the new shield) and wielding a twelve-foot rather than an eight-foot spear? or as (b) light-infantry peltasts, who thereby became pseudohoplites (Parke, *Greek Mercenary Soldiers* p. 80)? These possibilities are significant because it has long been argued that Philip II of Macedon copied his Macedonian phalanx from this new "Iphicratean Peltast"; see below, p. 417. But they might also have been (c) light-infantry peltasts who merely had their equipment standardized (Parke, *Greek Mercenary Soldiers* p. 80 n. 2), or (d) light-infantry peltasts whose way of fighting was somehow changed. Best's discussion (*Thracian Peltasts* esp. pp. 102–10) provides the essential insight: peltast equipment had always been mixed, and some Thracians, the original peltasts, had carried a long spear. I believe that (d) is most plausible and that the essence of the reform was making the *pelte* round rather than crescent-shaped, lengthening the swords and giving some peltasts a longer thrusting spear. But no reconstruction so far is satisfactory.

For Thessalian cavalry formations we rely on the tactical treatises of Asclepiodotus (first century BC; Loeb trans., 1923), Aelian (early second century AD; trans. A. M. Devine, "Aelian's *Manual of Hellenistic Military Tactics:* A New Translation from the Greek with an Introduction," *The Ancient World* 19 [1989] pp. 31–64), and Arrian, the historian of Alexander the Great (mid–second century AD; trans. J. G. DeVoto, 1993, with many inaccuracies). All are derived from a single lost work, usually thought to be by the early first-century BC philosopher Posidonius (A. Dain, *Histoire du texte d'Élien le tacticien* [Paris, 1946] pp. 26–40; N. V. Sekunda, "The *Taktika* of Poseidonius of Apameia," in id., *Hellenistic Infantry Reform in the 160's BC* [Lodz, 2001] pp. 125–34). The treatises describe the organization, formations, and tactical terminology of an army loosely based on the Macedonian model — a fading memory in Asclepiodotus's day and wholly gone in Aelian's and Arrian's. The historical value of the works is diminished by powerful idealizing and abstracting philosophical and mathematical glosses: overall the treatises describe no historical army but an ideal army (on the origins of the tradition, see E. L. Wheeler, "The *Hoplomachoi* and Vegetius' Spartan Drillmasters," *Chiron* 13 [1983] pp. 1–20 at p. 6; on its tenor, see P. A. Stadter, "The *Ars Tactica* of Arrian: Tradition and Originality," *Classical Philology* 73 [1978] pp. 117–28 at p. 118).

On Thessaly and its people, H. D. Westlake, *Thessaly in the Fourth Century BC* (London, 1935) is still standard; on Thessalian cavalry, Spence, *The Cavalry of Classical Greece* pp. 23–25 gives a good thumbnail sketch of what is known about their organization; for their equipment and dress, see N. V. Sekunda, *The Ancient Greeks* (Oxford, 1986) pp. 15–17, gathering evidence from art that Thessalian cavalry used long thrusting spears. On Jason of Pherae and his army, see S. Sprawski, *Jason of Pherae* (Krakow, 1999) pp. 102–14. He notes (p. 110) that Jason of Pherae is also credited with inventing a new piece of armor, the "half-breastplate," about which we know nothing (Poll. *Onom.* 1.134).

Study of the campaign and battle of Leuctra is famously bedeviled by contradictions in the four surviving accounts, the contemporary Xenophon (*Hell.* 6.4.4–16), whose partiality toward the Spartans deforms his version, and the later Diodorus Siculus (15.51–56), Plutarch (*Pel.* 20–23), and Pausanias (9.13). My account is brief, mainstream, and dodges many of the controversial points. For the controversies, see C. J. Tuplin, "The Leuctra Campaign: Some Outstanding Problems," *Klio* 69 (1987) pp. 72–107. For an evaluation of Epaminondas's tactics, see V. D. Hanson, "Epameinondas, the Battle of Leuktra (371 BC), and the 'Revolution' in Greek Battle Tactics," *Classical Antiquity* 7 (1988) 190–207. For the topography of the battlefield, see W. K. Pritchett, *Studies in Ancient Greek Topography* vol. 1 (Berkeley and Los Angeles, 1965) pp. 49–58.

On the Theban Sacred Band, see J. G. DeVoto, "The Theban Sacred

Band," *The Ancient World* 23 (1992) pp. 3–19; on its relationship to the "charioteers and chariot-fighters" at Delium, see Anderson, *Military Theory* pp. 158–59. For the role of homosexuality in Greek warfare, see D. Ogden, "Homosexuality and Warfare in Ancient Greece," in A. B. Lloyd (ed.), *Battle in Antiquity* (London, 1996) pp. 107–68. On the systematization of military knowledge in Classical Greece, see E. L. Wheeler, "*Hoplomachoi*" pp. 1–20.

The date of the establishment of the Athenian *ephebeia* is subject to long-standing controversy (the evidence is usefully summarized in English by R. T. Ridley, "The Hoplite as Citizen: Athenian Military Institutions in Their Social Context," *L'Antiquité Classique* 48 [1979] pp. 508–48 at 531–34; for the controversy and its literature, Burckhardt, *Bürger und Soldaten* pp. 26–75). There is no unequivocal inscriptional evidence for the institution before the 330s BC, and no literary evidence for ephebes (whatever the word then meant) existing at Athens before the 370s (Aeschin. *Or.* 2.167). Given the large impact of the full-blown institution when it did exist (two years and compulsory for all citizens) the argument from silence is compelling, especially given the extensive discussions of military training in Plato and Xenophon, who clearly assume that mass public training does not exist at Athens (e.g. Pl. *Lach.;* Xen. *Mem.* 3.5.15, 3.12.5): whatever may have gone before (something may be alluded to in Xen. *Vect.* 4.52, from the late 350s — but Xenophon is complaining that it was not fully funded, so it cannot have been compulsory — see N. V. Sekunda, "*IG* ii² 1250: A Decree Concerning the *Lampadephoroi* of the Tribe Aiantis," *Zeitschrift für Papyrologie und Epigraphik* 83 [1990] pp. 149–82 at 151–52), the course of mass ephebic training known to Aristotle (*Ath. Pol.* 42) dates to the 330s. And the spread of similar institutions through the Greek world seems to have been sparked by the Athenian *ephebeia* of the 330s (A. S. Chankowski, "Date et circonstances de l'institution de l'éphébie à Érétrie," *Dialogues d'histoire ancienne* 19 [1993] pp. 17–44), suggesting that what went before at Athens was far more rudimentary. But it may well be that all Classical Greek ephebic institutions took their name from a widespread archaic institution.

For the role of *techne* (skill or craft) in fourth-century Greek warfare, I draw upon P. Vidal-Naquet, "The Tradition of the Athenian Hoplite," in id., *The Black Hunter,* trans. A. Szegedy-Maszak (Baltimore, 1986) pp.

85–105 at pp. 93–97 (translating "La Tradition de l'hoplite Athénien," in
J.-P. Vernant [ed.], *Problèmes de la guerre en Grèce ancienne* [Paris 1968]
pp. 161–81). But I reject the tendency (e.g., E. Heza, "Ruse de guerre —
trait caractéristique d'une tactique nouvelle dans l'oeuvre de Thucydide,"
Eos 62 [1974] pp. 227–44 at 228–29) to oppose military *techne* to the
Greek agonistic military ethos: since Hesiod *techne* had been conceived
of as competitive. The conflict is not between competition and *techne*, it
is between different competitions.

For resistance to military change in the fourth century, see R. Schulz,
"Militärische Revolution und politischer Wandel. Das Schicksal Griechen-
lands im 4. Jahrhundert v. Chr.," *Historische Zeitschrift* 268 (1999) pp. 281–
310 at 286–304. For the decline of strict hoplite ethics even at Sparta, see
L. Piccirilli, "L'ideale Spartano della morte eroica: crisi e trasformazione,"
Annali della Scuola Normale Superiore di Pisa 25 (1995) pp. 1387–1400.

For Spartan education, see N. M. Kennel, *The Gymnasium of Virtue:
Education and Culture in Classical Sparta* (Chapel Hill, 1995). On *metis*
and Spartan views of *metis,* see above, p. 411.

Fourth-century trends in warfare are conventionally conceived in
terms of professionalization (e.g., Vidal-Naquet, "Tradition" p. 94), on
the face of it unexceptionable: mercenaries and some generals did make
a profession of fighting. But professionalism sneaks in an implicit explanation along with a description, making fourth-century developments
seem inevitable or part of a natural process of improvement and perfection: they were not, and they need to be explained, as I have tried to do
in this chapter. Yet the reader should be aware that (unlike the ethos of
hoplites) there is no direct evidence for the ethos of cavalry or peltasts.
So this chapter is necessarily speculative.

Chapter VI. Alexander the Great at the Battle of Issus

On Alexander the Great and his campaigns, see the magical account of
R. Lane Fox, *Alexander the Great* (London, 1973); for a more strictly military telling of the campaigns, see J. F. C. Fuller, *The Generalship of Alexander the Great* (London, 1958). Alexander's relationship with Homer and
Achilles and the Homeric tenor of Macedonian aristocratic society have
long been understood: the literature is gathered by A. Cohen, "Alexander

and Achilles — Macedonians and 'Myceneans,'" in J. B. Carter and S. P. Morris (eds.), *The Ages of Homer* (Austin, 1995) pp. 483–505, noting (p. 489) that Macedonian pottery suggests a conservative society preserving continuity with the Bronze Age rather than a self-conscious sixth-century BC revival. Specifically on Alexander and Achilles, W. Ameling, "Alexander und Achilleus: Eine Bestandsaufnahme," in W. Will (ed.), *Zu Alexander dem Grossen, Festschrift G. Wirth* (Amsterdam, 1988) pp. 657–92 is encyclopedic. In this chapter I bring out some military implications of this relationship.

On the army of Alexander, concise English descriptions are given by N. V. Sekunda, *The Army of Alexander the Great* (Oxford, 1984) and A. M. Devine, "Alexander the Great," in J. Hackett (ed.), *Warfare in the Ancient World* (London, 1989) pp. 104–29. A grasp of the large number of details in contention (and likely to remain so) must begin with H. Berve, *Das Alexanderreich auf prosopographischer Grundlage* vol. 1 (Munich, 1926) pp. 103–217; W. W. Tarn, *Alexander the Great* vol. 2 (Cambridge, 1948) pp. 135–69; P. A. Brunt, "Alexander's Macedonian Cavalry," *Journal of Hellenic Studies* 83 (1963) pp. 27–46; R. D. Milns, "The Army of Alexander the Great," in [no ed.], *Alexandre le Grand, Image et réalité* (Entretiens Hardt 22; Geneva, 1976) pp. 87–136; and G. T. Griffith in id. and N. G. L. Hammond, *A History of Macedonia* vol. 2 (Oxford, 1979) pp. 405–49, on Philip's reforms. On the phalanx reform of Philip II in particular I prefer the account of N. G. L. Hammond, "What May Philip Have Learnt as a Hostage in Thebes?" *Greek, Roman, and Byzantine Studies* 38 (1997) pp. 355–72 at 366–69, which also gathers previous discussions. I do not derive Philip's phalanx from hoplite-like "reformed" peltasts of Iphicrates (an old theory now championed by N. V. Sekunda, "Classical Warfare," in J. Boardman [ed.], *The Cambridge Ancient History*[2] *Plates to Volumes V and VI* [Cambridge, 1994] pp. 167–94 at 184–88) because I do not believe that Iphicrates' reform produced a new kind of hoplite (see above p. 413). Against this derivation see also G. T. Griffith, "Peltasts and the Origins of the Macedonian Phalanx," in H. J. Dell (ed.), *Ancient Macedonian Studies in Honor of Charles F. Edson* (Thessalonica, 1981) pp. 161–67.

On the Macedonian *telamon* (shoulder strap) shield I follow M. M. Markle, "A Shield Monument from Veria and the Chronology of Macedonian Shield Types," *Hesperia* 68 (1999) pp. 219–54 at 246–51. This arrangement seems to work in reenactment, see P. Connolly, "Experiments with the *Sarissa*—the Macedonian Pike and Cavalry Lance—a Functional View," *Journal of Roman Military Equipment Studies* 11 (2000) pp. 103–12 at 109–12, who notes that the *telamon* takes some of the weight of the *sarissa*. For possible nonepic inspirations, note that *telamon* shields are occasionally attested earlier in vase painting, e.g., H. van Wees, "The Development of the Hoplite Phalanx," in id. (ed.), *War and Violence in Ancient Greece* (London, 2000) pp. 125–66 at p. 135 fig. 8b (on a Boeotian shield, c. 530–520 BC), and straps may have been used by peltasts as well (Xen. *An.* 7.4.17). For discussion of straps and belts in epic, M. J. Bennett, *Belted Heroes and Bound Women* (Lanham, Md., 1997) pp. 61–175, with a full list of shield straps, p. 166 n. 30.

On the psychology of Alexander's army and especially on hunting and games, A. B. Lloyd, "Philip II and Alexander the Great: The Moulding of Macedon's Army," in id. (ed.), *Battle in Antiquity* (London, 1996) pp. 169–98. On the loose formal discipline—by modern standards—of Alexander's army, E. Carney, "Macedonians and Mutiny: Discipline and Indiscipline in the Army of Philip and Alexander," *Classical Philology* 91 (1996) pp. 19–44.

All the surviving chronicles of Alexander's campaigns describe the battle of Issus: Arrian's account (2.8–12) is fundamental; Quintus Curtius (3.7–11) and Callisthenes (as summarized and denounced by Polybius [12.17.1–12.22.7]) add useful details; Diodorus (17.33–34) and Plutarch (*Alex.* 20) contribute mostly air. Issus is the least contentious of Alexander's four great battles: see A. M. Devine, "Grand Tactics at the Battle of Issus," *The Ancient World* 12 (1985) pp. 39–57 for the issues and the scholarship. The major controversy is the degree to which it is allowable to supplement Arrian with details preserved in other traditions: I see no need for the extreme pessimism of, e.g., N. G. L. Hammond, "Alexander's Charge at the Battle of Issus in 333 BC," *Historia* 41 (1992) pp. 395–406. On the Alexander Mosaic, see A. Cohen, *The Alexander Mosaic* (Cambridge, 1997): Issus is the usual identification of the subject, but it might well be Gaugamela or a generic victory (pp. 130–31). The battle of Granicus River, on the other hand, is very confused and contentious: J. C. Yardley and W. Heckel, *Justin, Epitome of the Philippic History of Pompeius*

Trogus: Books 11–12, Alexander the Great (Oxford, 1997) p. 114 give references to modern discussions.

On the ranked arrays of Greek armies, see P. Vidal-Naquet and P. Lévêque, "Epaminondas the Pythagorean, or the Tactical Problem of Right and Left," in P. Vidal-Naquet, *The Black Hunter,* trans. A. Szegedy-Maszak (Baltimore, 1986) pp. 61–82 (trans. from *Le Chasseur noir* [Paris, 1981]). On the Macedonian battle line as a precedence system, see Devine, "Grand Tactics" p. 49 and Griffith, *History of Macedonia* vol. 2 pp. 711–12. On the practice of granting honorific titles to Macedonian units and their inflation over time, see R. D. Milns, "The Army of Alexander the Great" pp. 95–101.

Chapter VII. Hellenistic Warfare (323–31 BC)

For the relationship of war and athletics in the Hellenistic world, M. Launey, *Recherches sur les armées hellénistiques* vol. 2 (Paris, 1950) pp. 813–74, perhaps soon to be superseded by A. S. Chankowski, *L'Éphébie hellénistique* (forthcoming). For beauty contests, see N. B. Crowther, "Male 'Beauty' Contests in Greece: The *Euandria* and *Euexia*," *L'Antiquité classique* 54 (1985) pp. 285–91.

For Philip II's training of his army in the phalanx, see N. G. L. Hammond, "Training in the Use of a *Sarissa* and Its Effect in Battle," *Antichthon* 14 (1980) pp. 53–63; and for his cavalry, N. G. L. Hammond, "Royal Pages, Personal Pages, and Boys Trained in the Macedonian Manner During the Period of the Temenid Monarchy," *Historia* 39 (1990) pp. 261–90 at 261–64 gathers the evidence for an old system of training royal pages in Macedon that may be linked to Macedonian cavalry training.

For the Achaean leader Philopoemen, see R. M. Errington, *Philopoemen* (Oxford, 1969).

For the war of Paraetacene and Gabiene, R. A. Billows, *Antigonos the One-Eyed and the Creation of the Hellenistic State* (Berkeley and Los Angeles, 1990) pp. 82–109. The exact dates of these events are a muddle: it may well be that Paraetacene was in 316 and Gabiene in 315 BC (J. Hornblower, *Hieronymus of Cardia* [Oxford, 1981] p. 109 n. 8 gathers the scholarship).

For the battle of Paraetacene, the only account is that of the first-century BC Diodorus of Sicily (19.25–31), a derivative author usually no better than his sources. But in this case his source is the excellent Hieronymus of Cardia, who may well have been present and who was close to both generals (on Hieronymus and his relationship to Diodorus, see J. Hornblower, *Hieronymus of Cardia* pp. 18–62 and esp. 37–39; for a trace of his presence at the battle, p. 121; Hornblower is also excellent on Hellenistic thinking about what made armies win and the Hellenistic culture of command, esp. pp. 187–203). For discussion of the battle, see E. Kahnes and J. Kromeyer, "Paraetakene (317 v. Chr.)," in J. Kromeyer, *Antike Schlachtfelder* vol. 4 (Berlin, 1924–31) pp. 391–424, and A. M. Devine, "Diodorus' Account of the Battle of Paraitacene (317 BC)," *The Ancient World* 12 (1985) pp. 75–86, who deal ably with the many minor problems in Diodorus's account (which I have mostly ignored). I rely on Diodorus's editorial comments on the battle for a sense of the culture of Hellenistic warfare: but I do not care whether these comments come from Hieronymus's early Hellenistic account (as J. Hornblower, *Hieronymus of Cardia* pp. 196–99 implies) or are an addition in Diodorus's late Hellenistic account.

On the battle of Gabiene, see E. Kahnes and J. Kromeyer, "Gabiene (316 v. Chr.)," in J. Kromeyer, *Antike Schlachtfelder* vol. 4 (Berlin, 1924–31) pp. 425–34, and A. M. Devine, "Diodorus' Account of the Battle of Gabiene," *The Ancient World* 12 (1985) pp. 87–96. Hieronymus was certainly present, since he was wounded and captured by Antigonus (Diod. Sic. 19.44.3). Neither the battlefield of Paraetacene nor that of Gabiene can be located.

For interest in Homer and the Hellenistic "Bronze-Age revival," see, for popular, "reading" editions of Homer, K. McNamee, "Aristarchus and 'Everyman's Homer,'" *Greek, Roman, and Byzantine Studies* 22 (1981) 247–55. Royal benefactions to Troy, A. Erskine, *Troy Between Greece and Rome* (Oxford, 2001) pp. 232–34. For hero cults in Bronze Age tombs (late fourth century and after), see S. E. Alcock, "Tomb Cult and the Post-Classical *Polis*," *American Journal of Archeology* 95 (1991) pp. 447–67, and more generally on Hellenistic cults to Homeric heroes, id., "The Heroic Past in a Hellenistic Present," in P. Cartledge et al. (eds.), *Hellenistic Constructs: Essays in Culture, History, and Historiography* (Berkeley and Los Angeles, 1997) pp. 20–34. For Bronze Age or Homeric revival in architecture and vase painting, E. Vermeule, "Baby Aigisthos and the Bronze Age," *Proceedings of the Cambridge Philological Society* n.s. 33 (1987) pp. 122–52, esp. 131.

For surveys of Hellenistic warfare, still worth consulting are W. W. Tarn, *Hellenistic Military and Naval Developments* (Cambridge, 1930) and P. Lévêque, "La Guerre a l'époque hellénistique," in J.-P. Vernant (ed.), *Problèmes de la guerre en Grèce ancienne* (Paris, 1968) pp. 261–87. Now on all aspects except actual combat, and especially for the rich epigraphical evidence, A. Chaniotis, *War in the Hellenistic World* (Oxford, 2005), with full bibliography. On specific armies, see B. Bar-Kochva, *The Seleucid Army* (Cambridge, 1976), M. B. Hatzopoulos, *L'Organisation de l'armée macédonienne sous les Antigonides* (Athens, 2001), and J. Lesquier, *Les Institutions militaires de l'Egypte sous les Lagides* (Paris, 1911).

On specific topics: for mercenaries, see G. T. Griffith, *The Mercenaries of the Hellenistic World* (Cambridge, 1935); for military organization (and rich on many other subjects), see N. V. Sekunda, *Hellenistic Infantry Reform in the 160's BC* (Lodz, 2001); for generalship, see P. Beston, "Hellenistic Military Leadership," in H. van Wees (ed.), *War and Violence in Ancient Greece* (London, 2000) pp. 315–35; for the various types of Hellenistic infantry, see E. Foulon, "Contribution à une taxinomie des corps d'infanterie des armées hellénistiques," *Les Études classiques* 64 (1996) pp. 227–44 and 317–38 (but Foulon is not always to be believed); and for elephants, see H. H. Scullard, *The Elephant in the Greek and Roman World* (Ithaca, 1974) (with pp. 86–94 on Paraetacene and Gabiene); for Hellenistic cities' arrangements for war, see J. Ma, "Fighting *Poleis* of the Hellenistic World," in H. van Wees (ed.), *War and Violence in Ancient Greece* (London, 2000) pp. 337–76.

The Romans

On early Rome, see the survey of T. J. Cornell, *The Beginnings of Rome* (London, 1995), with pp. 204–7 and 351 on territory, citing earlier studies. On Rome's expansion under the middle Republic, see the accessible survey of R. M. Errington, *The Dawn of Empire* (Ithaca, 1972).

For accessible, sensible, well-illustrated chronological surveys of the history of the Roman army, see A. Goldsworthy, *Roman Warfare* (London,

2000) and *The Complete Roman Army* (London, 2003). L. Keppie, *The Making of the Roman Army* (London, 1984) has more scholarly apparatus but stops in the early empire. More usual are thematically organized books on the Roman army of the empire: on the army as an institution the best are G. Webster, *The Roman Imperial Army of the First and Second Centuries AD³* (Norman, Okla., 1998[1985]) with a *catalogue raisonée* of recent scholarship by H. Elton (pp. xi–xix), and Y. Le Bohec, *The Roman Imperial Army* (London, 1994; trans. R. Bate from *L'Armée romaine sous le haut-empire* [Paris, 1989]). Synchronic analyses of the Roman army in action are A. Goldsworthy, *The Roman Army at War 100 BC–AD 200* (Oxford, 1996), C. M. Gilliver, *The Roman Art of War* (Stroud, 1999), and P. Sabin, "The Face of Roman Battle," *Journal of Roman Studies* 90 (2000) pp. 1–17.

Putting sixteenth-century emphasis on Roman discipline in context is J. De Landtsheer, "Justus Lipsius's *de Militia Romana:* Polybius Revived or How an Ancient Historian Was Turned into a Manual of Early Modern Warfare," in K. Enenkel, J. L. De Jong, et. al. (eds.), *Recreating Ancient History* (Leiden, 2001) pp. 101–22. Doubts about the iron discipline of the Roman army go back to W. S. Messer, "Mutiny in the Roman Army: The Republic," *Classical Philology* 15 (1920) pp. 158–75. See also Goldsworthy, *The Roman Army at War* pp. 281–86 for pungent remarks. For the psychological "cohesion" theory of Roman success, see below p. 432 for the literature.

Chapter VIII. Early Roman Warfare

On dueling before or during battle under the Republic, see S. P. Oakley, "Single Combat in the Roman Republic," *Classical Quarterly* 35 (1985) pp. 392–410 (supplemented by id., *A Commentary on Livy Books VI–X* vol. 2 [Oxford, 1998] pp. 123–25), who gathers real and mythical instances and modern discussion (including the Corvus and Torquatus episodes, "Single Combat" pp. 393–94), emphasizes how common single combat must have been (p. 397), and discusses the conflict between single-combat and *disciplina* (pp. 404–7). Later Roman moneyers might allude to the single combats of ancestors on their coins: M. H. Crawford, *Roman Republican Coinage* vol. 2 (Cambridge, 1974) p. 860 collects instances s.v. "battle."

T. Wiedemann, "Single Combat and Being Roman," *Ancient Society* 27 (1996) pp. 91–103 at 98 argues that single combat was fundamental to Roman culture and manifested itself later in gladiatorial combat.

For speculations on the origins of the Corvus story, see R. Bloch, "Combats singuliers entre gaulois et romains: faits vécus et traditions celtiques," in id. and J. Bayet, *Tite-Live histoire romaine* vol. 7 (Paris, 1968) pp. 108–17 at 113–17, tracing it to a Celtic raven tradition. Oakley, "Single Combat" p. 394 gathers other suggestions.

On the literary presentation of single combat in Livy, see A. Feldherr, *Spectacle and Society in Livy's History* (Berkeley and Los Angeles, 1998) pp. 92–111 and J. Fries, *Der Zweikampf. Historische und literarische Aspekte seiner Darstelling bei T. Livius* (Meisenheim, 1985).

On the *spolia opima*, J. W. Rich, "Augustus and the *Spolia Opima*," *Chiron* 26 (1996) pp. 85–127 gathers the literature. On trophies attached to houses, see E. Rawson, "The Antiquarian Tradition: Spoils and Representations of Foreign Armor," *Roman Culture and Society* (Oxford, 1991) pp. 582–98 (reprinted from W. Eder [ed.], *Staat und Staatlichkeit in der frühen römischen Republik* [Stuttgart, 1990] pp. 157–73). For the argument that single combat was not confined to the aristocracy, pp. 583–84.

On the primitive quality of Roman fighting under the Republic, arguing that the wolfskin-clad Roman *velites* were a survival from Indo-European wolf-warriors, see M. P. Speidel, *Ancient Germanic Warriors* (London, 2004) pp. 13–17. Along these lines it is possible to speculate that the manipular age echelons were descended from Indo-European age classes. J.-P. Morel, "Sur quelques aspects de la jeunesse à Rome," in [no ed.], *Mélanges offerts à Jacques Heurgon II. L'Italie préromaine et la Rome républicaine* (Rome, 1976) pp. 663–83 gathers the literature on archaic Roman age classes.

On single combat among the Celts, see L. Rawlings, "Celts, Spaniards, and Samnites: Warriors in a Soldiers' War," in T. Cornell, B. Rankov, and P. Sabin (eds.), *The Second Punic War, A Reappraisal* (London 1996) pp. 81–95 at 86–87.

On *virtus*, see J. B. McCall, *The Cavalry of the Roman Republic* (London, 2002) pp. 83–99 and J. E. Lendon, "The Rhetoric of Combat: Greek Military Theory and Roman Culture in Julius Caesar's Battle Descriptions," *Classical Antiquity* 18 (1999) pp. 273–329 at 304–16. There is little written on *disciplina,* but on the word see O. Mauch, *Der lateinische Begriff* Disciplina: *Eine Wortuntersuchung* (Freiburg, 1941).

There are many good, accessible descriptions in English of the manipular legion and considerations of the problems it presents. See, for example, P. Connolly, *Greece and Rome at War*² (London, 1998) pp. 129–42; G. Daly, *Cannae: The Experience of Battle in the Second Punic War* (London, 2002) pp. 56–73; N. V. Sekunda, *Republican Roman Army 200–104 BC* (London, 1996); or L. Keppie, *The Making of the Roman Army* (London, 1984) pp. 33–40.

The details of the current conception of the manipular legion were thrashed out (and the insoluble problems fought over with admirable erudition and bile) by German controversialists around the turn of the twentieth century. Access to these debates is easiest through E. Meyer, "Das römische Manipularheer, seine Entwicklung und seine Vorstufen," *Kleine Schriften* vol. 2 (Halle, 1924) pp. 195–285 (reprinted from *Abhandlungen der preussischen Akademie der Wissenschaften* 1923, *philol.-hist. Klasse,* Abhandlung 3); J. Kromayer and G. Veith, *Heerwesen und Kriegführung der Griechen und Römer* (= I. von Müller and W. Otto [eds.], *Handbuch der Altertumswissenschaft* 4.3.2; Munich, 1928) pp. 288–373; and P. Fraccaro, *Opuscula IV: Della guerra presso i Romani* (Pavia, 1975) pp. 41–58. The arguments of one of the contributors to that controversy, H. Delbrück, are accessible in English: *Warfare in Antiquity,* trans. W. J. Renfroe (Lincoln, Neb., 1990) pp. 272–96, translating *Geschichte der Kriegskunst im Rahmen der politischen Geschichte*³ vol. 1 (Berlin, 1920).

The evolution of the Roman army prior to the manipular legion is murky indeed. P. Connolly, *Greece and Rome at War*² pp. 87–128 and N. V. Sekunda and S. Northwood, *Early Roman Armies* (London, 1995) gather the archeological and artistic evidence; E. Meyer, "Manipularheer" and P. Fraccaro, *Opuscula IV* pp. 11–40 gather the literary evidence; all theorize about developments. Essential as a guide to the literary tradition is E. Rawson, "The Literary Sources for the Pre-Marian Army," *Roman Culture and Society* (Oxford, 1991) pp. 34–57 (reprinted from *Papers of the British School at Rome* 39 [1971] pp. 13–31). On the "Servian" census, T. J. Cornell, *The Beginnings of Rome* (London, 1995) pp. 179–86, with n. 39 on the coming of hoplite equipment to Italy in the seventh century.

On the theme of the *furor* of Roman youth, contrasted with *disciplina,*

G. Dumézil, *Horace et les Curiaces* (Paris, 1942) pp. 11–33; J.-P. Néraudau, "L'Exploit de Titus Manlius Torquatus (*Tite-Live,* VII, 9, 6–10) (Réflexion sur la 'iuuentus' archaïque chez Tite-Live)," in [no ed.], *Mélanges offerts à Jacques Heurgon II: L'Italie préromaine et la Rome républicaine* (Rome, 1976) pp. 685–94; and id., *La Jeunesse dans la litterature et les institutions de la Rome républicaine* (Paris, 1979) pp. 249–58.

For the relationship of *disciplina* to the needs of the Roman phalanx, cf. G. Brizzi, "I *manliana imperia* e la riforma manipolare: l'escercito romano tra *ferocia* e *disciplina,*" *Sileno* 16 (1990) pp. 185–206 at pp. 191–92.

Chapter IX. The Wrath of Pydna

Polybius's account of the Pydna campaign is lost, except for fragments: but Livy (44.33–42), Plutarch (*Aem.* 11–22), and Cassius Dio (in the epitome of Zonaras, 9.22–23) based theirs upon Polybius, and their accounts survive, Livy's with gaps at crucial points and Dio's with nothing on the battle itself. For the literary tradition (and the modern bibliography), see F. W. Walbank, *A Historical Commentary on Polybius* vol. 3 (Oxford, 1979) pp. 378–91. N. G. L. Hammond, "The Battle of Pydna," *Journal of Hellenic Studies* 104 (1984) pp. 31–47 gathers attempts to locate and reconstruct the battle, but I prefer the treatment of the sources given by E. Meyer, "Die Schlacht bei Pydna," *Kleine Schriften* vol. 2 (Halle, 1924) pp. 465–94 (reprinted from *Sitzungsberichte der preussischen Akademie der Wissenschaften* 31 [1909] pp. 780–803). The ancient accounts present many insoluble problems, but these do not affect the argument made here.

Detailed military narratives of the Third Macedonian War (with discussions of the battle of Pydna) are given by J. Kromeyer, *Antike Schlachtfelder* vol. 2 (Berlin, 1907) pp. 231–348 and P. Meloni, *Perseo e la fine della monarchia Macedone* (Rome, 1953) pp. 211–440. For the literary tradition about Aemilius Paullus (overwhelmingly positive because he was a benefactor of Polybius and later authors drew on Polybius), see W. Reiter, *Aemilius Paullus, Conqueror of Greece* (London, 1988).

On the Second Punic War, accessible are J. F. Lazenby, *Hannibal's War* (Warminster, 1978) and A. Goldsworthy, *The Punic Wars* (London, 2000). To trace the scholarly writing, J. Seibert, *Hannibal* and *Forschungen zu Hannibal* (Darmstadt, 1993) and Y. Le Bohec, *Histoire militaire des guerres puniques* (Monaco, 1996) are essential. For Hannibal as a helle-nized general, see G. Brizzi, "Hannibal — Punier und Hellenist," *Das Alter-tum* 37 (1991) pp. 201–10 at 207–10 and Seibert, *Hannibal* pp. 32–33, 100.

The degree to which the Romans preferred to fight openly and with-out tactics and trickery is controversial (and parallel to the same contro-versy about the Greeks before the Peloponnesian War). For the tradi-tional view — that the Romans fought in a ritualized style until Hannibal or Scipio Africanus taught them better — see J.-P. Brisson, "Les Muta-tions de la seconde guerre punique," in id. (ed.), *Problèmes de la guerre à Rome* (Paris, 1969) pp. 32–59; H. H. Scullard, *Scipio Africanus: Soldier and Politician* (Ithaca, 1970) pp. 73–75; G. Brizzi, *Il guerriero, l'oplita, il legionario* (Bologna, 2002) pp. 35–78. But E. L. Wheeler, in *"Sapiens* and Stratagems: The Neglected Meaning of a *Cognomen," Historia* 37 (1988) 166–95, and *Stratagem and the Vocabulary of Military Trickery* (Leiden, 1988) pp. 51–52 demonstrates a venerable Roman tradition of trickery in warfare. Both sides see real phenomena, but they each see only one side of a conflict among the Romans themselves, a conflict with a long life ahead of it: see J. E. Lendon, "The Rhetoric of Combat: Greek Military Theory and Roman Culture in Julius Caesar's Battle Descriptions," *Clas-sical Antiquity* 18 (1999) pp. 273–329 at 306–9.

On the Roman use of elephants in battle, see H. H. Scullard, *The Elephant in the Greek and Roman World* (Ithaca, 1974) pp. 178–98. On the hellenization of Rome during the middle Republic, see E. Gruen, *Culture and National Identity in Republican Rome* (Ithaca, 1992).

Chapter X. Caesar's Centurions and the Legion of Cohorts

Our knowledge of Gergovia derives from Caesar's own account, *B Gall.* 7.44–53. On the battle and its location, see T. Rice Holmes, *Caesar's Con-quest of Gaul* (Oxford, 1911) pp. 149–58, 756–67. For the contrast between Caesar's aggressive centurions — described as "berserk" — and his passive military tribunes, see J. Harmand, *L'Armée et le soldat a Rome de 107 à 50 avant notre ère* (Paris, 1967) pp. 338–39, 356–57. On the generally unheroic practice of Roman higher command, A. Goldsworthy, *The Roman Army at War 100 BC–AD 200* (Oxford, 1996) pp. 150–63. For the change in Ro-man aristocratic attitudes to warfare and the abolition of the citizen cavalry, see J. B. McCall, *The Cavalry of the Roman Republic* (London, 2002) pp. 100–36.

There are many English descriptions of the legion of cohorts, including H. M. D. Parker, *The Roman Legions* (Oxford, 1928) pp. 26–46 and L. Keppie, *The Making of the Roman Army* (London, 1984) pp. 63–67. For the cohortal army in action, Goldsworthy, *The Roman Army at War*. We know even less of the internal workings of the cohortal legion than we do of the manipular: access to the fundamental German scholarship and areas of controversy is through Rice Holmes, *Caesar's Conquest of Gaul* pp. 587–99 or P. Fraccaro, *Opuscula IV: Della guerra presso i Romani* (Pavia, 1975) pp. 137–66. See M. P. Speidel, "The Framework of an Imperial Legion," in R. J. Brewer (ed.), *The Second Augustan Legion and the Roman Military Machine* (Cardiff, 2002) pp. 125–43 for thoughts on how the centuries which made up the cohorts went together (an extremely murky matter, but J. C. Mann, "Roman Legionary Centurial Symbols," *Zeitschrift für Papyrologie und Epigraphik* 115 [1997] pp. 295–98 offers new evidence) and the evolution of the legion after Caesar. For a gloomy survey of some of the unsolved problems, see B. Isaac, "Hierarchy and Command-Structure in the Roman Army," *The Near East under Roman Rule* (Leiden, 1998) pp. 388–402.

On the invention of the cohort, see M. J. V. Bell, "Tactical Reform in the Roman Republican Army," *Historia* 14 (1965) pp. 404–22, but I am less confident than Bell that the invention of the cohort can be localized to Spain during the Second Punic War. N. V. Sekunda points out to me that the Roman legionary cohort may have been copied from Rome's Italian allies, who supplied so much of Rome's army, but in contingents smaller than legions: perhaps their contingents were the original cohorts.

Traditionally (e.g., Parker, *The Roman Legions* pp. 21–46), the moment of final transition from manipular to cohortal array was thought to be a reform of the Roman army by Gaius Marius to face the Cimbri and Teutones (c. 104 BC). This is soon after the last appearance in literature of the *velites* and the gaps between the maniples, at Muthul river in 108 BC (Sall. *Jug.* 46.7 and 49.6 [written, of course, in the 40s BC]). But in reality the transition was not so crisp. The maniples maintain a shadowy existence in Caesar (*B Gall.* 2.25, 6.40; Harmand, *L'Armée et le soldat* p. 237 argues for their continued importance) and possibly later (Speidel,

"Framework" n. 7 gathers the arguments), although cohorts receive far more emphasis. And in his description of the battle of Ilipa (206 BC), Polybius notes in passing that the Romans call a group of three maniples and an accompanying segment of *velites* a cohort, explaining the Latin word (Polyb. 11.23.1; cf. 11.33.1; Livy too frequently uses the term *cohors* in his descriptions of the Second Punic War, but given his habit of anachronism in military terminology, no weight can be placed upon his testimony). Even if the cohort is anachronistic for the age of the Second Punic War, the deployment of thirty maniples plus *velites* as ten cohorts must have been known by Polybius's own day, the mid–second century BC (for second-century cohorts, cf. Cato Mai. fr. 128 [Peter], "turmam, manipulum, cohortem temptabam"). But when Polybius describes the Roman legion in detail, it is the manipular legion he depicts, with no mention of cohorts: maniples and cohorts must have coexisted. And in Sallust's account of the war against Jugurtha, both maniples and cohorts can be seen as well: both appear at the battle of Muthul river (Sall. *Jug.* 51.3; cf. 55.4, 56.4, 100.4; but C. M. Gilliver, *The Roman Art of War* [Stroud, 1999] pp. 18–19 does not trust Sallust to use the technical terms accurately). No pleasing sharp transition, then, from maniple to cohort. Rather, a messier picture: "an *evolution,* a slow, continuing process" (Bell, "Tactical Reform" p. 418, his emphasis) from the legion of maniples to the legion of cohorts. To insist that Marius turned the Roman army from maniples to cohorts to fight the Cimbri and Teutones — a position for which there is no ancient evidence — implies that the Germans fought in some unusual way that placed maniples at an unusual disadvantage. But so far as can be told, the Germans fought much like Gauls (Plut. *Mar.* 11.8, 19.3, 19.7, 20.5, 25.6–7, 27.1; Goldsworthy, *The Roman Army at War* pp. 42–60, esp. p. 50, 58–59). And the Romans had been defeating Gauls for centuries with the manipular legion.

On the question of the changing minimum property qualification to serve in the Roman army, the advance of scholarship has moved our understanding from artificial clarity to irredeemable confusion. The reasons, dates, property qualifications, and values of the coins in which the various qualifications are expressed are all in play. For the traditional, simple view, see E. Gabba, "The Origins of the Professional Army at Rome: The '*proletarii*' and Marius' reform," in id., *Republican Rome, the*

Army and the Allies, trans. P. J. Cuff (Oxford, 1976) pp. 1–19, arguing that lack of manpower required a series of reductions and that the qualification was abolished for good by Marius in 107 BC. For the appalling current state of the question, see J. W. Rich, "The Supposed Roman Manpower Shortage of the Later Second Century BC," *Historia* 32 (1983) pp. 287–331 at 305–16, denying the lack of manpower and arguing that the qualification was only finally eliminated during the Social War (90–88 BC), and D. Rathbone, "The *Census* Qualifications of the *Assidui* and the *Prima Classis*," in H. Sancisi-Weerdenburg et al. (eds.), De Agricultura. *In Memoriam Pieter Willem de Neeve* (Amsterdam, 1993) pp. 121–52 at 139–46. It is safe to conclude only that there used to be a qualification and that it ceased to exist sometime around the turn of the first century BC.

A case for Greek influence on Roman fighting in the first century BC was made by F. Lammert, *Die römische Taktik zu Beginn der Kaiserzeit und die Geschichtschreibung* (Leipzig, 1931), particularly with regard to Roman use of cavalry and light infantry. I welcome Lammert's inspiration without accepting the details of his argument, which are weak.

Chapter XI. Scenes from the Jewish War

The siege of Jerusalem is recounted by Josephus, who participated in the war, first on the Jewish side and then, after his capture, on the Roman. On Josephus as an author, begin with T. Rajak, *Josephus: The Historian and His Society*[2] (London, 2002[1983]) and P. Bilde, *Flavius Josephus between Jerusalem and Rome* (Sheffield, 1988).

On the Roman military history that can be mined out of Josephus, see M. Gichon, "Aspects of a Roman Army in War According to the *Bellum Judaicum* of Josephus," in P. Freeman and D. Kennedy (eds.), *The Defence of the Roman and Byzantine East* vol. 1 (BAR Int. Ser. 297[i]; Oxford, 1986) pp. 287–310 and esp. A. Goldsworthy, "Community under Pressure: The Roman Army at the Siege of Jerusalem," in id. and I. Haynes (eds.), *The Roman Army as a Community* (Portsmouth, R.I., 1999) pp. 197–209, upon whose analysis I draw heavily in this chapter.

For a fuller, popular account of the Jewish War, see N. Faulkner, *Apocalypse: The Great Jewish Revolt Against Rome* (Stroud, 2002) with illustrations; for scholarly accounts, B. W. Jones, *The Emperor Titus* (London,

1984) pp. 34–55 and especially the excellent J. J. Price, *Jerusalem Under Siege: The Collapse of the Jewish State 66–70 CE* (Leiden, 1992). Price discusses the credibility of Josephus's *Jewish War* (pp. 180–93): it is hardly perfect, but there is no reason for radical disbelief. He reasons (p. 186) that "a piece of information that contradicts any tendentious statement or motif can generally be trusted, for Josephus would have no reason to make up uncooperative details." Many of the details cited in this chapter — of Roman individual and mass indiscipline — fall into this category, given Josephus's editorial statements about the discipline and obedience of the Roman army.

On Roman imperial military training, see G. Horsmann, *Untersuchungen zur militärischen Ausbildung im republikanischen und kaiserzeitlichen Rom* (Boppard am Rhein, 1991). In English, see R. W. Davies, "Fronto, Hadrian, and the Roman Army," *Latomus* 27 (1968) pp. 75–95 (reprinted in id., *Service in the Roman Army* [Edinburgh, 1989] pp. 71–90), and P. Rance, "*Simulacra Pugnae:* The Literary and Historical Tradition of Mock Battles in the Roman and Early Byzantine Army," *Greek, Roman, and Byzantine Studies* 41 (2000) pp. 223–75. On drill fields and practice areas, see R. W. Davies, "Roman Military Training Grounds," in E. Birley, B. Dobson, and M. Jarrett (eds.), *Roman Frontier Studies 1969: Eighth International Congress of* Limesforschung (Cardiff, 1974) pp. 20–26. On excavated cavalry exercise fields, see R. W. Davies, "The Training Grounds of the Roman Cavalry," *Archeological Journal* 125 (1968) pp. 73–100 (reprinted in id., *Service in the Roman Army* pp. 93–123); for practice camps, see R. W. Davies, "Roman Wales and Roman Military Practice-Camps," *Archaeologia Cambrensis* 117 (1968) pp. 103–20, (reprinted in id., *Service in the Roman Army* pp. 124–39); for artillery ranges, see R. W. Davies, "The Romans at Burnswark," *Historia* 21 (1972) pp. 99–113.

On Roman siegecraft, C. M. Gilliver, *The Roman Art of War* (Stroud, 1999) pp. 127–60.

Of the frieze of Trajan's Column, of accessible editions, F. Coarelli, *The Column of Trajan,* trans. C. Rockwell (Rome 2000) has good photographs. On the column as a source for the study of equipment, see especially J. C. Coulston, "The Value of Trajan's Column as a Source for Military Equipment," in C. van Driel-Murray (ed.), *Roman Military Equipment: The Sources of Evidence* (BAR Int. Ser. 476; Oxford, 1989) pp. 31–44.

For the Roman practice of taking heads in war (in no way limited to auxiliaries, despite the convention of Trajan's Column), see A. Goldsworthy, *The Roman Army at War 100 BC–AD 200* (Oxford, 1996) pp. 271–76 and J.-L. Voisin, "Les Romains, chasseurs de têtes," in [no ed.], *Du Châtiment dans la cité: Supplices corporels et peine de mort dans le monde antique* (Rome, 1984) pp. 241–93.

On the increased use of auxiliaries to form the main line of battle, see C. M. Gilliver, "Mons Graupius and the Role of Auxiliaries in Battle," *Greece and Rome* 43 (1996) pp. 54–67.

On trends in recruitment to the legions, see G. Forni, *Il reclutamento delle legioni da Augusto a Diocleziano* (Milan, 1953); on recruitment of the sons of soldiers, pp. 126–29; this work is brought up to date in id., *Esercito e marina di Roma antica* (Stuttgart, 1992) pp. 11–141; see also J. C. Mann, *Legionary Recruitment and Veteran Settlement during the Principate* (London, 1983). On the auxiliaries, K. Kraft, *Zur Rekrutierung der Alen und Kohorten an Rhein und Donau* (Bern, 1951). On reluctance to serve under the Roman empire, conscription, and resulting revolts, see P. Brunt, "Conscription and Volunteering in the Roman Imperial Army," *Roman Imperial Themes* (Oxford, 1990) pp. 188–214 (reprinted from *Scripta Classica Israelica* 1 [1974] pp. 90–115).

On the competitive culture of the imperial Roman army, see J. E. Lendon, *Empire of Honour* (Oxford, 1997) pp. 244–64; O. Stoll, "'De honore certabant et dignitate,' Truppe und Selbstidentifikation in der Armee der römischen Kaiserzeit," in id., *Römische Heer und Gesellschaft* (Stuttgart, 2001) pp. 106–31. Specifically on decorations of individual soldiers and units, see V. A. Maxfield, *The Military Decorations of the Roman Army* (Berkeley and Los Angeles, 1981). On unit titles, see P. Holder, *Studies in the* Auxilia *of the Roman Army from Augustus to Trajan* (Oxford, 1980) and J. Fitz, *Honorific Titles of Roman Military Units in the 3rd Century* (Budapest, 1983).

S. P. Oakley, "Single Combat in the Roman Republic," *Classical Quarterly* 35 (1985) pp. 392–410 at 404–7 assembles literature on the question of how initiative — in his case single combats in the Republic — can be reconciled with Roman discipline. Goldsworthy, *The Roman Army at War* pp. 264–82 denies the tension, maintaining that the Roman concept of discipline allowed such individual aggressiveness. But Josephus's Titus reproves his men for it, and at one point they think he will execute them (*BJ* 5.126), so the tension did exist. But Goldsworthy is quite right that "discipline and the bold action of individuals were complementary factors in the success of Roman armies" (p. 281): I would extend that to the boldness of groups, units, and whole armies. For *virtus* the Romans were willing to put up with a great deal of disobedience.

In this chapter I question theories of the effectiveness of the Roman army that stress cohesion, horizontal bonds between soldiers, that descend particularly from S. L. A. Marshall's *Men Against Fire* (New York, 1947). Study of group solidarity in the Roman army begins with R. Mac-Mullen, "The Legion as a Society," *Historia* 33 (1984) pp. 440–56 (reprinted in id., *Changes in the Roman Empire* [Princeton, 1990] pp. 225–35) and cohesion has been advocated especially by Goldsworthy, *The Roman Army at War* pp. 252–57 and "Community under Pressure," and G. Daly, *Cannae: The Experience of Battle in the Second Punic War* (London, 2000), both influenced by J. Keegan, *The Face of Battle* (London, 1976). But the limitations of cohesion are beginning to be understood in other fields of military history: studies of forces which have taken such severe casualties that maintaining cohesion can hardly have been possible, but which continued to fight, have suggested other solutions. O. Bartov, *Hitler's Army: Soldiers, Nazis, and War in the Third Reich* (New York, 1991) argues that coercion or fighting for a cause was more important, while R. S. Rush, *Hell in Hürtgen Forest: The Ordeal and Triumph of an American Infantry Regiment* (Lawrence, Kan., 2001) pp. 309–47 stresses leadership, whether supplying encouragement or coercion. In the Roman context, the "buddy system" has been questioned by E. L. Wheeler, "Firepower: Missile Weapons and the 'Face of Battle,'" *Electrum* 5 (2001) pp. 169–84 at 173.

For the controversy about the "barbarization" of the late Roman army and more generally on the decline of quality and discipline, see, arguing yes, R. MacMullen, *Corruption and the Decline of Rome* (New Haven, 1988) pp. 199–204; A. Ferrill, *The Fall of the Roman Empire: The Military Explanation* (London, 1986) pp. 77–85 (barbarians, but dating it after Adrianople) and pp. 46–50 (earlier decline); J. H. W. G. Liebeschuetz, *Barbarians and Bishops* (Oxford, 1991) pp. 7–25 (barbarians); and arguing no, H. Elton, *Warfare in Roman Europe AD 350–425* (Oxford, 1996) pp. 136–52, 272–77 (barbarians), pp. 265–67 (decline); M. J. Nicasie, *Twilight of Empire: The Roman Army from the Reign of Diocletian until the Battle of Adrianople* (Amsterdam, 1998) pp. 97–116 (barbarians), 185–86 (decline).

For the reckless behavior of Titus in Judaea, see B. W. Jones, "The Reckless Titus," in C. Deroux (ed.), *Studies in Latin Literature and Roman History VI* (Brussels, 1992) pp. 408–20.

Chapter XII. Shield Wall and Mask

The main ancient account of the battle of Strasbourg (also called Argentorate after the Roman name of the city) is in Ammianus Marcellinus (c. AD 330–95), a contemporary soldier and historian who will have heard about it from many participants, including perhaps Julian himself (and he will certainly have read the account Julian wrote of it, Eunapius fr. 17 [Blockley]). His account is supplemented by the orator Libanius, also contemporary and close to Julian, who described it in his funeral oration upon the emperor (*Or.* 18.52–62). For a modern account of the battle, see M. J. Nicasie, *Twilight of Empire: The Roman Army from the Reign of Diocletian until the Battle of Adrianople* (Amsterdam, 1998) pp. 219–33. P. de Jonge, *Philological and Historical Commentary on Ammianus XVI* (Groningen, 1972) pp. 165, 210–11 and G. A. Crump, *Ammianus Marcellinus as a Military Historian* (Wiesbaden, 1975) p. 88 n. 72 collect older discussions, especially attempts to locate the battlefield.

For the fourth-century army in battle, Nicasie, *Twilight of Empire* pp. 185–219 and P. Rance, "Combat in the Later Roman Empire," in P. Sabin, H. van Wees, and M. Whitby (eds.), *Cambridge History of Greek and Roman Warfare* (Cambridge, forthcoming) should be a reader's first resort. For broader overviews of the late Roman army, see Nicasie, *Twilight of Empire,* P. Richardot, *La Fin de l'armée romaine (284–476)* (Paris, 1998), the articles in the late antiquity section of the *Cambridge History of Greek and Roman Warfare,* and P. Southern and K. R. Dixon, *The Late Roman Army* (New Haven, 1996), with good illustrations.

The Byzantine military treatises are translated by G. T. Dennis as *Maurice's* Strategikon (Philadelphia, 1984) and the first of *Three Byzantine Military Treatises* (Washington, D.C., 1985). The former is sixth-century, but the latter defies dating: compare C. Zuckerman, "The Military Compendium of Syrianus Magister," *Jahrbuch der österreichischen Byzantinistik*

40 (1990) pp. 209–24 with S. Cosentino, "The Syrianos's '*Strategikon*' [*sic*]: A 9th Century Source?" *Bizantinistica* 2 (2000) pp. 243–80 at 262–80.

For the late-Roman shield wall, see P. Rance, "The *Fulcum:* The Late Roman and Byzantine '*Testudo*' — the Germanization of Roman Infantry Tactics?" in *Greek, Roman, and Byzantine Studies* 44 (2004) pp. 265–326, who traces it back to earlier Roman formations. He attacks the interpretation now forcefully restated by M. P. Speidel, *Ancient Germanic Warriors* (London, 2004) pp. 103–109 that the late Roman shield wall was a result of Germanic influence. On the intermittent Roman use of phalanx-like arrangements (gathering evidence from the Republic and later second and third centuries AD), see E. L. Wheeler, "The Legion as Phalanx," *Chiron* 9 (1979) pp. 303–18, a paper upon which I have relied heavily. Arriving too late for full consideration in these pages is Wheeler's update, as rich and cruel as a double helping of Murder by Chocolate: "The Legion as Phalanx in the Late Empire (I)," in Y. Le Bohec and C. Wolff (eds.), *L'Armée romaine de Dioclétien à Valentinien 1er* (Paris, 2004) pp. 309–58 and "(II)," in *Revue des études militaires anciennes* 1 (2004) pp. 147–75.

On Arrian, see P. A. Stadter, *Arrian of Nicomedia* (Chapel Hill, 1980). For the *Deployment against the Alans,* see A. B. Bosworth, "Arrian and the Alani," *Harvard Studies in Classical Philology* 81 (1977) pp. 217–55, who discusses the political background to the Alan incursion, expanding Cassius Dio 69.15.1, and also (pp. 236–44) provides an essential philological commentary upon this difficult and lacunose text; and id., "Arrian and Rome: The Minor Works," *Aufstieg und Niedergang der römischen Welt* 2.34.1 (1993) pp. 226–75 at 264–72. For a translation of the *Deployment,* see C. M. Gilliver, *The Roman Art of War* (Stroud, 1999) pp. 178–80. The details of Arrian's array are controversial: see Wheeler, "Legion as Phalanx in the Late Empire (II)," pp. 152–9.

For debate over the significance of the *Deployment,* see F. Kiechle, "Die 'Taktik' des Flavius Arrianus," *Bericht der römisch-germanischen Kommission* 45 (1964) pp. 87–129, who argues that it implies a fundamental change of doctrine based on Hellenistic models (cf. F. Lammert, *Die römische Taktik zu Beginn der Kaiserzeit und die Geschichtschreibung* [Leipzig, 1931] p. 20); Bosworth, "Arrian and the Alani" p. 244 who guesses that these tactics might have originated in the reign of Trajan and "are most likely to be contemporary developments, which bore fortuitous resemblances to Hellenistic practices." I follow Wheeler, "Legion as Phalanx," who also gathers other contributions to the debate (pp. 303–4) and to whose position the revised position of Bosworth, "Arrian and Rome" pp. 255–57 is, despite Bosworth's protestations, very close.

The *corpus* of what are called cavalry sports helmets begins with J. Garbsch, *Römische Paraderüstungen* (Munich, 1978), with catalogue and map of findspots (pp. 92–93); this has a discussion of female (p. 24) and "mixed" sex (p. 21) masks, and "Greek-style" helmets (p. 7). His work has been extended through more recent discoveries by M. Junkelmann, *Reiter wie Statuen aus Erz* (Mainz, 1996), with superb photographs (pp. 46–47 on female masks). Junkelmann summarizes the controversy over the ultimate origins of the masks in the first century AD (pp. 22–26) — Eastern? Greek? Thracian? Italian? — a controversy that does not concern us here: our interest is in the classicizing trends of the second century. The major English treatment (the masks are mostly a German project) is H. R. Robinson, *The Armour of Imperial Rome* (New York, 1975) pp. 107–35, with discussion of female masks (pp. 124–25).

On Arrian's cavalry display — Arrian calls it the *hippika gymnasia*, and we do not know its Latin name — see Junkelmann, *Reiter wie Statuen* pp. 56–67 and A. Hyland, *Training the Roman Cavalry: From Arrian's Ars Tactica* (London, 1993), with a translation of the relevant parts of Arrian (pp. 69–77).

About the female masks, Junkelmann (*Reiter wie Statuen aus Erz* p. 47 and id. and H. Born, *Römische Kampf- und Turnierrüstungen* [Mainz, 1997] p. 103) has his doubts about Robinson's much-cited association of the masks with Amazons: to him the female masks look more like theatrical masks than traditional Amazon iconography because of the elaborate coifs on some of the masks. But in vase painting Amazons can sometimes have conelike hair (D. von Bothmer, *Amazons in Greek Art* [Oxford, 1957] p. 203 nr. 161=pl. LXXXV; cf. p. 162 nr. 15=pl. LXXVII.1), conical beehive-like headdresses (Bothmer p. 161 nr. 5=pl. LXXIV.3; *LIMC* s.v. *Amazones* 384), and quite elaborate hair (Bothmer p. 161 nr. 2=pl. LXXIV.2, p. 185 nr. 79=pl. LXXXI.4; *LIMC* s.v. *Amazones* 380a), which they can also have in sculpture (Bothmer p. 216 nr. 35=pl. LXXXIX.1, p. 219 nr. 67=pl. LXXXIX.3). For an analysis of the mythical motifs on horse armor,

E. Künzel, "Zur Ikonographie römischer Pferdestirnpanzer," in M. Kemkes and J. Scheuerbrandt (eds.), *Fragen zur römischen Reiterei* (Stuttgart, 1999) pp. 23–30.

It is generally accepted that Roman imperial officers wore muscle cuirasses and pseudo-Attic helmets and that some auxiliary cavalry wore pseudo-Attic helmets to battle. But there is controversy about whether the Praetorian Guard actually wore the pseudo-Attic helmets in which they are depicted in metropolitan art: G. Waurick, "Untersuchungen zur historisierenden Rüstung in der römischen Kunst," *Jahrbuch des römisch-germanischen Zentralmuseums Mainz* 30 (1983) pp. 265–301 at 288–301, in the absence of any archeological examples, suspects they are Greek-influenced artistic convention; B. Rankov, *Guardians of the Roman Empire* (Oxford, 1994) pp. 19–20 follows Waurick. *Non liquet*. Evidently great care must be exercised in drawing evidence for equipment from Roman official art (see J. C. Coulston, "The Value of Trajan's Column as a Source for Military Equipment," and G. Waurick, "Die militärische Rüstung in der römischen Kunst: Fragen zur antiquarischen Genauigkeit am Beispiel der Schwerter des 2. Jahrhunderts n. Chr.," both in C. van Driel-Murray [ed.], *Roman Military Equipment: The Sources of Evidence* [BAR Int. Ser. 476; Oxford, 1989] pp. 31–44 and 45–60), which seems to overrepresent Greek-style equipment. Yet since the taste for antiquarian and hellenizing equipment was shared by artists and officers, who themselves used such gear and might impose it on their troops, it is hard to tell where the taste of officers stops and that of artists begins.

On Roman soldier poetry, see J. N. Adams, "The Poets of Bu Njem: Language, Culture and the Centurionate," *Journal of Roman Studies* 89 (1999) pp. 109–34.

For the tactical manuals of Arrian and Aelian, see above, pp. 413–14. Onasander is translated in the Loeb volume with Aeneas Tacticus and Asclepiodotus. For an introduction, see C. J. Smith, "Onasander on How to be a General," in M. Austin et al. (eds.), *Modus Operandi: Essays in Honour of Geoffrey Rickman* (London, 1998) pp. 151–66 (with pp. 152–55 on Onasander's dedicatee). On Onasander's reliance on Greek material (despite his claim to have drawn on Roman experience, *pr.* 8), see D. Ambaglio, "Il trattato 'Sul Commandante' di Onasandro," *Athenaeum* 69 (1981) pp. 353–77 at 358–64. Polyaenus is translated in P. Krentz and E. L.

Wheeler, *Polyaenus, Stratagems of War,* 2 vols. (Chicago, 1994). Julius Africanus is available in a French edition with translation, J.-R. Viellefond, *Les "Cestes" de Julius Africanus* (Florence, 1970); for an introduction, see E. L. Wheeler, "Why the Romans Can't Defeat the Parthians: Julius Africanus and the Strategy of Magic," in W. Groenman-van Waateringe et al. (eds.), *Roman Frontier Studies 1995* (Oxford, 1997) pp. 575–79.

On the lack of military specialization and experience among the imperial Roman aristocrats who held high commands in the first and second centuries, see B. Campbell, "Who Were the '*Viri Militares*'?" *Journal of Roman Studies* 65 (1975) pp. 11–31 and "Teach Yourself How to Be a General," *Journal of Roman Studies* 77 (1987) pp. 13–29.

On the mindsets created by Roman aristocratic education, see A. Alföldi, *A Conflict of Ideas in the Late Roman Empire* (Oxford, 1952) pp. 96–124; R. MacMullen, *Roman Government's Response to Crisis AD 235–337* (New Haven, 1976) pp. 24–58 (esp. for government); and S. P. Mattern, *Rome and the Enemy: Imperial Strategy in the Principate* (Berkeley and Los Angeles, 1999) pp. 1–80 (esp. for foreign affairs).

On the culture of archaism of the second century AD, for the Greek side, see E. L. Bowie, "Greeks and Their Past in the Second Sophistic," *Past and Present* 46 (1970) pp. 3–41; S. Swain, *Hellenism and Empire* (Oxford, 1996) pp. 17–131; and especially for monuments, S. Alcock, *Archaeologies of the Greek Past* (Cambridge, 2002) pp. 36–98; for the Latin side, L. Holford-Strevens, *Aulus Gellius* (London, 1988), esp. pp. 1–6.

For Vegetius, see the convenient translation, with introduction and commentary, of N. P. Milner, *Vegetius: Epitome of Military Science* (Liverpool, 1993), with arguments as to the date of the work (pp. xxv–xxix). Trying to discern which bits of Vegetius are copied and adapted from which earlier authors (once a fashionable game) produces few reproducible results. Compare Milner pp. xvi–xviii to D. Schenk, *Flavius Vegetius Renatus: Die Quellen der* Epitoma Rei Militaris (Leipzig, 1930). No argument should hang on such attributions.

On Hellenistic fortifications, see A. W. McNicoll and N. P. Milner, *Hellenistic Fortifications from the Aegean to the Euphrates* (Oxford, 1997) and A. W. Lawrence, *Greek Aims in Fortification* (Oxford, 1979). Lawrence translates and elucidates Philo's treatise on fortification and siegecraft (with omissions) pp. 73–107 (to be read with Y. Garlan, *Recherches de poliorcétique grecque* [Paris, 1974] pp. 279–404). Whether the diversity of designs of late third- and fourth-century fortification rules out central planning (as I think) is controversial. H. von Petrikovits, "Fortifications in the North-Western Roman Empire from the Third to the Fifth Centuries AD," *Journal of Roman Studies* 61 (1971) pp. 178–218 at 204, thought that "military architects on the different sectors were evidently given a free hand in the execution of their duty." J. Lander, *Roman Stone Fortifications* (BAR Int. Ser. 206, Oxford, 1984) made a heroic but futile attempt to deduce a logic that would restore central direction (pp. 305–8). S. Johnson, *Late Roman Fortifications* (Totowa, N.J., 1983) pp. 97, 113–14, 260 thinks that only small, localized direction can be detected (which I find plausible).

On cavalry in the fourth century, see Nicasie, *Twilight of Empire* pp. 194–95: its numbers were somewhat larger than earlier, but infantry remained the core of the Roman army. On heavy-armored cavalry and its origins, M. Mielczarek, Cataphracti *and* Clibanarii (Lodz, 1993) gathers the evidence. For growing specialization of unit functions in the late Roman army, see P. Brennan, "Combined Legionary Detachments as Artillery Units in Late-Roman Danubian Bridgehead Dispositions," *Chiron* 10 (1980) pp. 553–67.

The anonymous *de Rebus Bellicis* is edited, translated, and discussed in M. W. C. Hassall and R. I. Ireland, *De Rebus Bellicis* (BAR Int. Ser. 63, Oxford, 1979).

Chapter XIII. Julian in Persia, AD 363

For Julian's campaign in Persia, the major ancient accounts are those of Ammianus Marcellinus (23.2–25.8), who was present, the early sixth-century Zosimus (3.12–31), who adapted the lost account of the contemporary Eunapius, and Libanius in his funeral panegyric upon Julian, *Or.* 18.212–80. There are many minor discrepancies between their accounts and between their accounts and other sources (catalogued by L. Dillemann, "Ammien Marcellin et le pays de l'Euphrate et du Tigre," *Syria* 38 [1961] pp. 87–158 and wisely discussed by C. Fornara, "Julian's Persian Expedition in Ammianus and Zosimus," *Journal of Hellenic Studies* III [1991] pp. 1–15). Such issues and others are properly treated in J. den

Boeft et al., *Philological and Historical Commentary on Ammianus Marcellinus XXIII* (Groningen, 1998) and *XXIV* (Leiden, 2002), and, one assumes, in the forthcoming volume on book XXV. Like nearly all modern readers, I base my account on Ammianus and supplement it with Zosimus and Libanius, usually believing Ammianus in cases of disagreement.

On Ammianus as a historian of war, see G. A. Crump, *Ammianus Marcellinus as a Military Historian* (Wiesbaden, 1975); N. Bitter, *Kampfschilderungen bei Ammianus Marcellinus* (Bonn, 1976); N. J. E. Austin, *Ammianus on Warfare* (Brussels, 1979); and F. Trombley, "Ammianus Marcellinus and Fourth Century Warfare," in J. W. Drijvers and D. Hunt (eds.), *The Late Roman World and Its Historian* (London, 1999) pp. 17–28, with interesting thoughts on how Ammianus's particular duties as a *protector* (honorary imperial bodyguard/staff officer) may have influenced his coverage.

For an up-to-date scholarly description of the campaign and the problems of geography and sources it presents, see J. Matthews, *The Roman Empire of Ammianus* (Baltimore, 1989) pp. 130–79. R. Browning's narrative in *The Emperor Julian* (Berkeley and Los Angeles, 1976) pp. 186–218 is a pleasure to read; the brief account of B. S. Strauss and J. Ober in *The Anatomy of Error* (New York, 1990) pp. 217–43 is acute.

On Julian's education and erudition, see J. Bouffartigue, *L'Empereur Julien et la culture de son temps* (Paris, 1992): enough of Julian's writings survive and enough was written about him that he is, after Cicero, the Roman figure whose intellectual world we can reconstruct most fully. At pp. 496–97 Bouffartigue offers speculations about Julian's military reading. W. E. Kaegi, "Constantine's and Julian's Strategies of Strategic Surprise against the Persians," *Athenaeum* 69 (1981) pp. 209–13 speculates that Julian's strategy may have been inspired by writings of the first-century AD Cornelius Celsus or the emperor Constantine (cf. Lydus, *Mag.* 3.33–4).

There is an old controversy about the degree to which Julian sought to imitate Alexander the Great: R. Lane Fox, "The Itinerary of Alexander: Constantius to Julian," *Classical Quarterly* 47 (1997) pp. 239–52 at 248–52 and J. Szidat, "*Alexandrum Imitatus* (Amm. Marc. 24.4.27). Die Beziehung Iulians zu Alexander in der Sicht Ammians," in W. Will (ed.), *Zu Alexander dem Grossen, Festschrift G. Wirth* (Amsterdam, 1988) pp.

1023–35 gather the references and literature. Certainly Libanius had reason to emphasize this link, to make Julian a hero (esp. *Or.* 18.260), and Christian authors had reason to overemphasize it, to make Julian appear mad (esp. Socrates *Hist. eccl.* 3.21). But for our purposes the controversy misses the point: Julian was an omnivorous imitator of past generals, hardly limiting himself to Alexander. Julian wrote to a friend, "Of old I used to think I was a rival to Alexander and [the emperor] Marcus [Aurelius] and anyone else excelling in excellence" (*Epist. ad Themist.* 253A-B). If his particular interest in Alexander had declined over time (as Lane Fox argues, pp. 248–52) his catholic taste in subjects for imitation had not.

For the size of the Roman armies brought to battle in the fourth century, see R. MacMullen, *Corruption and the Decline of Rome* (New Haven, 1988) pp. 173–74 and M. J. Nicasie, *Twilight of Empire: The Roman Army from the Reign of Diocletian until the Battle of Adrianople* (Amsterdam, 1998) pp. 202–7. It cannot be too much emphasized that the total strength on paper of the fourth-century army, estimated between four hundred thousand and one million (Nicasie p. 75 gathers estimates; the lowest are most plausible) is quite beside the point (except perhaps to the empire's taxpayers): what matters is how many soldiers came to fight. MacMullen argues that the totals are smaller than in the earlier empire; Nicasie responds (pp. 202–3) that there is not really enough information on early imperial armies to tell. But certainly fourth-century armies were smaller than attested Republican and late-Republican armies, see P. A. Brunt, *Italian Manpower 225 BC–AD 14* (Oxford, 1971) pp. 416–512.

Reasons for the small size of the late-antique army: for economical discussions of tax collection, army pay, supply, reluctance to serve, conscription, and desertion (with literature), see the late-antique chapters of P. Sabin, H. van Wees, and M. Whitby (eds.), *The Cambridge History of Greek and Roman Warfare* (Cambridge, forthcoming). For corruption, MacMullen, *Corruption,* esp. pp. 171–77.

INDEX

Charidemus (Greek mercenary
commander), 354 n.16
chariots: Alexander, sporting use
of, 118, 128; in *Iliad*, 29, 30, 35, 55;
mingling in early phalanx, 344
n.25; not revived by mainland
Greeks, 56, 159; in tactical treatises,
159, 288; Theban infantry unit
called "charioteers and chariot
riders," at Delium, 85
cheiroballistra ("hand ballista"). *See*
catapult; technology, siegecraft
chiliarchs ("commanders of a thousand"), 127
Cimon (Athenian general): celebrating victory with a monument, 84;
as hoplite, 44
civil officials, in late-Roman warfare,
303
Claudius Quadrigarius, 363 n.1,
363 n.3
Clearchus (Greek mercenary
commander), 73, 76, 77
Cleombrotus (Spartan king) at
Leuctra, 107
Cleomenes (Spartan king), 82
clibanarii ("oven men," late-Roman
heavy cavalry), 288
Clitus (officer of Alexander), 119, 129
Coenus (officer of Alexander), 125
Cohen, A., 416–17
cohesion, 3; overemphasis upon in
modern writing, 255, 432; Roman
indifference to, 184–85; theory of
success of Roman army, 171, 255,
432. *See also* Goldsworthy, A.
cohort: in action, 427; *genius* (spirit)
of, 231; independent use of, 228.
See also Goldsworthy, A.; legion,
of cohorts

coins: Achilles, use of image on, 149;
single combat of Roman ancestors
alluded to on, 422
comitia centuriata, 365 n.21
commanders
—Homeric, ethos of, 28, 30, 32–33,
86–88, 158
—Greek, competitions of, 74, 89,
105, 144, 148, 150, 152. *See also*
arraying; Antigonus; competition;
cunning (*metis*); Eumenes; single
combat
—Greek, Archaic and Classical,
ethos of, 74–77, 89, 409
—Hellenistic: emulation of Alexander, 148–49; ethos of, 147–49,
420, 421; heroic command, culture
of, 128, 132, 136–37, 148–49
—Roman, ethos of, 167, 185, 188, 199,
200, 207, 215, 219; ethos, changes
in, 202, 205–6, 221, 229–30; heroic
command, imperial culture of,
259–60; heroic command, lack
of, 426
—late-Roman, heroic ethos of,
302–4
—obedience to. *See* insubordination;
obedience
communications, effect on innovation, 13, 157
companies. *See* units
competition: athletic, 73, 84, 128,
151, 419; beauty, 141, 419; in Greek
cavalry, 104–5; city contingents,
among Greek, 40, 62, 63–65, 105,
157, 403, 404, 406; commanders,
among Greek, 76–77, 84, 89, 106,
144, 145, 148, 152; between commanders and hoplites, 136; commanders, among Roman, 167, 201,

cowardice (*continued*)
52–53; Roman, definitions of,
201–3, 207. See also *kakos; virtus*
Crastinus (centurion), 217–18
Crawley, R., 409
Cretans, as mercenaries, 196, 205
Ctesiphon, battle of, 295, 296, 297,
299–301; Julian's decision not to
attack, 300–301
cultural history of war, 2, 393
culture: "agonistic," in Greece, 45–
46, 48, 62, 85, 103–4, 157, 260, 403;
influence on warfare, 3, 28, 36–38,
159, 175, 191, 194, 197, 312, 393. *See
also* past
cuneus, 368 n.18
cunning (*metis*), 3, 411–12; of Alexander, 131; commanders, competition
in, 85, 89, 106, 146, 152, 154; conflict with hoplite ethos, 87–88, 147;
distaste for, Greek, 27, 86, 88–89;
distaste for, Roman, 194, 426;
in Homer, 24, 28, 158; in hoplite
battle, 41, 80, 410, 411; later imitation of Homeric, 86, 89, 112, 146–
47; prizes for, 85–86; Roman tradition of use of, 175, 205, 211, 426; at
sea, 67–68; use of before Delium,
82–83. *See also* Spartan, cunning of;
tactics
Cynoscephalae, battle of, 167, 194,
204. *See also* Macedonian Wars

Dacians, 242, 243
Darius III, 118, 120, 132, 133–36, 138
Dark Ages, Greek, 21, 402
dead bodies, recovery of: U.S., 2–3;
Classical Greece, 3; at Delium,
permission denied, 81; Homeric,
3; in hoplite battle, 42, 64, 108,

152; Leonidas, 66; at Plataea, 69;
Roman, 3
decimation: described by Polybius,
170; misunderstood by Julian, 295
decorations, Roman, 46; for cavalry,
188; formalized in empire, 248;
late-antique, 297, 383 n.19; preserving reputation of victor, 188; for
Roman soldiers, 187, 248, 431;
worn by victor's father, 189
Delbrück, H., 394
Delium, battle of, 79–83, 89; "chariots and chariot riders," 85, 348 n.11;
site of, 79, 410; unconventional
elements of, 80, 81–83
Demetrius Poliorcetes ("the
besieger"), 153, 241, 294, 295
Demosthenes (Greek orator), on
courage, 55, 58
deployment. *See* array
Deployment Against the Alans, of
Arrian, 266–69, 288
Dercylidas (Spartan officer), 86
de Rebus Bellicis, Anonymous, 288,
438
Detienne, M., 44
Diocletian (Roman emperor), 284
Diodorus of Sicily: on Gabiene, 420;
on Iphicrates, 413; on Issus, 418;
on Leuctra, 414; on military
innovation, 10–11; on Paraetacene,
419–20; on Philip II, 11; on
Persian Wars, 405
Diomedes, abuse of Paris, 33–34,
35–36
Dionysius of Syracuse, 160
disciplina: auxiliaries, Roman, of, 252,
432; competitive, 252, 256, 312; as
a divinity, 252; *labor,* included concept, 251; legionaries, associated

eris ("strife"), 314, 362 n.1

esthloi ("the brave"), in *Iliad*, 29, 32, 47, 130

ethics, Greek. See *sophrosyne*; values, martial, Homeric

Eudamas (officer of Eumenes), 150

euexia ("male beauty contest"), 141

Eumenes (Hellenistic warlord), 143–53; emulating Alexander, 147–48; capture at Gabiene, 153; cunning of, 143, 144, 152; description of, 143; friendship with Antigonus, 143; "out-generals" Antigonus, 152; single combat with Neoptolemus, 148

Eunapius, 433, 438

Euphorbos, 20, 21, 27, 397

Euripides: on archery, 47; on hoplite fighting, 47, 80, 150; on holding one's place in the phalanx, 50, 52

eutaxia ("discipline"), 74, 141, 142

euxos ("claim to glory"), 26, 27

Evangelos (tactical author), 147

exempla: in Ammianus Marcellinus, 292–93, 296; in education, 283–84; and Julian, 296; in Vegetius, 283

experimentation with modes of fighting, 154–55, 156

Fabius, L. (centurion), 216, 217, 221

Fabius Maximus (Roman general): army of, opposition in, 202, 207, 229, 307; Fabian strategy of, 201–2, 205, 307

ferox ("ferocious"), traditional quality of Roman youth, 188

Ferrill, A., 395, 412

fleeing: dishonor of, 2, 36–37, 50, 51, 87, 178; phalanx, 41, 52–53, 132 (see also *lipotaxion*)

fleet. See Agathocles; Julian; riverboats, use of; technology, naval

formations, military: cavalry, Greek, 98–102, 124–25, 126; hoplite phalanx, 41–42, 43–44, 69–70, 124, 126; infantry, 29, 421; keeping place in phalanx, 40, 41, 50–52, 53–55, 61, 63, 71, 72, 74, 94; "rectangle," 98, 99; "rhombus," 98–100; "wedge," 98. See also array

fortification. See technology, fortification

Forum Gallorum, battle of, 221

Fox, R. Lane, 416

Frazer, J., 186

Frontinus (S. Julius Frontinus): and Aelian, 279, 282; attitude toward siege technology, 7; stratagem collection of, 279–80, 283, 296

funeral games, 34, 48, 57

Furius Purpurio, L., 197

furor: of Roman youth, 188, 209, 424; *disciplina*, opposition with (see *disciplina; virtus*, opposition to)

Gabba, E., 428–29

Gabiene, battle of, 144, 152–53, 419, 420; date of, 419; site of, 420

Gamala, battle of, 236–38, 253, 257, 266; similarity to Gergovia, 237, 241; topography and archaeology of, 372 n.7

games: on Alexander's campaign, 57, 116, 418; in Classical Greece, 48, 49, 56; competition of soldiers in, 73, 128–29, 142, 158; funeral, 34, 48, 57; in Hellenistic era, 141; of Julian, 296, 298; Paullus, offered by, 206

Gaugamela, battle of, 125, 138, 418;

121, 125, 355 n.20; at Paraetacene, 144

Idomeneus, 25, 26

Ilerda, battle of, 222–24, 231; Gergovia, contrasted with, 224; site of, 222–23

Iliad

—compostion of, 21

—contradictions in, 21, 30, 32, 33–36, 38, 48, 397

—date of, 17, 396

—dominance over *Odyssey* in education, 36

—fighting in, 30, 32, 34, 48; massed, 29, 30, 31–32, 34, 66–67; one on one, 22–25, 32

—imitation of in sixth century AD, 310

—imitation of by later Greeks, 157–58; Alexander, 116–18, 129–31, 137–38; Archaic, 36–37, 40, 45–46, 48, 51, 409; Classical, 65–67, 84–85, 87, 403, 405; fourth-century, 36–37, 75, 96, 105–6; Hellenistic, 146–47, 148–49, 420; Philip II, 11, 122–24, 138, 158

—literary representation of fighting in, 22–23, 32, 36, 48

—society depicted in, 21

—unreality of competition in, 46–47, 49, 52, 57

—use of shield straps in, 418

—values, Greek, vector for, 36–38, 45, 56–57, 102, 105, 157–60

Ilipa, battle of, 228, 428; Scipio's tactics as perhaps copied from Marathon, 385 n.35

imitation. See *Iliad*; past

initiative of Roman soldiers, 187, 202,

208, 214, 231, 307; in Jewish War, 237, 240, 241–42, 253, 255, 431

inscriptions: as evidence for date of *ephebeia*, 415; as evidence for Roman fighting techniques, 264–65; on Greek gravestones with Homeric language, 45, 46; of Hadrian's address at Lambaesis, 251; revival of Greek dialects on, 281; revival of term *triarii* on, 284; of victors of contest at Samos, 141

insubordination

—Greek, 409; of Antigonus's troops, 152; of mercenaries, 102; Spartan, 72; of Ten Thousand, 74–75, 77

—Roman: in Jewish War, 240–41, 248, 257, 430; in late Antiquity, 258, 262; in late Republic, 218, 219, 302; in middle Republic, 186, 196, 199; tradition of, 200, 202, 208, 257. See also *disciplina*; initiative; *virtus*

inventions, military: go out of use, 8, 9; never used, 9, 13, 288. *See also* Iphicrates; Philip II

Iphicrates: generalship of, 10, 93; innovations of, 10, 96–97, 413, 417; on mixed army, 92, 106; training peltasts, 96, 105

Ipsus, battle of, 140

Issus, battle of, 121–25, 131–36, 418; controversies in traditions about, 418

Jason of Pherae: intensity of training of troops, 100; inventions, 414; and "rhombus," 98; treaty with Sparta, 106; use of mercenaries, 102

javelin, 412; Greek hoplite, 43; Roman *pilum*, 8, 178, 180, 263, 434; training in, Hellenistic, 142,

craft, 120, 160, 222, 235, 241,
248–50, 253–54, 292, 294–95, 298,
306, 430; treatises on (*see* stratagems, military, books on; tactical
treatises)
telamon (shoulder strap for a
shield), 124, 417–18. *See also* shield,
Macedonian
Ten Thousand, the: culture of, 73,
74, 76–77, 409; cunning, using,
86; as a *polis,* 73, 409
Terentius Varro (Roman general),
200, 207
testudo (shield wall): in early empire,
237, 266; late-Roman, 262, 266, 285,
287, 292, 297; origin of, 266, 285,
434; as phalanx, 263, 267–68, 434
Teucer, best of Achaeans in archery,
34, 48
Teutomatus, 216
Thapsus, battle of, 221
Thebans: cavalry of, 107; at Delium,
battle of, 79–81; at Leuctra,
battle of, 84, 106–7; Sacred Band
(*see* Sacred Band); tactics of,
80–81; at Thermopylae, 60
Themistocles: cunning of, 112;
receives prize for cleverness, 85–86;
at Salamis, battle of, 67, 73
Thermopylae, battle of, 59–61, 63,
76, 82, 405; Homeric depictions
of, 66–67, 69; list of bravest
fighters at, 45; topography of,
60, 405
Thersites, 24
Thessalians: equipment and dress of,
414; famed for cavalry, 98, 99–100;
Homeric qualities of, 102
Thracians, as peltasts, 95–96
threats, exchange of, in *Iliad,* 23

Thucydides: on cunning, 85; on
Mantinea, battle of, 91; and
"mature" phalanx, 401; on *Pitanate
lochos,* 279; on *polis* as an individual,
62; on Spartans, 74, 87–88, 110;
on Sphacteria, battle of, 47
thureomachia (fighting with a long
shield), 141, 154
thureophoroi (long-shield-bearing
soldiers), 154
Thyrea, battle of champions at,
39–41, 44, 108, 399–400; conflict
over who won, 51–52, 399–400;
different versions of in sources,
399–400; rules agreed to in advance at, 41, 83. *See also* Orthryades
Ticinus, battle of. *See* Punic War,
Second
timē ("honor, worth, worthiness"),
in *Iliad,* 24, 33. *See also* competition; *kleos*; *kudos*; ranking
Titus (Roman general and emperor),
236, 238, 241; fighting hand to
hand, 236, 237, 240; heroic mode
of fighting of, 237, 259–60, 278–79;
judging competition of units, 250;
leading the charge, 236, 241, 250,
256, 278; reckless behavior of, 240,
248, 260, 433; reproving soldiers
for aggression, 248, 431 (*see also*
initiative; *virtus*); strategy of,
in Jewish War, 250, 253, 255; on
swiftness, 307. *See also* Jerusalem,
siege of
Torquatus, T. Manlius, 174, 177, 188,
296
tragedy, Greek: depictions of heroic
age, 11, 37; depictions of hoplites
fighting, 45, 53, 61, 66–67. *See also*
Aeschylus; Euripides